A look into the art of
David J. Vanderpool

Second Edition - 2013

Visit the artist's web site at www.paper2pencil.com

Some of the drawings found in this book are available in print at
http://paper2pencil.redbubble.com

Pencil Drawings - a look into the art of David J. Vanderpool
by David J. Vanderpool

ISBN 978-0-578-02528-5
Second Edition | Paperback

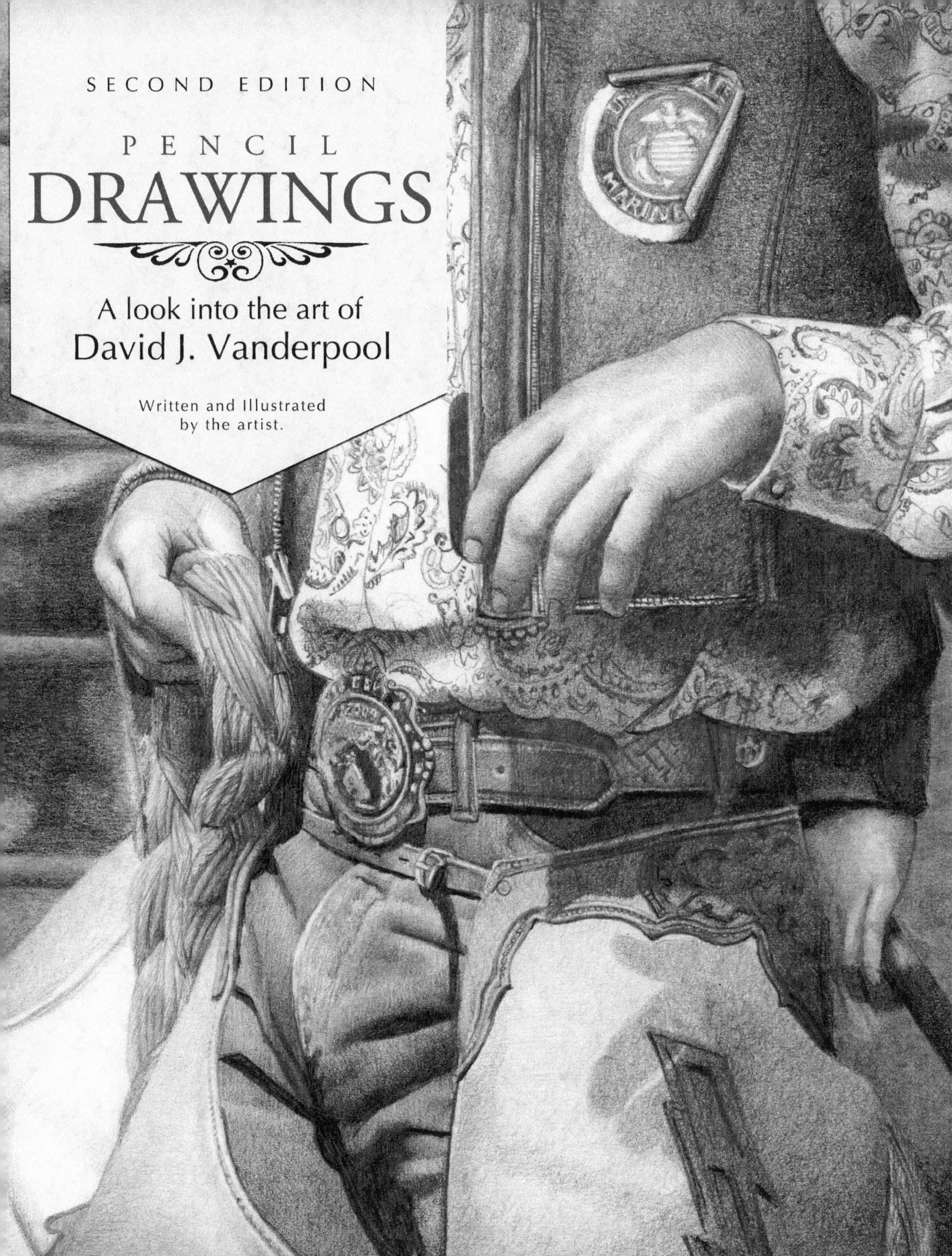

SECOND EDITION

PENCIL DRAWINGS

A look into the art of
David J. Vanderpool

Written and Illustrated
by the artist.

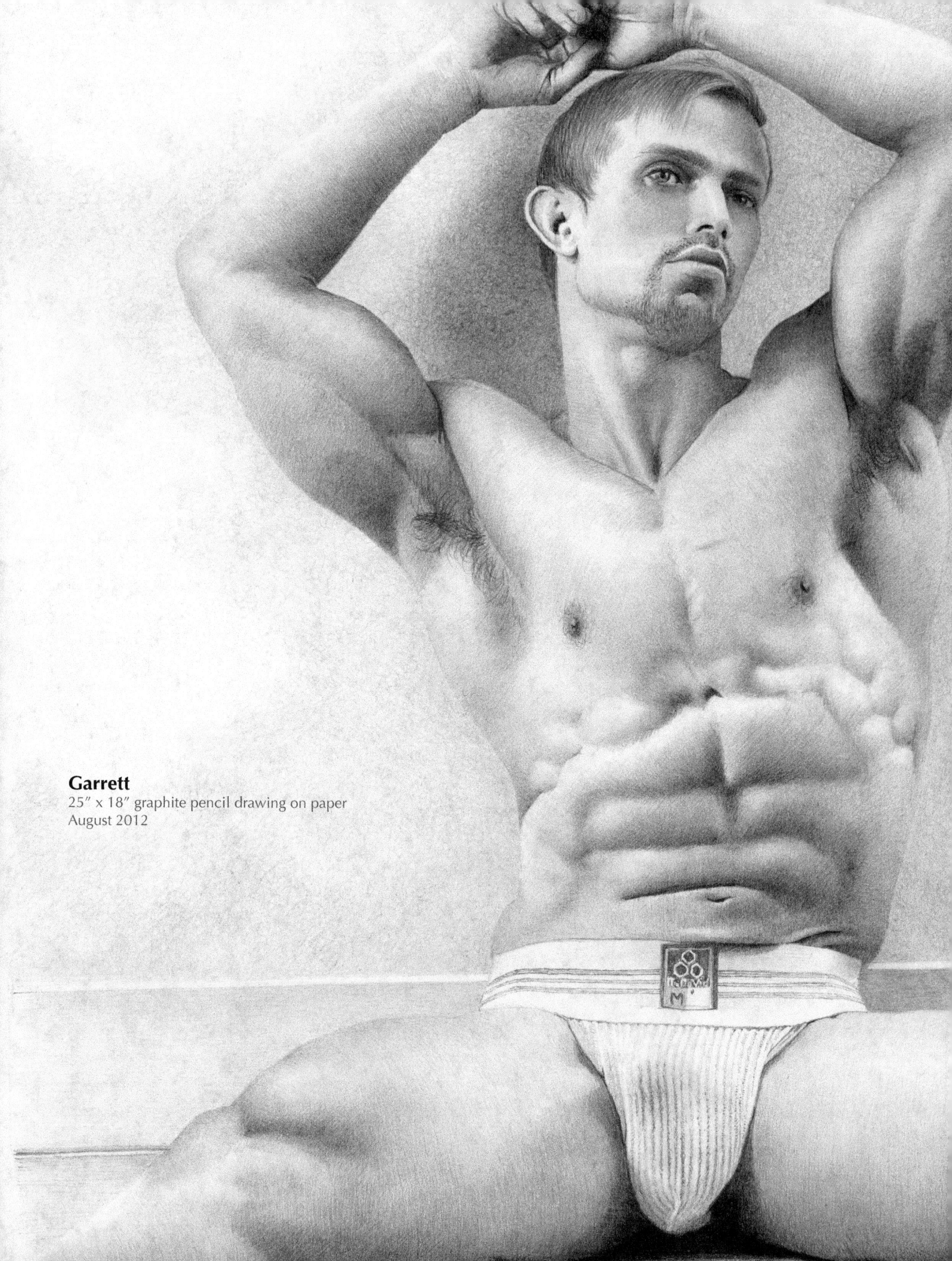

Garrett
25" x 18" graphite pencil drawing on paper
August 2012

CONTENT

Chapter One
We will be judged for the art we create.

Art isn't always about who the artist is. But rather who catches his attention at that moment.

- David J. Vanderpool

Standing at a distance and looking into the eyes of the couple displayed before you, it's easy to want to question how much of the artist was put into that piece, what motivated him to create such beauty, and why was this subject chosen over another? However doing so, we often over look the beauty and subject for what it is - art.

Art isn't always about who the artist is but rather who catches his attention at the moment. No hidden messages. Nothing to reveal to the world in regard to secrets or unspoken desires. Just art, for the sake of art.

Just a drawing for the sake of taking on a challenge of duplicating what God had already blessed us with.

Well - just a drawing most of the time.

Hidden messages or bold statements can and often are found in today's pop culture art, as the artist uses his skills to express himself. However, in a more classic or traditional form of art, the sole purpose can be as simple as just trying to capture the beauty around him.

Traditional art, or classical revival pieces, are rare in today's art scene as art galleries focus on nearly mass produced pieces and those they can easily sell without having to educate the public.

Not to hold or say anything against such art galleries and those who favor modern or contemporary art, but as explained to me by an art gallery in London; a gallery will sell a painting at a higher margin than a drawing because of the time put into a painting can be, and often is, far less than the time put into a drawing.

Therefore, as an artist, one must make a choice; to create for himself and focus on the overall quality of his work with the hope it becomes an heirloom for the generations to come, or create to meet the demands of the current market.

I suppose this statement could easily explain what separates commercial artists from fine art artists, and why taking on commissioned assignments are not for every one.

No matter the creative level an artists is at, or the

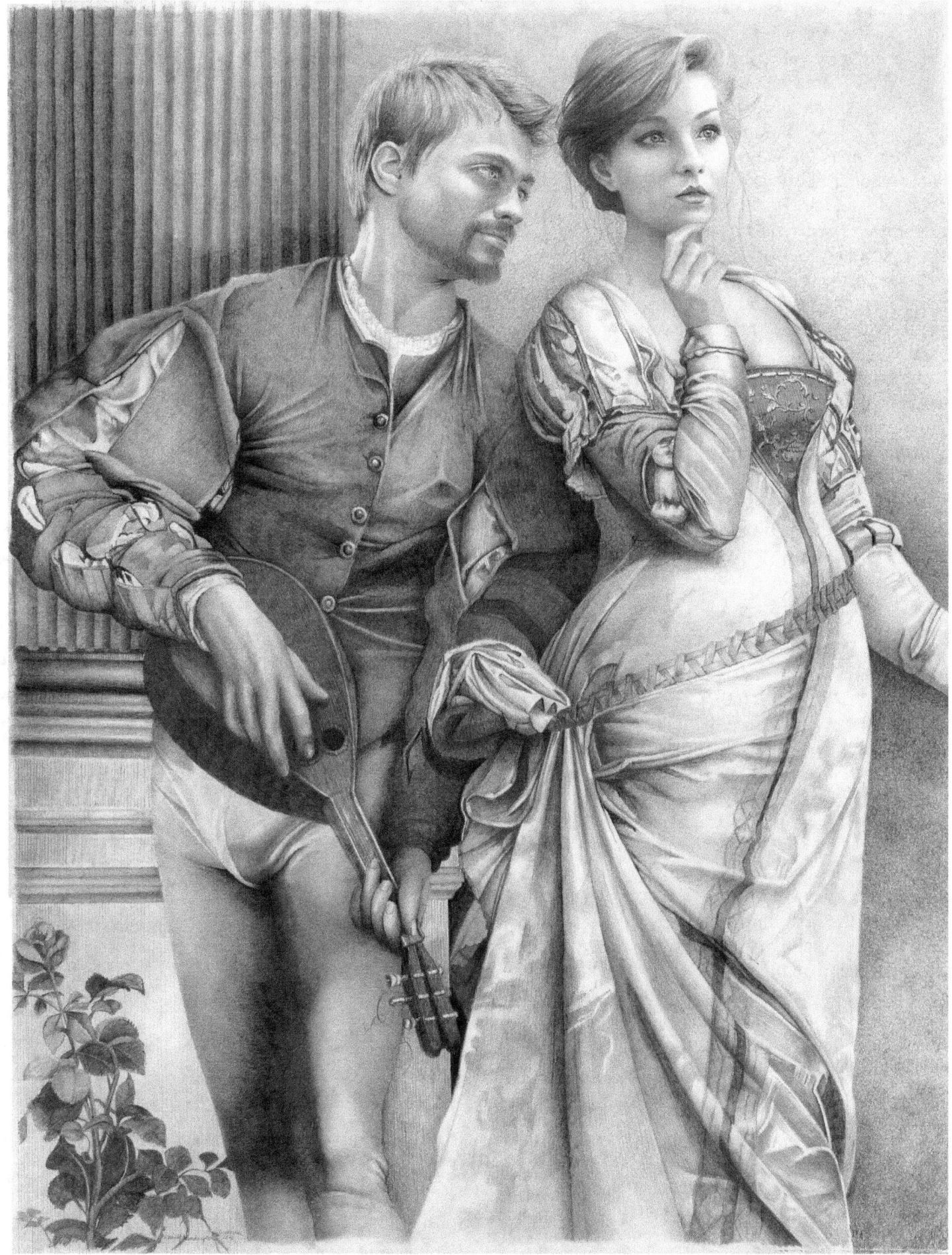

Courting

18" x 25" graphite pencil drawing on paper. June 2012

reason behind what motivates him, without passion for what he does the desire to improve and the over all quality will become a challenge that will either make the piece or break the artist.

My drawings have evolved and changed through the years - they had to! For without growth and learning from ourselves, what is the point in doing what we do?

And of course - life and the circumstance put before us effects the outcome to what we do, how well we do, and whether or not we allow it to tear us down or turn that obstacle into a challenge that makes it work for us.

Fine examples of adapting to ones circumstance are the four drawings seen in the first eleven pages of this book. The drawings of "Garrett", "Courting", and "Kevin - Repose" were all drawn on 25" x 18" Bristol paper. "Rodeo", was a smaller piece on the same type of paper, at 15" x 11".

A paper I had never used, but had waited several years to try my hand at.

Why the need to change?

As a diabetic, and dealing with it's effects, I was diagnosed in April of 2012 with the early stages of Diabetic Neuropathy, Diabetic Retinopathy, and Posterior Subscapsular Cataract. This explained why it was becoming harder to see and capture the detail I had become known for.

And yes - the first thing to come to mind was, "Oh great, I get my hearing restored in time to go blind!"

Then it really hit me! If I don't take this serious and work at getting rid of this curse I had inherited from my mother's family, not only will it kill me, but far worse - it will prevent me from drawing!

The use of Bristol paper came highly recommended from an artist friend by the name of Cory Wilaby. Not only had he been the subject of a few of my earlier drawings, but a fine pencil artist in his own right.

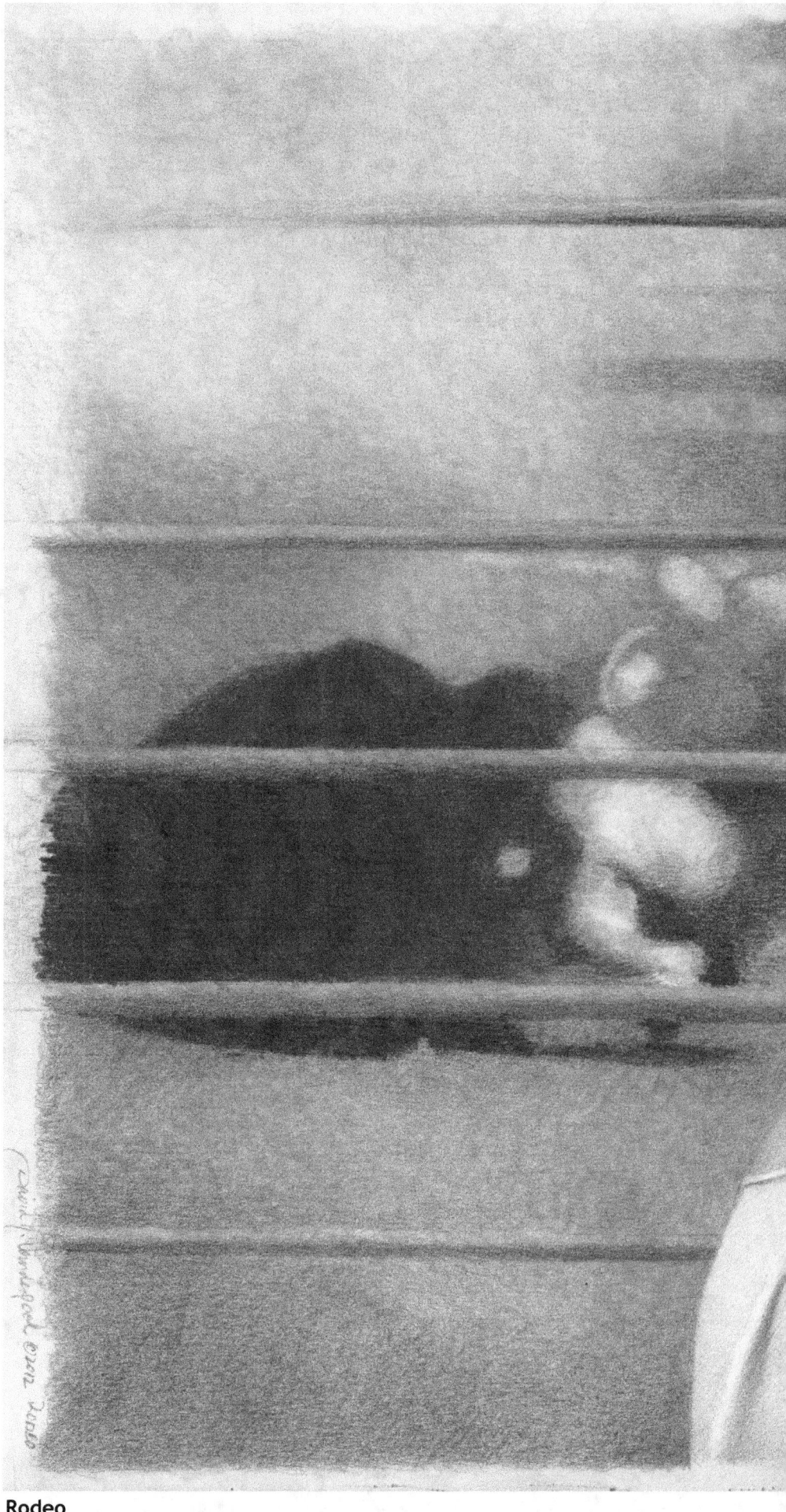

Rodeo

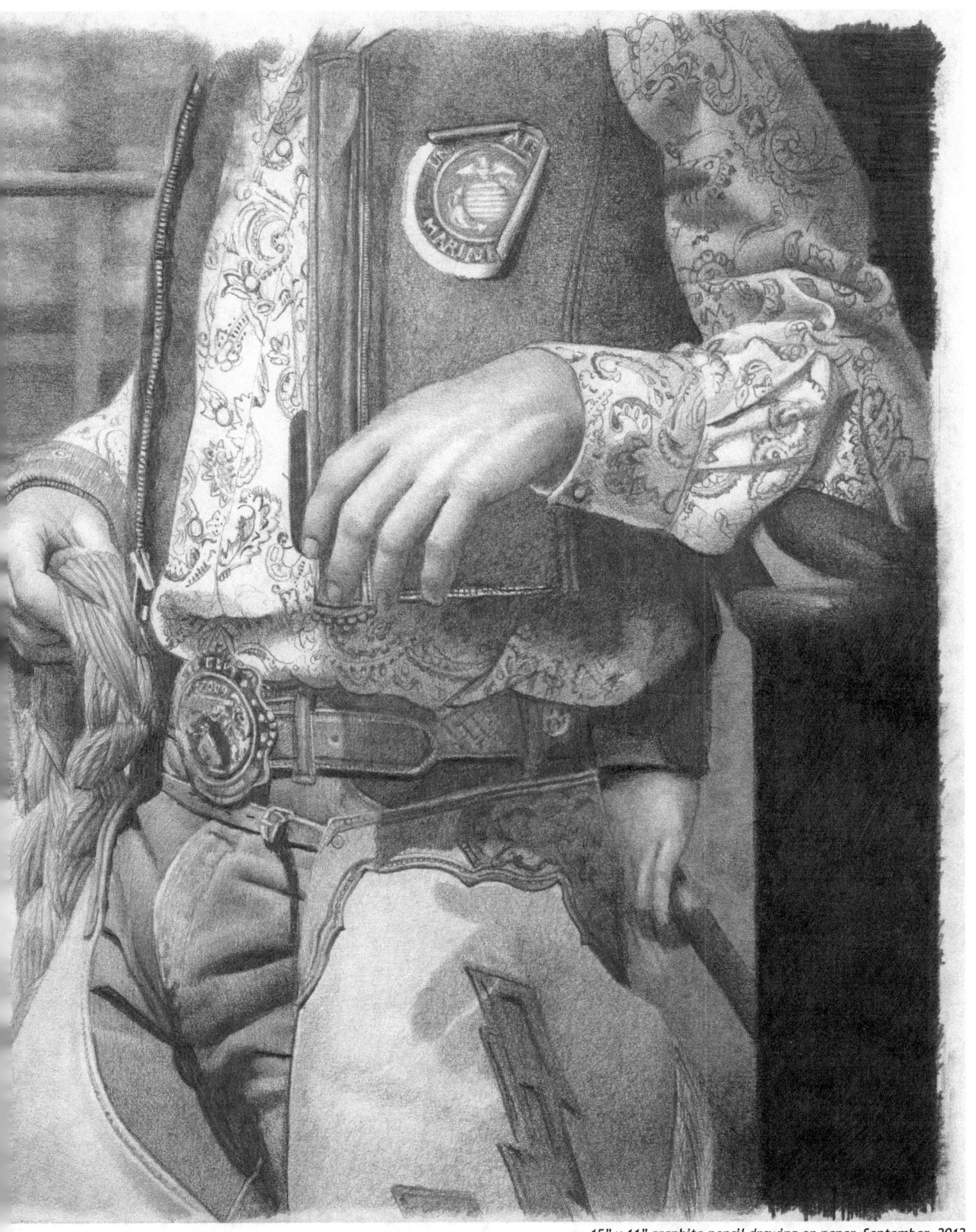

15" x 11" graphite pencil drawing on paper. September 2012

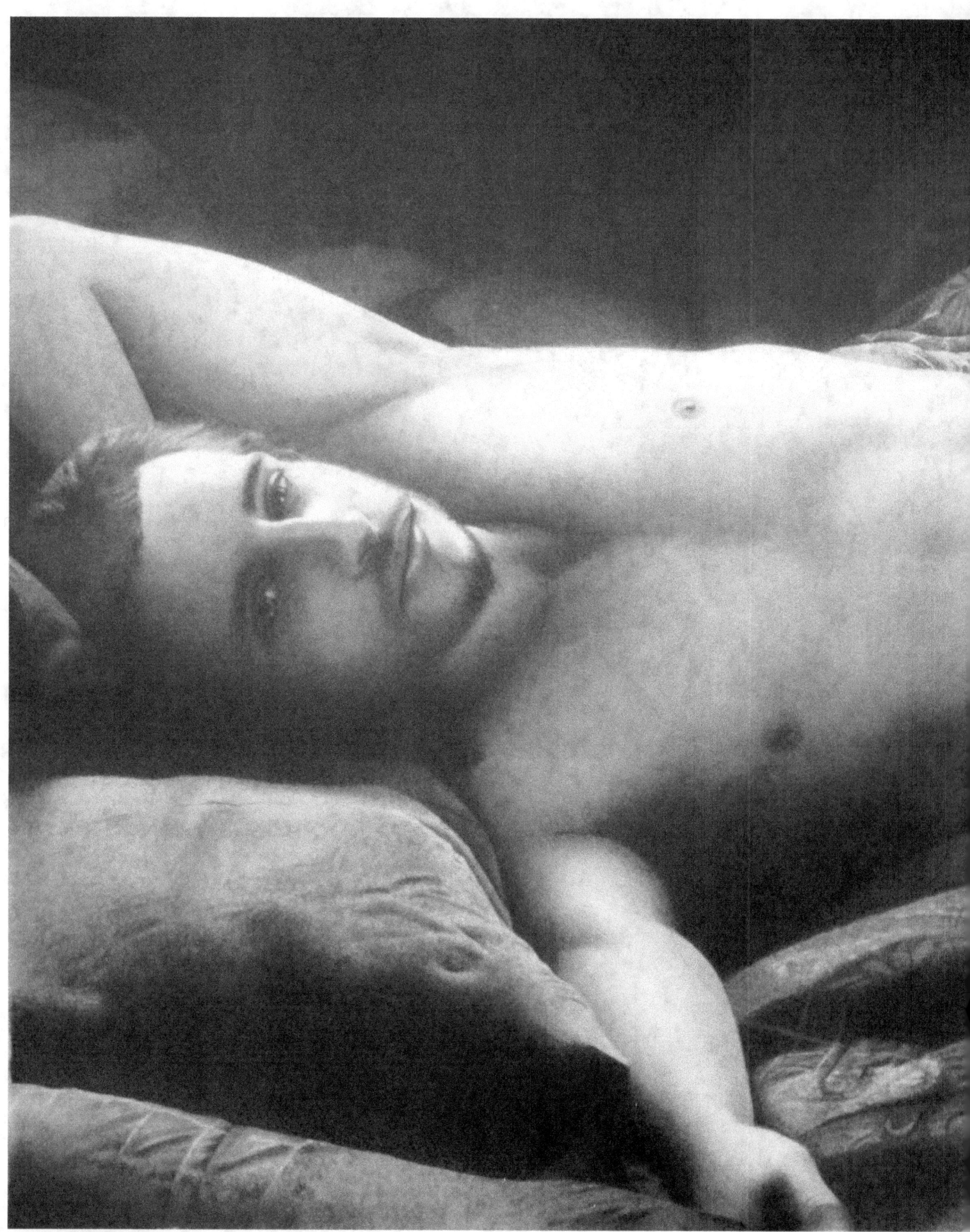

Kevin - Repose

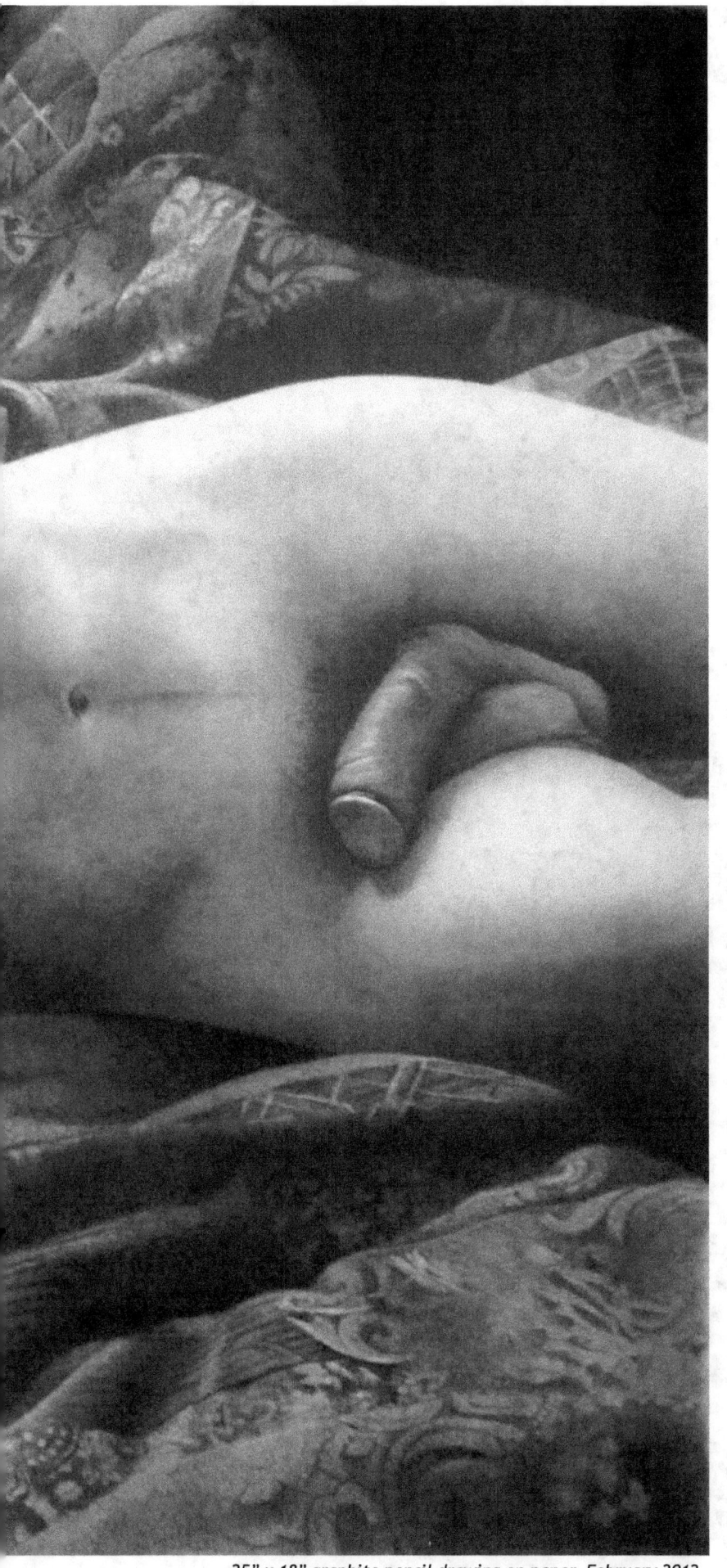

25" x 18" graphite pencil drawing on paper. February 2012

With this paper I was able to enhance my drawing skills, since I draw with all lines and never smear the graphite, as well as pull out more of the detail on this smooth hard pressed surface.

An instant hit for me as an artist and for those who call themselves fans of my work.

The drawings of "Courting" and "Rodeo" were entered in the 2012 Kern County Fair, and both won first place for professional artists.

"Courting" taking the winning trophy for "Best in Show", for the professional fine arts division, as well as first place for professional drawings.

"Rodeo" took home first place for the fair's theme "Best In The West." It also was awarded the Bakersfield Art Association Award.

Granted - It might not sound like much to most artists but for a community event, and dealing with a "small town attitude", this was good exposure.

"Garrett" had not been drawn by the time the entries for the Fair were being accepted and the drawing of "Kevin - Repose" would never have passed the judges or censors. All drawings for the Fair must be family friendly. Too bad.

So, I guess "Garrett" wouldn't have been accepted either. Again. Too bad.

The drawing, "Kevin - Repose" was saved for last. My last full frontal male nude.

Far too many times people judged, condemned, and even limited my potential as an artist because of the male nudes I had drawn. Therefore it was time to accept this may well be one of my best drawings ever. And what better place in my career as a professional artist than now to move on and let this be my last!

So how does one draw so much detail on paper this size? The same as any size. You focus in the various shades of grey, lights, shadows, and details that most people over look - one section at a time. And often with the drawing and reference photo, upside down, and sideways.

The proper tools and supplies are a must for any fine arts project. And the type of paper does effect the piece you are working on. I learned that the hard way, on several drawings with in the past three years, including the figure drawing of Kevin. Which I ended up stopping half way through capturing his facial features before I realized I was using the wrong paper.

Heavy weight drawing paper was just too

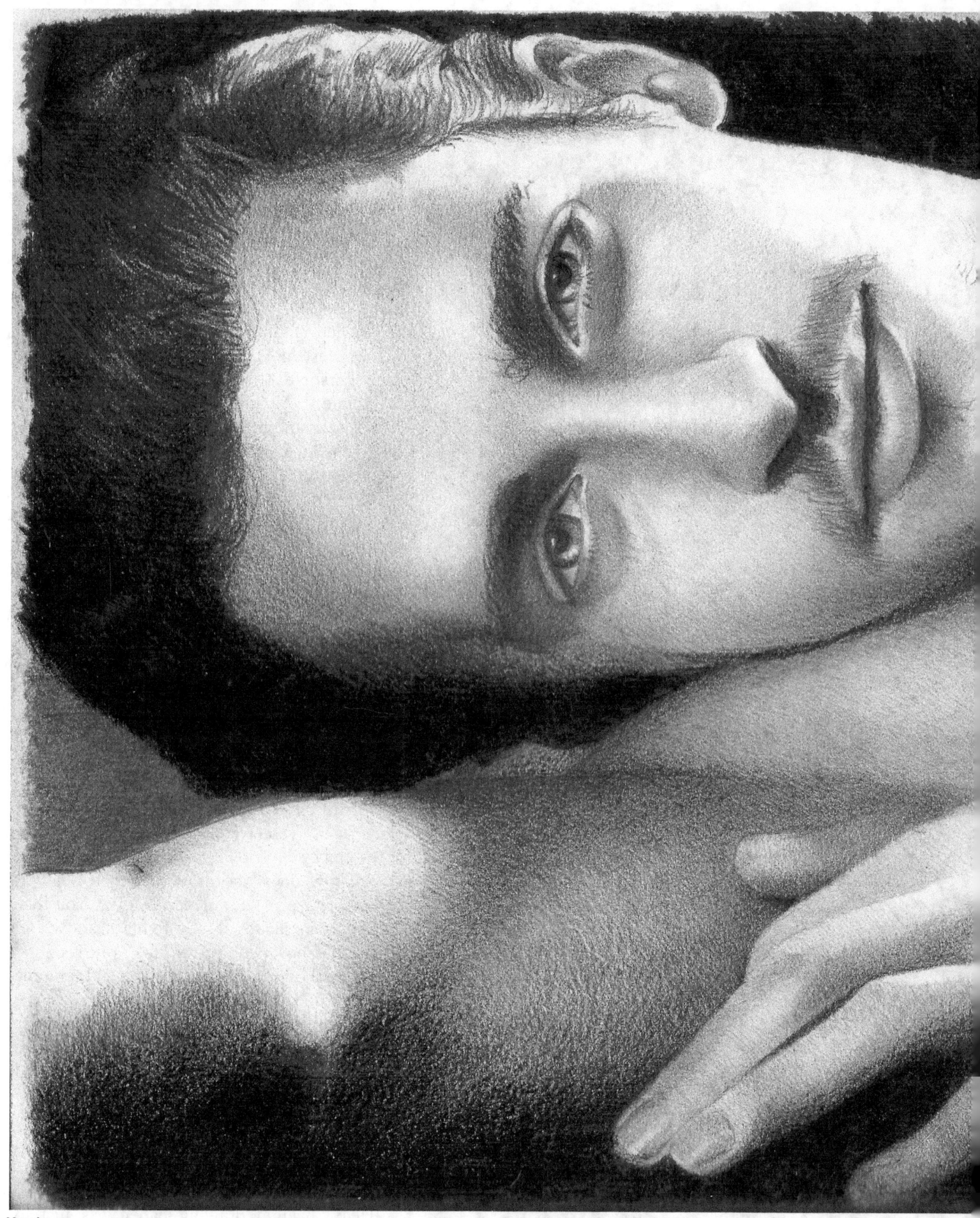

Kevin

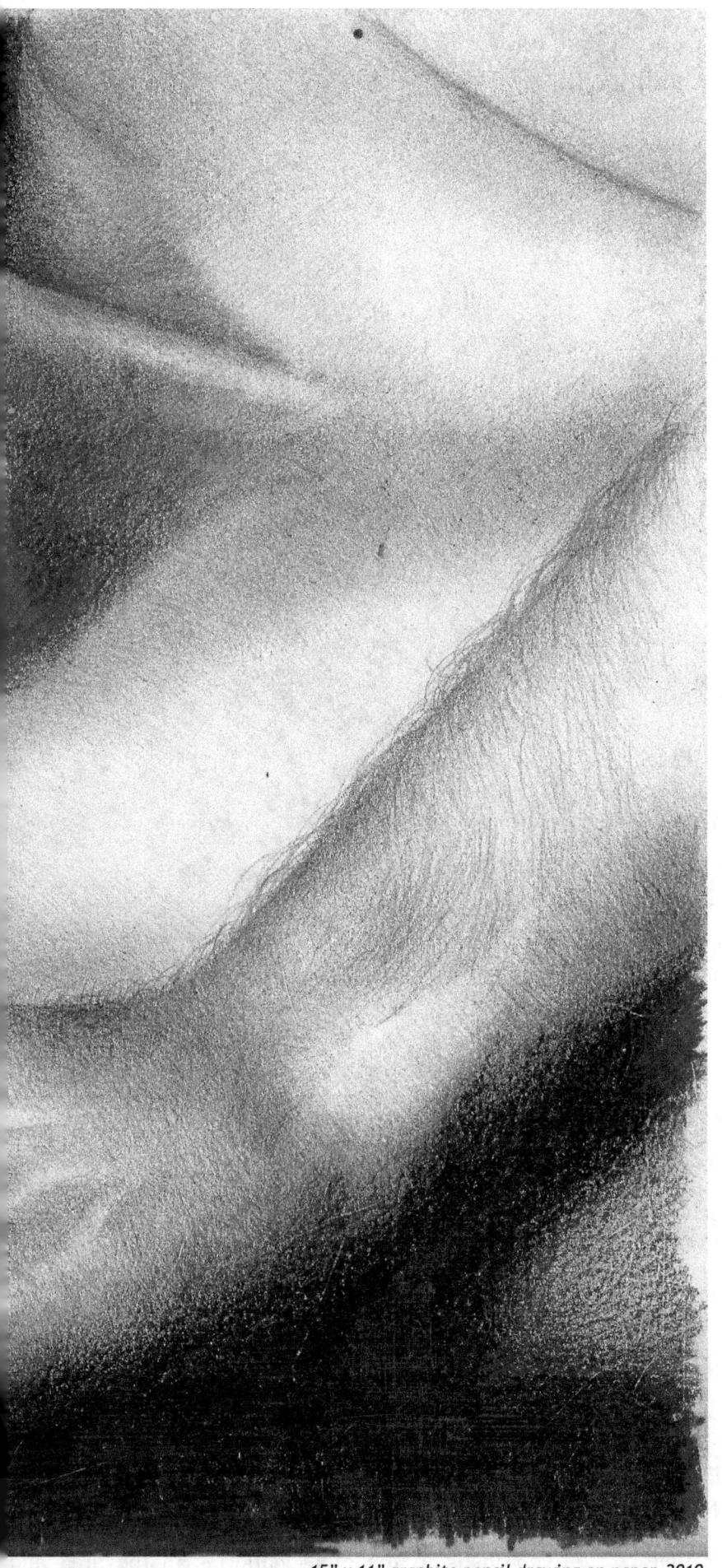

15" x 11" graphite pencil drawing on paper. 2010

rough a texture to capture the detail I wanted from his eyes. And if the eyes were not right, what was the point of continuing the drawing? Especially if it wasn't going to look like him?

Fact - the texture of the paper, as well as it's color, effects not only the quality of the drawing but the style the artist is accustom to working with.

So why the delay or limiting the sizes to my drawings? Simple. The three earlier books were limited to the home scanner I had. Keeping most of the drawings at an 8.5" x 11" or risk damaging the drawings. I felt that it was best to keep the drawing the actual size when it came to showing the detail and explaining how they were created.

As to why these people or the poses were selected? I knew that if these were to be my final drawings they had to be my best!

G. T. Anderson, "Garrett", introduced himself after commenting on the posting a censored version of "Kevin-Repose" on Facebook, which lead me to his profile and the fitness and modeling photos he had posted of himself taken by various photographers.

Never one to just draw anyone, and seeking permission first, I commented on how I'd love to draw one of his photos some day, and before the evening had ended, photographer Dave Ouano emailed me a high resolution jpg of the photo I had commented on.

The drawing of "Garrett", "Courting", and "Kevin - Repose" were the inspiration to updating this book as a second edition.

"Kevin - Repose" was inspired from the works of photographer Robert James and the model being a young man by the name of Kevin J. Gadzalinski.

Both men I came to know separately, via the internet, as the result of networking with other artists, photographers, and models. It wasn't until I came across a series of photos of Kevin, taken by Robert James, that I realized they knew one another.

Award winning drawings.

It was the portrait of "Kevin" (shown here) that convinced me it was time to start showing my work locally. Even if it was just at the County Fair.

Yes, I had art galleries in Los Angles, San Francisco, the Central Coast here in California, and even in NYC and London interested in my drawings, but to get my work shown locally was not practicable at a time when our economy was demanding financial cut backs. I just couldn't afford the rental fees that most galleries were collecting, with one up to $500 a month!

However, I could afford the Fair's five dollar entry fees for each drawing.

2010 was the first year I entered drawings in the Kern County Fair, in Bakersfield, California. Two of which were created for and used in my pencil drawing books.

The portrait of "Kevin" which was created for "Pencil Drawings - a look into drawing portraits", won first place for professional drawings, as well as taking "Best In Show" for professional fine arts.

The drawing of "Cory", featured in "Pencil Drawing volume 2- a look into drawing men", and "Felix - Cowboy II took second pace.

"Cory" for professional pencil drawing.

"Felix - Cowboy II" for miniature art.

In 2011, I entered three more drawings that were created for my pencil drawing books. A portrait of a local friend named "Augie", my second drawing of "Chris" and for the fair's theme entry, I submitted "As The Worlds Fall Down."

"Augie" brought home first place for the professional drawing category.

"Chris II" brought home second place in that same category, and "As The Worlds Fall Down" took first place for the Fair's theme for that year, which was "magic".

Seeing the winnings that summer night, I called my sons from the Fair, and after telling my oldest son that I did not bring home "Best in Show" for the second year, he playfully informed me I was a disgrace and could not come home that night.

In 2012, when I had called him to inform him my drawing of "Courting" took first place as well as "Best In Show", I asked if it was okay to come home this time? He had forgotten his sarcastic comment from the year before, so the humor was lost in that phone conversation.

As with all first place winners at the Fair, each piece has the opportunity to be on display at The Bakersfield Art Center, starting the week after the Fair and run through the month of October.

Great exposure for local artist, however, not always a welcoming feeling.

As I stood back and watched people approach the drawings of "Courting" and "Rodeo", I noticed three middle aged adults, who I thought were educated judging their appearance, verbally attack my drawings. As one man pointed to the crotch of the men in the two separate drawings I could hear the woman comment that "that"

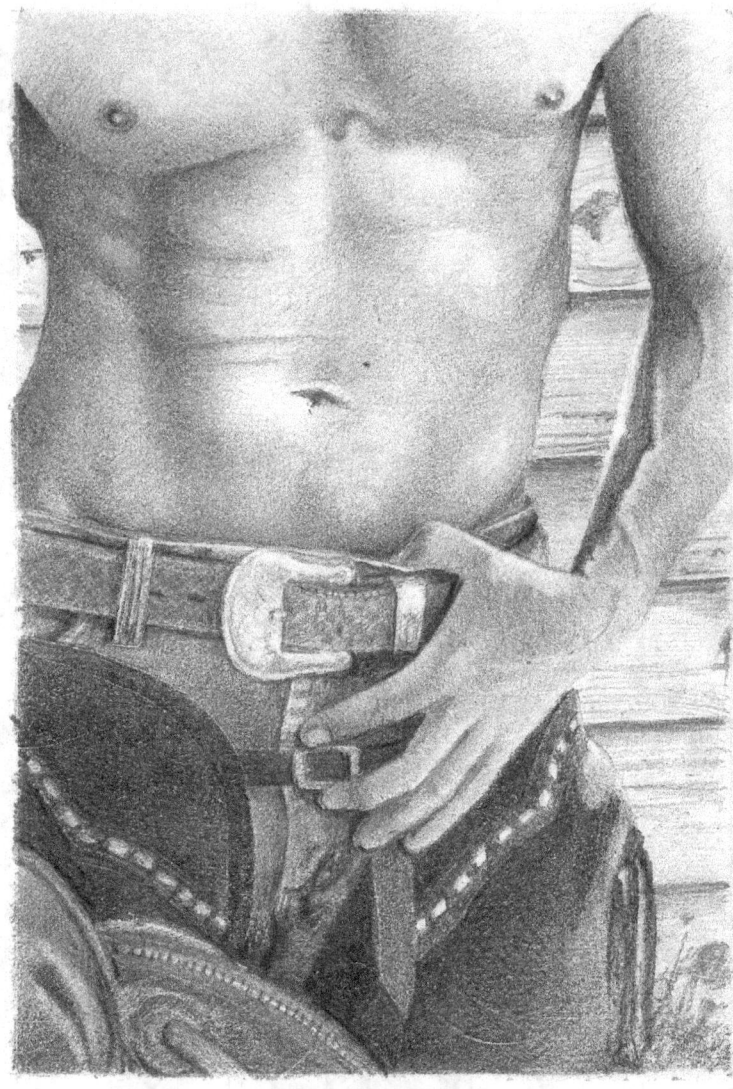

Felix - Cowboy II
4.25" x 6.25"" graphite pencil drawing on paper. 2009

was what she too had noticed first.

Attacked again for the beauty I had placed on paper!

Without a second thought to how others would perceive my two drawings when I first entered them in the Fair, for the first time I realizes that what and who I drew may have been my downfall and why my work was not accepted locally.

Leaving the gallery feeling dirty, condemned, and questioned how others perceive me through the work I create, I knew it was better not to listen to them anymore before I said something I shouldn't have.

Followed by my wife and youngest son, who came along for the showing, we left the gallery as quickly as we had entered.

It was Bakersfield's "First Friday" so the streets in the local art district were packed with local artists and their crafts as well as admirers and buyers. However no matter how hard I tried to put the "crotch watchers" comments at the gallery behind me, I couldn't.

Even visits to the other galleries in the area and

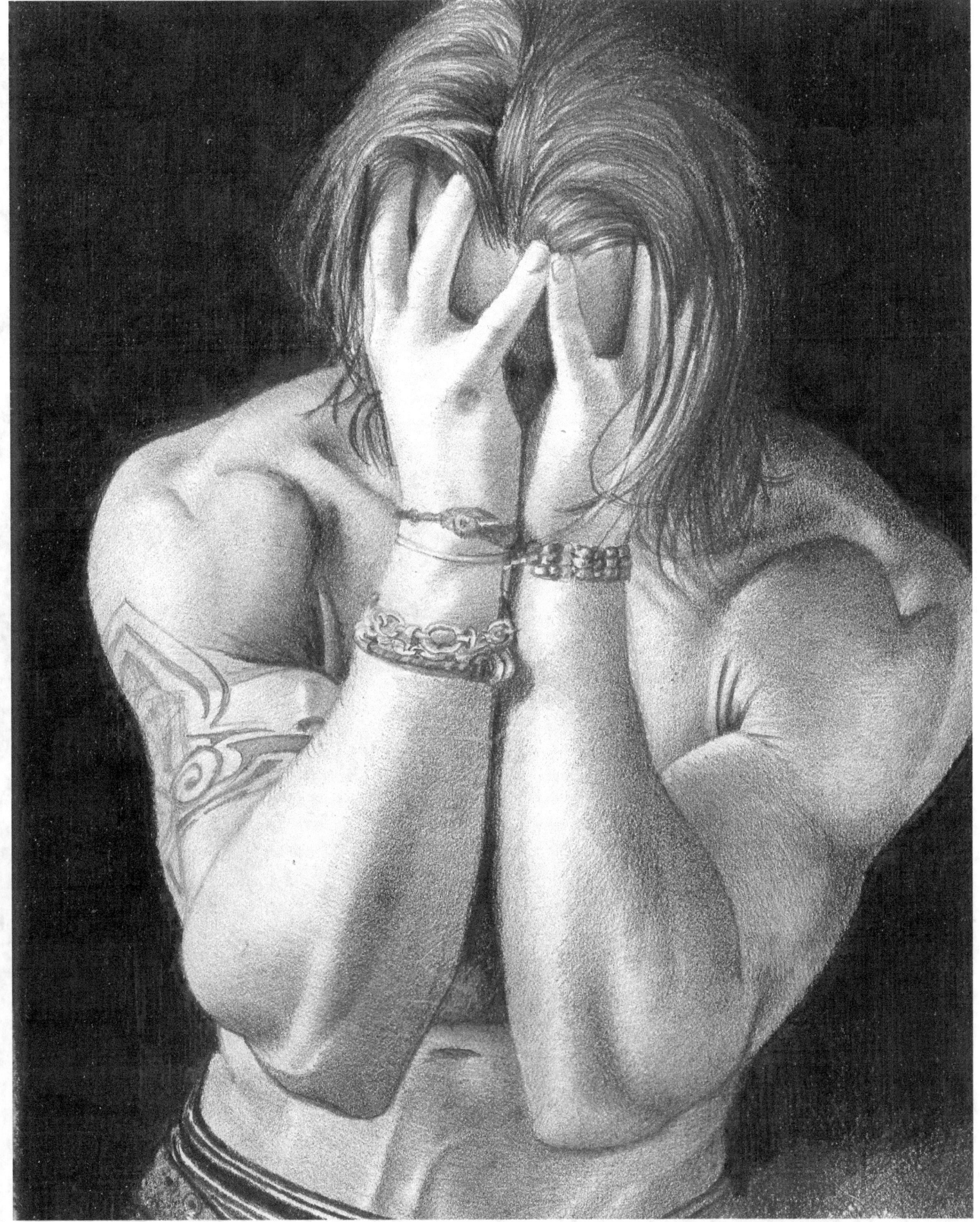

Cory

8.5" x 11" graphite pencil drawing on paper. 2009

A look into the art of David J. **Vanderpool**   15

meeting up to some of my wife's family didn't help. At least not at that point.

Not wanting to go back in fear of further judgment, and out spoken comments, I knew I had to. Not for me, but for my family who came to see not only my drawings but the other pieces on display.

Once inside, my wife's brother was there to offer support in a way only Robert could do. And that was to attract a group and get people to take notice of the two drawings that were displayed center of the exhibit.

Not sure where he was going to take this, and just how far he would go, I played along and answered his questions as to how each drawing was completed.

Taking this opportunity to down play the "crotch-watcher's comments from earlier I reminded them how the human anatomy is different from one sex to the other.

For a man without a bulge in his jeans can easily be, and often is, mistaken as a woman.

Yes they were still there. However they became silent and lost in the crowd as others openly commented on quality of each the drawings and how accurate the costumes were for the period.

Catching on to what Robert was doing, and how the 'crotch-watchers' began to fall out of the group, one gentleman took notice and with a smirk that only those facing him would see playfully asked if the two men in the drawings were self portraits.

I thanked him but politely said, "No, they were not. Well... at least not the cowboy".

That silenced the 'crotch watchers'. In fact they were never seen again that night. Good!

Yes we will be judged for the art we create.

No matter the reason we give, as to why we do what we do, as artist we seek attention, recognition, and if possible, acceptance among our peers as well as the community who stands back and watches what we create.

Interesting people were met that night.

A woman approached me that night and asked me if I went to one of the high schools in the area. Her husband was a teacher and had a student with the same name as

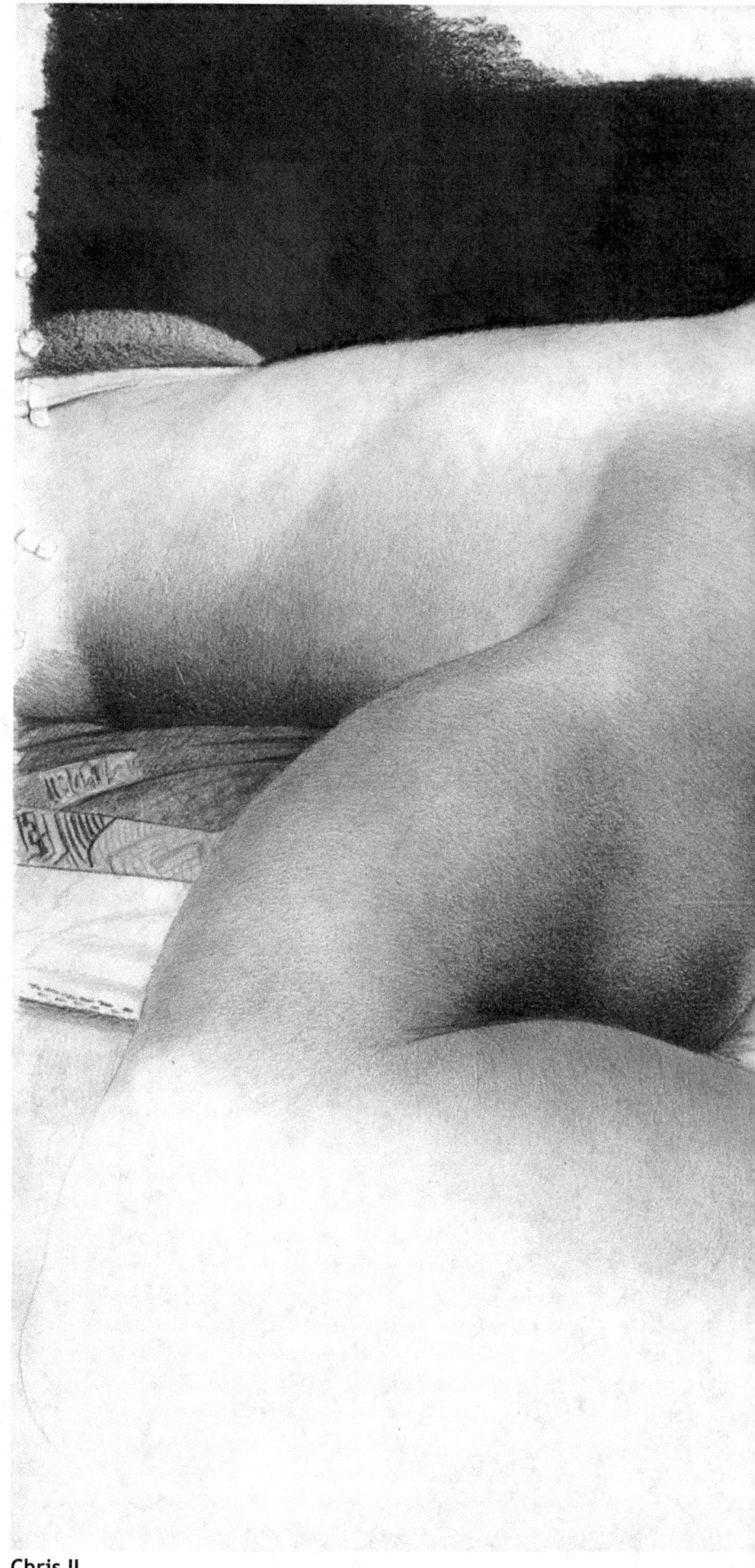

Chris II

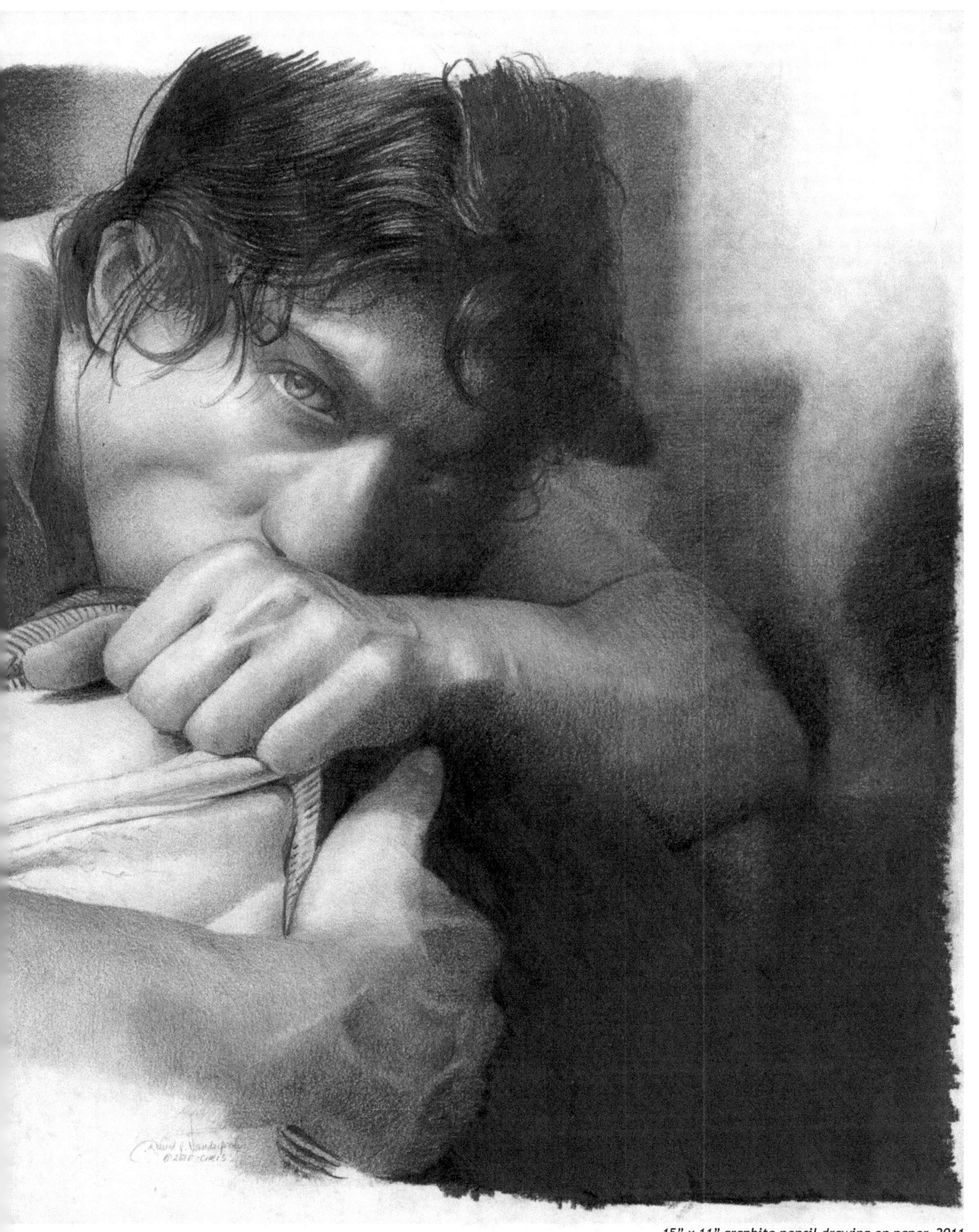

15" x 11" graphite pencil drawing on paper. 2011

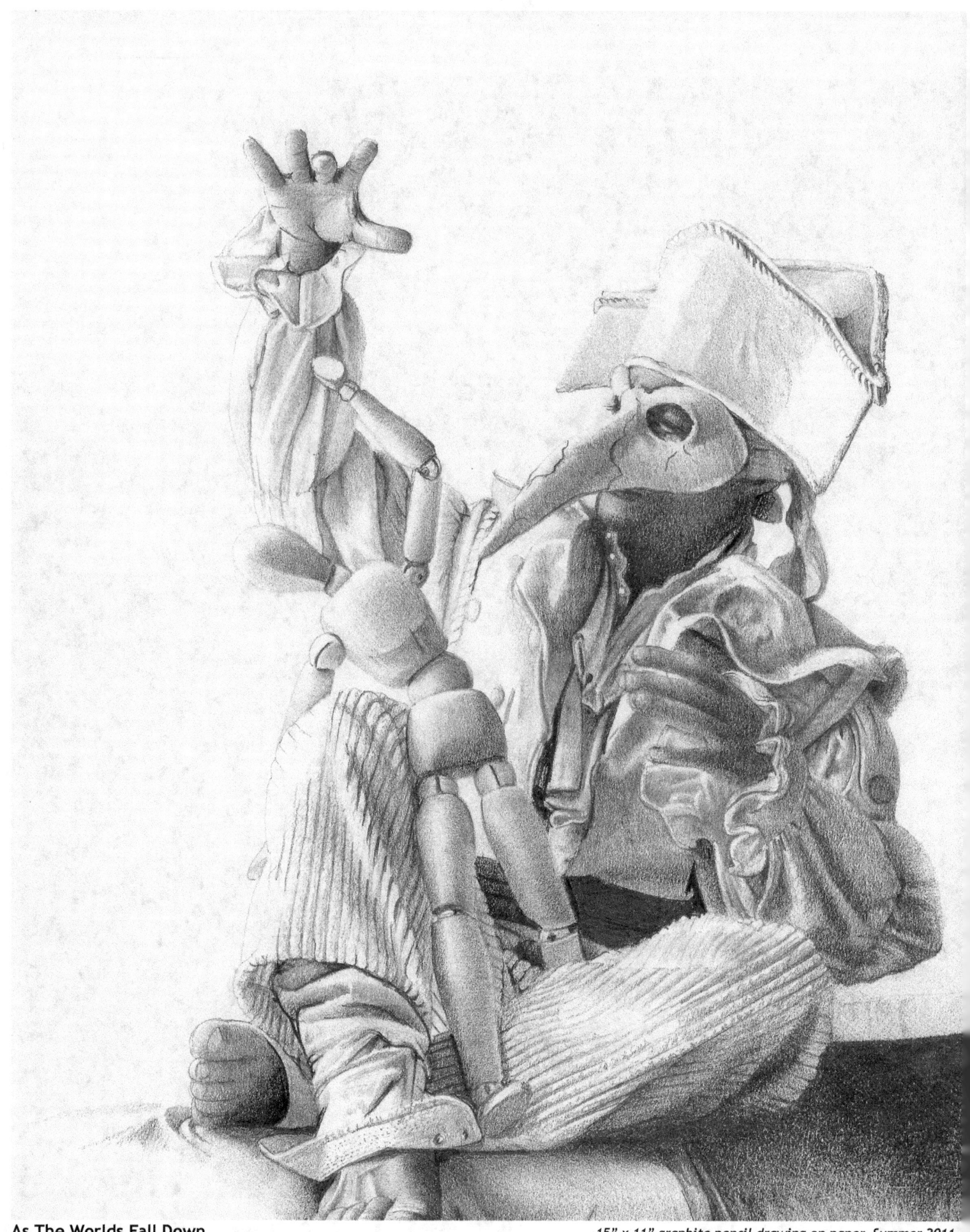

As The Worlds Fall Down

15" x 11" graphite pencil drawing on paper. Summer 2011

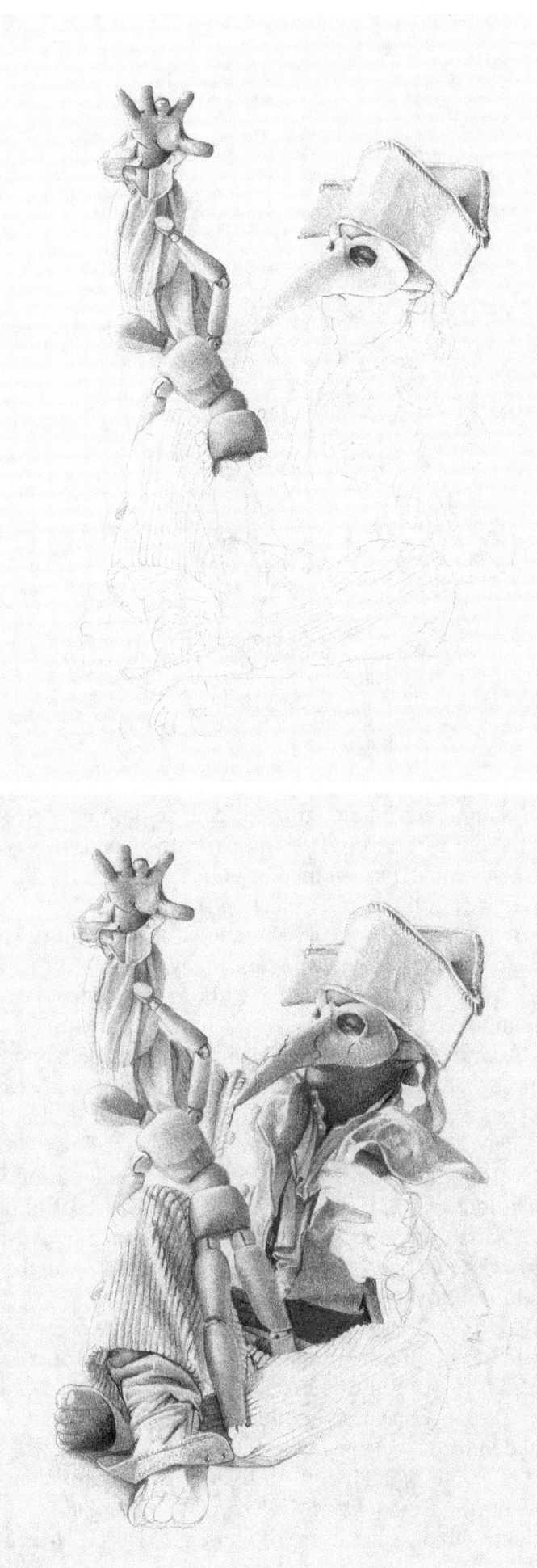

mine.

I informed her it wasn't me. I like to tell people I was kidnapped and held hostage here because I was born and raised in San Jose.

Her husband approached me and started an interesting conversation, and before the end of the night was over I was in a far better mood than earlier.

"That turned out nicely", my wife had said as we headed towards our SUV that night. Better than earlier, wasn't it? "They really liked your work"

She too had noticed the infamous "crotch watchers"

"Yes. It turned out better than I feared."

Who catches who's attention?

So just how much do we reveal who we are with the pieces we create? And what do we do when our work speaks louder than we want it to?

Do we change, tame or alter what we want to create, based on how we want others to see and accept us as an artist? Or do we be ourselves and accept who we are as a person, and create based on how we feel and who catches our attention?

As a graphite pencil artist I knew early on, and was repeatedly told over and over again, that my drawings would never be accepted commercially. Not just because collectors do not want portraits or figure drawings of people they don't know, or the fact they are in black and white, but because they are only drawings!

Young and passionate at the time, I took this as a challenge rather than an obstacle and put away my paintings, brushes, and focused on my drawings. Making sure each drawing was better than the last.

If I couldn't be good at all I attempted, I was going to be good at least in one area. And it just so happened that drawing was my escape -- I didn't have to think and figure out what to do with each step as I would if I were painting.

However this was not until I hit a period in my life when frustration and despair took over and one day in the mid 1990's I just stopped drawing. Promising myself that I would never draw again.

I had reached my early 30's and I was still unknown and my art career was going nowhere. We had moved to a part of California where quality art supplies were as limited as the Arts themselves.

Taking on my first professional job as an illustrator for a furniture store that advertised in the major newspaper for Bakersfield. I would stay after work and began teaching myself the programs needed to layout ads and instantly Photoshop was a hit for me!

By the end of nearly three years I was doing most of

the ad layouts. What started as illustrations of furniture for the store's newspaper ads taught me how to use Photoshop to create the pieces and change the fabrics.

As to why the manager and owners never purchased a digital camera was beyond me! And yes this was asked many times by me and the other artist that worked there.

That job ended when the local newspaper, *The Bakersfield Californian*, called me a week before Christmas and asked me to work for them. I didn't have to think twice. They knew my work by the ads I created and since they came to me, that must have been a good thing?

The start of 2000, I found myself wanting, needing, to get back into drawing again. I was no longer interested in using it as the escape I sought as a child. I came to realize I was missing out on the simple pleasures drawing had provided for me.

Knowing my drawings would never take on where I had left off well over six years ago I was ready for wherever it would lead me.

My style had changes - and for the life of me I could not draw as I had before. What was once a smooth and soft feel to my drawing, blending the graphite and focusing on the eyes, the drawings took on a life of their own and I had no idea where this was coming from.

A self taught artist, I learned by sight and not by reading. Even the books I collected as a child, I would see and copy, rather than read and learn. Which may explain why it took me so long to reach this level of artistry.

I was drawing now with all lines and no longer smearing, blending the graphite with a finger, or using a blending tool.

I started to use the lighter pencils and worked in layers by going over the darker graphite that had been placed on the paper. My blending tools had now become the pencils I had been working with all along.

What did not change was the focus on the eyes. If the eyes did not turn out perfect the first time, then there was no need to continue the drawing. When drawing portraits I always start with the eyes.

What did not change was who attracted me when it came to, not only my drawings, but people in general. There has to be an attraction, an interest in who they are, both in physical appearance as well as character.

Character and emotion make for a better drawing rather than beauty alone.

As an artist who started off as a shy child, I learned early on that people paid attention to me when I drew. Granted it wasn't focused on me, but rather what I was doing, but none the less it was some attention and usually positive.

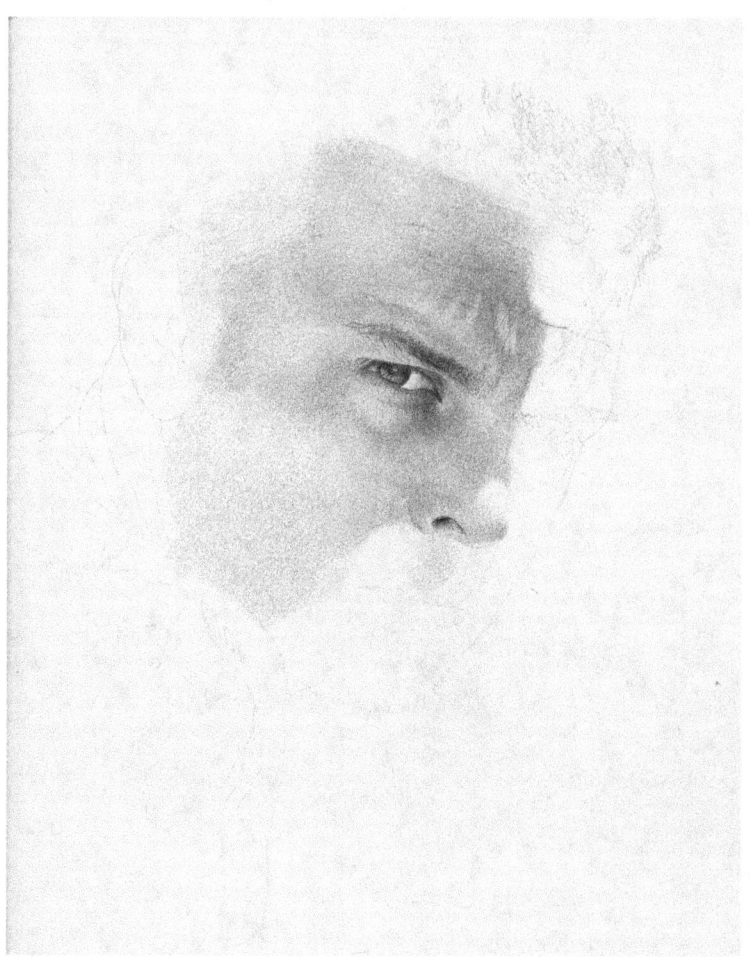

As an adult; habits, good or bad, seldom change and to this day I find myself using my drawings as a way to introduce myself when meeting others.

As was in the case of meeting Augie.

Being called to a jury summons one should always bring something to pass the time away. A book for some, work for others, and in my case I brought my pencils and drawing pad.

Instantly people would take notice. Some bold enough to ask what I was working on while others stood back at a distance and took notice. Augie was one that kept his distance but his interest was noticeable.

Not on the same trial, but passing in halls during the lunch hour break, it wasn't hard to take notice of him as well. Attractive, masculine, and he had amazing eyes. I fall back to old habits when I see people and thought he would be a good model and great to draw.

However this wasn't the place or time because I would never approach a man to draw as I would approach a friend. It wouldn't be proper, and worst of all, what if he took the request as another motive than what it was intended for?

Or worse what if my motivation was other than to draw him? After all having been in this county and still no contact with others outside of work and church. Meeting

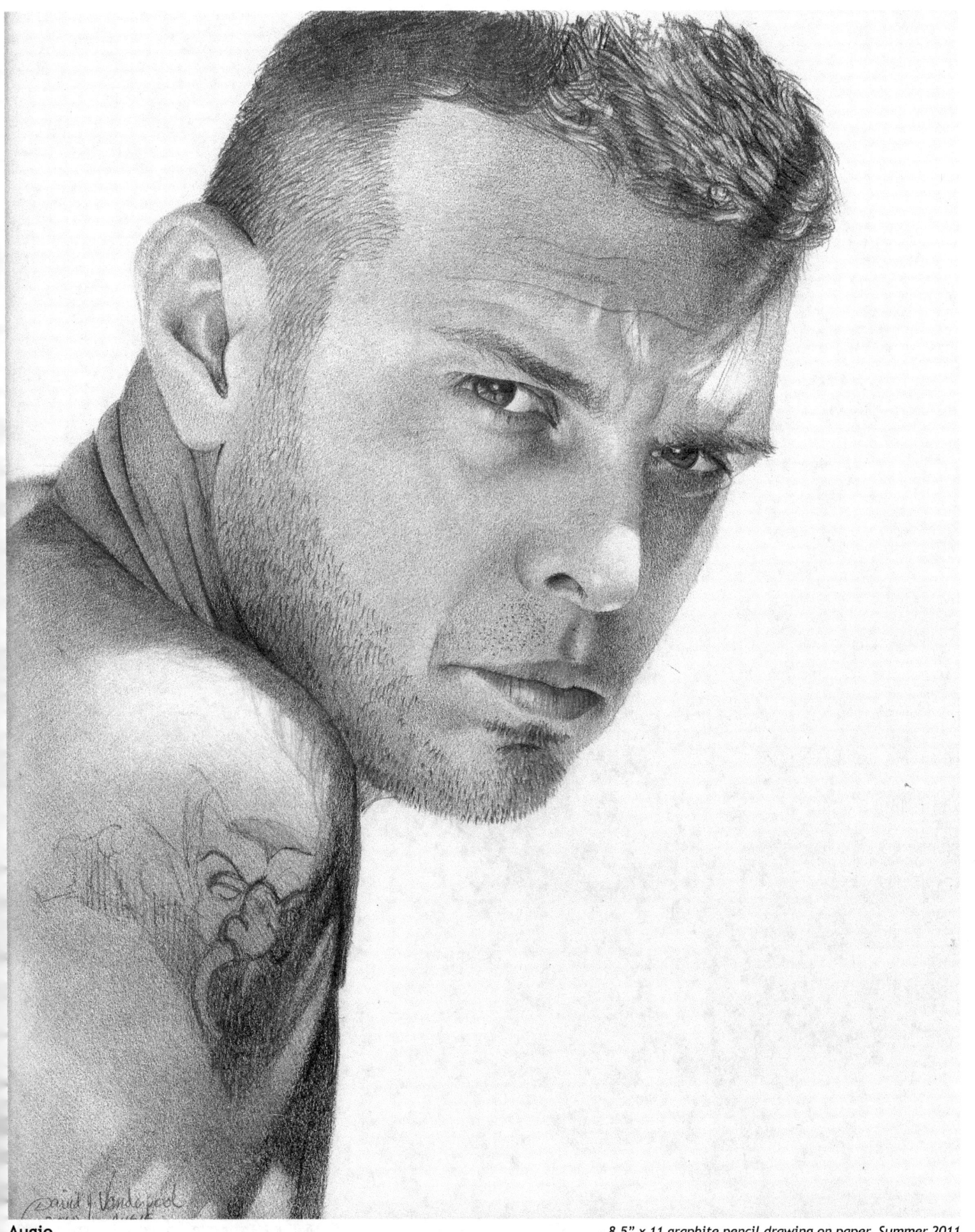

Augie

8.5" x 11 graphite pencil drawing on paper. Summer 2011

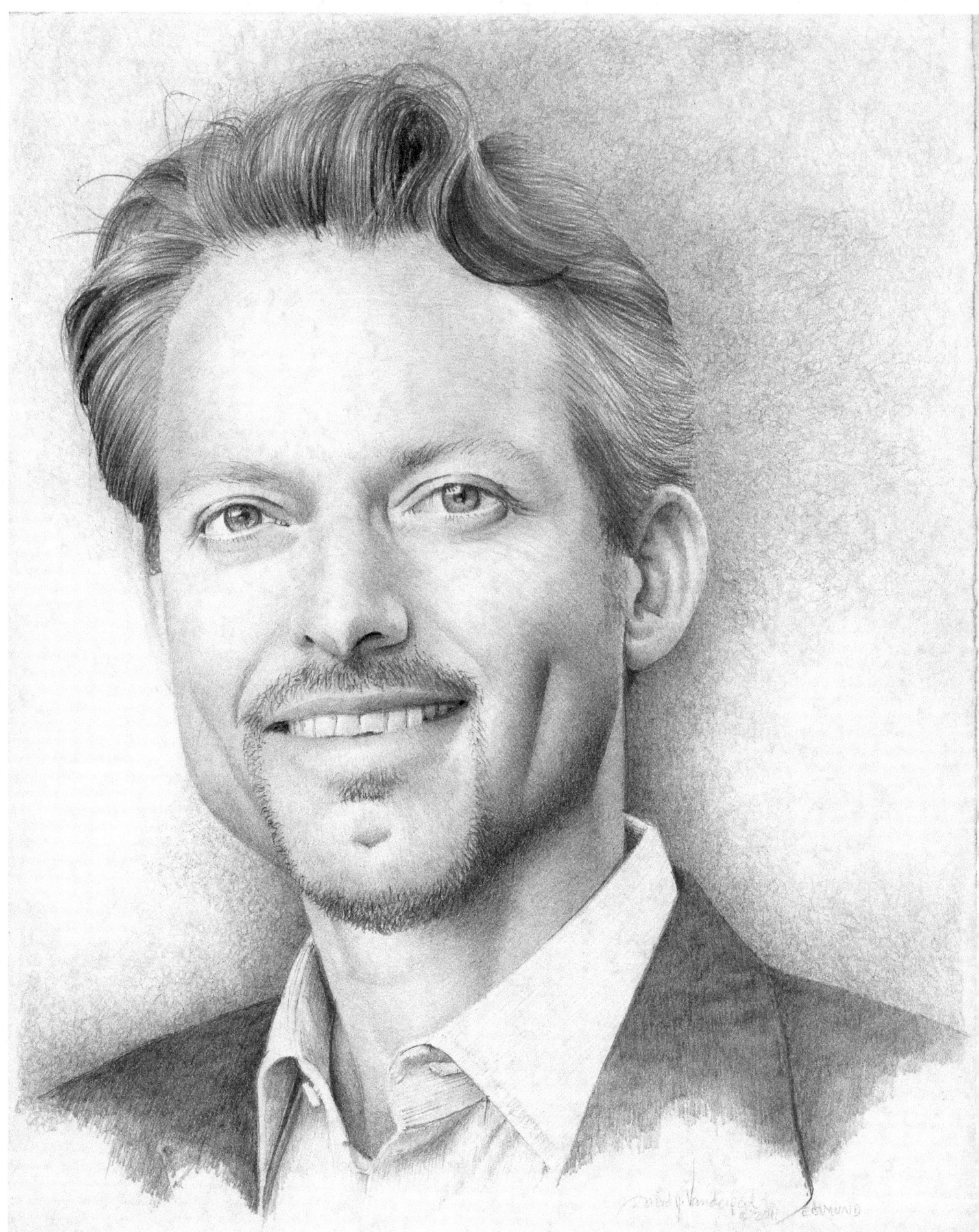

Edmund

8.5" x 11" graphite pencil drawing on paper. 201

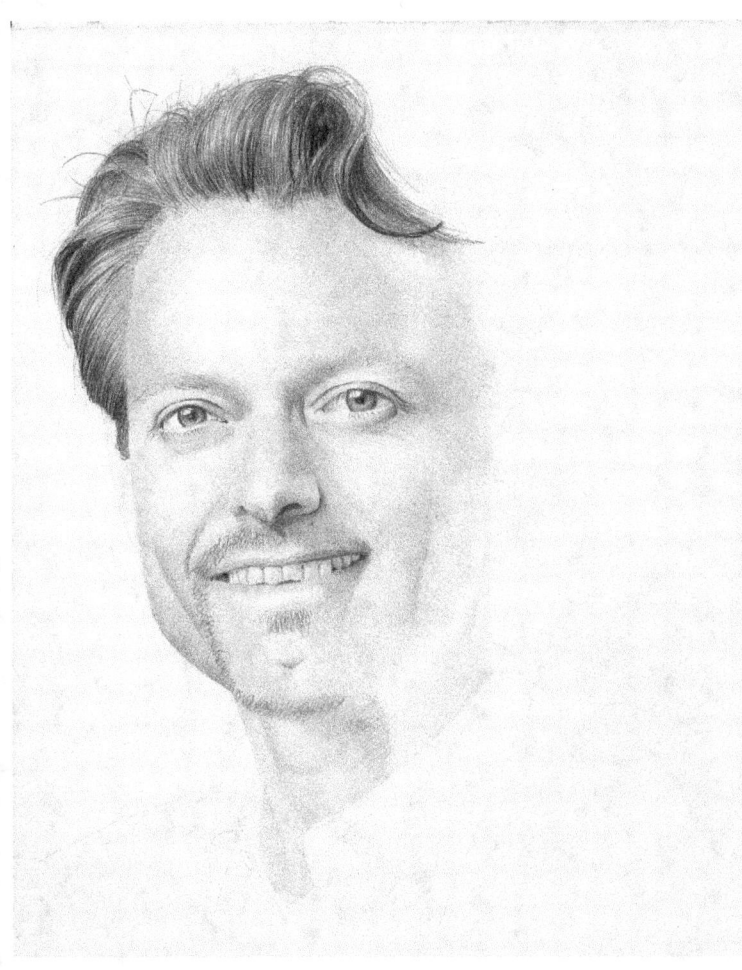

subconsciously brought into the world where adults often find themselves over work and little time for themselves.

Keep in mind though - not all drawings lead beyond what is seen on paper. Nor were they intended!

I met Dr. Fisher as the result of an audiologist who asked me one afternoon why hadn't I had surgery to correct my hearing? I told him in the six years or so of wearing a hearing aide no one informed me I had the option and so I had no idea my hearing lose could be corrected. It would be wonderful if my hearing could be restored.

As a male artist drawing men I find myself defending who I am as a person both sexually and artistically. However this man was different. He was my doctor and I could not risk offending someone who had the potential to change my life.

Yes he was very attractive, but more than that, his eyes lit up when he talked about his work and what he could do for me. It wasn't a sales pitch but a man who had passion for what he did for a living. A man that found passion in helping others. That is exactly what I look for in models for my drawings. Emotion and a passion for life!

The first surgery to rebuild the bone behind my ear drum occurred June of 2010 but there had to be a six month waiting period before a second surgery could take place.

It was during this waiting period, and our first meeting after the operated on my left ear, we discover my hearing went from about a 92% loss to where I could get by without a hearing aide.

Tears filled my eyes the minute I could hear him for the first time without a hearing aid. And when he saw this his eyes sparkled and the smile on his face told me this man was for real. A man that loved not just his work, but the look on the patients face when the surgery was a success.

It was also a smile that took me beyond a doctor patient relationship and "pushed" me to ask him if I could draw him for a book I was working on.

Instantly I knew I had stepped out of line, or so I thought.

He already knew about my book on 'portraits' that went on the market not long before our first meeting. So before any regret of asking him could set in he asked what did he have to do to be drawn?

I was caught off guard and said he just needed to e-mail me a few photos that I could draw from. When in reality I wanted to say that I would be willing to take some photos of him like I had done with Augie.

Two drawings were created of Edmund (Dr. Fisher).

someone to talk to and share a smile would have been nice?

Nonsense, just a foolish thought, I went back to work on my drawing of "Cory". That first afternoon of Jury Duty my focus was on what was in front of me rather than on the man across the hall taking stolen glances of me.

Surprisingly, that evening a message in my e-mail from Augie revealed that I wasn't wrong. That he in fact had taken an interest in what I was doing and accepting a friendship can occur in the most unlikely places.

Odd that he would go online to look for me and search for more of my drawings? Not really. Later I would discover he had an interest in art and would go back to college and take art classes.

With e-mails exchanged we kept in touch so when it came time for me to work on the portraits for my book on drawing men I knew I had to draw him.

Besides things were changing. He was no longer a stranger taking notice of me and my drawings at a distance. He had become an acquaintance with the potential of becoming a friend within time.

Again I found myself using my ability to draw to meet others in the hopes of making a friend. In hopes to be appreciated and accepted. A childish behavior

I was never pleased with how the first one turned out. The quality was not good enough to show my appreciation towards what he had done for me.

Therefore an e-mail went out to him shortly after he received the first drawing requesting if I could try just one more time.

The final drawing reflects the man I saw the day we discovered how well I could hear once again.

No personal friendship was made after the doctor and patient relationship came to a close other than what was excepted between an artist and one of his models.

Not all drawings lead to friendships, nor are they intended!

Same sex attraction vs. the opposite sex.

Same sex attraction, or attraction to the opposite sex can often lead to very powerful drawings if the subject is approached carefully, respectfully, and in most cases, none sexually. Allowing the model to speak for themselves and not for the artist.

Whether it's a sensual pose, as seen in this drawing of Cristina, or of Stephen from Palm Springs, California (pages 26, 27), keeping away from sexual themes or poses and focusing on the emotion or character captured in the original photograph can be enough to catch the viewers attention. And leaving them to want for more.

Questioned, judged or perceived, in regards to who we may or may not be, has always been something an artist has had to deal with when it came to selecting who he works with

Too often are we judged and labeled by what we create. And granted most artists welcome and in fact encourage it when their works take on social issues - but as mention early in this chapter - sometimes art is just art!

Years ago I received two e-mails on the same day. One from a young Christian man and the other from a woman.

The young man questioned my sexuality and then stated that my drawings caused him to sin and that I should remove my drawings of men from my web site. I wrote back, in defense, and told him if he has a problem with his sexuality that was an issue between him and God.

The next e-mail was from a woman who called me a sexist for the women I drew and that I should be shamed of myself.

I never replied back to her. The Christian in me knew better than to go there. At least at that moment and especially after the earlier e-mail.

Sexuality and drawings.

Cristina

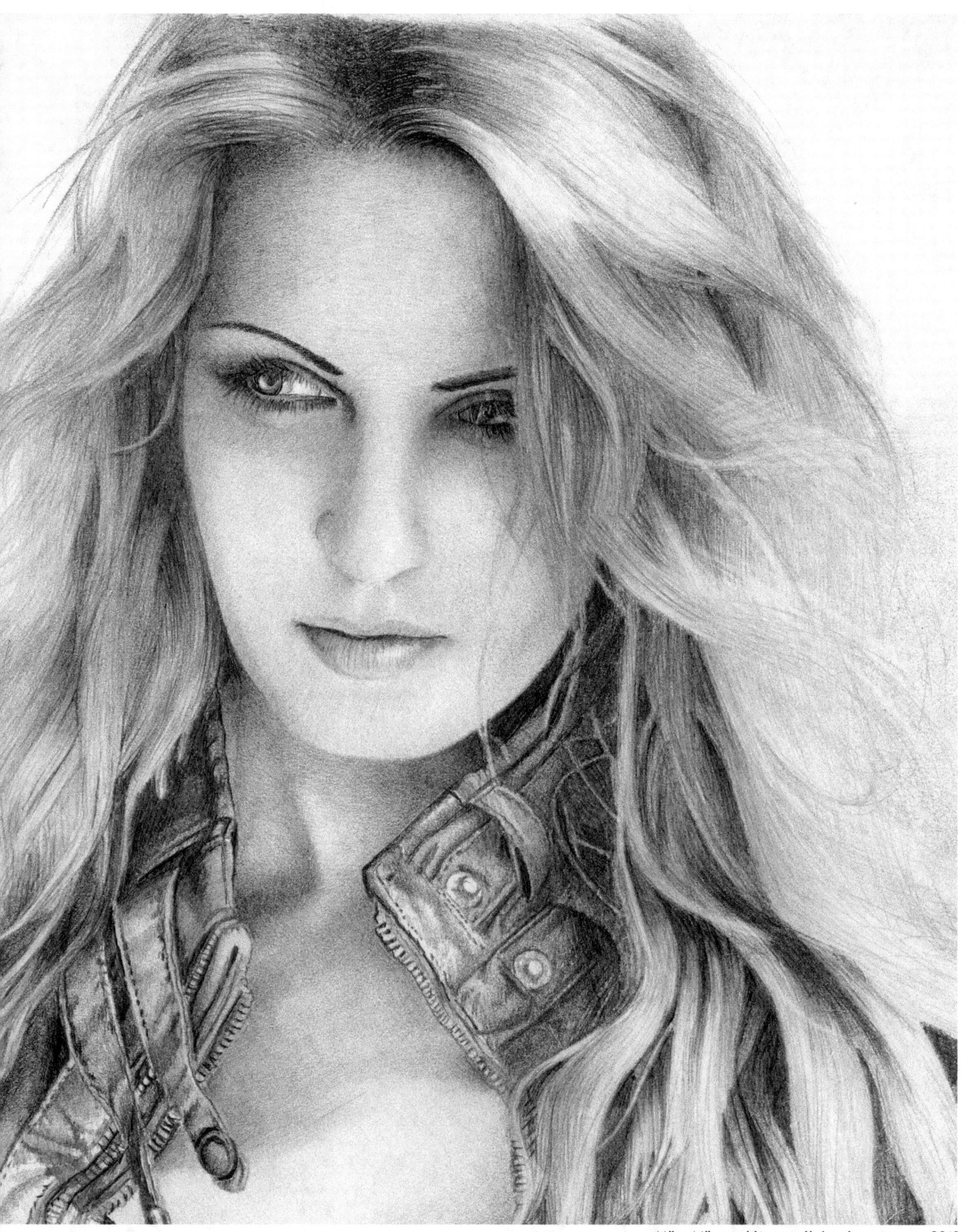

11" x 14" graphite pencil drawing on paper. 2013

A look into the art of David J. **Vanderpool**   25

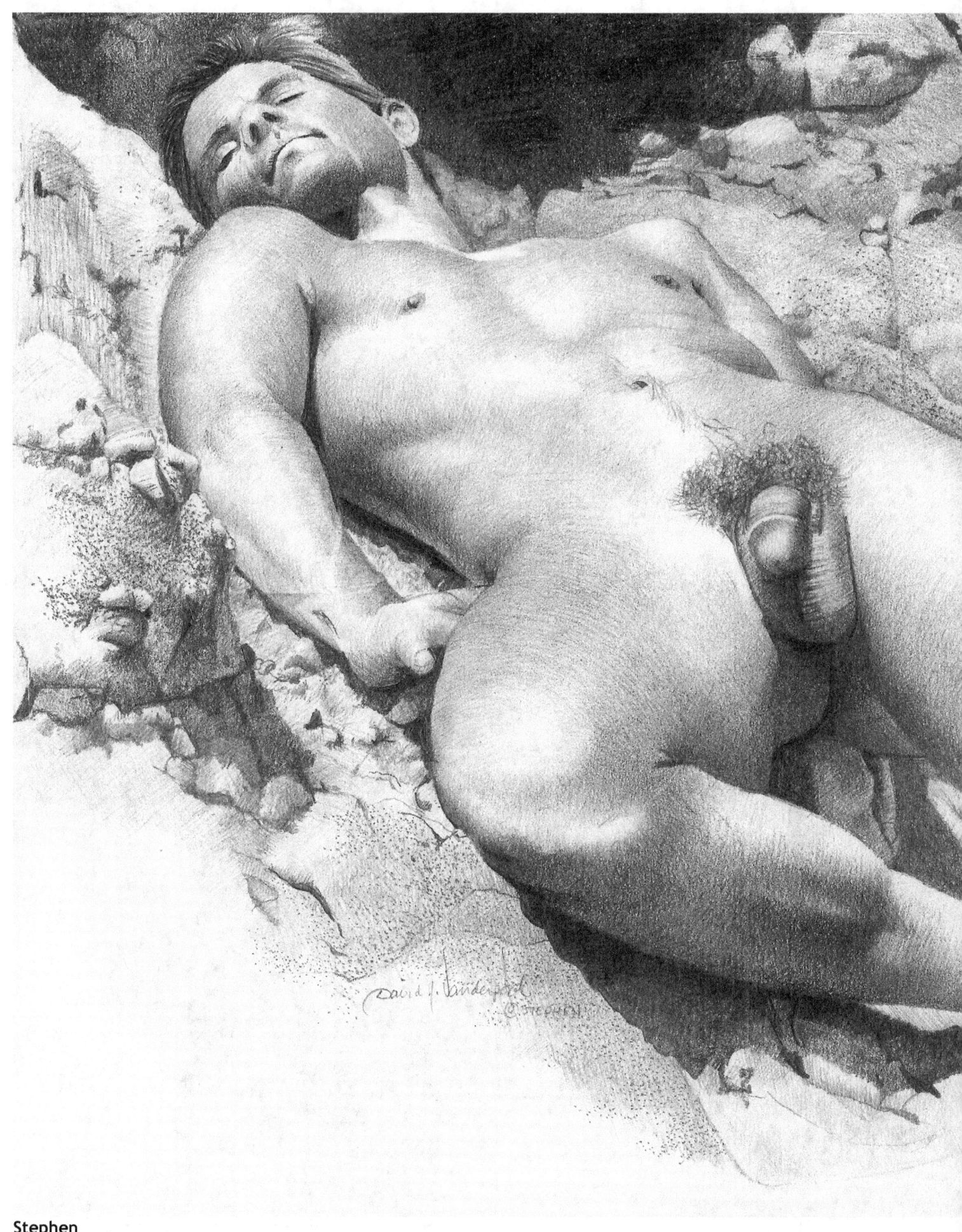

Stephen

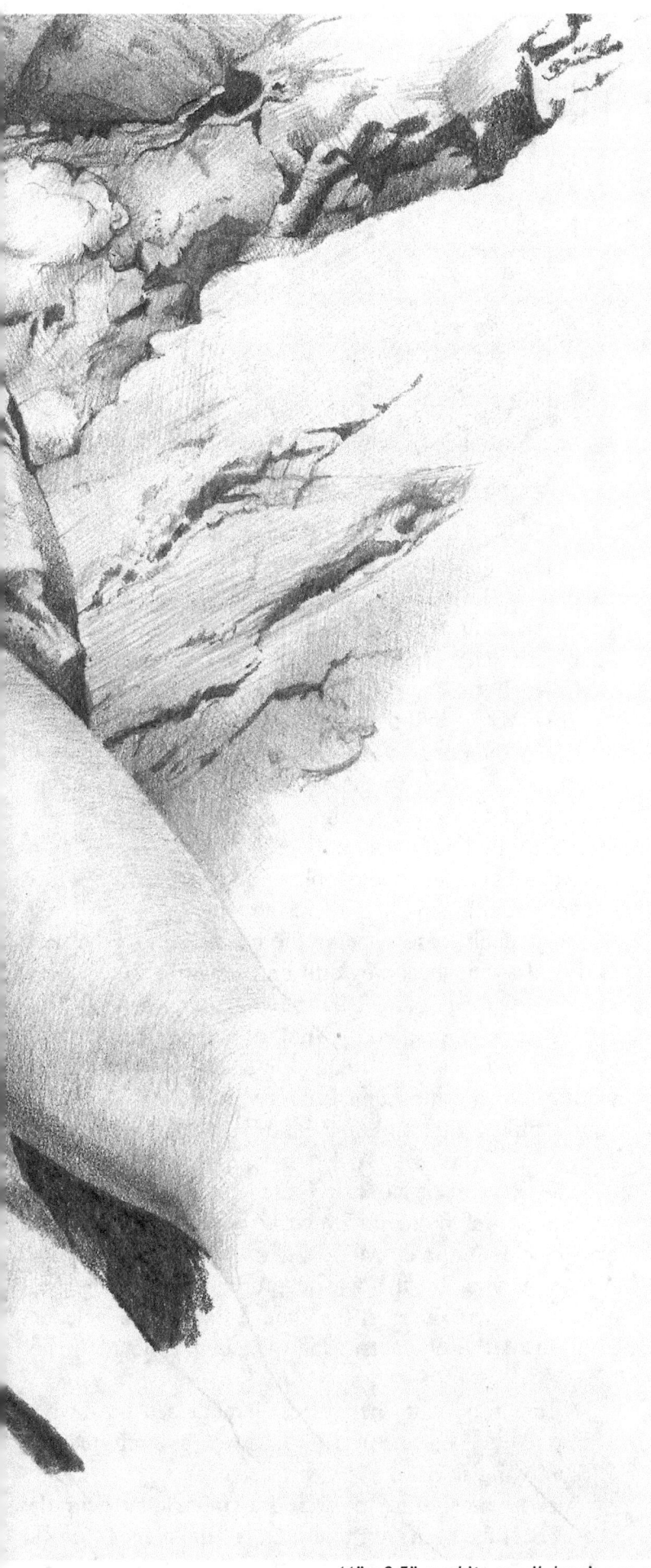

For some people they see only what they want, seek what they desire, and assume the hearts of others without knowing who that person is personally, solely on the bases of what the artist is able to put on paper, with just a few pencils in hand.

Is the drawing of Stephen sexually appealing? To most people of course it is?

Does the drawing make people uncomfortable seeing a full frontal male nude? That all depends on where you are in life socially and where you live physically? What is rejected in America is appreciated in Europe. Just as the education man will see the detail in the side of the mountain he is resting on others will take first notice of his penis - and never see past it.

However, in all fairness to those who see "that" part of the drawing first, it is in the center of the drawing and masterfully drawn with all its detail so how could you not see the drawing for what it is?

A nude man.

Nude, not crude.

As art should be!

For where others see a naked man in the drawing shown here I see a portrait of a man asleep in the sun.

But no matter what I see, or why I draw who I draw, there will always be people who question my interests and motivation behind male drawings. And in doing so they limit themselves from seeing the rest of the drawing and the effort that was put into creating the art.

Point given: When working on the book on drawing men I was asked why didn't I draw women? For goodness sake man where you not paying attention! The book is on drawing men, for crying out loud! Or course you wouldn't see as many drawings of women during that period!

Yes there will always be beauty in both sexes to catch an artist's attention and therefore we will be judged for the art we create.

And that is the difference between commercial art and fine art! To work with those who catches the artist's attention and allow others to react to what they see before them.

For good or bad - that's up to the viewer.

11" x 8.5" graphite pencil drawing on paper. 2006

Chapter Two
Portraits

Drawing is one of the first skills children pick up and one of their first experiences in acceptance and recognition. Instantly the refrigerator door becomes their gallery, a place to show off their latest masterpiece as new pieces are added daily. It's as if the refrigerator was created just for that purpose.

As an adult, for those of us who continued to explore our creative side, the desire for acceptance and recognition never leaves us.

Towards the middle part of my childhood I discovered what was intended as my way of escaping those around me, I could use it to get attention and acceptance by sharing what I do with a single pencil and a piece of paper by those who would take notice.

And of course when people would ask how I did this, I would simply say "it's all in the pencil", which really is pretty much close to being the truth. Without the right tool, a drawing becomes dull and flat - no life to it no matter how much one wishes they could do better.

When people generally think of a portrait, they think of a painting created from an old master – something one would find in a museum. Rarely would they consider a pencil drawing capable of capturing life and passion. That is until now!

This portrait of Nonna, created for my book "Pencil Drawings - a look into drawing portraits", was taken from a photograph by Matt Bottos. A photographer from Australia who, by the way captures some of the best photos you will ever get the chance to see, was selected because of the character, charm, and the detail in her face.

All are important when selecting models to draw, when adding to one's private portfolio, as well as strengthening ones drawing skills.

As with most of my portrait drawings, I start with the eyes. For if the eyes aren't perfect, a true likeness to who you are trying to capture on paper will not be achieved,

> " I have come to realize that one should never assume you are at your best! Even though what you have completed might be your best at that moment. Time will prove that your best is yet to come ...

- David J. Vanderpool
November 25, 2012

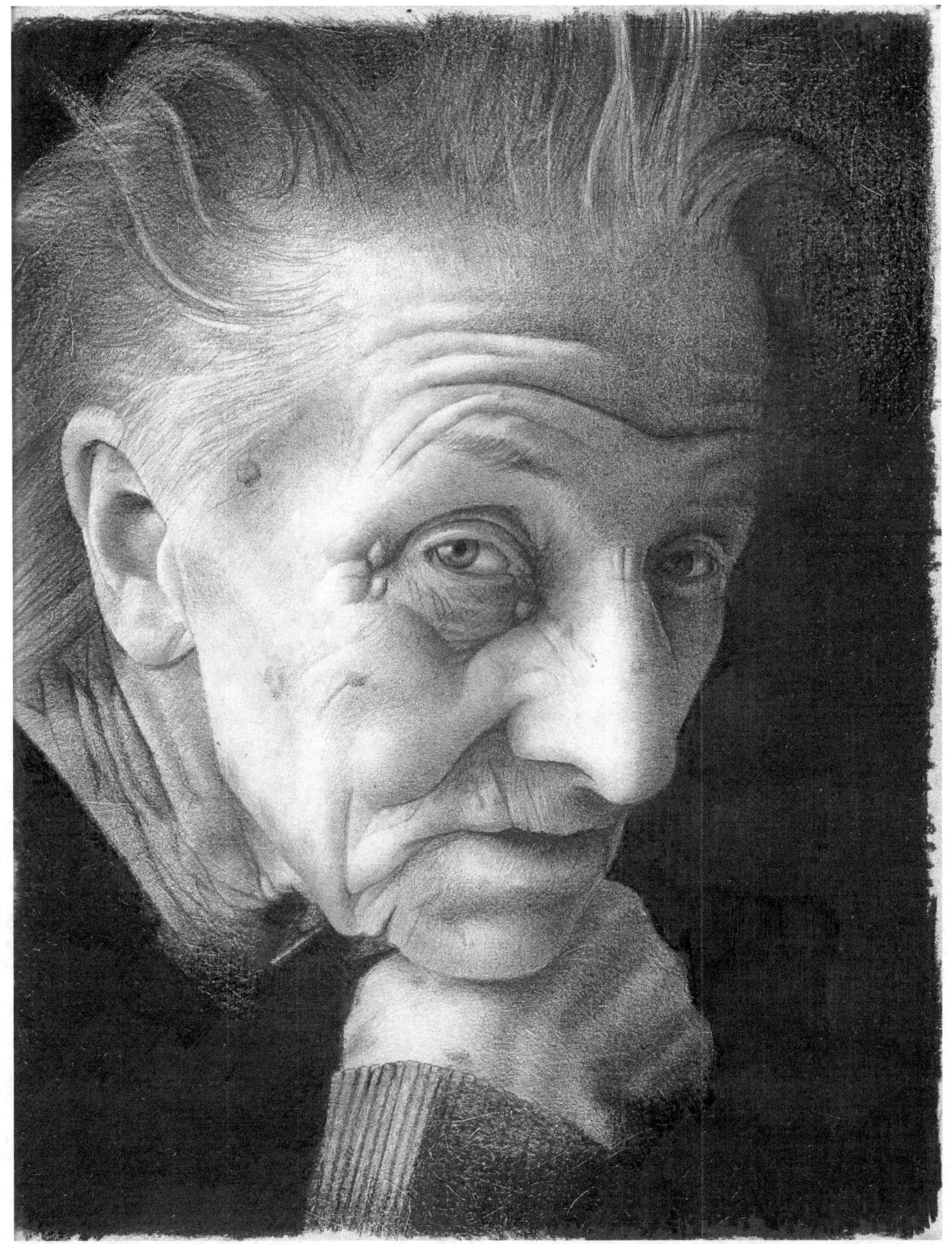

Nonna

8.5" x 11" graphite pencil drawing on paper. 2007

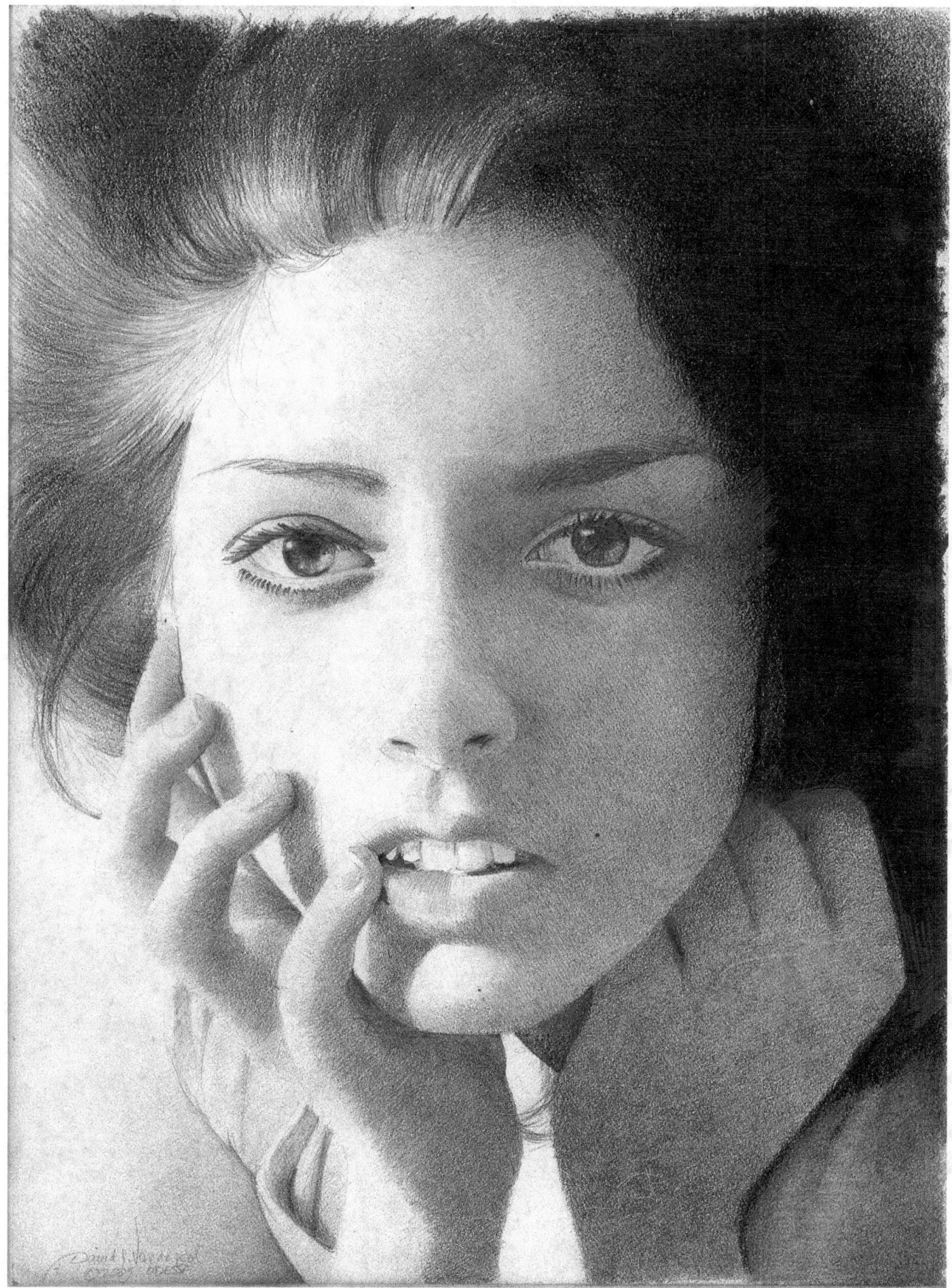

Odessa

8.5" x 11"graphite pencil drawing on paper. 2007

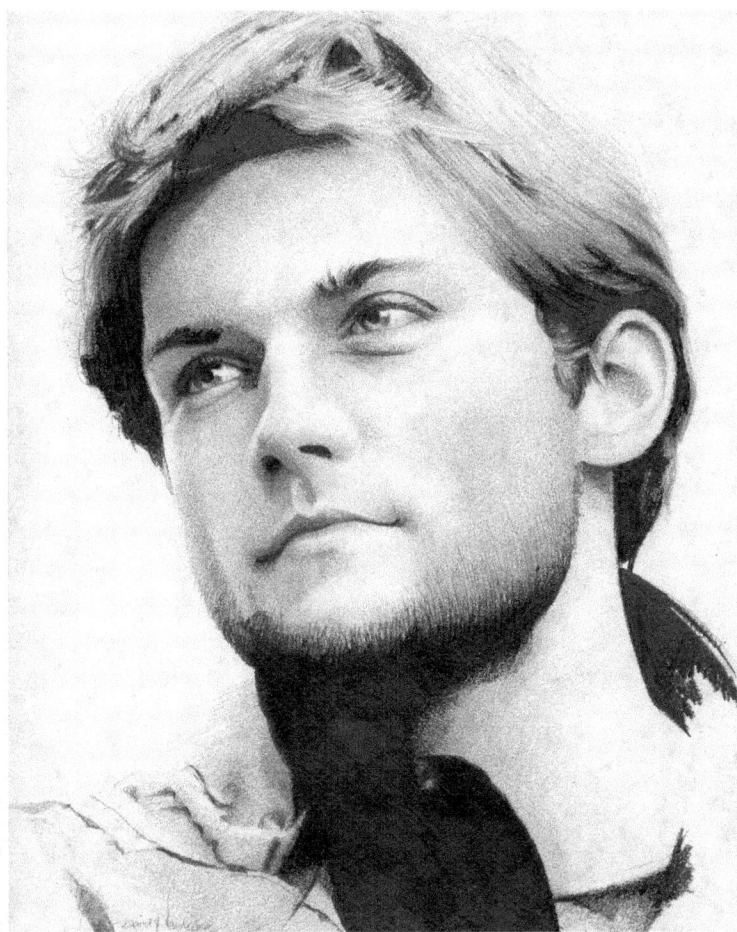

Allan - 8.5" x 11" graphite pencil drawing on paper

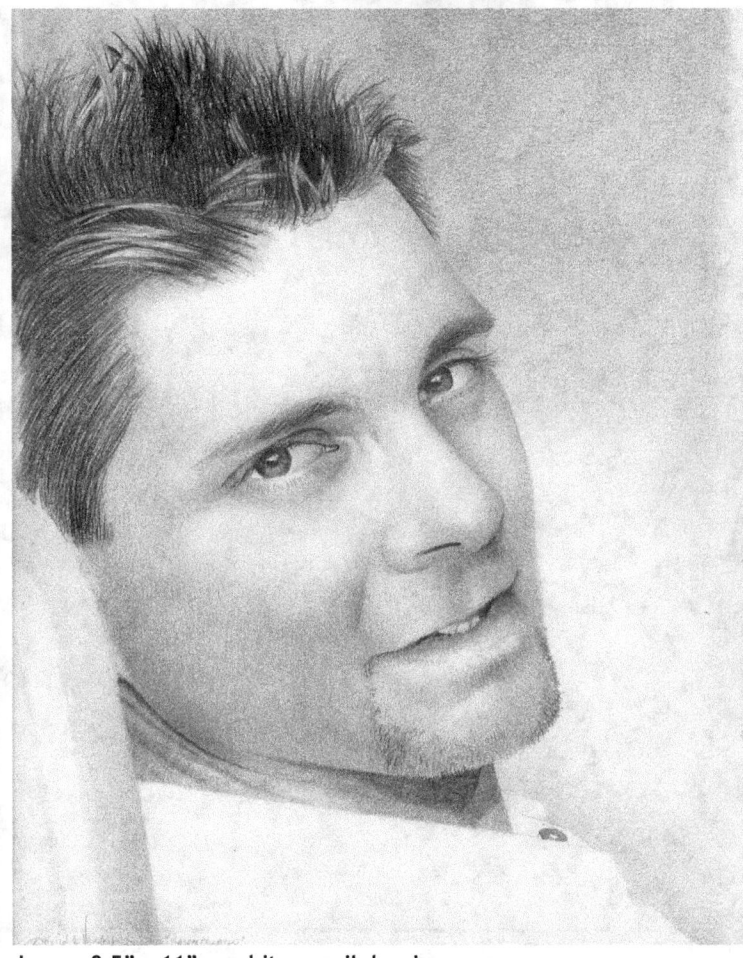

Jason - 8.5" x 11" graphite pencil drawing on paper

then there is no point in continuing the drawing.

Besides, art is far more interesting based on actual people rather than what the artist can create alone. Leaving it to the artist, you may well just end up with how they want to see people, rather than the reality of people around him.

And that usually means a whole lot of self portraits, whether they intend to our not.

Much like working with people that pass in and out of my life, if the eyes do not catch my attention first, chances are nothing else will.

Character, personalities, life's day to day issues, as well as passion - or lack of - are shown in the eyes. Which is what makes being a portrait artist so rewarding as well as challenging.

Whether it be seductive (Odessa), casually captured in a photo while working (Allan), or relaxing in a chair with one of his daughters (Jason), each drawing became that person because of what was revealed through their eyes. It's the first thing you take notice when looking upon each drawing for the first time.

Seldom do I take on a drawing where the model's head is positioned straight towards the camera (viewer), for the fact most end up looking like mug shot's at your local post office, or from the F.B.I's most wanted list, with an exception of a few.

Odessa is one of them. Her hand resting on her cheek, her small finger resting lightly at the edge of her lips and reflection from the light off to the side reveals a young woman who can look beyond the lens of the camera, and right through the person looking at her.

Giving you the opportunity to look a little longer, a little deeper into her eyes, which you would not dare to attempt in person.

Mike Musick.

The most challenging portrait drawings are those you aren't comfortable doing or think you can't pull off. And for me, this was the case of Mike Musick's portrait, as seen on page 32.

My second portrait of this singer and the better of the two, I had decided midway with the first drawing that I wanted my drawing to take on more emotion, show more passion and reveal a part of who the person was since a single pose alone could not offer the viewer.

The first drawing was pretty much a 'mug shot' with little expression, where as this drawing shows a cheerful expression you can't help but enjoy viewing. It took longer to get his hands just right but it was well worth the

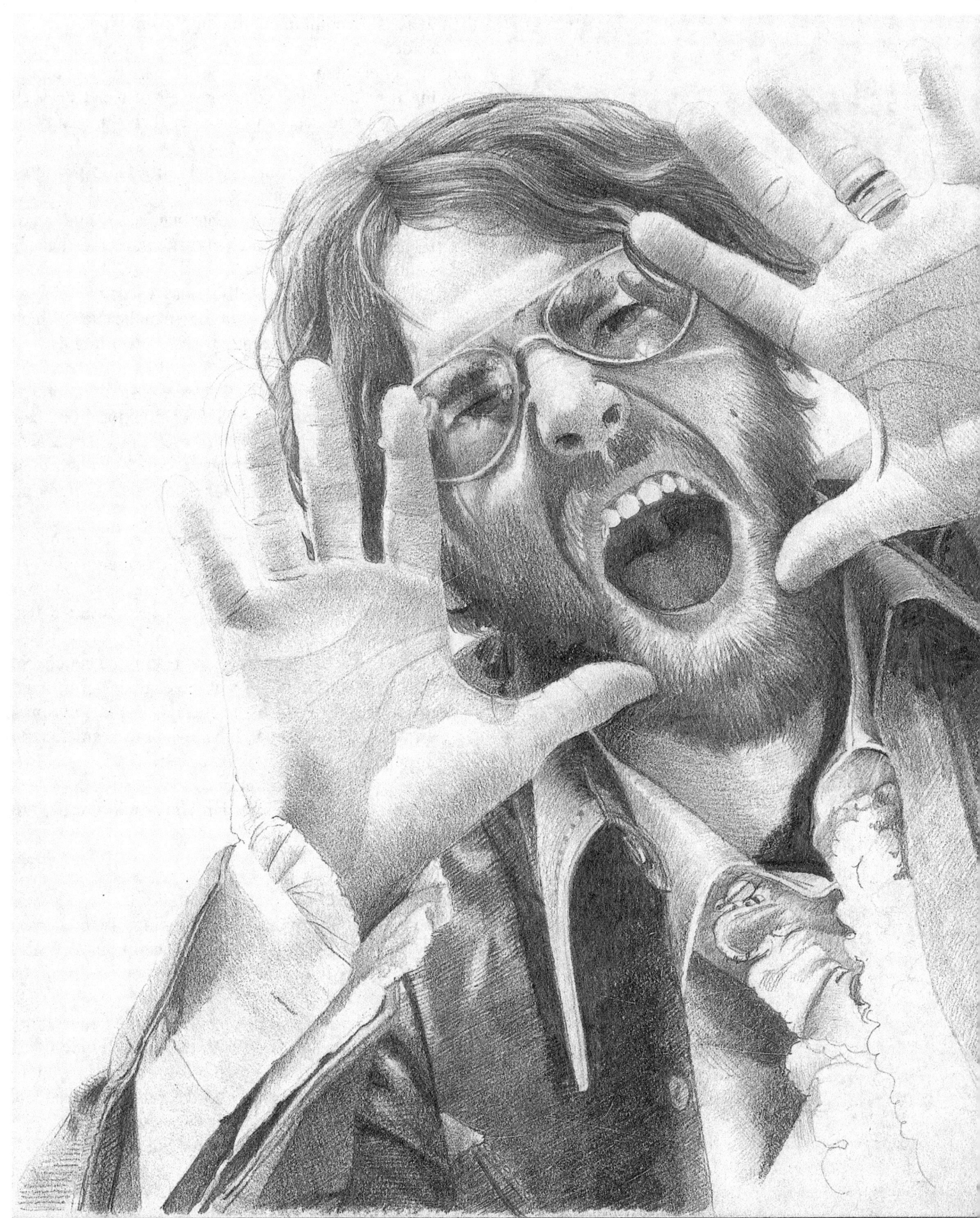

Mike Musick

second attempt.

Starting any project you need the correct tools: quality drawing paper that will stand the test of time, a set of pencils ranging from 2H to 8B, a kneaded rubber eraser, a pencil sharpener and an interesting photograph of a friend.

As an artist, I prefer to draw from photographs even over the live models I work with. Using a photograph I can get up close when drawing the eyes and other personal details that need to be seen up close. It also allows the model to pose only once and I can draw when I feel like it - be it after work in the evening or during a six hour drawing marathon on a lazy Saturday.

What sets me apart from most pencil artists, is my drawings are all lines. Each line placed on the paper follows the object I am trying to duplicate, be it a strand of hair, a fabric he might be wearing, a well sculpted chest muscle or the man's face. From short lines to long flowing lines as seen in his hair, each line is carefully placed on the paper. The entire time I'm thinking where the next line will go, as I draw from the first line to the last, keeping three steps ahead of the last move I made.

It's not important to capture every strand of hair but it is important to take the time to get the hair flowing in its natural direction. Keep in mind that hair grows from the scalp out, and so should your pencil lines. This is especially true when dealing with eyelashes and facial hair.

The eyes are the most important feature in any portrait. The eyes are what captures who that person is. Start off with your lighter pencils, as you will with the entire drawing. Use every pencil you have, from 2H to 8B, and gradually add layers of darker graphite until you get the shade of grays you are looking for.

The trick to creating any realistic and almost three dimensional look to any flat pencil drawing is to follow the contour of the face. Therefore, knowing the human anatomy is a must. From the bones to the muscles, you need to know what's hidden beneath your drawing as you attempt to draw the skin and fabrics that cover the body.

Again, this is game of seeing something that's not on the paper yet and your challenge is to bring it out for others to see.

For the sake of creating so many drawings for this book project in a very short time, a light table was used to lay down a light outline of the person. From there I quickly sketched the remaining detail I needed.

Yes, I know ... I can already hear the loud sound of people gasping from such shocking news. But keep in mind the goal here is to see how I use lines and

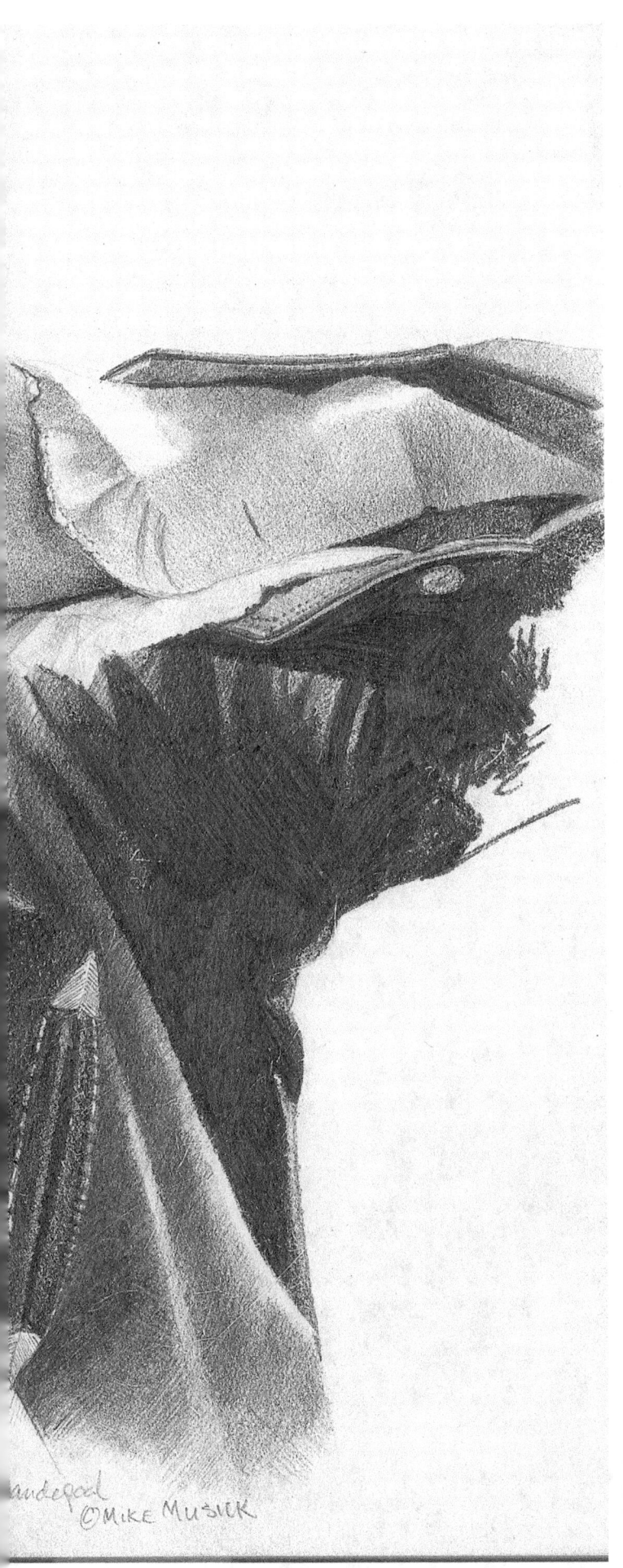

11" x 8.5"graphite pencil drawing on paper. 2006

crosshatching to create a realistic pencil drawings.

Besides, it's been discovered that the great Masters in Europe used mirrors on their paintings. Which is why for the longest time art scholars questioned why there were so many left handed people in the paintings they were studying. Upon proving to myself and others that I could draw freehand, the next issue was completing a drawing in a timely manner to meet clients' needs.

With that being said, use whatever tool you are comfortable with to start your drawing, be it a quick sketch, a light table, a grid or even a mirror. But this should only be done after you have learned to draw freehand! Drawing freehand is a must for any artist.

No matter where you start or what part of the body you are drawing, be sure to follow the contour of each muscle, hair or even an eye.

I have been told I draw oddly. I start from the center of the eye and draw outwards, making each line close to each other as possible for a smoother feel on the skin, and harder more solid lines when the drawing is to be more masculine or have a harder feel to it.

I suggest drawing from a black and white photograph so you can see the grays you are trying to capture. That's not to say you can't create a good black and white drawing from a color photograph. But with a black and white photograph your brain doesn't have to figure out the shades of grays you need to place down on the paper.

Use a 2H or 4H pencil to lay the foundation for the skin, again, it is important to know the anatomy and where the muscles under the skin are. Since there aren't any flat surfaces on the human figure or face, make your lines with a slight curve to them.

Once the eyes are established, I work out from the cheeks and up along the forehead. There is no need to worry about the eyelashes and eyebrows until the skin has been completed.

Taking your time, keep your lines sharp and clean as you work across the face. Crosshatching comes into play only when you wish to give the appearance of a shadow; or later, fabric. The rest of your drawing will be all lines – very fine lines. In fact they should be so fine that at the first glance people won't notice them but rather think you had blended the graphite or assume they are looking at a photograph.

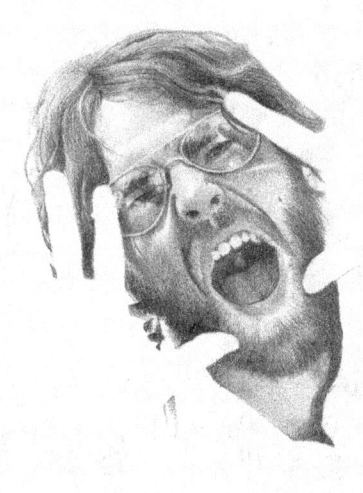

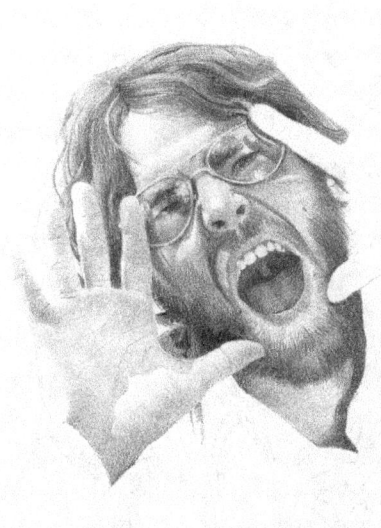

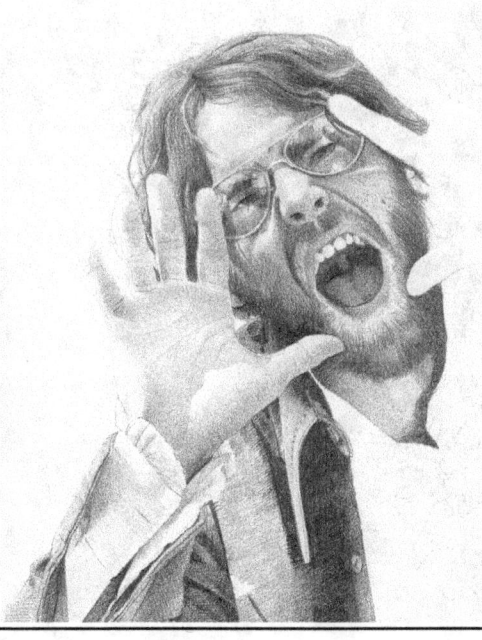

Shadows and lighting come hand in hand. You can't have one without the other. As for his teeth, highlights off his nose or even the reflection off his glasses, allow the natural color of the paper to come through. Let the paper be your whites while using your other pencils for the skin and shadows.

Since the whites of the eyes and teeth aren't really white, use your 2H pencil to create a shadow that covers part of them. Each tooth has a shadow and light so take your time.

Remember, it's always best to go light when applying the graphite and add a darker layer over that as you work toward a realistic appearance. Starting off with your darker pencils leads to a very dark portrait, which may not be the look you want. Similarly, drawing with a single lighter pencil makes for a flat illustration with no depth.

To bring out your highlights, use a kneaded rubber eraser. This method is great for keeping your drawing clean. Press gently to lift your highlights; with the right planning you will have reserved the natural color from the paper to do most of your work. The eraser will help bring a cleaner look to your blending from light to shadow.

Hair grows from under the skin and out, and so should your lines when drawing facial hair, eyelashes and other body hairs. Remember it is important to draw one strand at a time.

Don't panic just yet! You don't have to draw every hair on his head, but at least keep to the style, texture and flow that is there naturally.

Again, start off light and work your way to darker layers as the hair starts to take on its form. Keep the lighter highlights in place and work the shadows and darker strands under it.

Your kneaded rubber eraser can be used to bring out any highlights you need, but again, use your 2H or 4H to place the fine lines over those highlights in order to blend the lighter hair color with the highlights.

Hair is made up of lines so be sure to show the lines in their proper flow on the body. It will take some time and practice to get hair just right. Even though I know of some artists who feel it's not important to draw everything they see in the photograph or the live model in front of them, I say it is, since we are going for a realistic look here folks.

Okay, now it's time to panic! Facial hair is drawn one hair at a time so take your time and enjoy. Again, with a sharp but darker pencil, start at the skin and pull away from the face, following the natural course of how his hair is growing. And, yes, facial hairs grow in a direction that is very noticeable with close-trimmed beards or those just starting to grow.

As with the hair on his head, the model's facial hair has several shades of color - or in our case here, grays - so use several pencils, from 2B to 8B through the face.

Okay - I'll be the first to admit it, drawing hands has always been a challenge for me, simply because of the many bones and muscles one must know, even if it's just the skin that is shown in the drawing.

As a young artist in high school I'd draw people with hands in their pockets. This was a quick solution to a problem I avoided for years. It wouldn't be until I made myself look for photos that featured hands did I realize how more interesting the drawing turned out. It soon became a challenge worth taking on in nearly every drawing after that.

With your lighter pencils, follow the curve of each finger as the skin wraps around each digit. Stop short of the highlighted areas - the paper where you will not be penciling over. Take on one muscle at a time, or in this case, one joint or digit that makes up his hands.

A simple contour line works great for the outline of his hands, even when it's up against the whitest whites used for highlights. Be sure it's a 2H pencil. It's not important to see the line but just know it's there.

They say clothes make a man, but in this case they make the drawing, especially when the person is a rock singer and costumes are a part of his expression. Here, Mike is wearing a ruffled shirt with long sleeves. Sorry, but there was no way I was going to draw his entire shirt. In this case the detail in his cuffs and the start of his collar was enough to show what he is wearing.

His jacket is a fine corduroy, and there was no way of faking that. So once the first layer of shading was added, deeper lines were set into place for the shadow between the lines of the corduroy. A medium shaded pencil was placed next to that one to give it a more rounded shade for a more dimensional drawing.

Since the shirt was unfinished there was no real need to finish the jacket, either.

Choosing the right pose to draw.

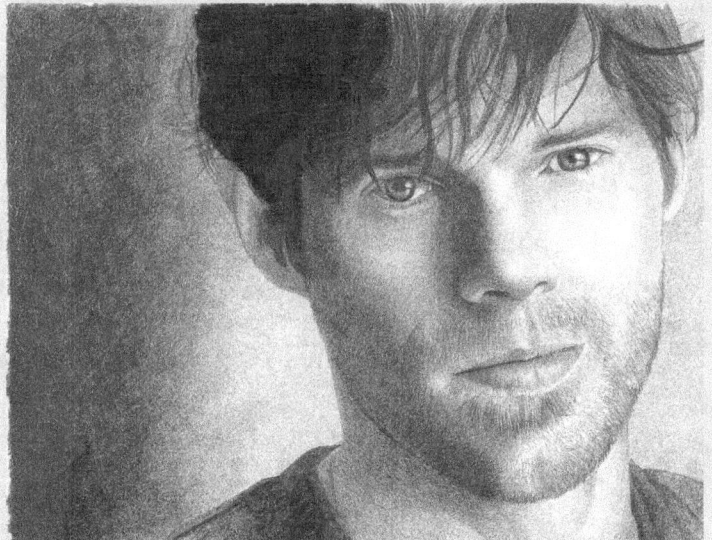
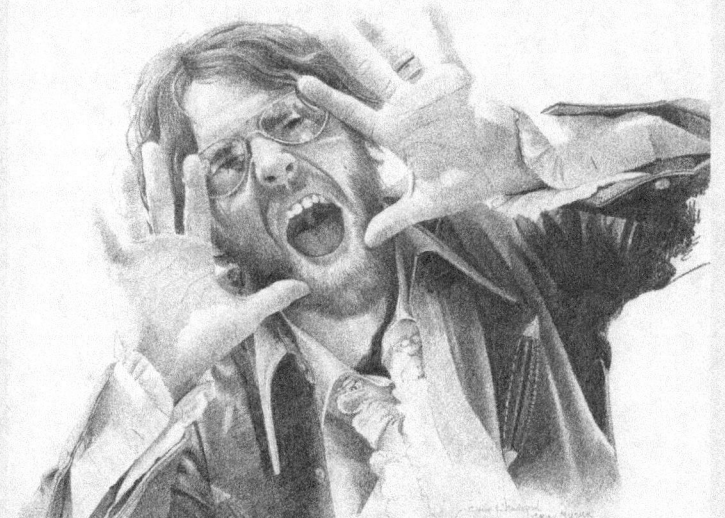

It's very important to pick the best photo when working on a commissioned drawing. One that shows a little more than just a 'mug shot' is usually more of a challenge but the results reveal a stronger impact on what you are trying to achieve.

Not to say the first pose was bad, it's just that the when dealing with a portrait, you don't have to limit yours to something simple - when a loud expression can often work best!

This first drawing of Mike is a great example for drawing facial hair. However, the second goes beyond the face and allows you to see a more emotional, funny side of the singer. This by the way, may end up on his next CD cover or used to promote his latest work.

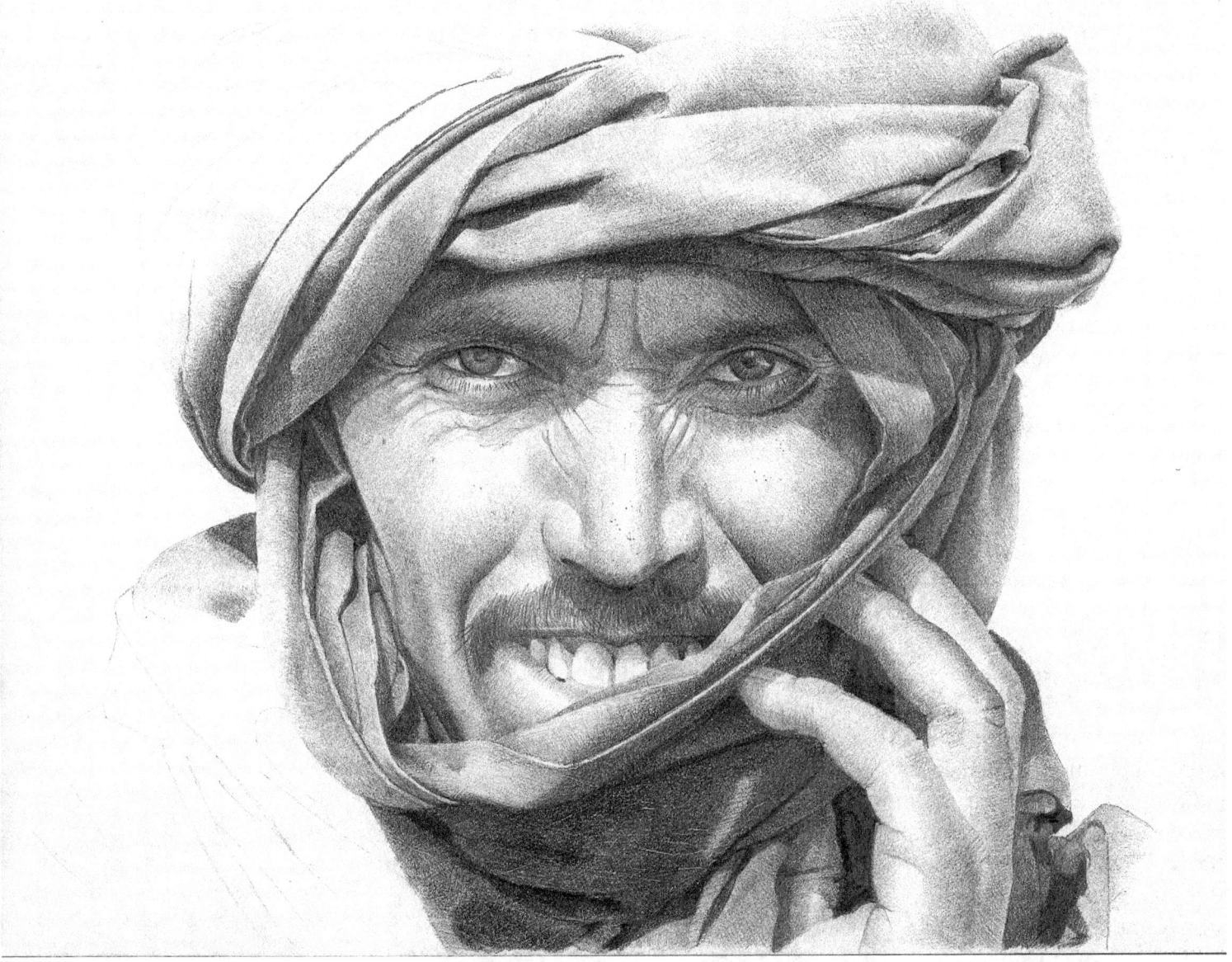

Abdel Rahman

11" x 8.5"graphite pencil drawing on paper. 2007

Abdel Rahman.

On the way to Tombouctou, photographer Wim Denijs came across this cattle man who was from a rich Bedouine family, but preferred to live with his cattle in the desert - away from the big cities, its smells and pollution.

"He had something royal about him and it showed in his eyes proudly" Wim reported. Stating " It was as if he was a desert Prince", which can be easily imagined from this portrait of him.

Skin, facial hair and cloth all required working with several different textures. It also requires working with the lighting, and the shadows where they cover his eyes as a result of his turban and the reflection of the sun on his face.

Much like the drawing of Odessa, shown earlier, when drawing portraits that focus on large eyes, it is very important to be sure that eyes appear moist and

reflect the light around them.

The whites of his eyes will have several shades of gray. The eyeball itself will have a layer from your 2h pencil so that the light reflection can be seen later in the final stages. A shadow just under the upper eye lid can be seen on each eye you draw, so that the lid doesn't appear flat against the ball of the eye.

The same ability to work with shadows and lighting is a must when it comes to drawing the lines in his face. Opposite of what cosmetics and beauty magazines tell people, lines are a must. At least when it comes to deal with every day people and art. Lines tell a person's age, character, and often the their personality.

The deeper the shadow beside each highlight, the deeper the line. As shown around his eyes, and most likely as the result of the bright sun he works in.

I don't know if it's the smile on his face, or the look in

his eyes or a combination of both, but I knew this was a man I had to draw, and not one who could afford to be shy when it comes to approaching people to draw, I emailed the photographer to get his permission.

To my surprise, Wim emailed me several high resolution photos of people from various countries while on his business trips.

As mentioned earlier, it is important to like what you draw and be comfortable within yourself when your drawing will you out of any comfort zone you find yourself in.

To go out of one's comfort zone and draw something that others may not accept or possibly judge you for, is something every artist needs to take into consideration. This is especially true when displaying his work in public.

In this case - in a time of war - an American artist drawing a man wearing a turban - the artist must understand that some people will see what they want no matter what the artist's motive or personal views are.

When drawing people of various ethnic backgrounds it's important to bring out their strongest features, from their nose to their forehead and cheeks. Taking what we know about contours and the needed steps to capture a realistic image that you want to pop off the page. This drawing uses more of the whites within the paper to help bring out the drawing.

This doesn't mean you leave all the white spots on his face alone. You need to decided what will be the whitest in the entire drawing and shade the rest even if they appear to be white. Look closely and you will see the reflection off his teeth and the spot near his right eye are the whitest. This will draw them into studying your work even closer.

Don't worry about the shadow across his face until the object making the shadow is in place. Which in this case in the man's turban.

If you find yourself drawing the shadow first, once the turban is in place, you will end up going back and work the shadow over his eyes again, until you get it right.

His mustache has some gray to it, so be sure to leave enough of the white from the paper and use only your darkest pencil for the whiskers in the shadow under his nose.

The turban of course is a different texture from his face so work just the lines you need to make

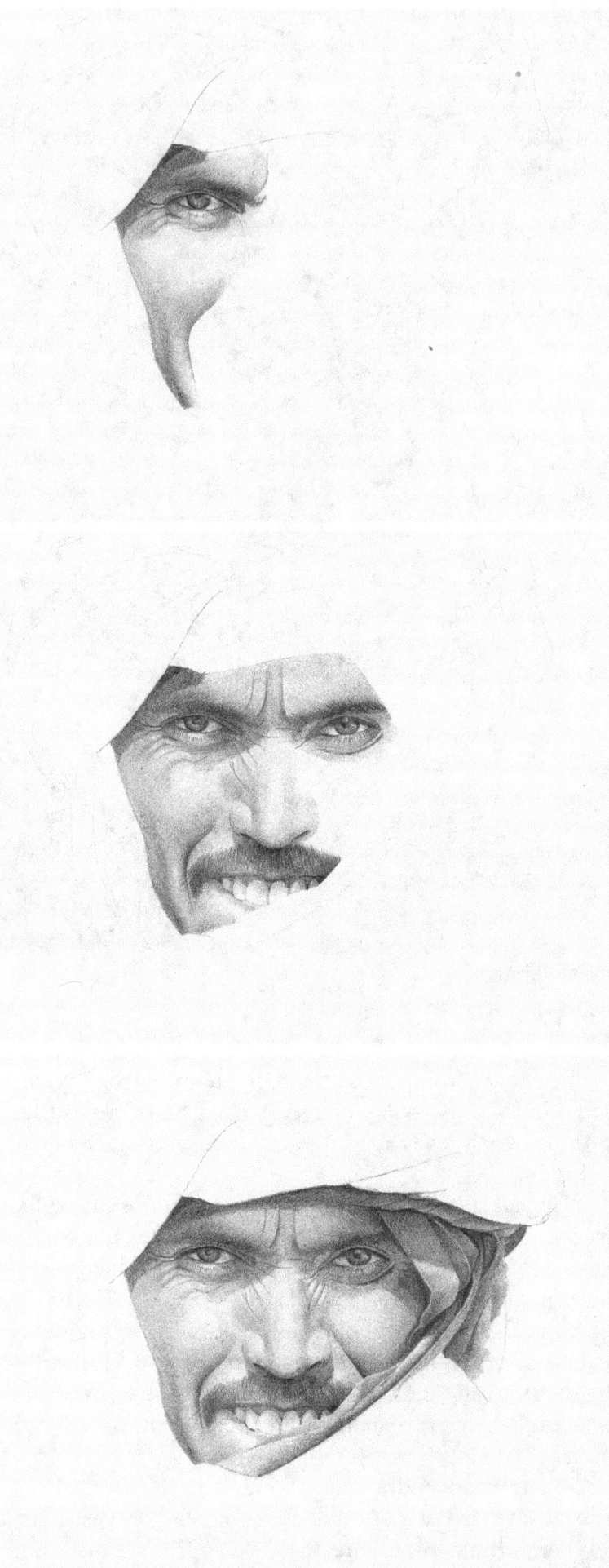

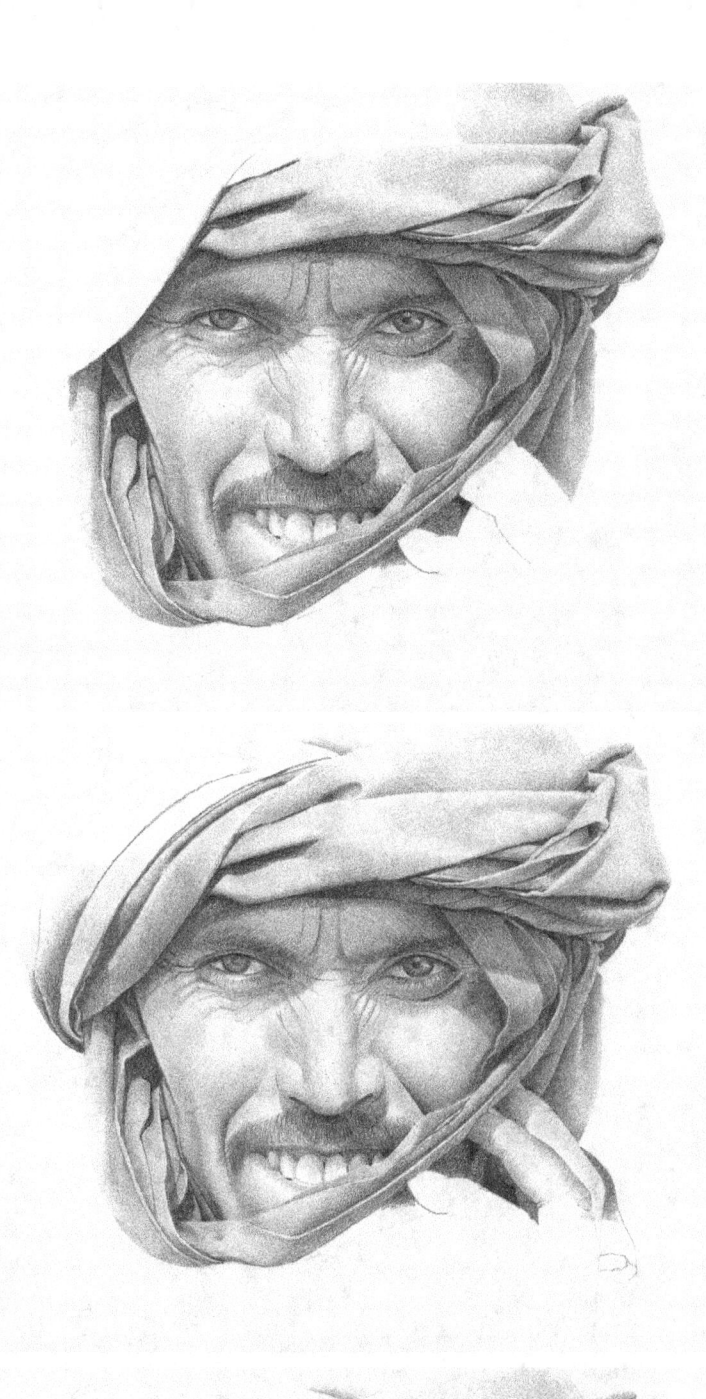

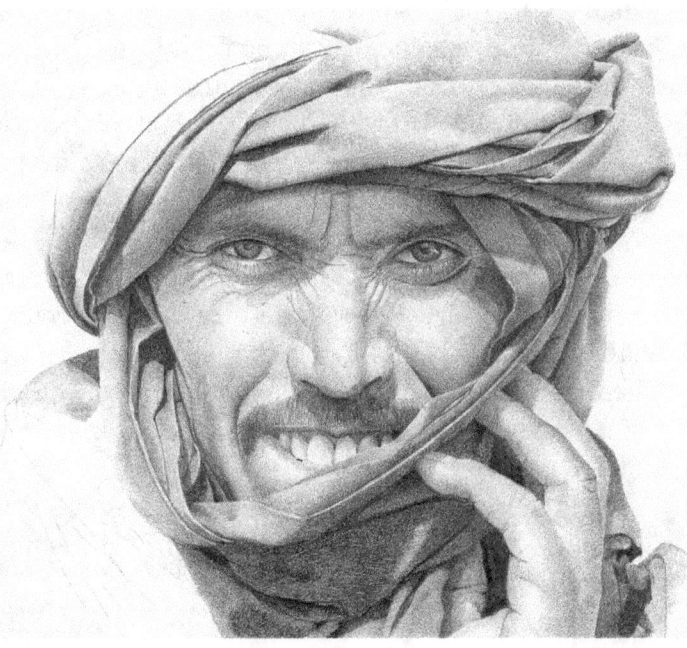

sure the viewer can tell the difference. As the face is created with single lines that follow his facial form, the lines in the turban are a combination of lines and crosshatching that wrap and twist as the fabric folds.

Use single lines for the lighter areas of the fabric, and crosshatching in the shadows and the design of the fabric, it's very important to capture the actual fabric he is wearing.

I decided ahead of time that I was going to leave half this drawing unfinished therefore it was important to know where, and how much, I was going to omit. Since I work top to bottom, left to right, the bottom right hand corner is usually left unfinished when I do something like this. However, to do that with this drawing, it would have left too much detail unfinished. His hand holding onto the fabric of his head piece is a major part of the drawing and couldn't have been left untouched.

I chose to leave the top left corner of his turban unfinished and the bottom two corners of the drawing. This gives the drawing a sense of still being created as you view it

Studying the drawings created for this book you will see that there is one thing in common. Almost all of the drawings have hands. I am not too sure how much of that I planned, or if it just worked out that way. I do know that by the time the fourth drawing was completed for this book project, I found myself sitting back and taking note of the photos that were sent for me to draw from.

Hands in this case work well in capturing a mood within the drawings. You know this herdsman is outside in the sun on a daily basis, as he holds on to keep the wind from blowing dust in his face ... or perhaps in this case, allowing a warm smile to escape for the photographer to capture as the sun shines high in the afternoon sky.

Old Man from Morocco.

One of my earliest drawings of an older person, perhaps second best followed by the drawing of Nonna, was this man that photographer Wim Denijs had meet through his business travels in Zagoram, south of Morocco.

Even though the name of this old tradesman is long forgotten, the photographer remembers

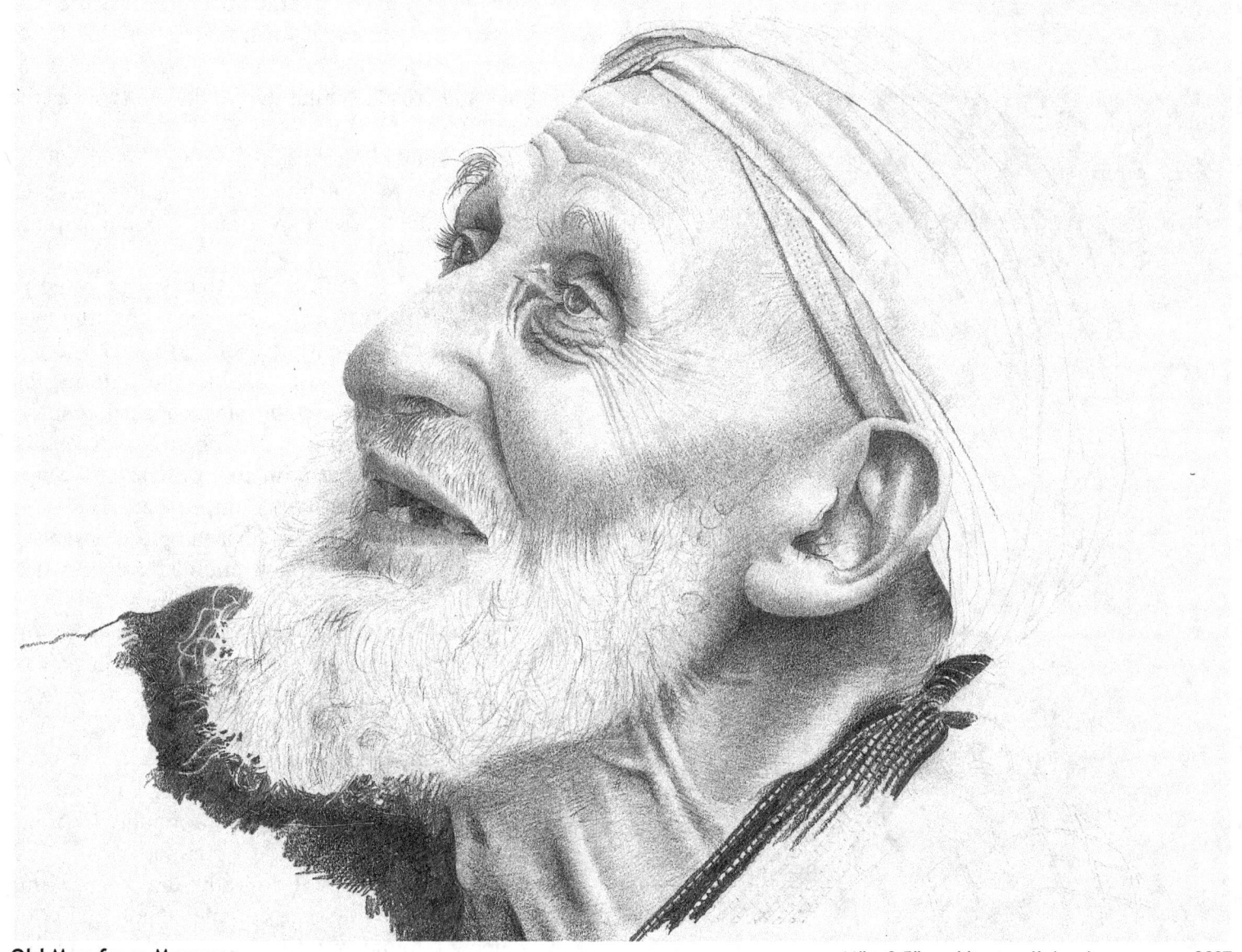

Old Man from Morocco

11" x 8.5"graphite pencil drawing on paper. 2007

him as being a trader of herbs. He was on his way to Tombouctou, an old ancient race of Bedouines and traders, where he was trying to convince an old lady, who was probably sick, to buy his herbs.

Blending a drawing doesn't take a stump and heaven forbid should you use a finger! In fact the best tool to us for blending is a lighter pencil.

The cheek of this man took four pencils to complete. 2H for the first layer, then 4H over that. But be sure not to cover the area where 2H and the whitest of the paper meet. Your "F" pencil is next. Keep the strokes shorter than the prior pencils you used. Keep this up using all your pencils until you get the right shade and tone of the skin you are drawing

Keeping your pencil sharp is important, especially when drawing the flesh. You can use a dull pencil for fabric but to blend the graphic in order to capture the skin tones the pencil must be sharp at all times. The blending

comes into effect by using your 2H or 4H over the harder pencils you just used. This process may take several layers and crosshatching can come into play depending of the shadow effect you are looking for.

And yes, even if you started your drawing with 2H or 4H and then added darker pencils over the first layers, you finish it with the same lighter pencils you started off as your tool to blend.

Think of your drawing in layers. Several layers!

For some artists, a three-quarter view can be a challenge, yet once completed, can be very rewarding. There is nothing worse than drawing a portrait that turns out looking like a mug shot on display at your local police station.

You guessed it - I start off with the eyes and work my way out. Keep in mind the focus of this drawing is his eyes and the lines surrounding them.

Capturing his age through the lines in his face you

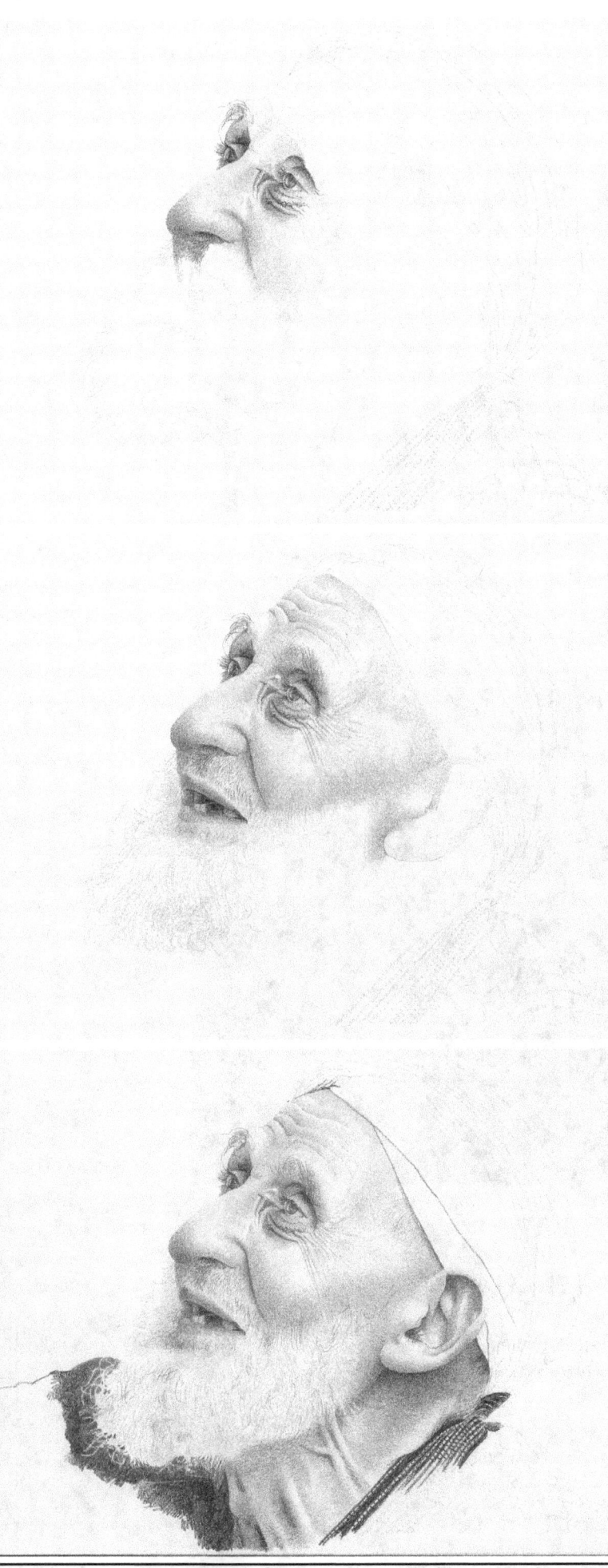

must try to get each line in place. Then you have to make them appear they belong there. This means knowing where to put the shadows and highlight for each wrinkle.

Different from any other drawing displayed in this book, this man's face does not follow a smooth cheek or forehead, so when drawing his face your lines must go up and over the small hills and valleys naturally put in his face. This takes longer so be patient.

Blending on any drawing will depend on the subject and effect you are working with. Here I want to be sure to blend his cheeks with his beard and the challenge being his beard is white and so is his face.

The technic in all the drawings shown within these pages are the same but the effects are different. Be it an old man or a youthful bodybuilder how you approach your drawing will affect the final outcome.

You will find some portraits will require a lot of graphite, while with other drawings you can use the white from paper. This method isn't based on the ethnic background of the person but rather the dramatic look you are wanting to reveal in your drawing. His ethnic or ancestral background will show through his facial features.

Often times you will want to leave your drawing unfinished while other times a black background is desired in order for the person to jump off the page. Shadows make for powerful drawings and so can the effect of natural lighting across a person's face as in the case of his white beard and his shirt.

Because I have yet to discover a pencil that draws well enough over graphite, and be as sharp and hard as one, here I allowed his neck and shirt to bring out the white in his heard.

Yet another man in a turban. Perhaps this book should have been on people from around the world. That might not have been a bad idea but with this being my first book I left it open to friends, fellow artists, and photographers to send me photos. This would challenge my creativity and give me more opportunity to draw.

As I mentioned before, one thing in most of the drawings in this book are hands. The most powerful drawings, be it a portrait or nude, hands help create an emotion when a simple smile or look can not.

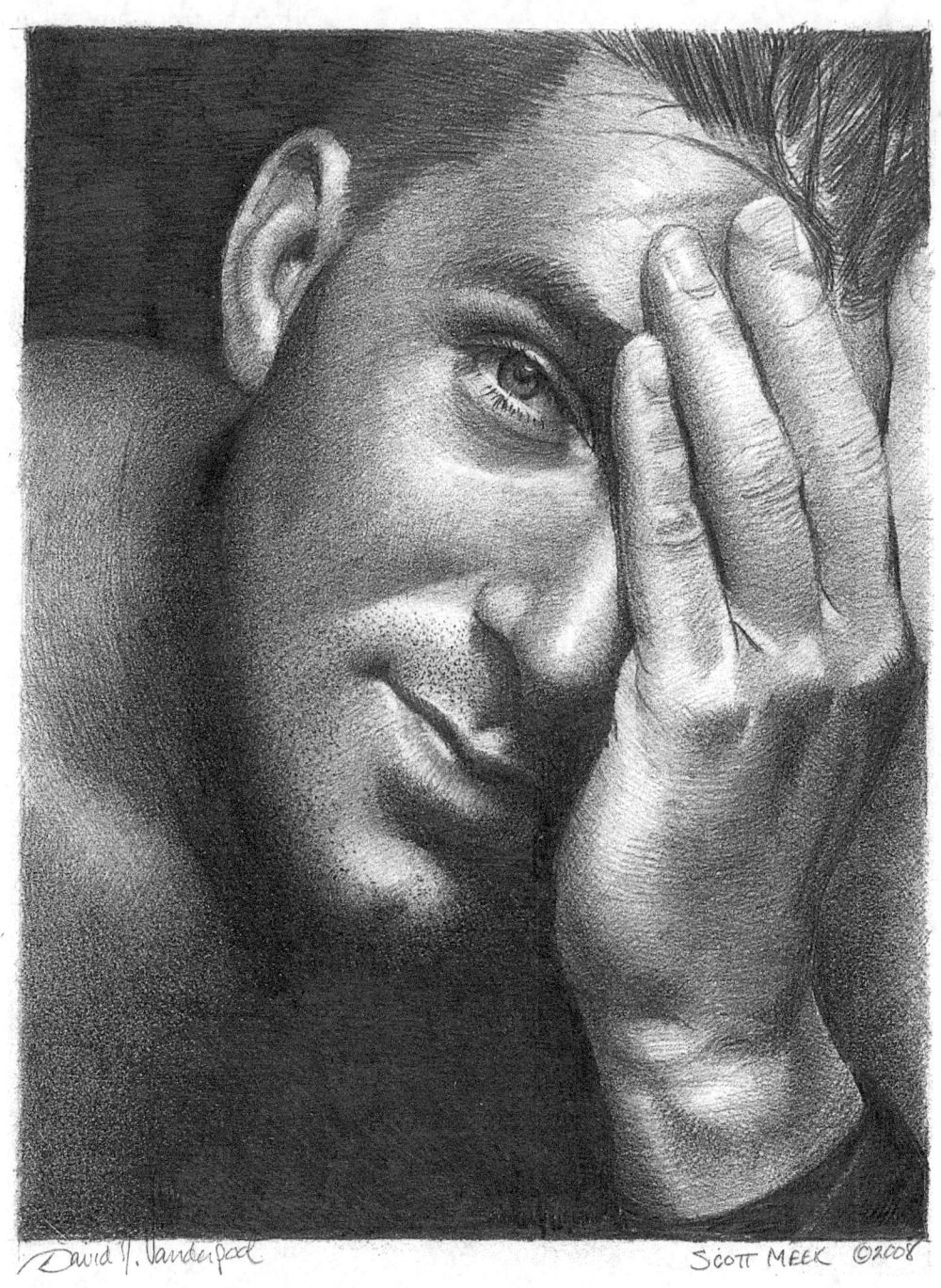

Scott Meek

Copyright 2008. David J. Vanderpool
Shown actual size.

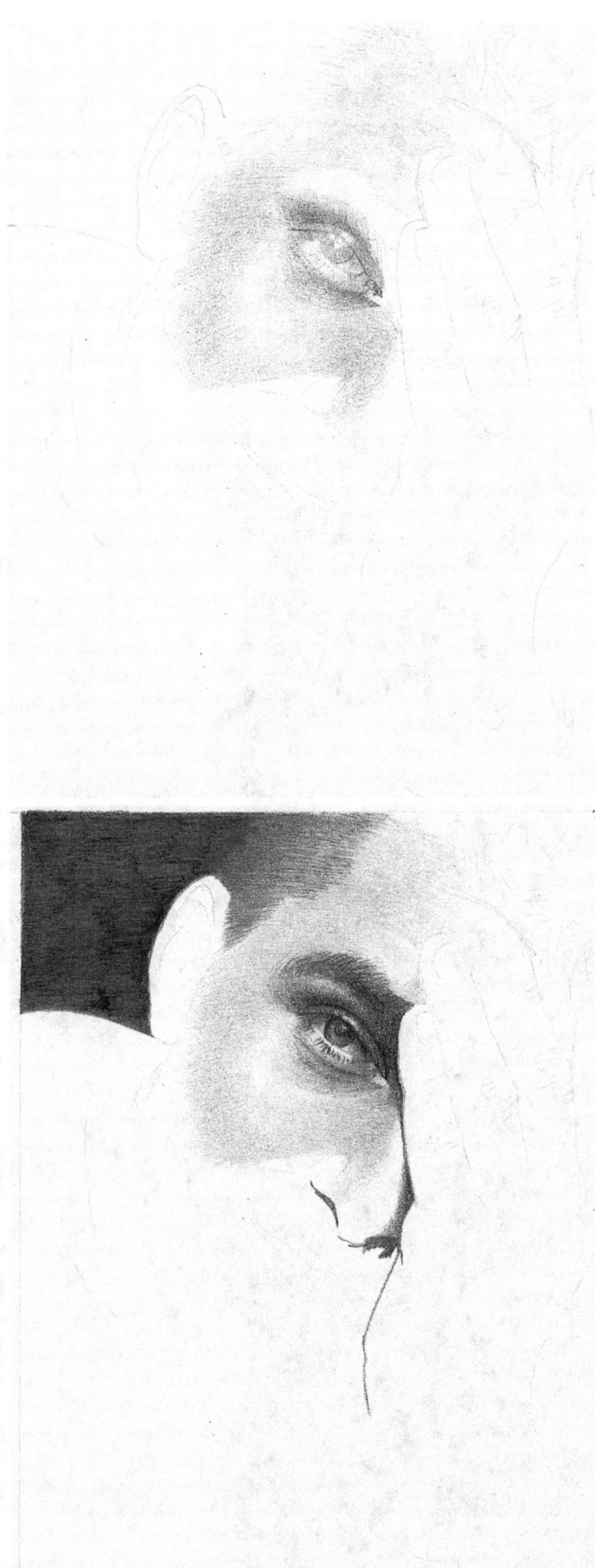

There are always exceptions and it was, for me, showing all the years of his life experiences in his face. When you can capture life through a pencil you have duplicated life as art. I accomplished this by creating the shadows around his eyes, neck, and the edge of his beard.

Scott Meek.

One of my earliest experiences in networking with others allowed me to meet Scott Meet, who to this day we continue to keep in touch.

This is rare since most people tend to fade off in the distance once they have been drawn. Busy life for some, while others sought just to be drawn by an artist, and that's okay too.

Portraits work best when you can focus on an expression, as with the energized laughter we saw with Mike, or the in deep-thought seen in the portrait of Odessa. You can't help but stop yourself from questioning what was going through their mind when such images are captured and this drawing of Scott is no different.

Here we find not an actor, model, or photographer, but a writer and even more rewarding, a teacher.

Unlike most of the drawings created for my book projects, where they were created at 8.5" x 11" in order to show the drawings full size, this drawing was 5" x 7" as I have done with many others.

I felt this was the perfect size for a close-up view showing off his eyes, and the slight smirk on his lips, while pursuing the challenge of the line work in my drawings small enough for such small projects.

Looking through the progression stages shown here it's easy to see how one mistake can alter an entire drawing, and yet, not necessarily destroy the drawing.

Starting off light and keeping to the contour and shape of his facial features, I made a mistake near the end of the drawing and picked up the wrong pencil to work on his cheeks. As a result, the drawing turned out darker than I wanted.

I wasn't about to start over nor was I going to allow it to ruin the drawing. It did require that I had to shade the rest of the drawing to match the error I made. In the end I was able to maintain his strong facial features that were still the focal point to the drawing.

I wasn't happy with how his fingers were coming along and therefore was worried how the drawing was going to turn out.

Drawing hands and feet were never been my strong point so all of my attempts were to find people to draw where their hands were not part of the drawing. No longer allowing my fears to limit what I create I actually learned to enjoy the challenge of drawing hands and feet.

The further into this drawing the darker it was becoming. Another problem I realized was knowing that this drawing would continue to get darker. Especially after I completed the shadows under his chin and most of his chest.

I knew before I started this drawing, a dark photo was going to be a challenge, I was not prepared to see how it would alter my style and effect drawings that would come later.

As I found my drawings evolving and I wasn't too sure where this change would take me.

Not to put blame in the photo this was inspired from. In fact, it's one of the better photos I have seen for a small portrait in a long time. I just wanted to make sure I could do it justice and not get carried away with the Ebony pencil.

Once you go dark with an Ebony pencil you can't go back. There is no erasing. Only starting over. Yet this drawing did not display a reason to start over.

Ebony graphite pencils. The darker the pencil the softer the graphite and soft graphite makes for poor lines. At least the type of lines I was using in my drawings.

A drawing that becomes too dark in some areas is seldom a total loss when you have a clean kneaded rubber eraser and a few lighter pencils at hand.

Shaping the eraser to have a flat tip, then pressing against a unused part of the paper and making sure it was even, I was able use the eraser to slowly lighten the areas. I was looking to bring out the necessary highlights. Making sure to press easy and gradually lifting as much as I needed - one step at a time.

By the way - never rub an eraser across your drawing but gently press the kneaded rubber eraser (cleaning it as you continue) until you have your highlights back.

Once that was completed, I was able to use the harder pencils such as 2H or 4H and lightly draw over the areas I had just lightened. Following the shape of the muscle as I slowly started to blend the various shades of gray together.

With a little patience, and being aware of where you went wrong, it is possible to save a drawing from total destruction usually.

Not giving up, and in fact taking on several other small drawings including my wife, seen to the right of here, I made it a goal to get these right.

So what makes it right? The proper tools, correct paper, pencils, and keeping the pencils sharp at all times, as well as remembering the finer and cleaner the lines, the clearer the drawing will turn out.

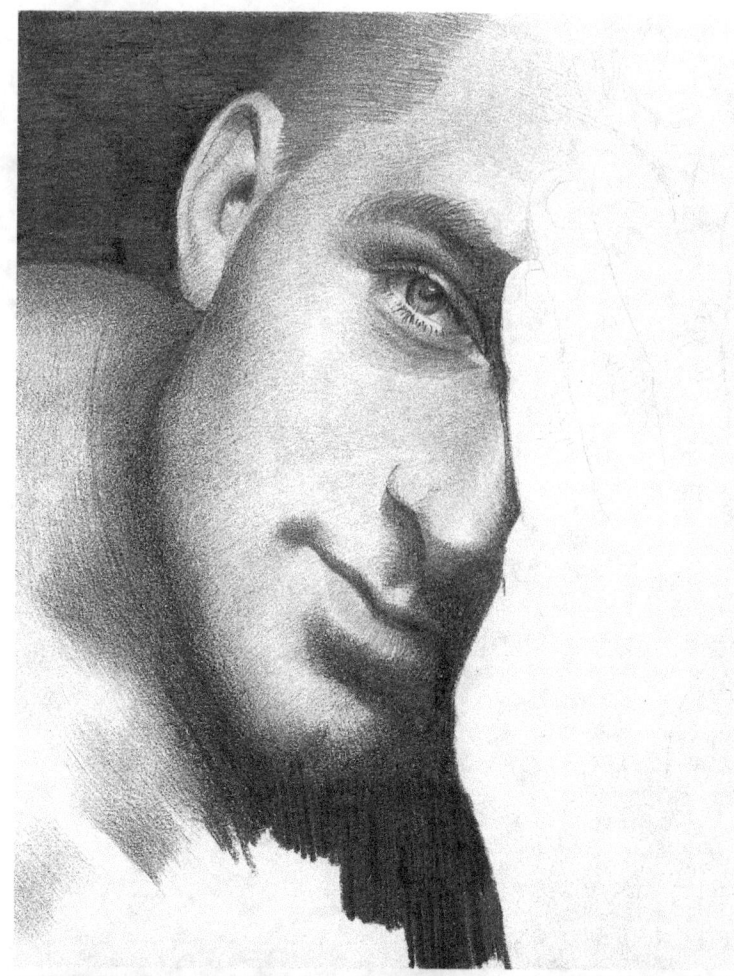

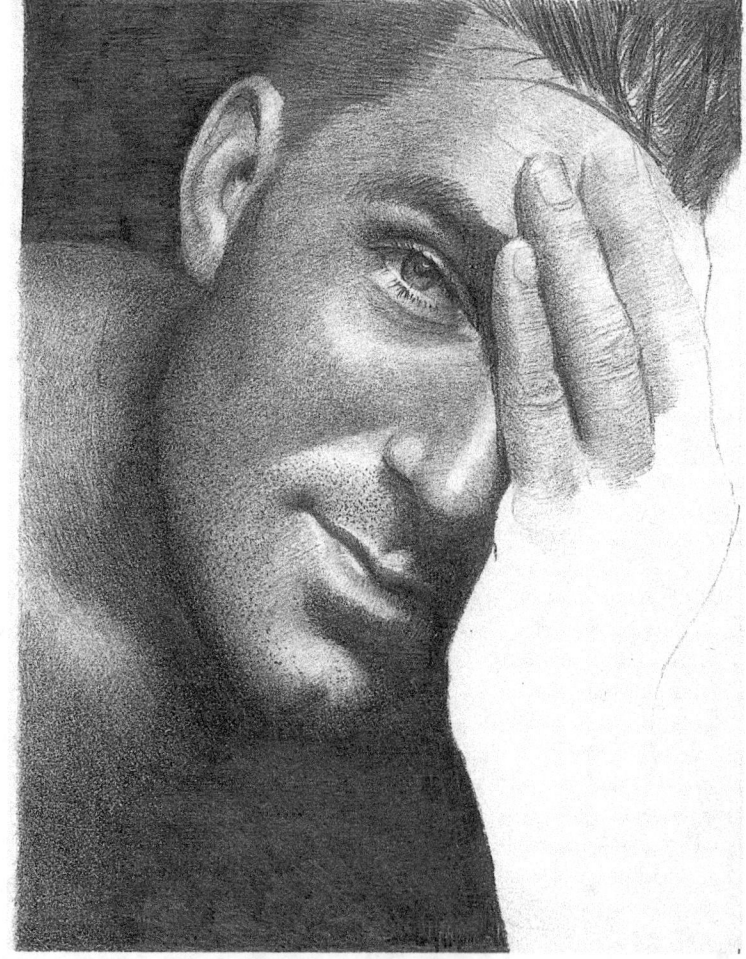

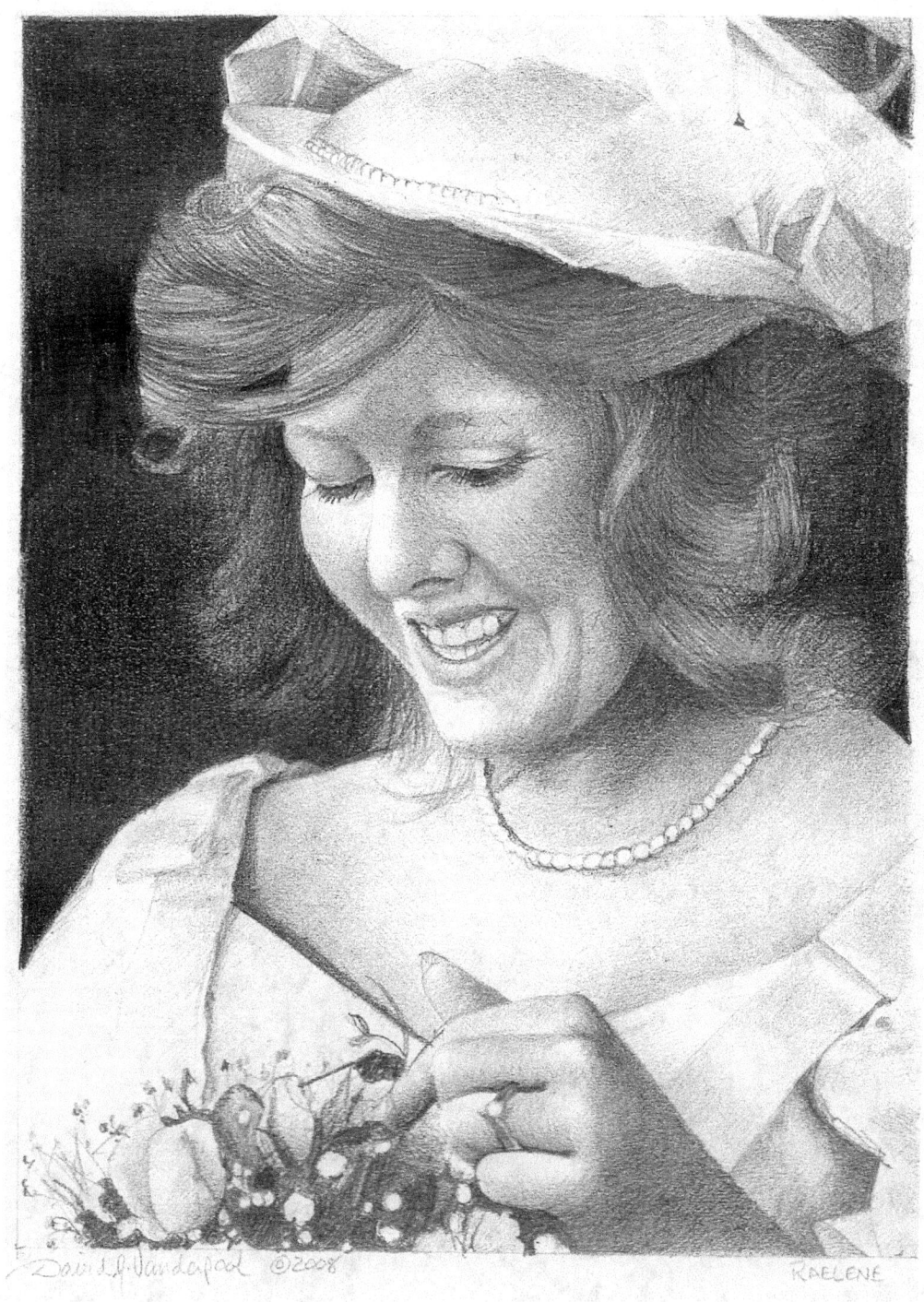

Raelene

Copyright 2008. David J. Vanderpool
Shown actual size.

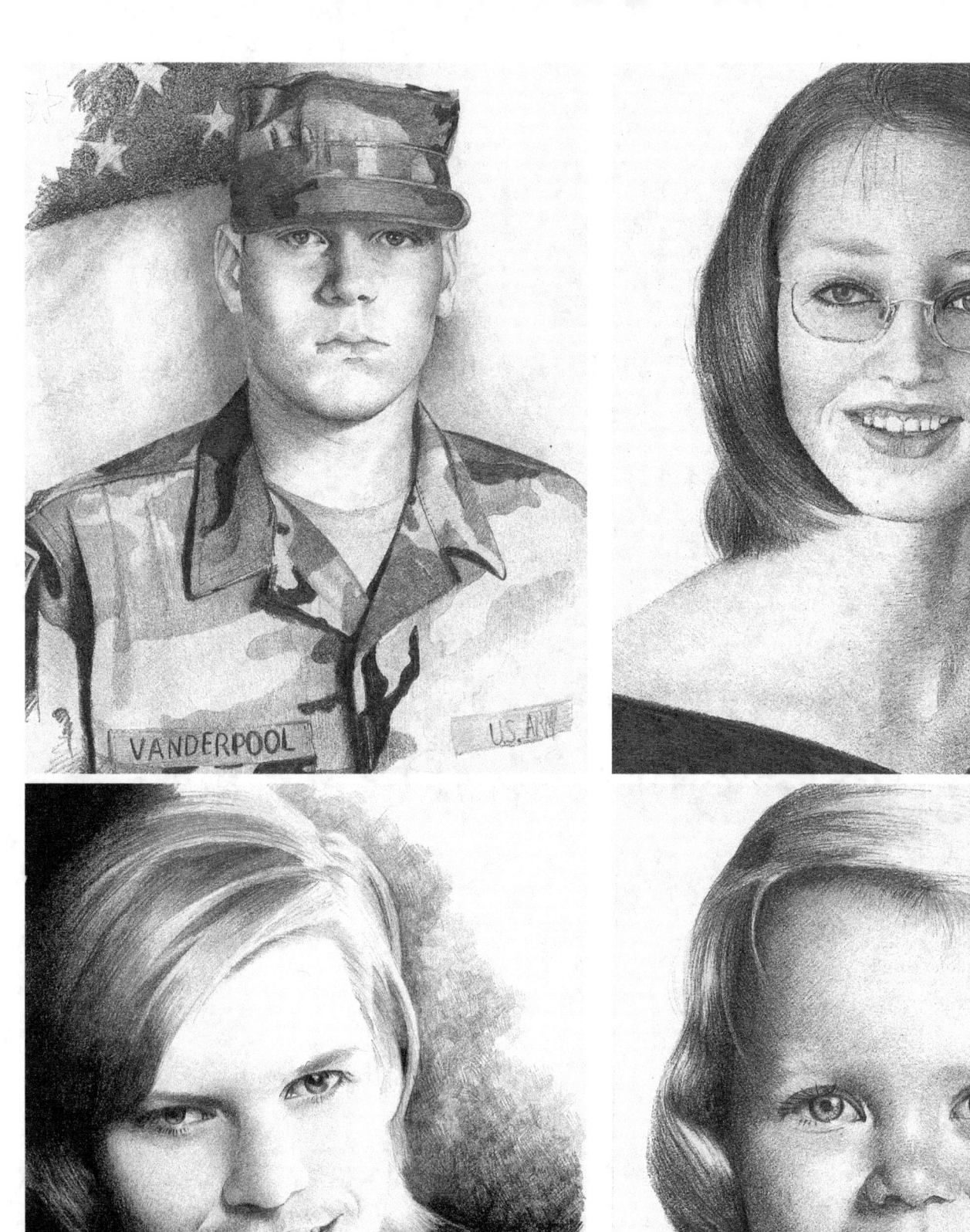

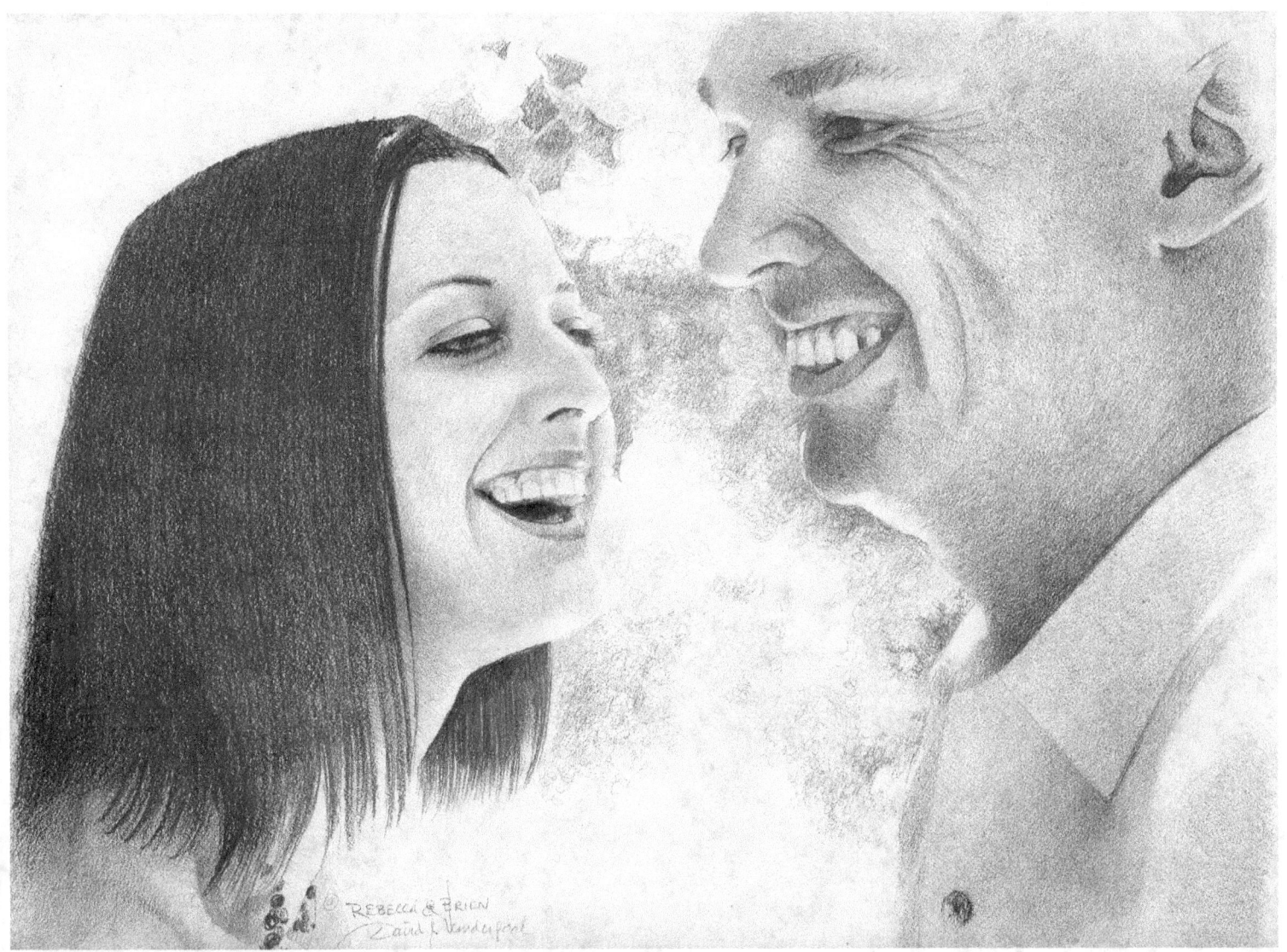

Family heirlooms or another mug shot?

The most challenging obstacle for some artists, when it comes to taking on commissioned assignments, is they are dealing with so many non creative photographers. Yes that means those studio shoot where they hire anyone to focus and click.

Sit, look this way, no that way, then click. Who's next?

Leaving little for the artist to work from unless capturing a person for a potential heirloom is enough? Which in most cases suites the clients needs but leaves an artist empty.

Just keep in mind that when taking on commissioned assignments and using a photographers work there are copyright laws. Always know the updated copyright laws in your country if you intend to sell prints of your drawings.

In regards to drawing created for the artist's own personal collection, either of family or fan art, there are limited exceptions since the work is not intended for sale or copies made for profit. However, when in doubt it's best to check national and international copyright laws when it comes to using photos you personally did not take.

An artist who is serious with his work will either get out there and take his own photographs or meet some pretty talented photographers who are willing to allow their work to be duplicated in a drawing.

Ideally, the artist can do both!

The drawing of Rebecca and Brien, seen above, was inspired by a photograph take by her sister Amanda. All three were visiting Catalina Island, off the coast of Los Angles, California, with a photographer who was setting up a photo shot shortly after they were engaged.

page 45: Raelene Vanderpool
Page 46, top left: Andrew vanderpool
Page 46: top right: Rebecca Shafner
Page 46, bottom left: Jared Vanderpool
Page 46, bottom right: Amanda Shafner
Page 47: Rebecca and Brien Roth

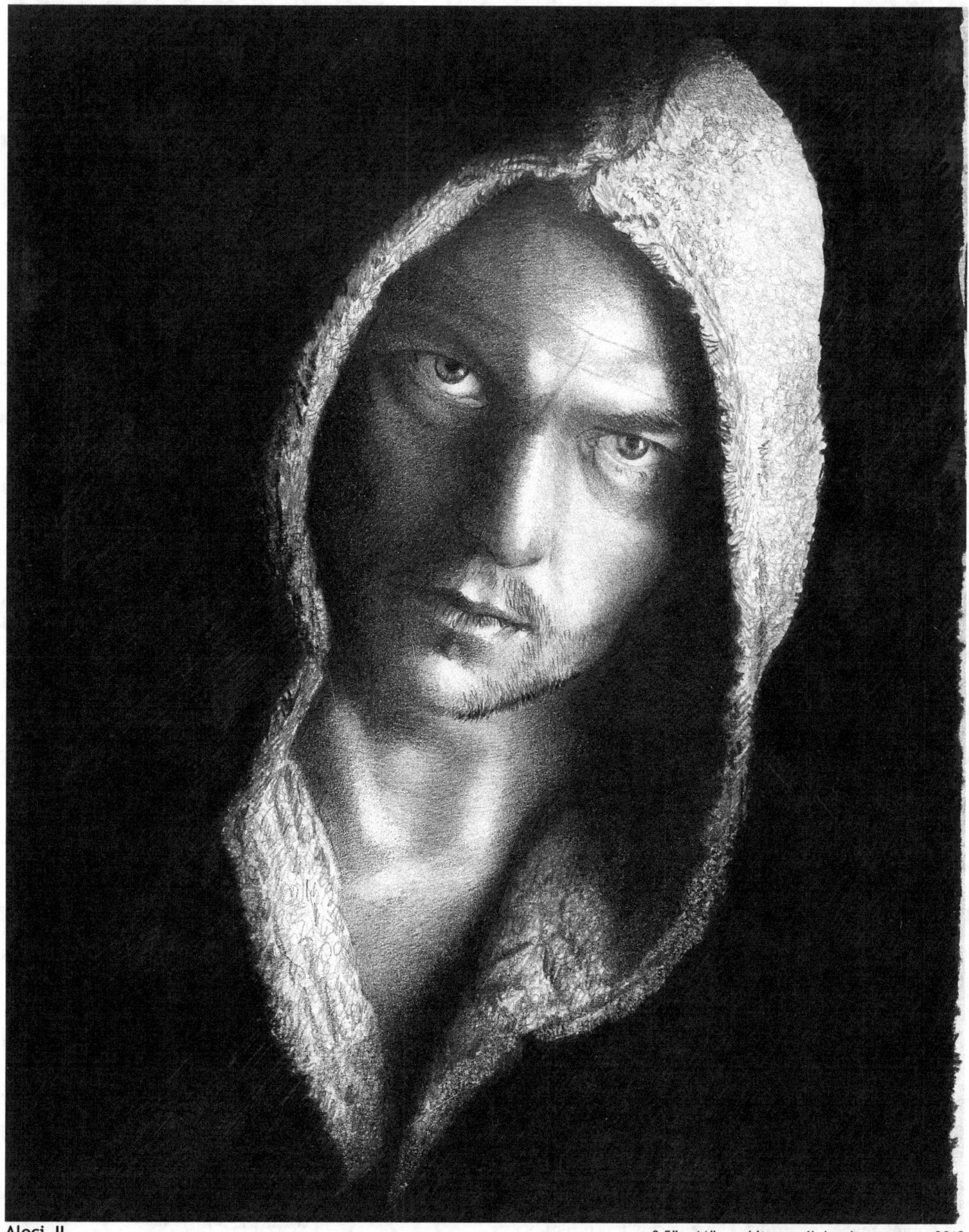

Aleci II

8.5" x 11" graphite pencil drawing on paper. 2010

Needless to say the photo taken by Amanda was perfect to draw from and made a nice wedding gift.

So why draw from photos rather than live models?

As with the drawing of Augie (page 21) he and I were able to meet one Saturday morning and in the privacy of his home. Taking well over 150 photos of him, in a wide range of poses, both inside and outside, and near his pool.

This required the model to pose only once and allowed me, as the artist, to draw when time best suited my busy schedule. In my case that was a few hours a night after work and weekends.

Photos also allows the artist to work with people outside of his physical location. Expanding to other cities, states, and even countries. This give the artist the ability of adding various ethnic groups and cultures to his collection of drawings and life experiences.

Aleci.

Proving drawing portraits doesn't have to be your traditional boring poses that resemble a wanted poster at your local post office. Add a little mystery and drama to your poses by using the right amount of lighting in an already dark setting.

This portrait is one of two I drew of Aleci, a photographer from Lokeren, Belgium, who likes to see himself as a player of light in every form of creativity. This drawing is from one of his self-portraits.

Even though eyes are the main features that attracts me to a person I try to stay away from stiff poses where the person is looking directly into the camera. Here is a perfect and excellent example of an exception to that rule.

Dark and mysterious, with a sense of overwhelming power, this portrait draws one directly to his eyes. A true classic from the start!

With the eyes as the main focal point it is imperative that the drawing be large enough to capture the detail of his eyes so that it will pull you into the image. On 8.5" x 11" size paper that in itself can be a challenge!

Another challenge was drawing the black background evenly and without appearing too glossy or with lines going in different directions. As you can see I kept the shading for the background in the same direction since lines are bound to appear no matter how hard you try to eliminate them.

The majority of this drawing was completed with a Design Ebony pencil by Sanford. It's a jet black graphite which is extra smooth and perfect for deep shadows and bringing out the eyes and edges of his lips.

The first thing to do when beginning to draw is a

contour drawing, which is another name for drawing the outline. With contour drawing you are focusing on the edges, the outside of an object, or the line made by a fold or pattern. The line that goes across an object, hinting at the form, is called a cross-contour.

Using a 4H pencil the first layer is set in place as I made sure to follow the shape and direction of each muscle. Slowly I went from light to dark, using the same pencil, as each shape and parts of his face came to life.

In regard to drawing his face, the darkest pencils were used for his eyes, the edge of his lips, and the shadow created from the hood he was wearing. It is important in this step to pay extra attention on the shades of gray placed down on the paper. Too dark too soon and there becomes a high chance of ruining the drawing before it's halfway done.

His eyes are drawn using a 2H, H, B, 2B, 4B, 6B and the Ebony pencil. As tempting as it may be never use charcoal on a graphite drawing! It's too messy and you will lose any detail you want in drawings of this size.

Working in layers, use each pencil, going from light to dark, when drawing his eyes. Keep the Ebony for the pupil, the edge of the iris, and his eyelids.

A little known fact in regards to men's eyelashes; they are normally longer than women's.

Therefore be careful when drawing them, that he doesn't look like he is wearing makeup. To accomplish this, use a pencil a few shades lighter than the one used for his hair, or in this case, his eyebrow.

The whites of his eyes aren't white at all. Use your 2H to draw the eyeball in curved cross lines to give shape. Use your F pencil for the shadow that his eyelid and lashes give off.

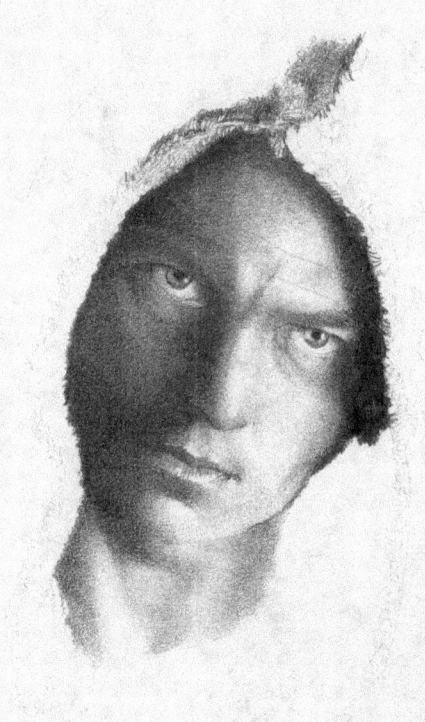

The kneaded eraser is perfect to lift highlights in the iris of the eyes to give it more of a wet appearance, and don't forget to bring out the color of the paper just below the iris and above the bottom eyelid.

It is very important to keep your pencils sharp when drawing his eyes as it is with most of his features. However, be careful, drawing lines with a sharp pencil will leave an impression on the paper. Even with erasing there may be no going back if you make a mistake. Once again, another reason to start off light.

Once the eyes are perfected the rest of the drawing can fall into place!

As you work down and away from the eyes his nose and cheeks will fall into place. Always follow the shape of the muscles to keep a realistic three-dimensional look to what really is a two-dimensional drawing.

After his eyes, his lips are the next focal point, and

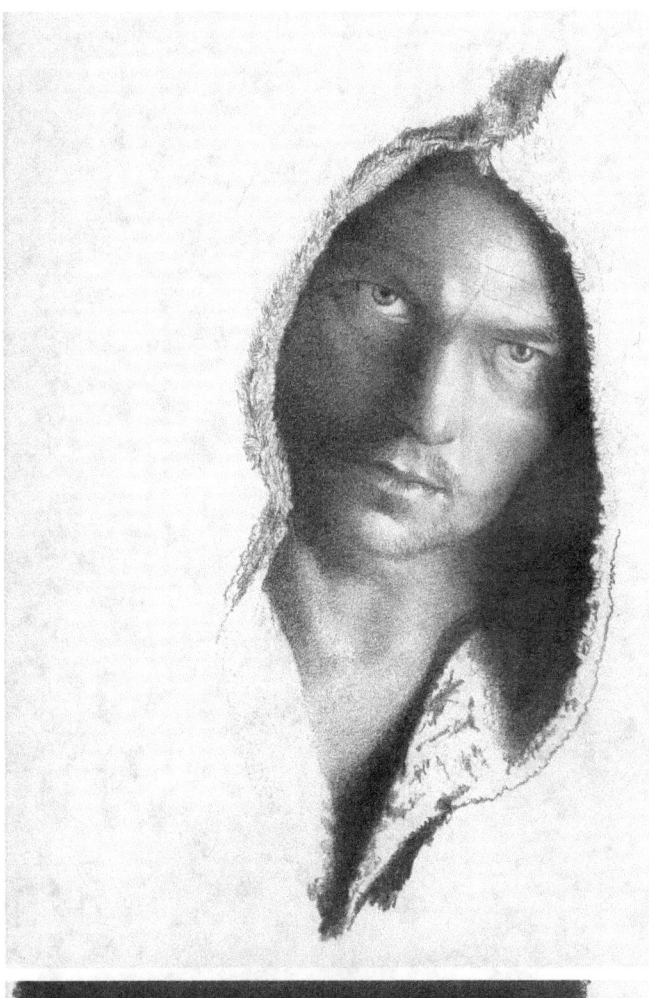

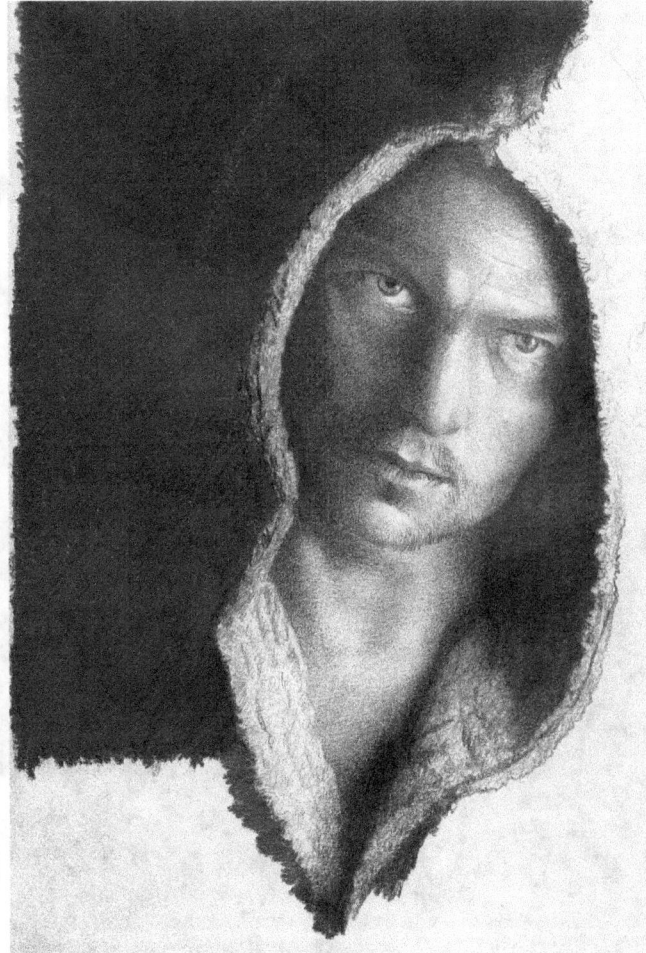

they need to be drawn perfectly.

With lips it's important not to draw a hard outline around them (unless the drawing is of a woman wearing make-up) but rather use shades of gray to follow the shape. Using your kneaded eraser for highlights will be "your lines".

Keeping your pencil sharp bring out the deep lines found in lips. Just be sure to follow the shape of the model's lip. Lighter lines will help make the lips realistic and not appear smooth. Use your kneaded eraser to bring out a moist highlight and give a pouting appearance.

Another area where no lines are drawn is his chin. Use the shadows on his neck to help define where his chin ends, then with one facial stubble and whisker at a time, his chin will start to take shape.

Using several of your darker pencils, draw the hairs coming from his face in various lengths, from a simple dot of the pencil to a sharp bold line. Keep the longer of the strokes to the edge of his chin.

The deep rich shadows surrounding his face may well be the most important part of this drawing since they circle his entire face as the hooded robe covers his head. These deep rich shadows are what draws your attention to his face as it appears to be coming out of the darkness when the drawing is complete.

The hood he is wearing is a terry cloth style fabric so the best way to create the fabric is by using twisted and circular motions, with various pencils, once the detail around the edge of the hood has been established.

Looking closely you can see that the edge of the hood are not circular but rather strands of yarn. The technique is like drawing hair by drawing out from the base of the fabric. For this, each strand will need to be drawn separately but don't feel as if you must draw each strand in the photo. You just have to draw enough to make it look real.

Draw the shadows that each strand brings out rather than the strand itself. It is not as complicated as it seems.

The dramatic look of this drawing is a the result of deep rich shadows and the highlights off the side of his face and eyes. To achieve this use your kneaded rubber eraser is used to gently lift up the graphite from the area you want lighter. Shape the eraser to fit the area you want to lighten, press gently and often, until you have the desired look. Then using your 2H and 4H pencils, gently go over the area once more, so that the lines can give shape to the final touches of your drawing.

Three drawings of Aleci were completed in the series from the same photo shoot. Each offering me the ability to work with very dramatic poses. This one being my

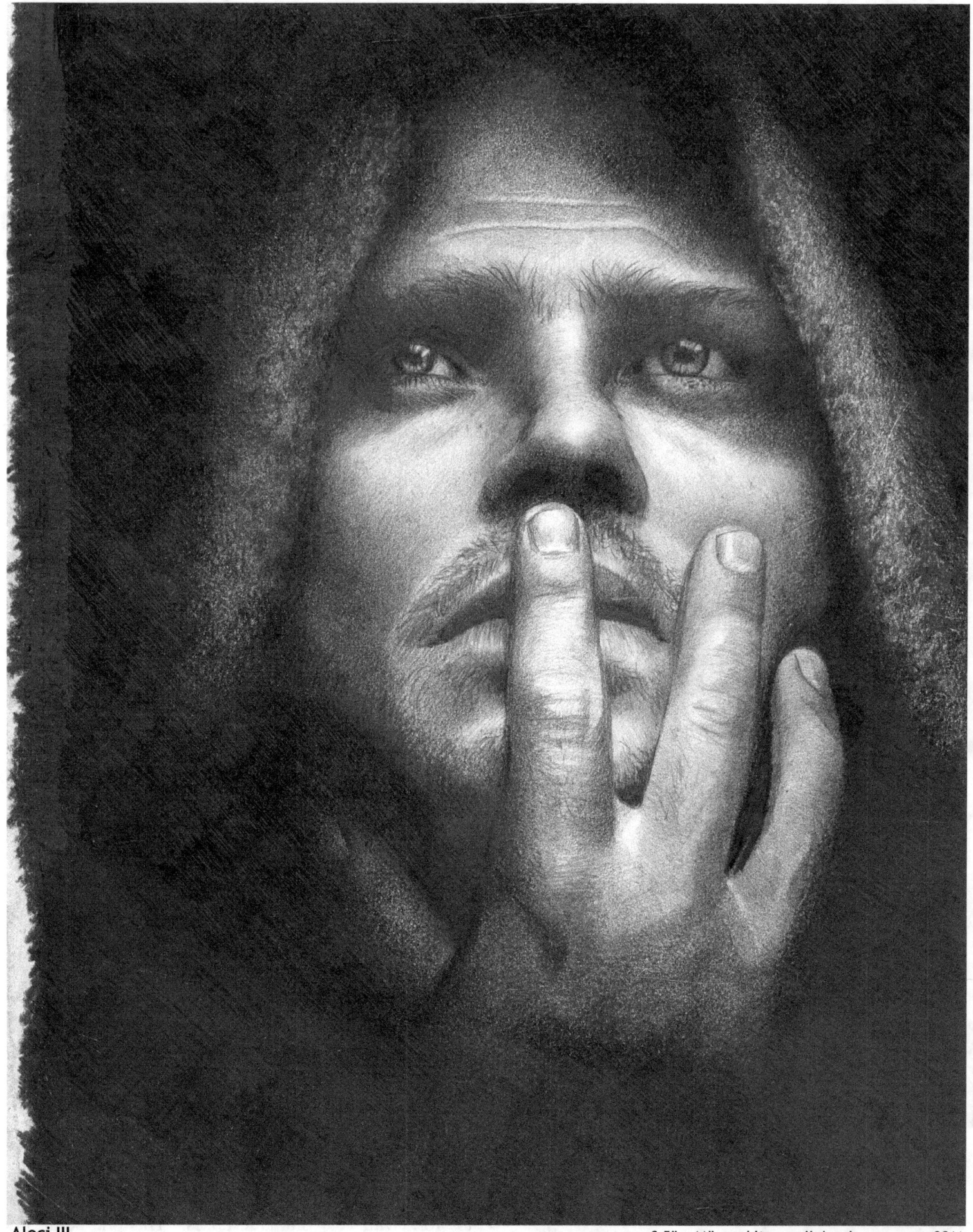

Aleci III

8.5" x 11" graphite pencil drawing on paper. 2011

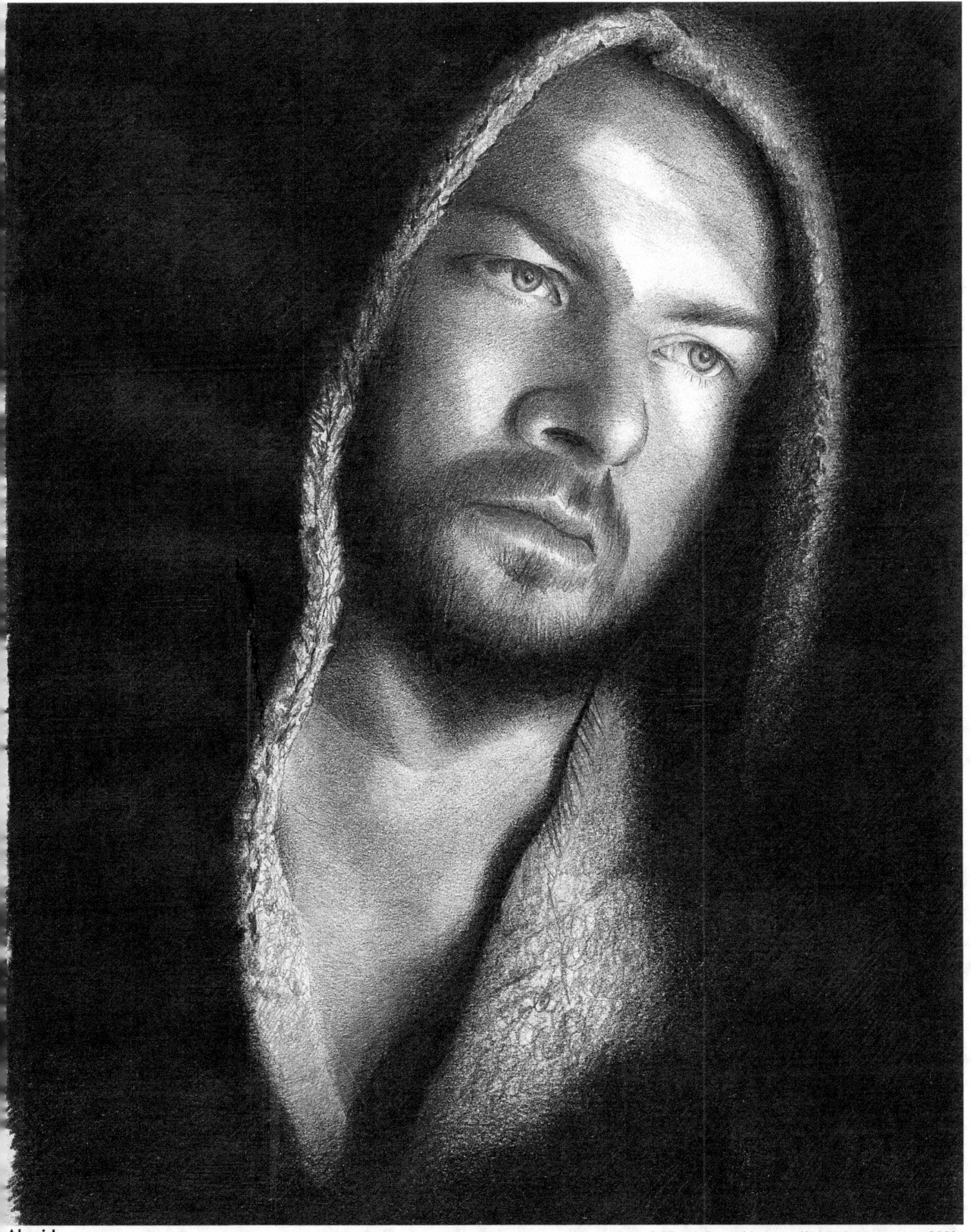

Aleci I

8.5" x 11" graphite pencil drawing on paper. 2009

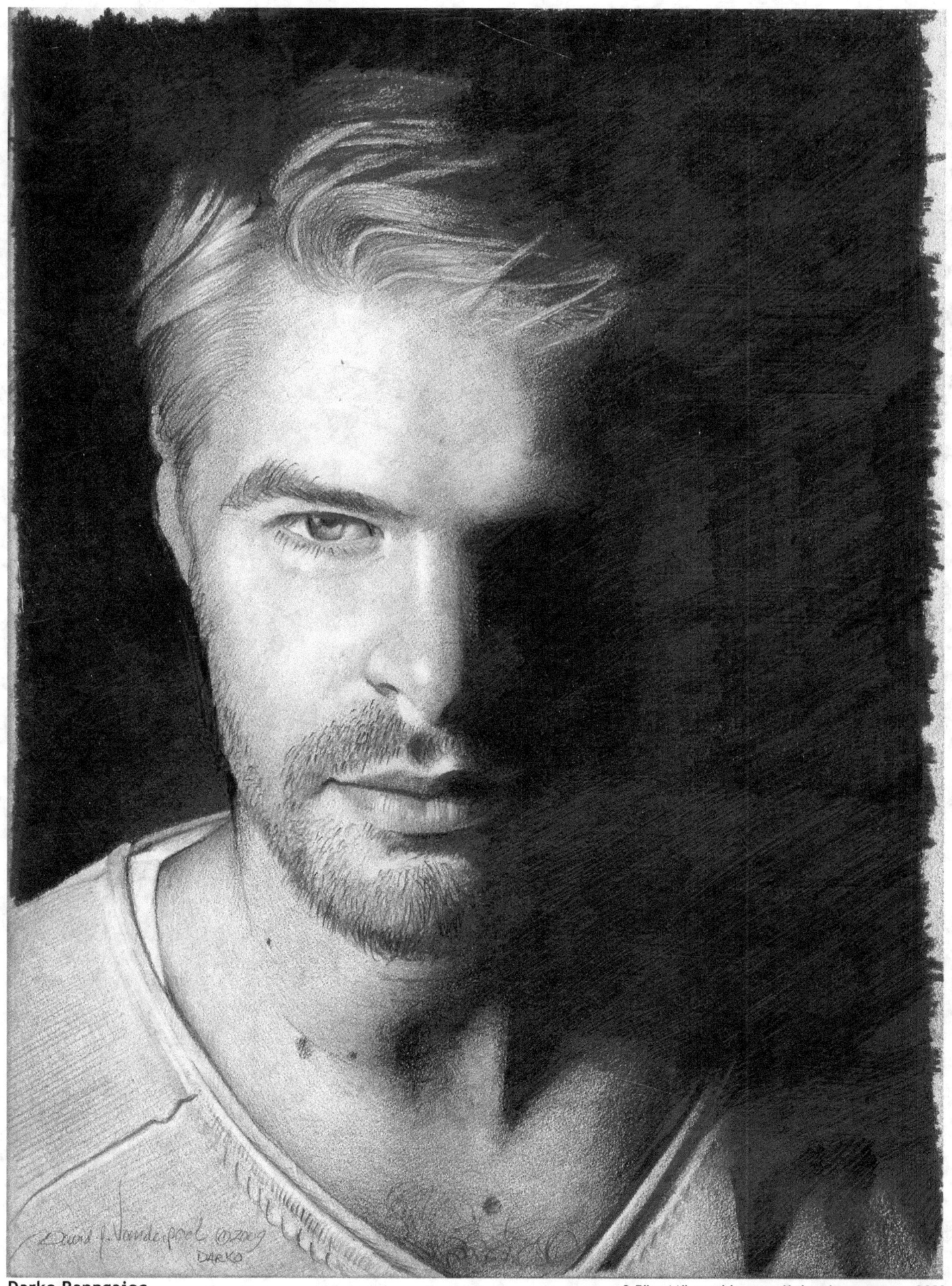

Darko Ranpgajec

8.5" x 11" graphite pencil drawing on paper. 2009

favorite of the series.

I will leave judgement of which is the best up to the art collector and those who have followed my drawings this last decade.

Darko.

As easy as it is to tell others that beauty can be found in the average person, there comes a time when we must admit, at least to ourselves, that a handsome face is preferable to look at!

One must realize that handsomeness in itself can be a challenge. Far too often a model can be too pretty, or too "posed", to fit into the art the artist is looking to create. This was the case with Darko.

After trying to draw him from three different photos, and nothing working out, I was just about to give up on ever capturing Darko's likeness on paper. But then he sent me one that was more like the portraits I had been creating of others.

He told me to stop trying to create a style seen in the other photos and draw what I am becoming known for: capturing mystery in such away that people question what the model is thinking or may be up to?

Darko Ranogajec: This young model and I met online after seeing his likeness in a painting by another artist. After further research on him, and instantly liking what I saw, I sent my request to draw him. I knew from experience that many requests to professional models or actors are usually denied or ignored. This wasn't the case with Darko.

Little did I know that finding the right photo to draw would be harder than getting permission. But once the right photo was discovered everything else just fell into place.

To present a light complexion man from Switzerland with Croatian parents this drawing had to start off light, and remain that way throughout the process, if the dramatic shadows surrounding him were going to work.

Not to be compared to the drawings of Aleci this young man had a romantic appeal to him. Where as with Aleci there was a darker and overpowering emotion that took over the drawing. With Darko there was passion in his eyes, and slight smile to his lips, that gave me a completely different feel from start to finish.

Knowing that the darkest part of the drawing would be the background and the one visible eye, the first layer to his portrait needed to be established using a 4H pencil, followed by a 2H over it.

Starting off with a 4H, the paper itself becomes the highlights reflected off of his nose and forehead, as well as the reflected light in his right eye. Establishing the muscles in his cheek and forehead the portrait quickly took on a three-dimensional look especially as darker pencils were introduced to the drawing.

Working in layers, each layer using a darker pencil, the shadows across the bridge of his nose and forehead gave a flatter appearance to where the side of his face was more rounded as it moved toward the center of the portrait.

Do keep in mind that nothing is really flat on a face as it appears. Even the bridge of his nose and his forehead follow the curves of bones and cartilage.

Blending with lighter pencils over the darker graphite allows a more natural blending effect and it keeps the lines left behind from the pencils. The lines must be slightly visible in the portrait to allow the drawing to take shape and "come alive" off the paper.

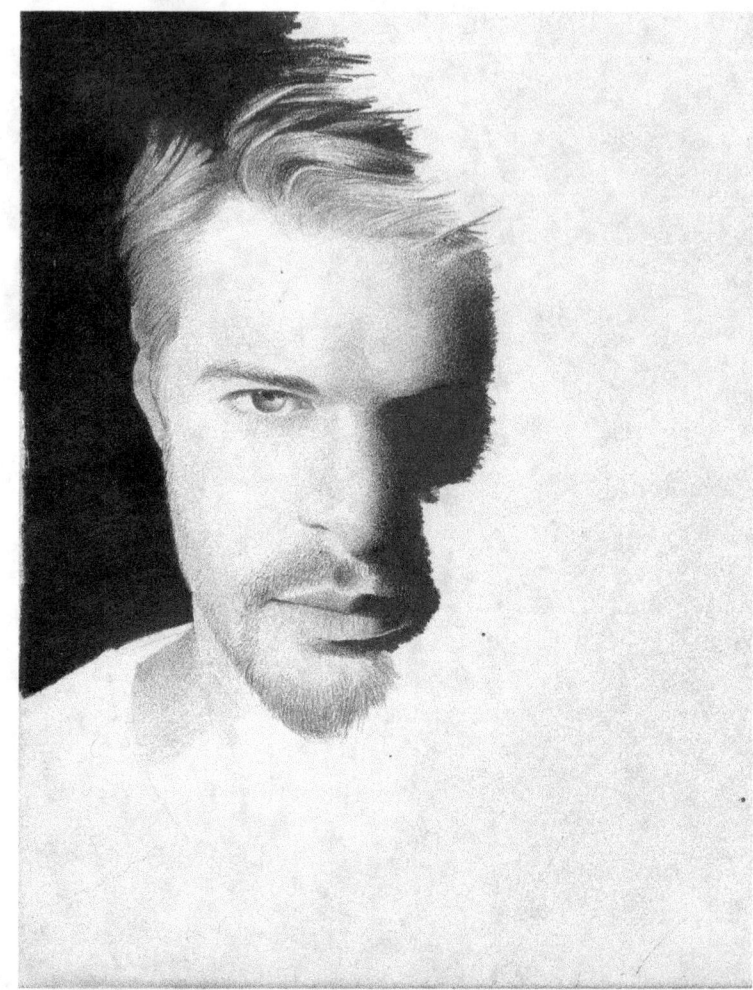

As with the drawing of Odessa, and a few others who's eyes attracted and inspired me to draw them, I jumped ahead of the required steps to complete the drawing and finished his eye(s) first.

Both eyes were drawn to establish placement for his eyebrows, as well as some reflection shown in the original drawing, that may not be noticeable here.

Unlike most of the drawings featured in books, where I started off with the darker shadows of the model's hair and worked outward toward the lighter shades, with Darko, the placement of each hair is started on his natural hair line. Just as hair grows each strand is lifted from the base and falls into place.

When drawing strands of hair various pencils are used. This allows the light to shine through the layers as well as give depth where color and shadows are the strongest.

As the shadows are slowly introduced, a kneaded rubber eraser is nearby to lift any necessary highlights, before a lighter, harder, well sharpened pencil follows the flow of his hair to set in any detail the eraser many have removed.

Facial hair – separating the boys from the men.

Facial hair in a blonde-haired man usually will be darker and thicker than the hair on his head. However, be careful not to start off too dark. With a sharp medium range pencil, such as a B, place one whisker at a time. starting from the pores and working your way our.

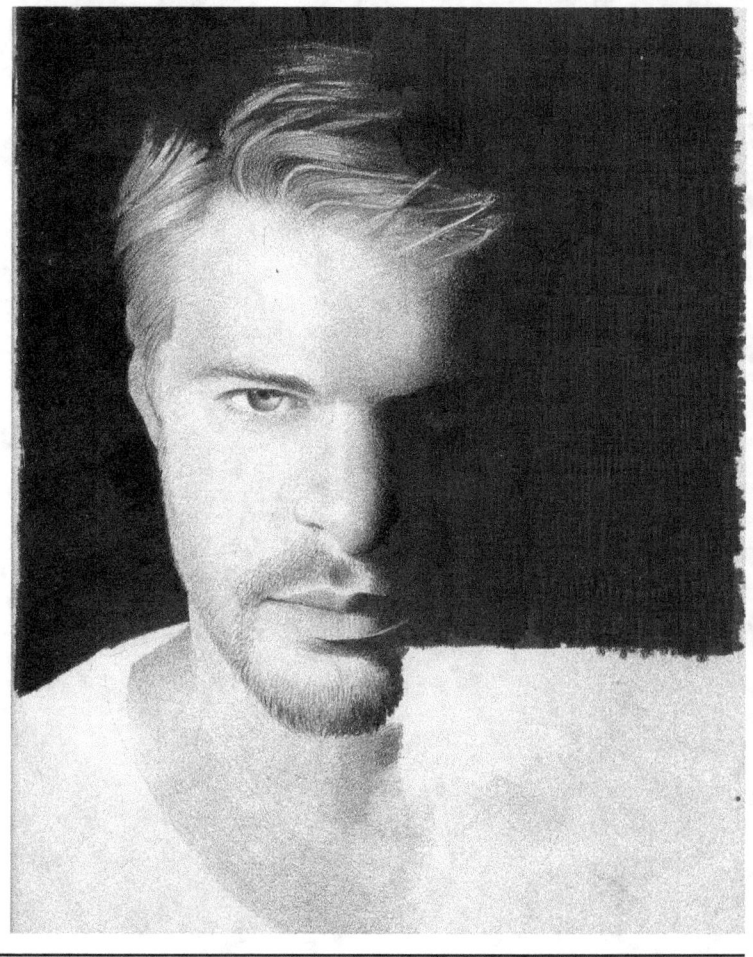

With short, well trimmed facial hair, whiskers tend to follow a natural direction so be sure your pencil follows the same direction. In Darko's case the hairs grew out and toward his neck.

Drawing his neck, I used a darker pencil than I used

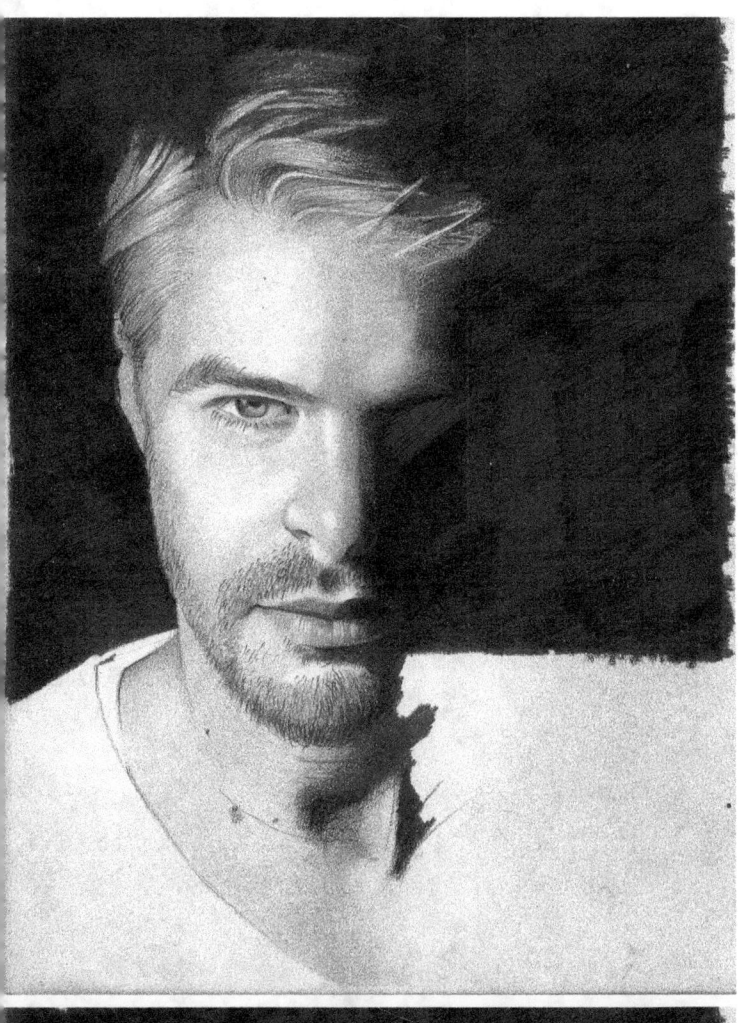

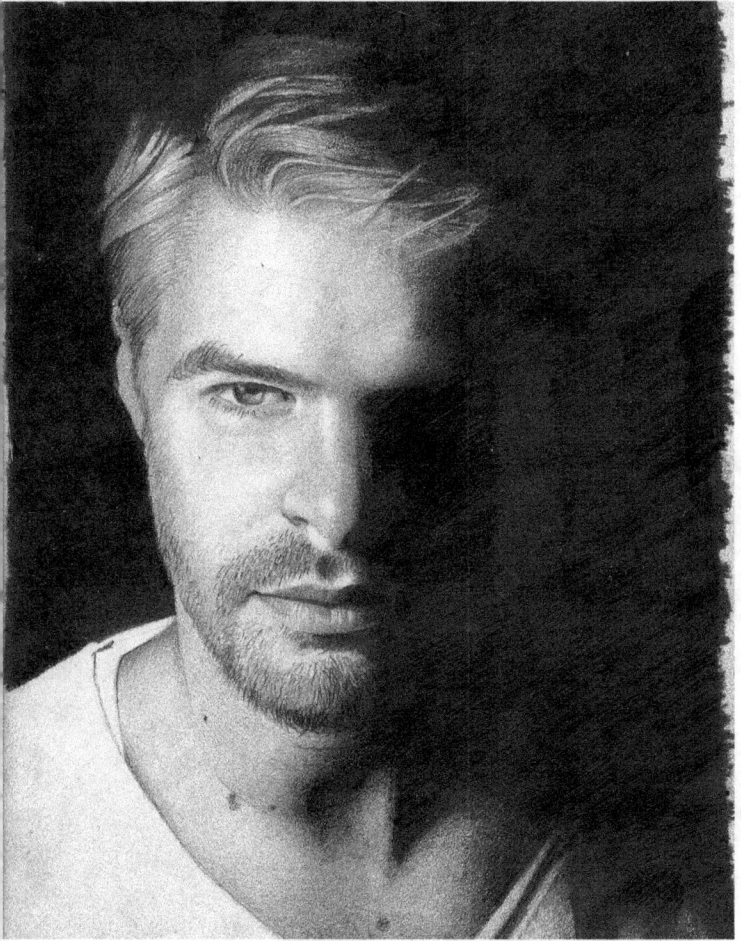

for his face, and be sure to follow the muscles in his neck, shoulders, and breast bone. Maintaining a sharp pencil follow the neck starting below the right ear and then go along the side of his neck until you wrap around his Adam's apple then up toward the other side. Draw much in the direction of a "U".

Fabrics have their own texture. Cotton blends to a smooth surface, tweeds have a pattern, and denim has a thick appearance to it. What they all have in common is they need lines to attain character.

With this portrait of Darko one can see that he is wearing a cotton shirt under a knitted shirt or light sweater. Using lighter pencils, the shadows, and then the white shirt are established first. However, make sure the pencil lines are not too noticeable and save the bolder lines for the outer shirt.

Work the layers backwards – shadows first and then the lighter shades of gray allows the graphite to blend more smoother.

Your darker graphite pencils are softer and tend to leave a harsher pattern on the paper. By using the lighter pencils over the darker graphite that section of the drawing slowing begins to smooth out allowing a smoother transition from your darkest shadows to your lighter shades of gray.

As you already may have noticed most of the drawings created in the last eight years have taken on a dark appearance. Not so much a theme in regards to good over evil but the use of darker backgrounds.

This not only helps to create a mood and some mystery at times (As in the three drawing of Aleci) but it helps bring out highlights and features that a lighter model with an all white background will tend to get lost and appear flat on the paper. (See the drawings of Eric and Russell).

We all have heard the saying that opposites attract and this applies to black and white art as well.

In order for highlights to be strong on a drawing dark shadows must be placed side by side in order for this to happen. This can be seen in the various works in progress showing the develop of Darko's portrait. His features do not begin to stand out until the surrounding darkness begins to take over the paper.

Where the model appears as though he is approaching you from the other side of a dark room, allowing the darkness in the background to pull away from him, as if unwrapping it's self from around him as he approaches the light. To achieve the darkness in this drawing an Ebony pencil was used for the deepest shadows in his hair, his eye lashes, eye brows, edges to his lips, and select whiskers on his chin.

Drawing women.

Through the years I have been questioned why I draw more men than women. Well it's quite simple - you draw not only who you know but who allows you to draw them.

Sure, I could have easily drawn celebrities. But fan art can only go so far before critics question your seriousness when it comes to being a professional artist. That plus the fact one has to deal with copyright laws, celebrities, movie studios, and their lawyers when going beyond drawing for your personal collection.

The women who did contact me after my drawings reached global distribution were quite frankly - scary! It reached the point I would not open an e-mail from a woman I did not know and Heaven forbid should an attachment be opened from one that insisted I draw her!

As with the men, of which I had developed a friendship via networking proved to be a success, I started to network with professional female models and the photographers who worked with them. As a result some of the worlds most beautiful women started to discover what I could do with a few pencils in hand.

Starting with Odessa, then onto Christina, each young lady offered their own individual beauty. They each allowed, not only this artist to look into their eyes to discover any passion deep within, but through each drawing they allowed the world to enjoy what God had blessed them with. True classic beauty!

The difference in drawing men and women is not a style or method of drawing but rather in the selection of who to draw.

Where as, the drawing of men filled a gap in my life where a male role model was lacking since my early teenage years, the selection of drawing women was completely different and for various reasons.

Convincing myself that I had developed a higher level of respect in woman than with men, both in a personal level and professionally, I later came to the conclusion that it most likely was a cover up for fear and therefore less women were approached or even drawn.

And error on my part that limited not only who I worked with but it limited the audience my work would possibly have reached.

And in all fairness to women, as an artist, I selected models based on the style I had developed through the years. No longer having a softer gentle look to my drawings, but a dark, bolder, and often harsher look, men were just more suited for my style of creativity.

It would not be until people started to questioning why I didn't draw more women did I notice what they may have been seeing. I reached the conclusion that I

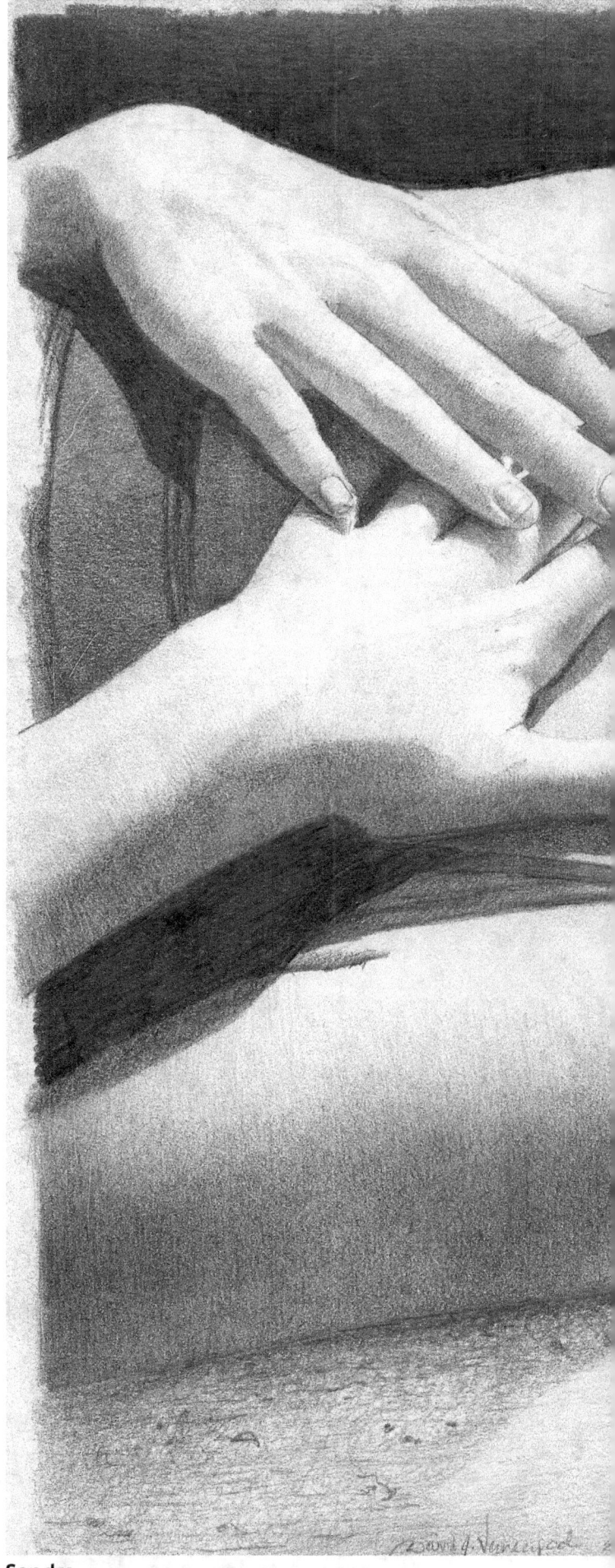

Sandra

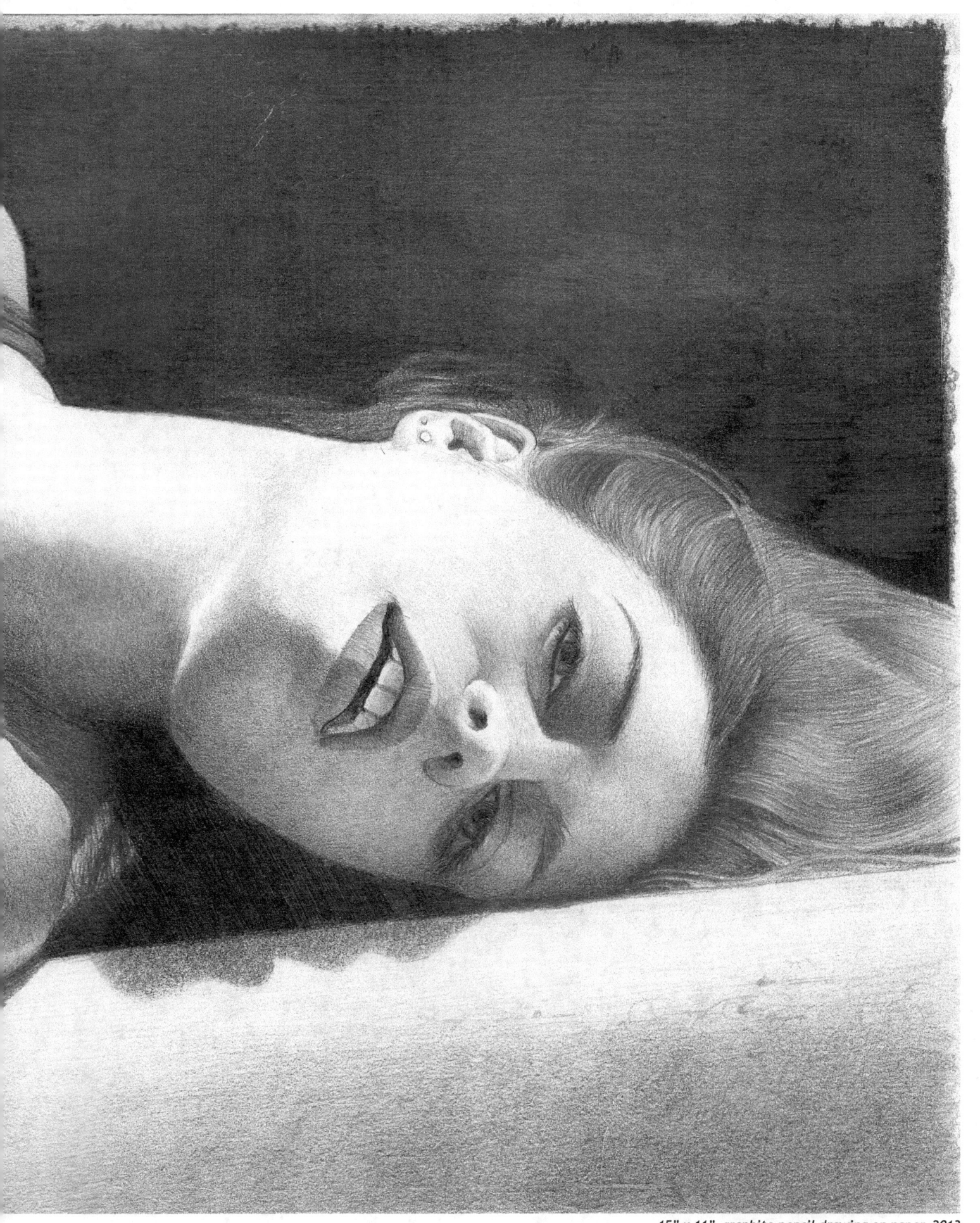

15" x 11" graphite pencil drawing on paper. 2013

A look into the art of David J. **Vanderpool**   59

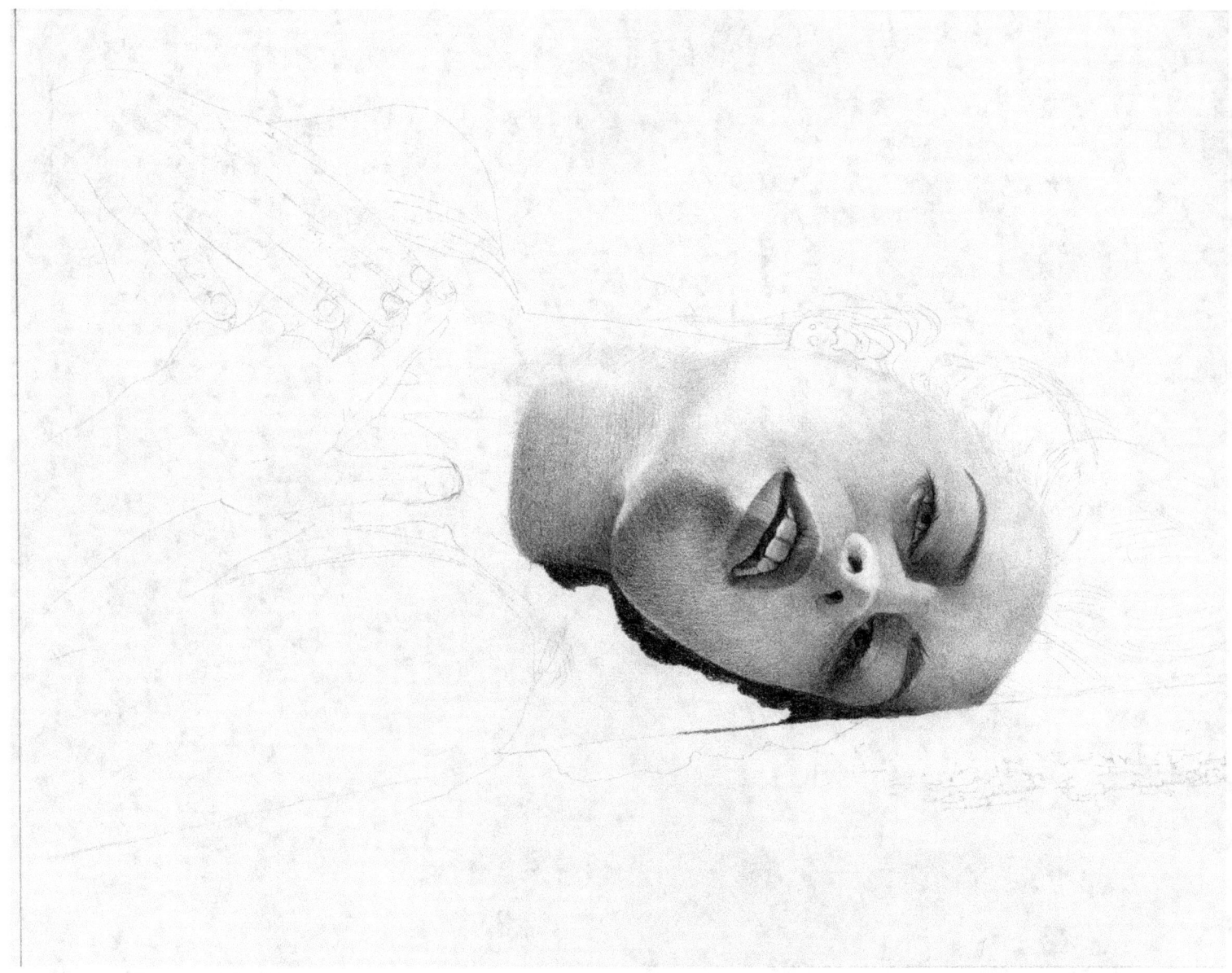

Sandra - work in progress - 1

needed to look into this more, not just as an artist but a more in-depth look from my personal point of view.

With no solid answer to why, other than my projects didn't leave opportunity to work with more women, I made an effort to make time in capturing perhaps one of the more attractive and powerful species on the plant - women!

Sandra

Knowing the drawing of Sandra would take on the style seen in the portrait of "Kevin" or even "Chris", I started the drawing as light as possible, and kept it as light as possible with every stage I advanced to.

Adjusting my drawing style was going to take some time if I was going to get this brain to work as it had done so many decades ago. Therefore, this drawing of Sandra was going to be perfect for this gradual transition from a

dark, bolder, and even sometime reported erotic look as in the drawing of men; to a softer more sensual look of these timelessly classic beauties.

Keeping her hair and skin lighter than how she appeared in the photograph was going to be the key factor in making this work. (See page 58)

Too dark too soon and the drawing would be destroyed at the start!

Once the background and shadows were set in place the grays used to draw her slowly fell into place. A slow process since the background and deep shadows would be the last to be placed in the drawing.

I had to trust what I was doing and not go by what I was seeing at the moment.

Working in layers I made sure the lines used in the drawing followed the curves of her skull and neck so that the drawing did not become flat. A repeat method

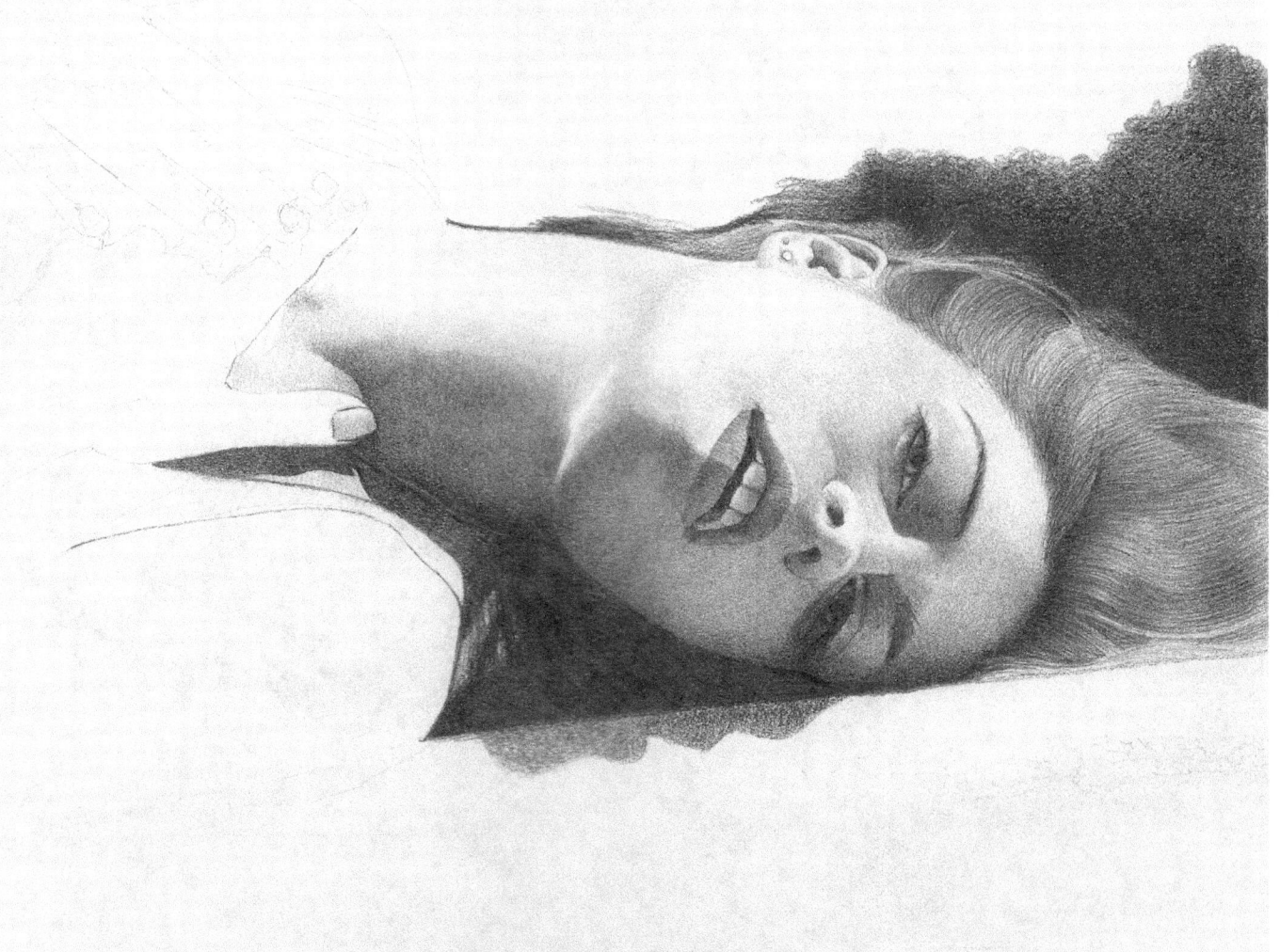

Sandra - work in progress - 2

through out the drawings as throughout all my drawings.

Knowing the drawing would be dark due to the lighting I made sure that her eyes kept true to the photograph and not embellished as I had done years ago with the portrait of "Kevin". In that drawing (See page 12) his eyes were lighter in order that they stood out strong in the drawing.

With this drawing I wanted the passion she was displaying be what caught the viewer's attention. Yes, passion sells, too, in art - If you haven't already noticed?

Placing the mid-range shading of gray into place, the lighter 2H and 4H pencils were used to blend as well as place the lightest of the graphite across her cheek and upper lips and the bridge of her nose. Gradually introducing the pencil to the paper, and with every layer, pressed a little harder.

The same pencils were used for her neck and shoulder. Keeping the drawing as light as possible and still keeping

About the model:

Sandra Falga is a model, actress, and presenter residing in Barcelona, Spain. After modeling for six years, she already enjoyed good fortune and success in her career.

As a on-camera TV and video reporter, this exciting reporting work enables her to pursue both her modeling and acting goals full-time.

As you might expect, she is hard working, determined, and goal-oriented. To further her career, she continually searching for opportunities to to network with professionals in the fashion, artistic and entertainment industries.

"ONE OF THE SIX SEXIEST SPANISH WOMAN BY ESQUIRE magazine, April 2012

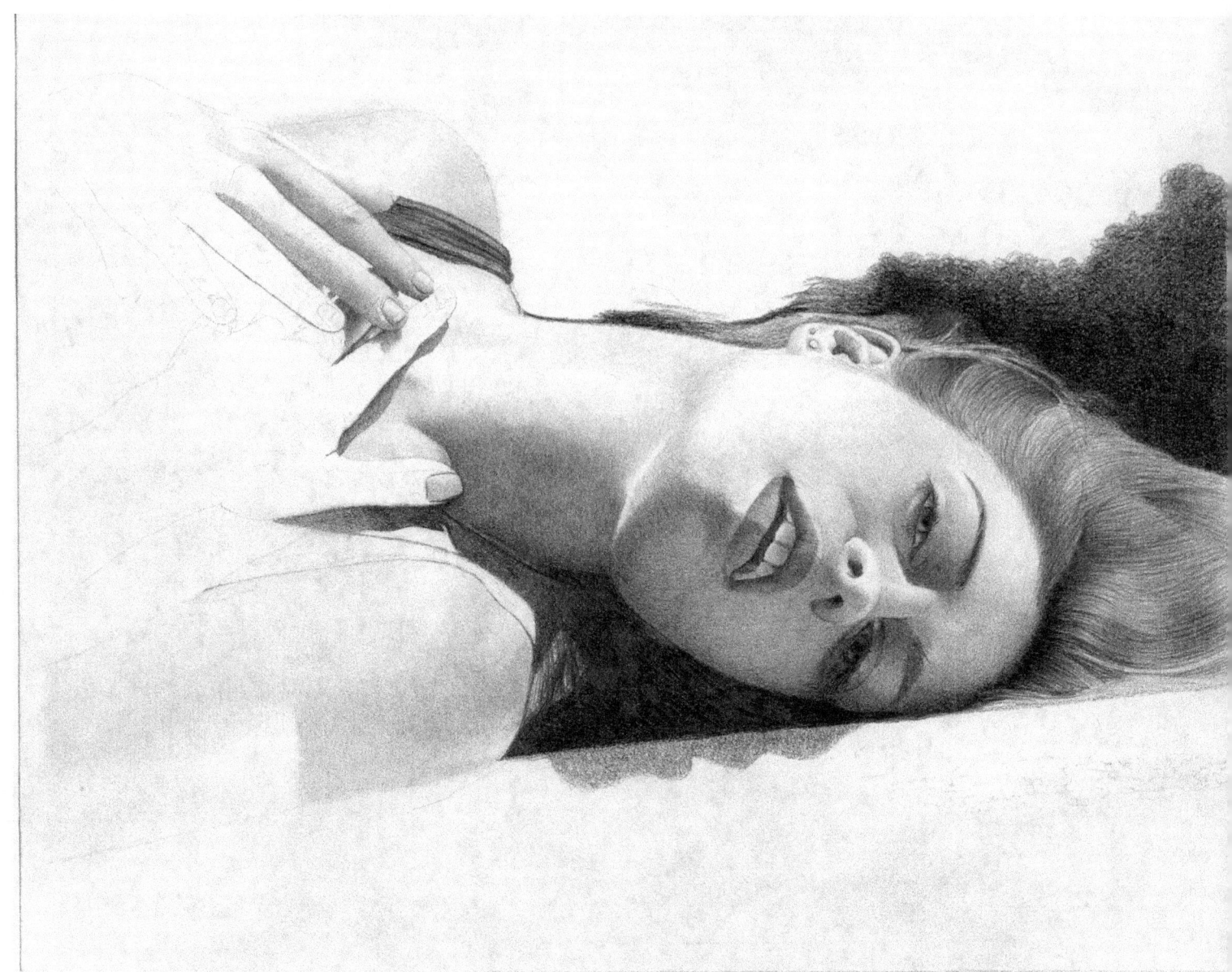

Sandra - work in progress - 3

About the photographer

The photograph used for this portrait was taken by Dutch photographer., Alfredo OP,

"Through my lens I want to convey the feelings of the artist and models .. go further and seek to create the details of the perfect time to transmit in one picture my passion for photography. To relive the most beautiful moments of a lifetime, is often as enriching as the experiences themselves. The distractions and emotions which accompany them give full appreciation to all the special details, while the event is occurring."

www.ajgfilmproductions.com

to her shades of gray presented in the black and white photograph.

Yes - when drawing from a photograph it is best to convert the image into black and white before printing it for easy reference as you work on the drawing.

Just be sure the images are at least 200 dpi or higher and printed on quality paper in order to see the detail in the model's eyes. Anything less than 200 dpi and the detail is lost and nearly impossible to make an exact duplicate of what sits in front of you.

This also apply when working with live models. Take as many photos as possible in one or two sittings. Then the model is no longer needed to pose, and you as an artist can drawing whenever you have time that is better suited your busy schedule.

By keeping the medium to light pencils for the skin and lips of the model, the remaining pencils in the

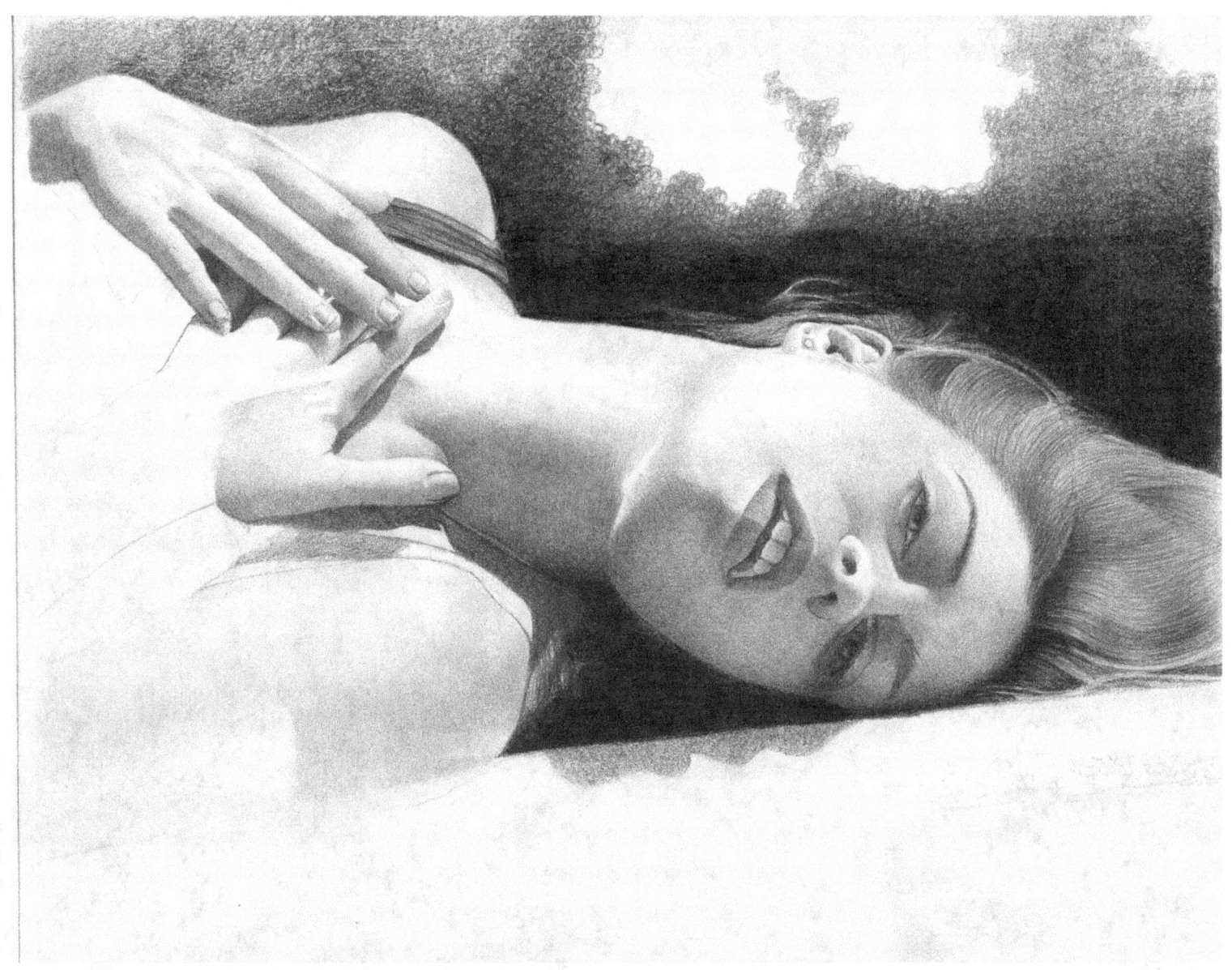

Sandra - work in progress - 4

collection (H through 8B) are used for her eye lashes, pupil, nostril, mouth, and the deeper shadows under her fingers, as well as the outfit she is may be wearing.

Keeping the darker 8B and Ebony Design pencil for the deepest of the shadows and the background, the medium shades of gray will final all come together and no longer looking too dark for the drawings.

If I had chosen not to draw the dark background she would have come across too rough in appearance.

Well enough if it was a man, but for a woman of this beauty, she needed to be perfect. And in this case - for this pose - a darker background make for an excellent over all mood for this drawing.

Sandra - A drawing that helped me make the transition from drawing what appeared to be all men with darker and harsher moods, to one that presented a model to be softer, and sensual - and a woman!

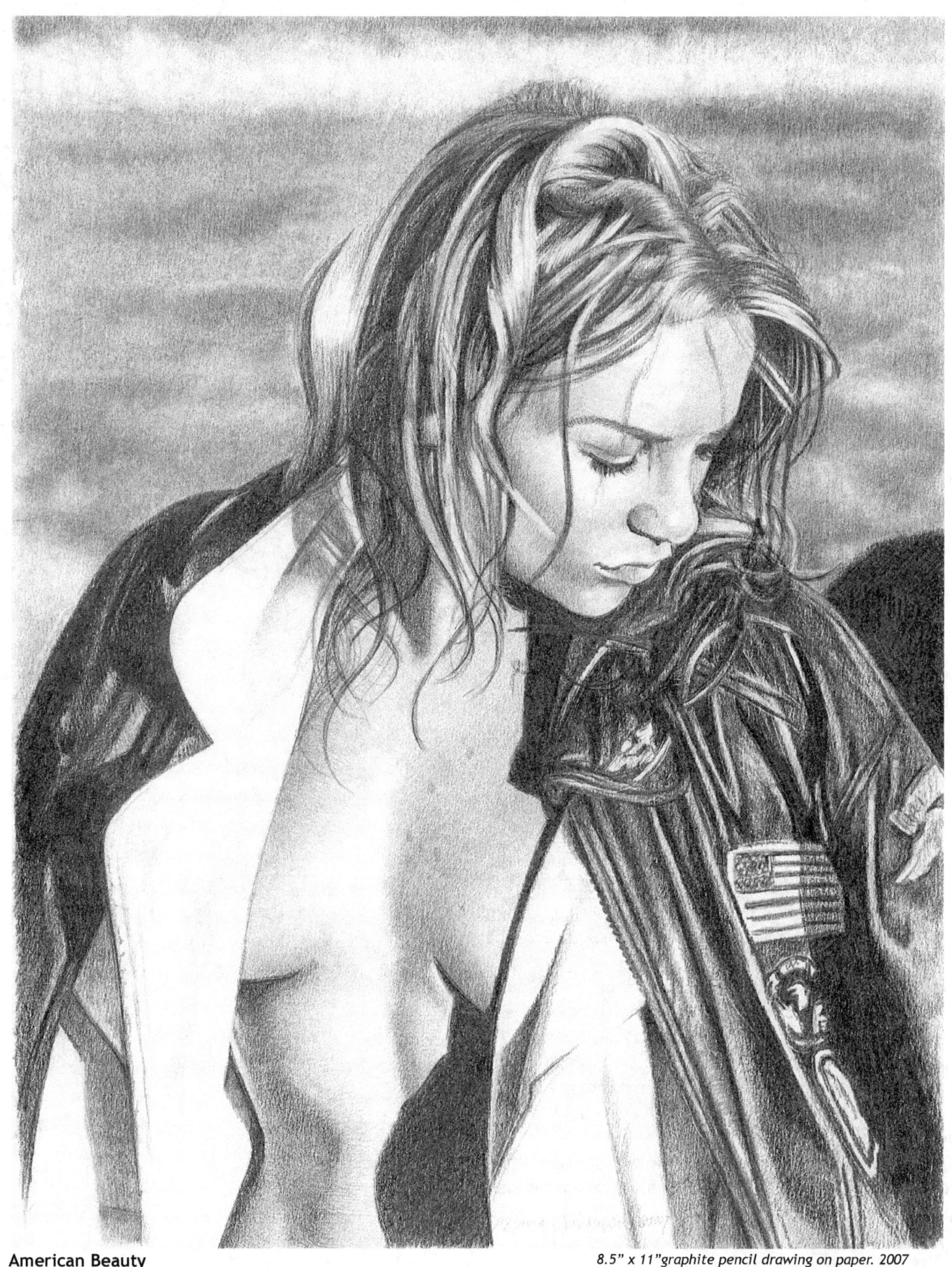

American Beauty

8.5" x 11"graphite pencil drawing on paper. 2007

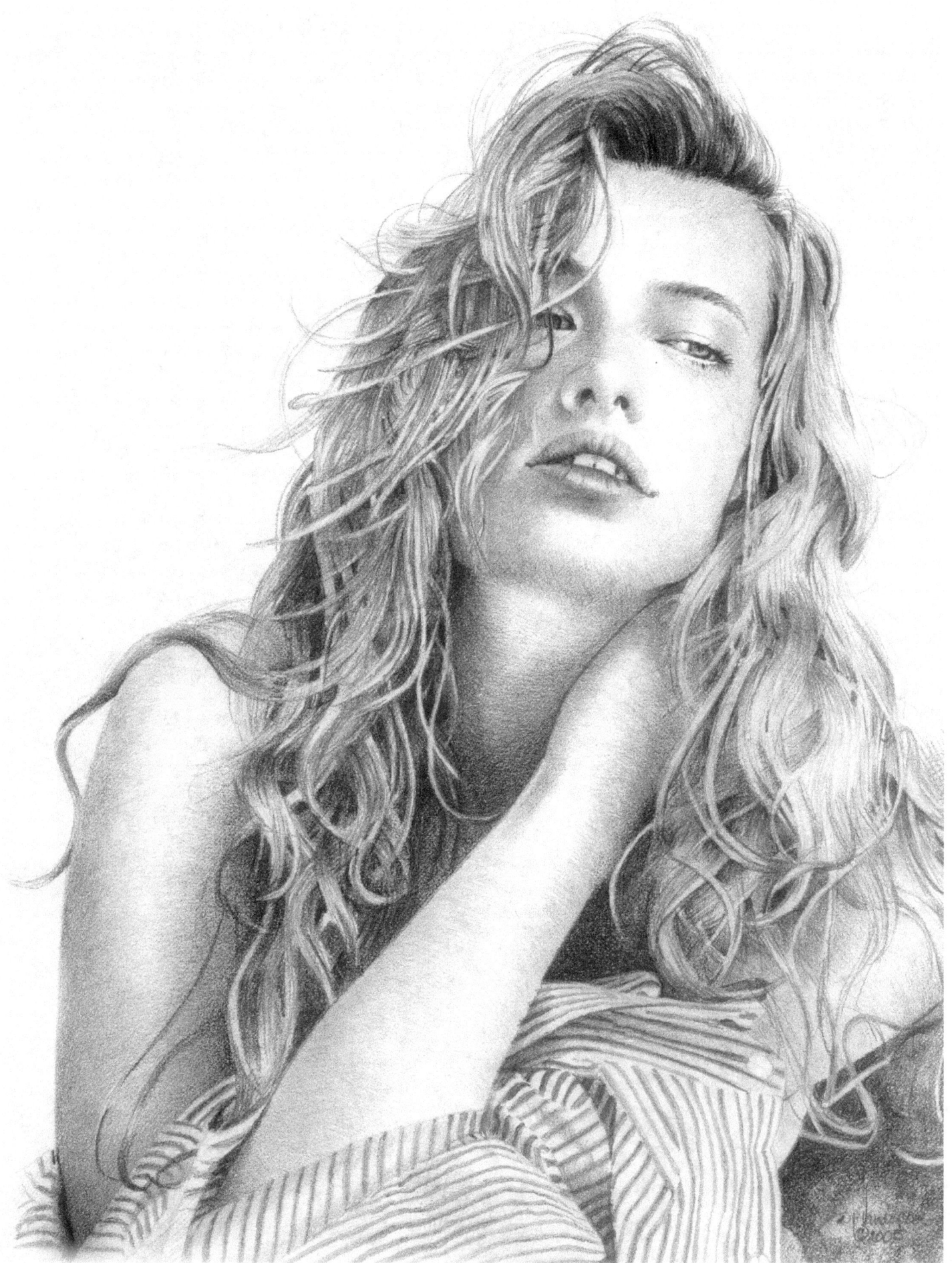

DressShirt 2

apprx 11" x 15" graphite pencil drawing on paper. 2005

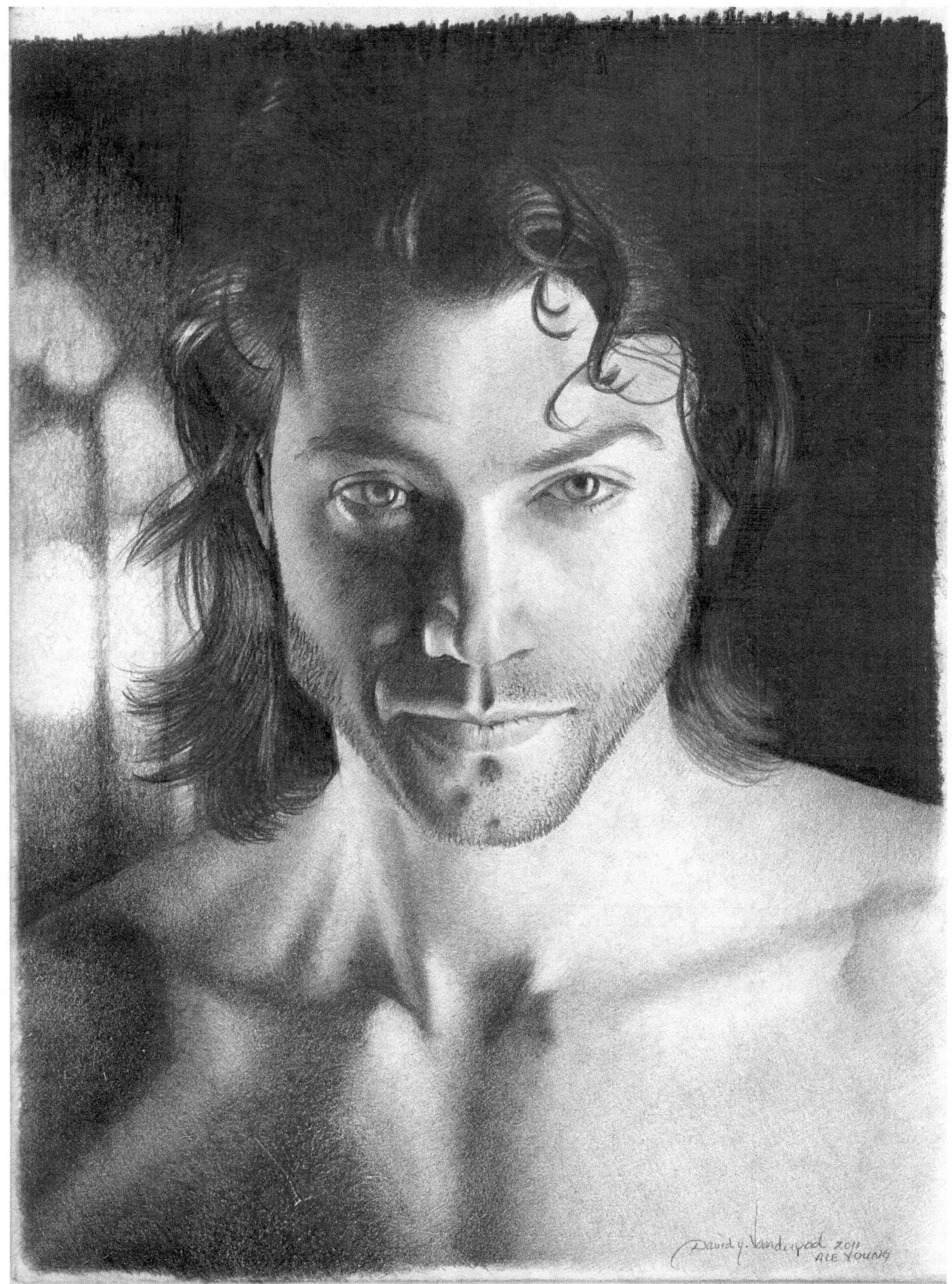

Ace Young

8.5" x 11" graphite pencil drawing on paper. 2011

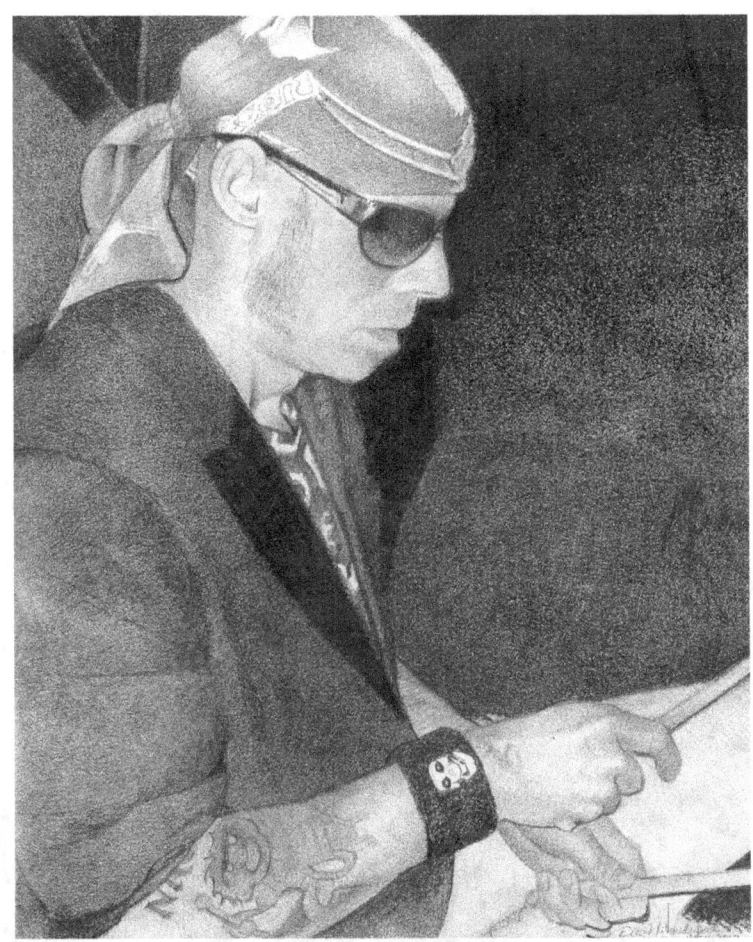

Preston - 8.5" x 11" graphite pencil drawing on paper

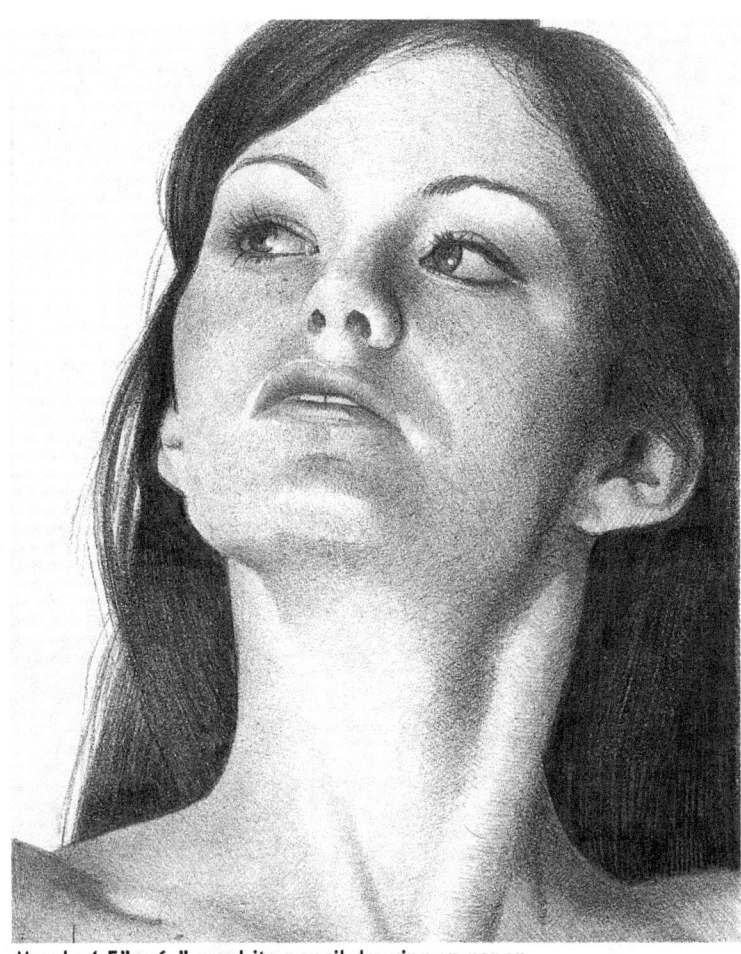

Mandy 4.5" x 6." graphite pencil drawing on paper

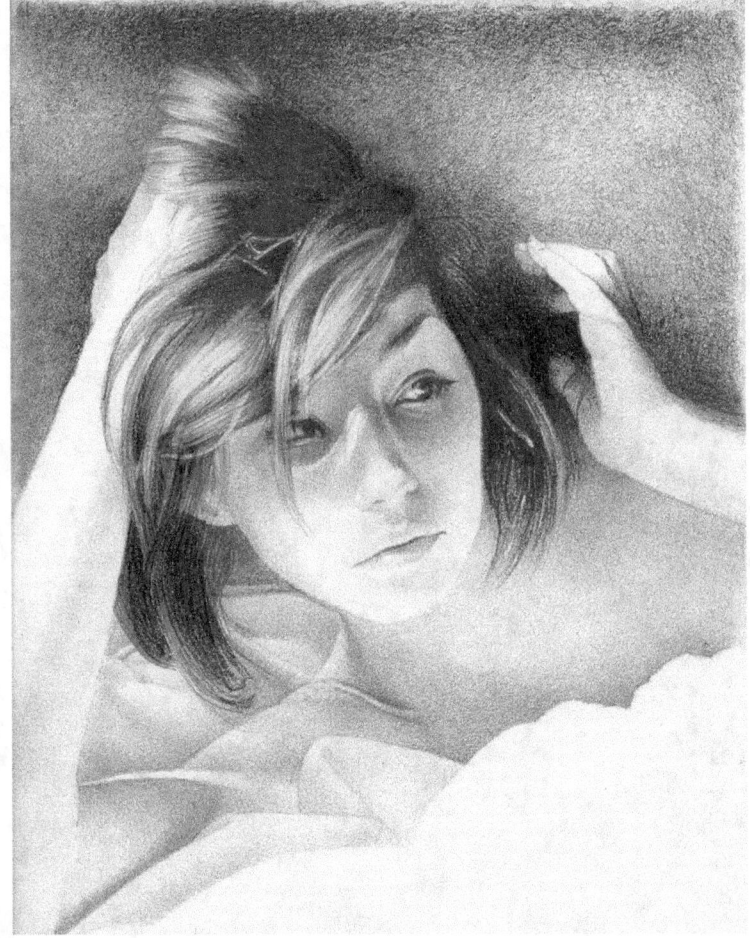

Christina - 8.5" x 11" graphite pencil drawing on paper

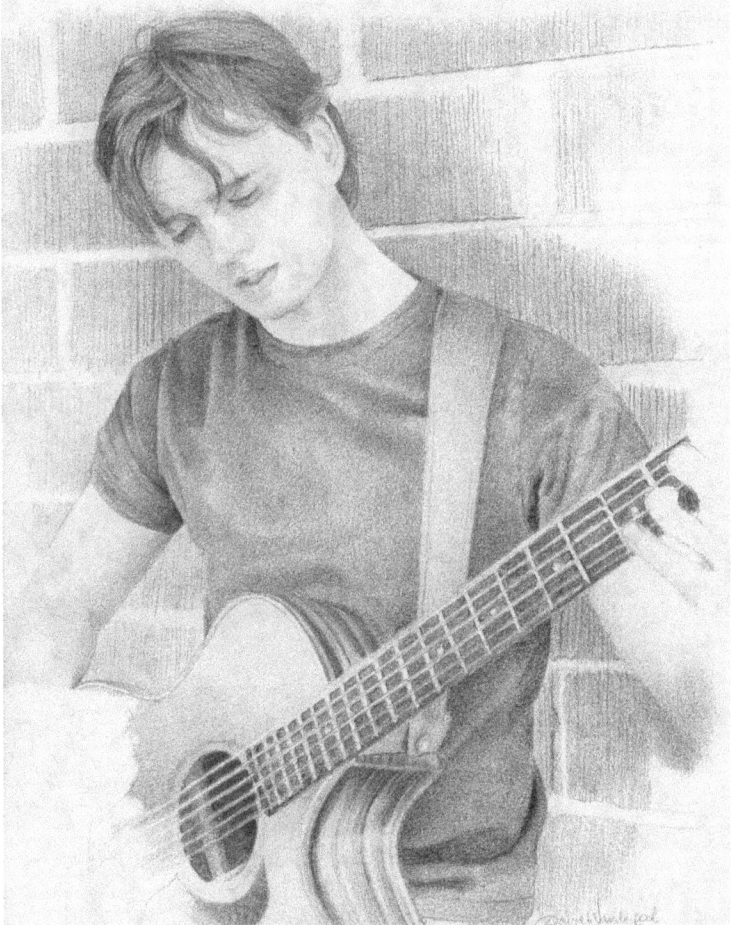

Peter- 8.5" x 11" graphite pencil drawing on paper

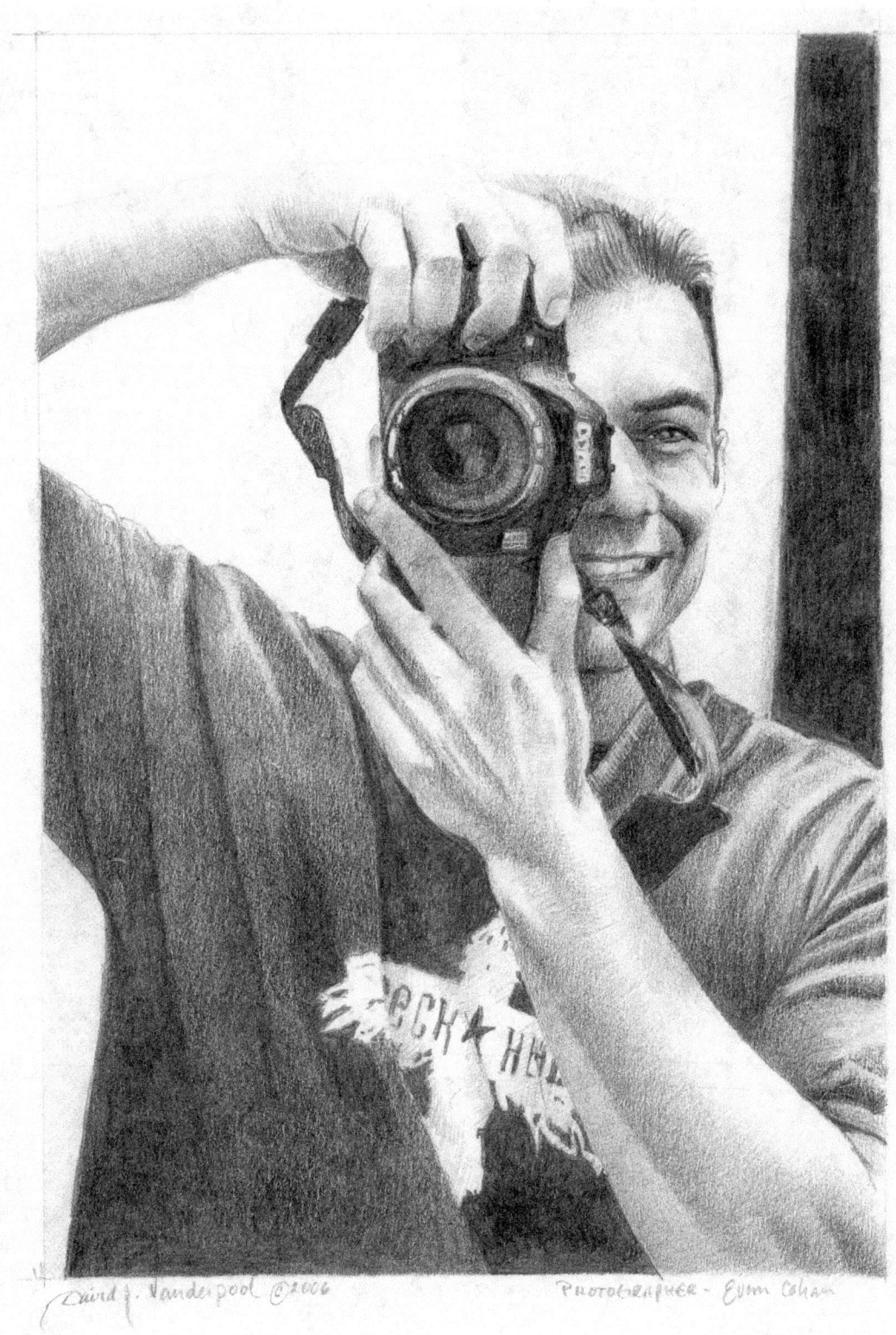

David J. Vanderpool ©2006   PHOTOGRAPHER - Evan Cohan

Evan

Copyright 2006. David J. Vanderpool
Shown actual size.

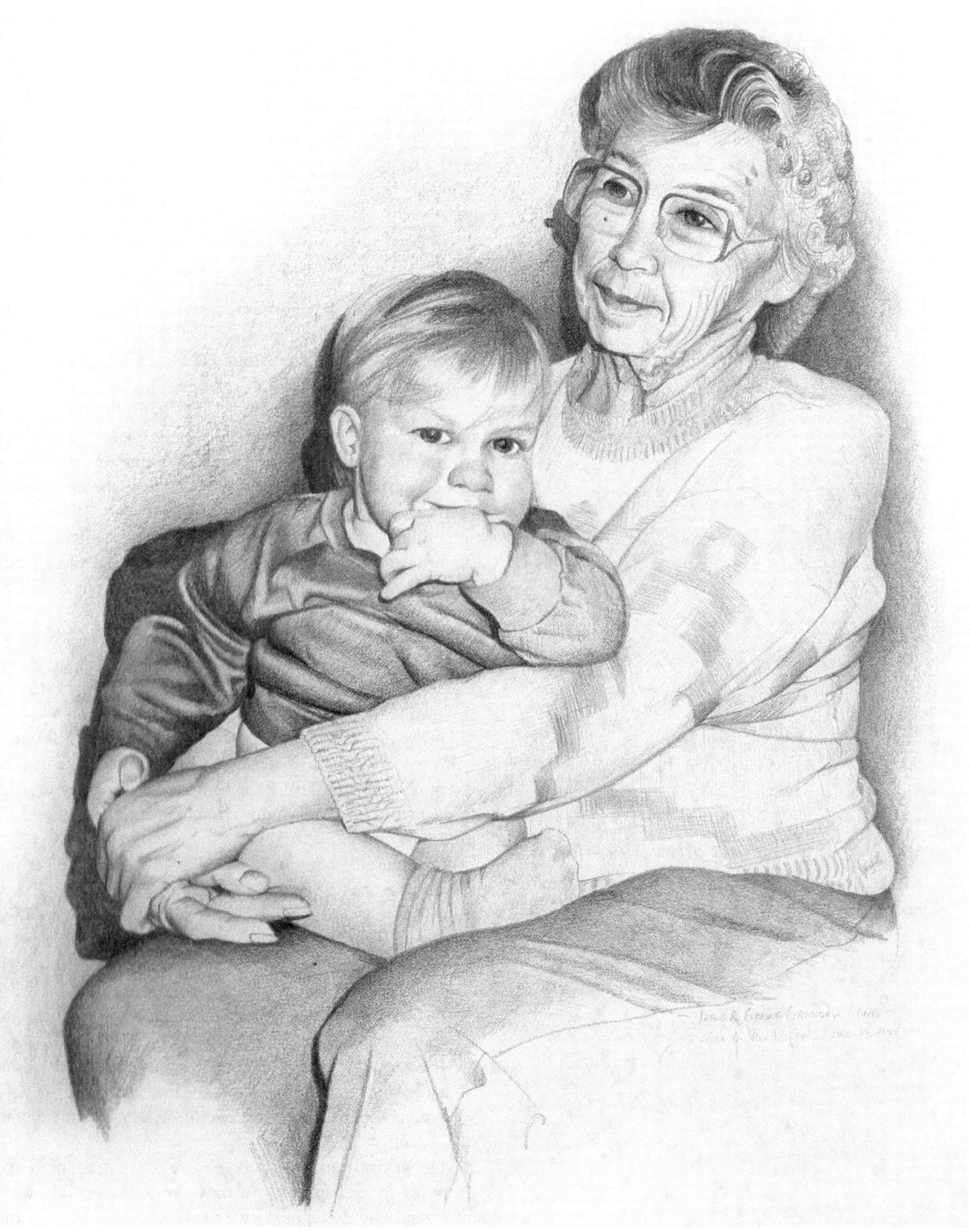

Jared and Great-grandma Long

8.5" x 11" graphite pencil drawing on paper. 2004

Chapter Three
Figure Drawings

Not all pencil drawings are created equal. Nor should they.

Where some drawings require being completed to the point where it's difficult at first glance to tell if it is a photograph or a drawing, some drawings are left incomplete as seen here in this drawing of Gordon, each drawing will determine just how much the artist will work on it. Especially when it comes to figure drawings.

Figure drawings are a wonderful opportunity, to show off not only the artist's skill but, to welcome the chance of duplicating the beauty God has already placed on this earth for man kind to enjoy.

Even if the enjoyment is at a distance.

Never to touch or embrace, but rather to see, up close, a piece of paper that reveals to each viewer what the artist saw in the models who entered his world.

Fully dressed, without a shirt on, or even a full nude, a figure drawing allows each of us to become the voyager we may never think of becoming. As the model reveals to the world a side of themselves that others would never dream of doing.

We secretly become pleased that someone else had the courage to do what we could not have done. Giving us a chance to see outside the world we have created for ourselves.

However, as an artist, how far does one go when it comes to art and drawing the human figure?

Do we limit ourselves, or our work, when it comes to what may or may not be socially acceptable?

Do we worry about what others may or may not think of us, let alone allowing them to discover more of who we are, as the result of those we draw, or even those who follow our work?

Do we draw only for the pleasure of creating, or do we draw for the acceptance we may potential receive when all is said and done, or do we draw who we draw for the reaction we may get from those around us?

"
...so long as we strive to make each piece better than the last, our best may not be determined when we stop ... proving that we can grow - no matter who we are and how long we have been drawing.

- David J. Vanderpool
November 25, 2012

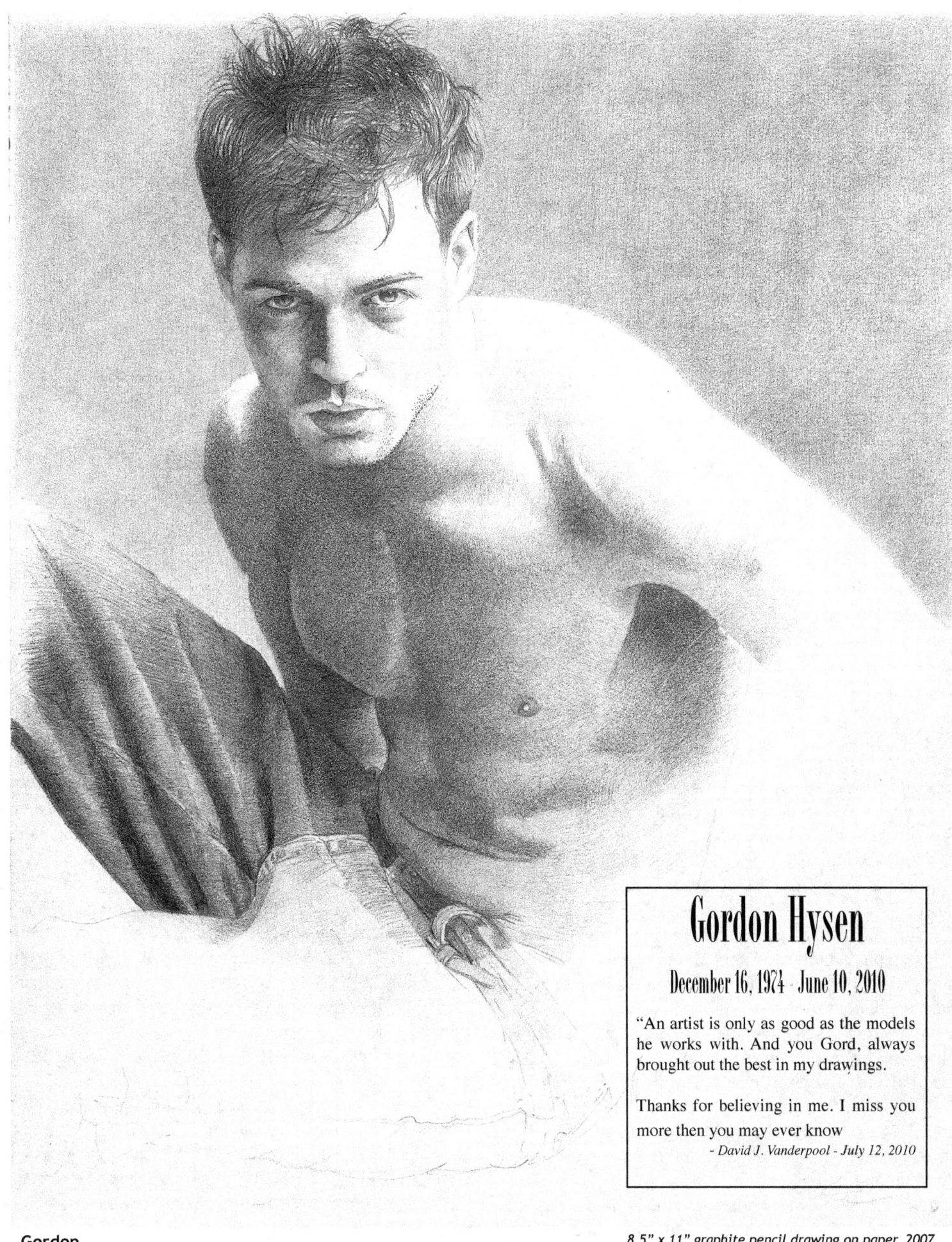

Gordon Hysen

December 16, 1974 - June 10, 2010

"An artist is only as good as the models he works with. And you Gord, always brought out the best in my drawings.

Thanks for believing in me. I miss you more then you may ever know
- David J. Vanderpool - July 12, 2010

Gordon

8.5" x 11" graphite pencil drawing on paper. 2007

Gordon.

Gordon Hysen was a Canadian model and actor I had the pleasure of knowing for many years and worked with him when I first started to get back into drawing.

At a time when I was discovering what I could or could no longer do Gordon would usually send me new photos of himself, of which he held the copyrights, for me to draw.

His timing was always perfect!

Each time I wanted to give up drawing for good Gordon was there to encourage me to draw "just one more time", and always without me asking.

I had no idea how important he was in the development of the artist I would later become. How much one person, how each person, we encounter in our daily life effects the person we eventually become.

For this I will always be eternally grateful for the opportunity to draw him, to know him, and see the faith he had in me as an artist and a person.

With Gordon there would be no better model, or friend, when the time came to reestablishing myself as a pencil artist - a fine arts figure drawing artist!

When drawing a portrait or figure the chest and forehead of a man is usually the only place on the body you can use a straight line when drawing. Dead center of the chest aligning with the dead center of the forehead before they wrap around the body.

I mainly use lines in all my drawings but I do use crosshatching for the shaded areas and fabrics.

Cross-hatching is as old as drawings it's self and no longer, or seldom, taught in schools since it required time and patience. A drawing could take a few days, a few weeks such as Gordon, or even a month as was the case of drawing "Courting". All depending on the detail required and how much you are willing to put into the work.

This 8.5" x 11" pencil drawing was created from a photograph that reflected light off of the models shoulders and yet kept enough shadows over his face and legs to offer some depth.

Capturing his likeness comes in a few easy steps, and once I was pleased, I was able to move on to the rest of the drawing. Keeping in mind even the smallest detail was important I made sure not to rush drawing his facial hair. Instead of blending the shadows, I had to draw one whisker at a time, or in the case of this small drawing, one dot at a time.

Drawing messy looking hair is much harder than hair that is combed. Light must be able to bounce through that careful styled 'mess' as well as the shadows that help some of it stand out. Take your time by tackling one section at a time. Much like muscles in a hand or chest hair needs to be drawn in sections too.

When the subject in your drawing has more light reflecting off his body than grays it is best to off set the reflection with a gray background. Just be careful not to get carried away and make your background appear like a wall that has been attacked with graffiti unless that's the look you want.

The trick to using a crosshatch method for a background is to start off with a pencil closest to shade you will be duplicating. In this case, a medium pencil such as a "B" or "F", and each pencil to follow in the remaining layers will be lighter than the last one used. Descending until you have used your 2H over the entire area you wish to cover.

Remember your best tool for blending is a lighter pencil.

You will notice with Gordon I had the perfect chest to draw! Not round as a woman's should be, or perhaps a younger man, but the muscles in his chest are solid and slightly flat across the top before rounding off to the sides. Be sure to follow those contours and draw the muscles as they are or the pose won't be as bold.

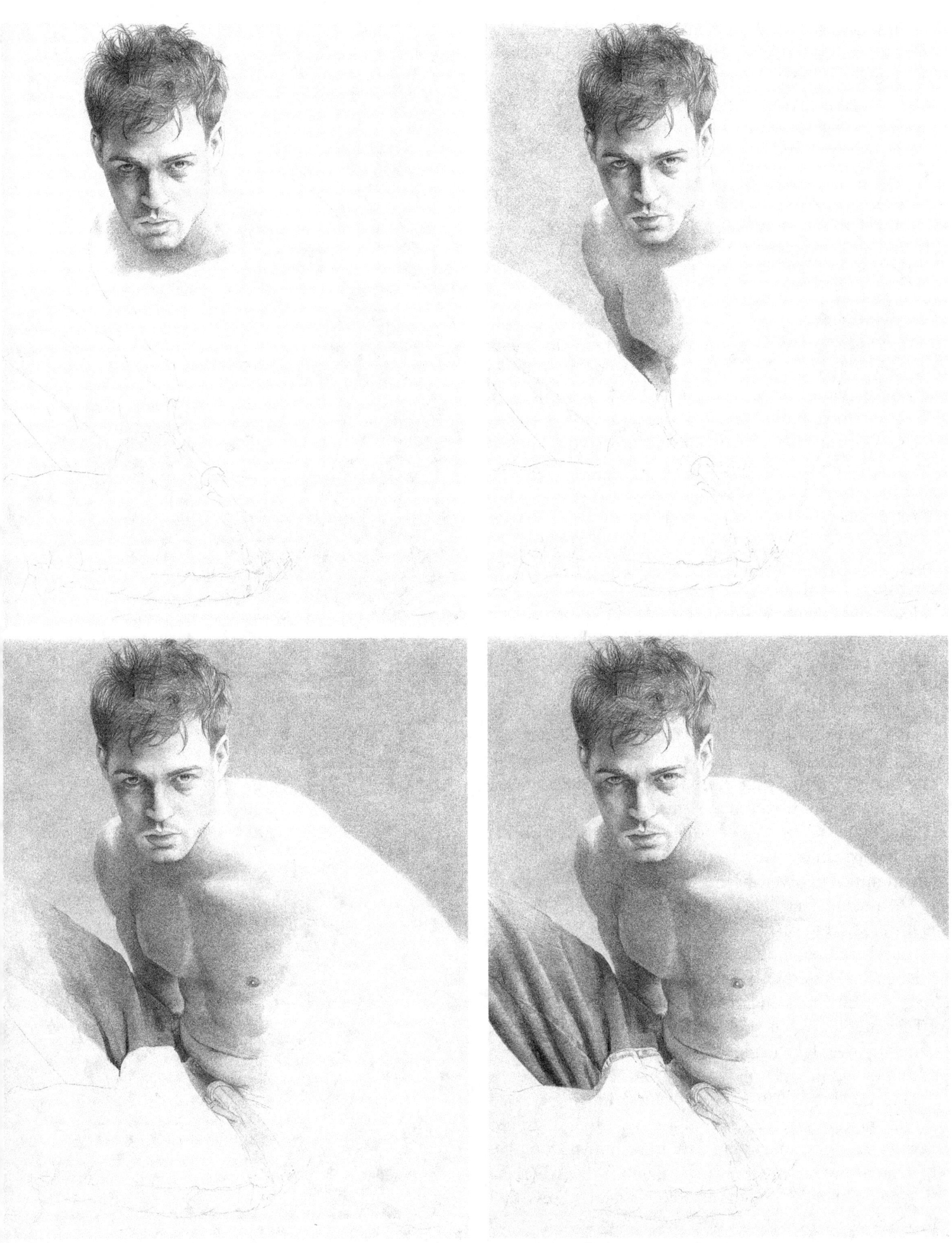

Gordon was a bit disappointed that I drew his belly and promised to be in better shape the next time I drew him. However there is nothing wrong with his stomach for the sitting position he was in. When your back moves in towards a center sitting position the stomach muscles have no where to go but pushed to the side. Or in this case, out front.

Drawing is stages, such as picking sections of his chest muscles and abs, is a good way to work. Just be sure to over lap each section with your blending pencils.

Be careful not to leave breaking points in your drawings which will happen if your pencil strokes vary from layer to layer.

Your kneaded rubber eraser will come in to play many times with this stye of drawing. Where the white from the paper is shown over the left side of his face (your right side as you look at him) and along his arm.

Use your darkest pencils only in areas you want to stand out the most. His eye lashes and brows, the shadow under his nose, the dark shadow between his lips, and lets not forget his nipples.

Shadows can be a tool to help bring out items in the foreground, such as the nipple on his right side, or in the deep folds of his jeans.

Jeans are actually fabric created in a crosshatch method if you look close at them, which makes drawing denim an easy task. Simply follow the curves and dips of the jeans and you can't go wrong.

Here is another example of why you must keep your pencil sharp at all times. Using the finest lines start off with a medium pencil and cover the area you want to draw the jeans. Keeping in mind to follow the contour and set the stage for your highlights.

Highlights in pants aren't the same as those on his face or upper body. Here you can cover the paper with a medium pencil, even where the highlighted areas will be. Then using your darker pencils, start to pull out the shadows. Making sure the lines follow the curves of each fold or where the fabric gathers.

Detail is important when drawing denim especially along the belt loops and zipper. There is a natural bulge in the materials when smaller pieces are sewn together. So again you will be using your kneaded rubber eraser to pull out the white lighting you may have covered over.

This drawing of Gordon was the first drawing created for this book project. It is part of a series of photographs he owns the rights to and the third to be drawn from that set. One of my favorite drawings of him is one where he is laying on his back and the camera is looking down and over his body as one hand rests across the crotch of the

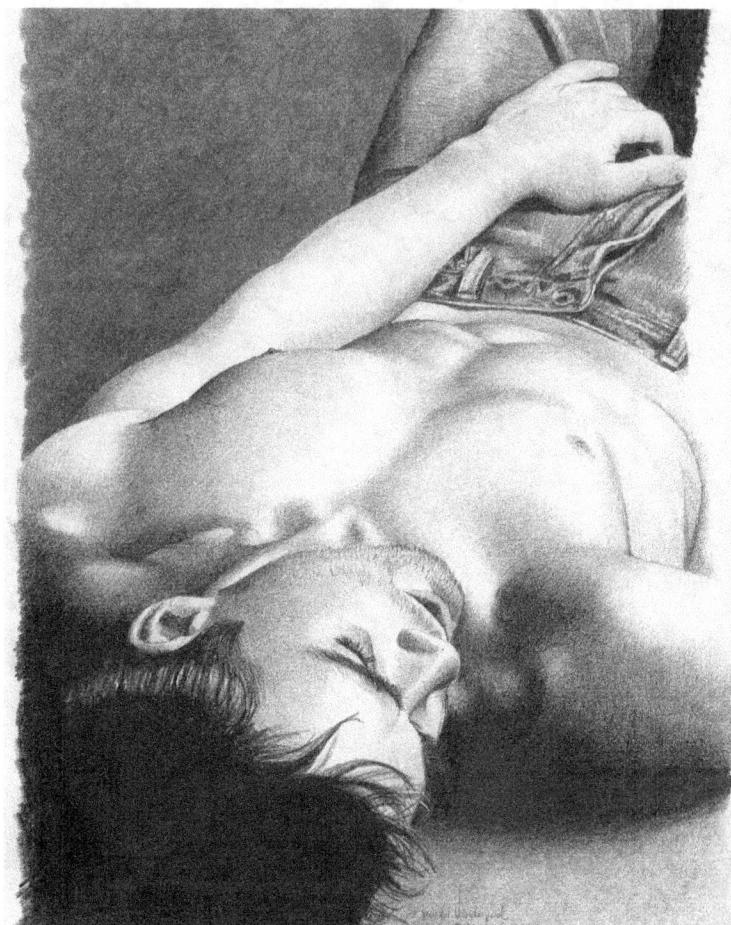

Gordon I - 8.5" x 11" graphite pencil drawing on paper

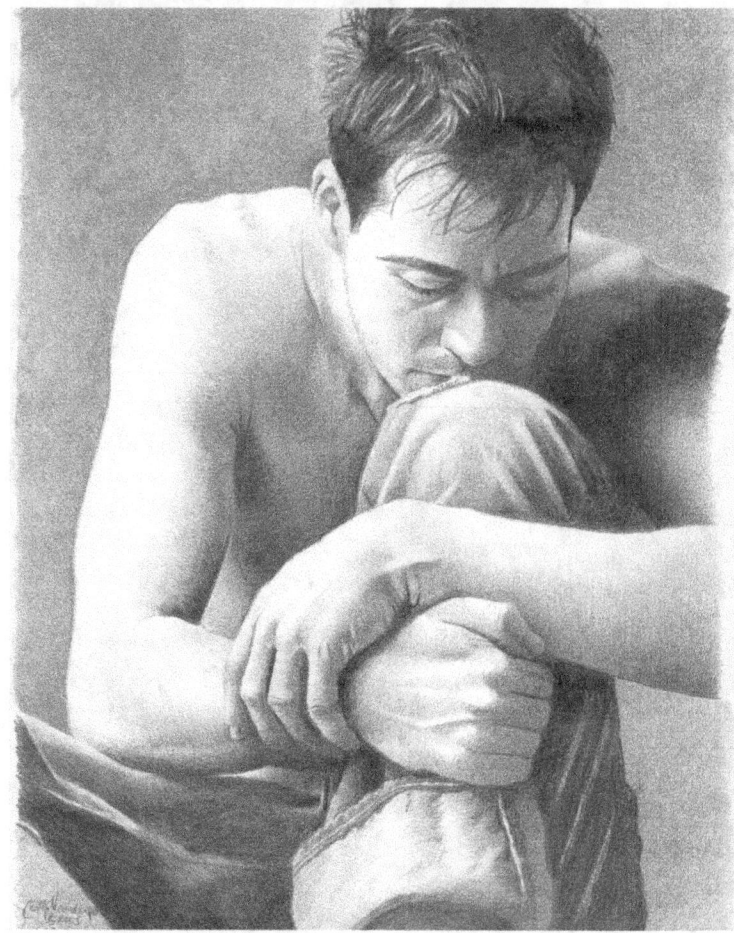

Gordon III - 8.5" x 11" graphite pencil drawing on paper

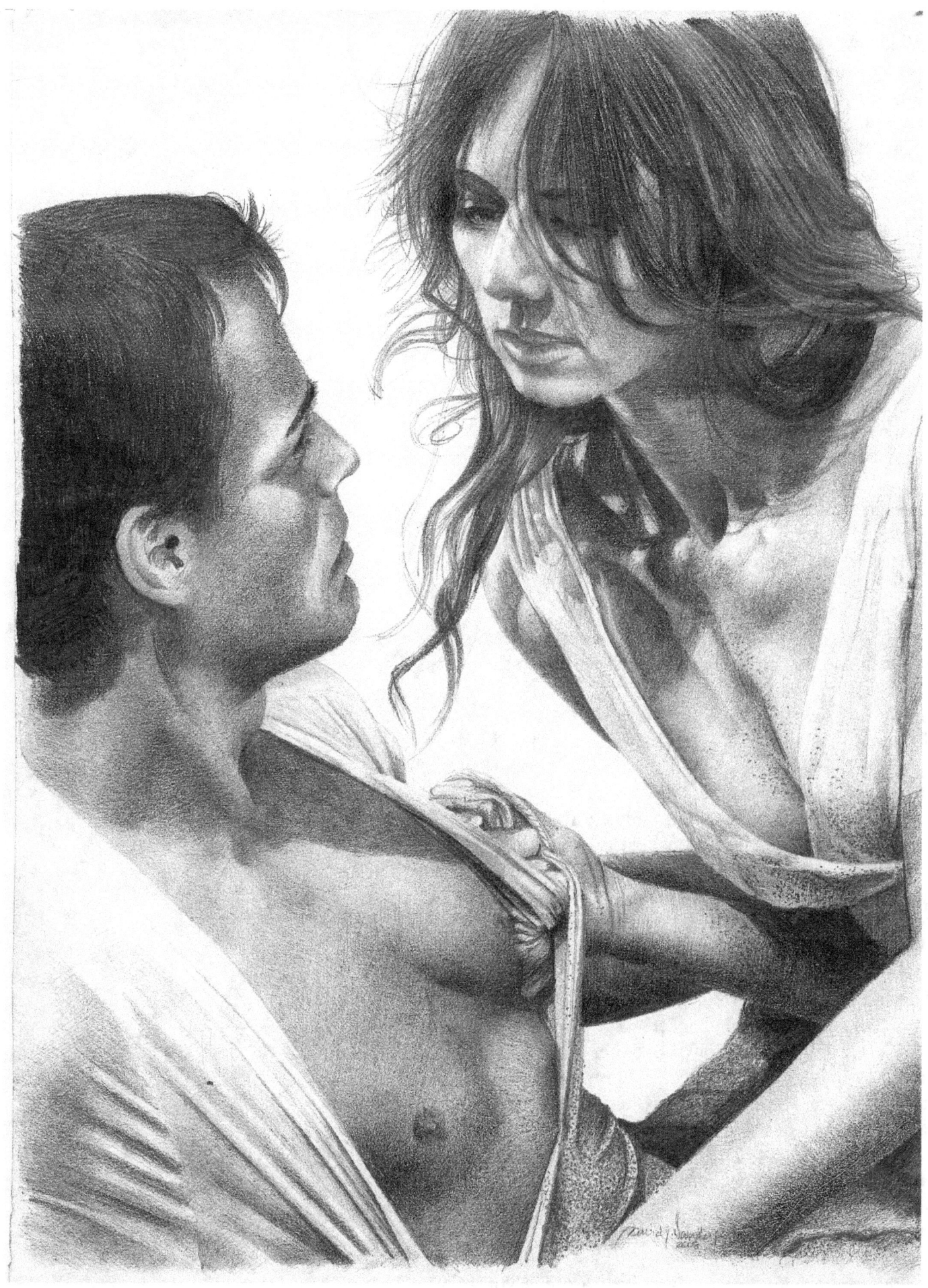

A Day At The Beach

8.5" x 11" graphite pencil drawing on paper. 2008

jeans.

Which proves a point. The model doesn't have to be nude to be erotic.

One of the best things about drawing from a photograph is the fact your models are frozen in time and you now have the freedom to draw when you want to and at your own pace.

Photographs also allows you to get closer to the model and capture the expressions on their faces, the air blowing in their hair, or count the grains of sand on both their upper bodies as a result of rolling on the beach. You may not get the chance to do so should the pose be live with the models directly in front of you.

When Gordon was approached by Nancy about doing a photo together he instantly knew he wanted it taken on a beach.

After researching online for poses and ideas Gordon sent his suggestions to Nancy for her feedback. Together, along with the photographer, they found the perfect place on a beach in Scarbourgh, just outside of Toronto, where they started shooting a bunch of pictures and got the chemistry flowing right away.

As if nobody else was around the two just did their thing while Vasko took different pictures from a variety of angles. The result is perhaps one of the most dramatic and power photographs a pencil artists can ever ask to draw from. And ask I did!

Instantly I knew I had to draw this photograph, and with Gordon's help, I contacted the photographer who responded back with a high resolution digital image for me to draw along with his blessing.

The photograph showed the couple on a beach with water at their feet and sand all over them as a result of playfully rolling around. The most powerful statement was her straddling over him and ripping off his wet shirt and that is exactly what I wanted to capture on paper!

She being the main focus in this drawing I started with her first. I knew that later it would be a challenge keeping the drawing clean and making sure I didn't smear the graphite since I am right handed.

Once her eyes were drawn and her likeness was captured I went right to her hair. I slowly drew each section of hair as it draped across her face due to the wind blowing in from the beach behind her.

As I mentioned earlier hair must appear as if it's being drawn one strand at a time. This requires several levels of my sharpest pencils. Because of her hair coloring I started off with my medium range pencil and drew one section of hair at a time. This is easy to choose since the highlights and shadows naturally in her hair give you a

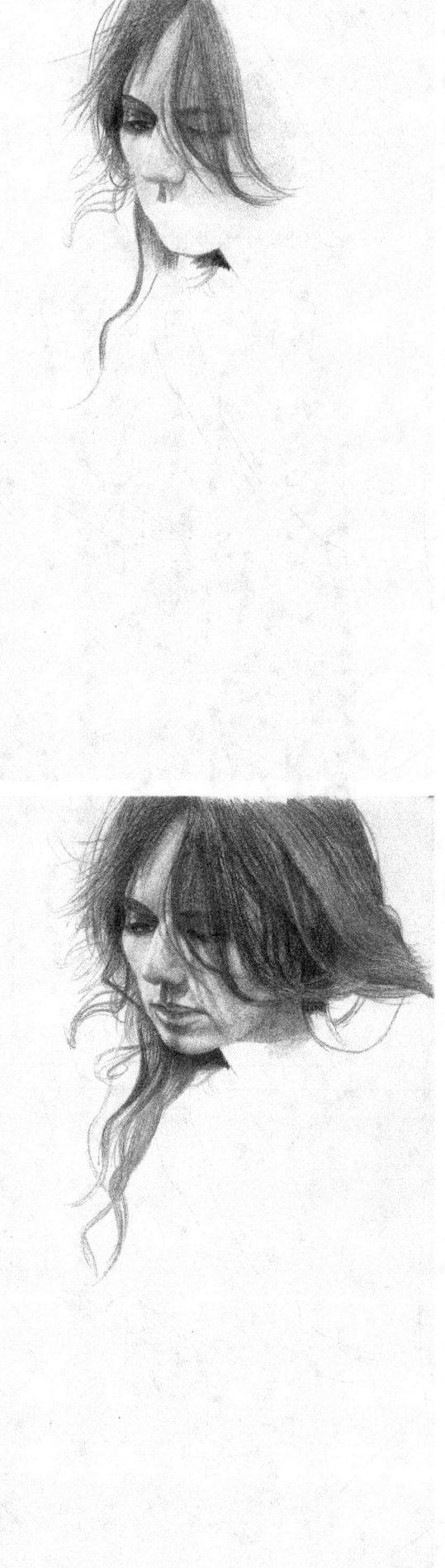

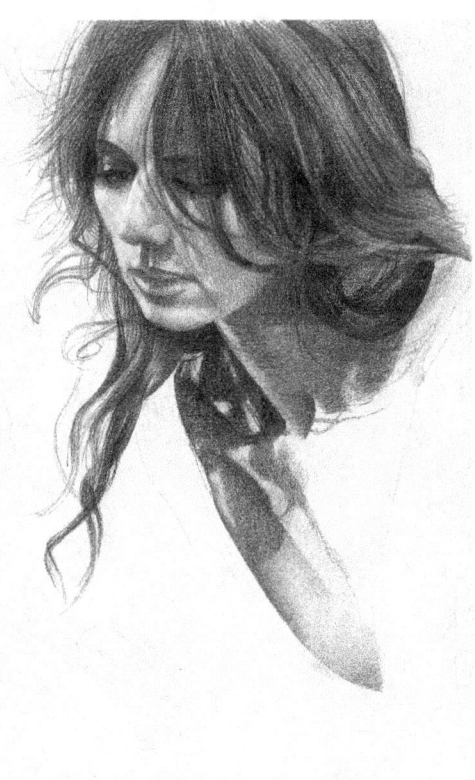

break and the ability to section the areas off.

I used my darker pencils to separate the hairs that appear to be combed while the lighter pencils offer the wind blown look of each strand as it blew in the wind.

The lighter pencils are also used to blend the darker and medium range pencils that were previously applied. Again your lighter pencils becoming your blending tool.

Using a 4H and "F" pencil for the foundation of her face I was able to pull out the highlights from the bridge of her nose and far cheek with the kneaded rubber eraser as well as the natural color of the paper I was using.

The whites of her eyes and teeth are hidden in the shadows on her face so several layers from the "F" pencil were used while making sure the eyes and teeth were still noticeable.

The darkest pencils were saved for her eye lashes, brows, just under her nose, and around the inner edges of her lips and teeth. Even the shadows within her hair is a lighter shade that what was just used.

As with any pencil drawing it is very important to know the human anatomy. Placing the right muscles over the bone structures before drawing the skin.
Now you don't have to know the names of each muscle or bones but you do need to know what is required to make that muscle stand out and keep its shape.

Her skin was tight and firm so I had to be sure to follow the contour of each muscle especially as is shown in her neck. Without her collar bone drawn she would appear to be overweight and you would lose the shadows that appears as a result of her hair.

The shadow seen here is a major factor in getting this portrait done right. It allows the shape if her bones and breast muscles to stand out. Just make sure they aren't too dark so the contour of the muscles can be seen as well as the hair within the shadows.

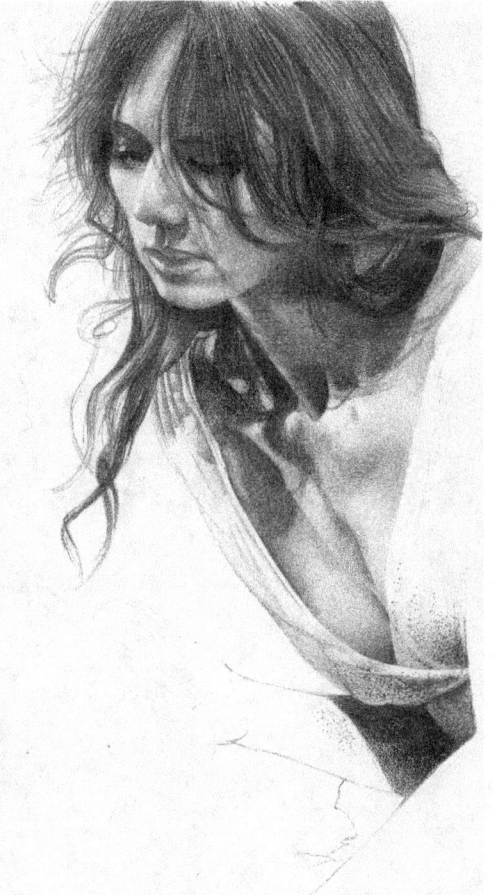

There is nothing flat about her therefore make sure all your lines are curved or arched and remember when using crosshatching this applies even more. Far too often it's easy to crosshatch a shaded area and forget to follow the muscles giving the appearance of a flat surface.

I suppose this statement could be argued since the closer you look at a person you are bound to find a flat surface. In reality even a flat surface such as her forehead, the bridge of her nose, or her front teeth, have a curve to them.

Covering the front of her blouse and her breasts are thousands of grains of sand. Don't feel like you have to draw each one but be sure you capture the look and appearance of the sand. You can achieve this by placing fine dots in the pattern of the sand as you see it before you.

Sand comes in various colors and this is a black and white drawing limiting the shades of grays I can use. I could have used a white pastel pencil or acrylic paint to capture the white or yellow gains of sand but I choose not to. I'll save those techniques should I someday recreate this piece in full color.

Starting on the left side of the paper isn't the best choice for a right handed artist but I felt it was important to capture her likeness at first. After all I have drawn Gordon more times than any model I have worked with so I knew I could draw him in my sleep. It was her likeness I was wanting to capture perfectly.

Starting on the "wrong side of the paper" means turning the paper and photo I was working from at various angles throughout the process of this drawing. This is something I do no matter where I start a drawing. It allows me to see the drawing using the other side of my brain and seeing areas that I might otherwise have missed.

Far too often we look at a drawing and our brain tells us what we think we are seeing. Putting shades of grays or lines where they might not really be but we do it anyhow because that's where it should be.

By seeing the drawing and photo upside down, sideways, and other various degrees, we start to look at shades and patterns rather than a person. And before you know it we have captured the image through the pattern we just drew.

When drawing Gordon I wanted to make sure there was just enough of him for others to enjoy seeing. I was careful not to let him take over the entire drawings because I wanted Nancy to do that!

With Gordon I made sure to crop the original photo just under his right nipple and get as much as his head in the pose as possible. To capture his expression was important in this pose and so was revealing what she was after!

When drawing their arms in the shaded area it was very important that the viewer would see two arms rather than one fat arm on her. When I was showing one of the early stages to an artist friend he pointed out that her arm was too fat. He had no idea of what was coming next when in fact he was seeing two arms. One arm was just hidden more within the shadow between them.

To keep the arms separated, and still be drawn in the same shades of grays, it's a must to follow the contour of each arm even within the shadow. His being the darker and a thicker rounder shape to it while her's being smaller wrist and lighter as the arms comes out of the shadows of

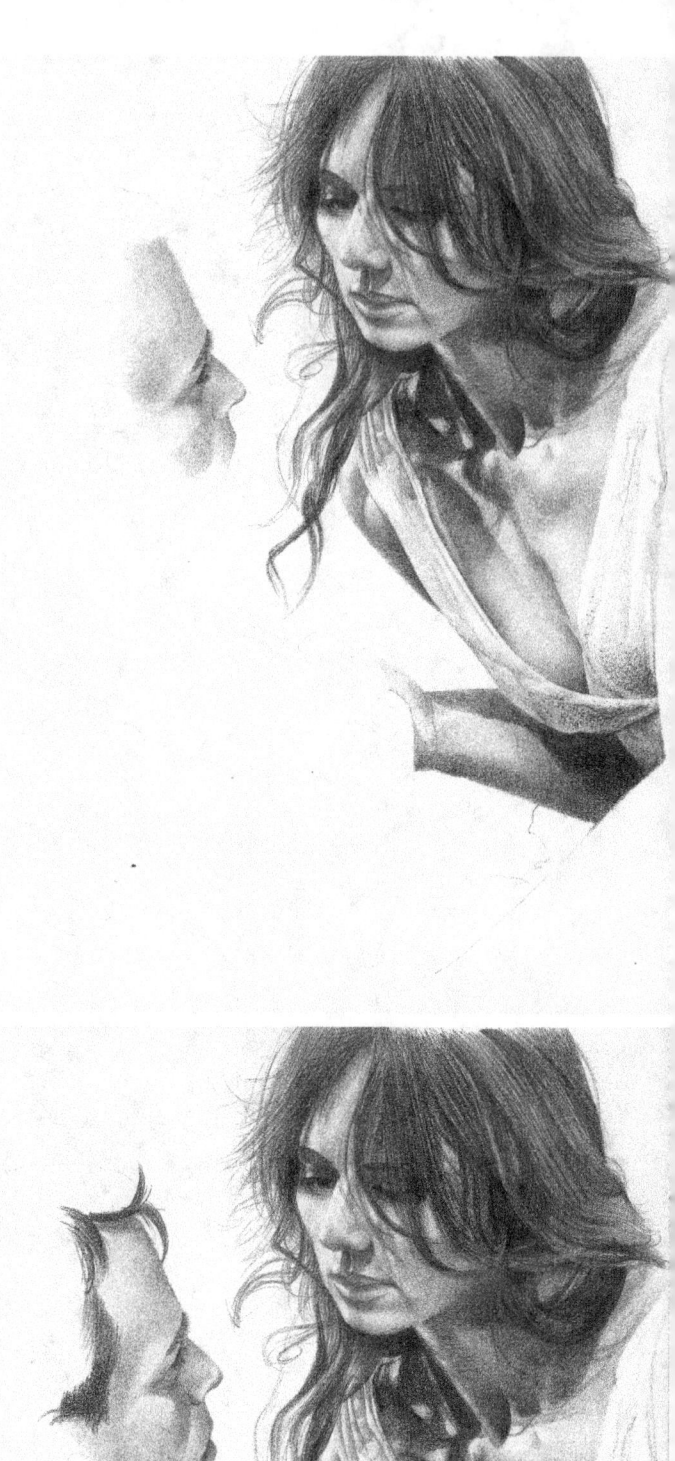

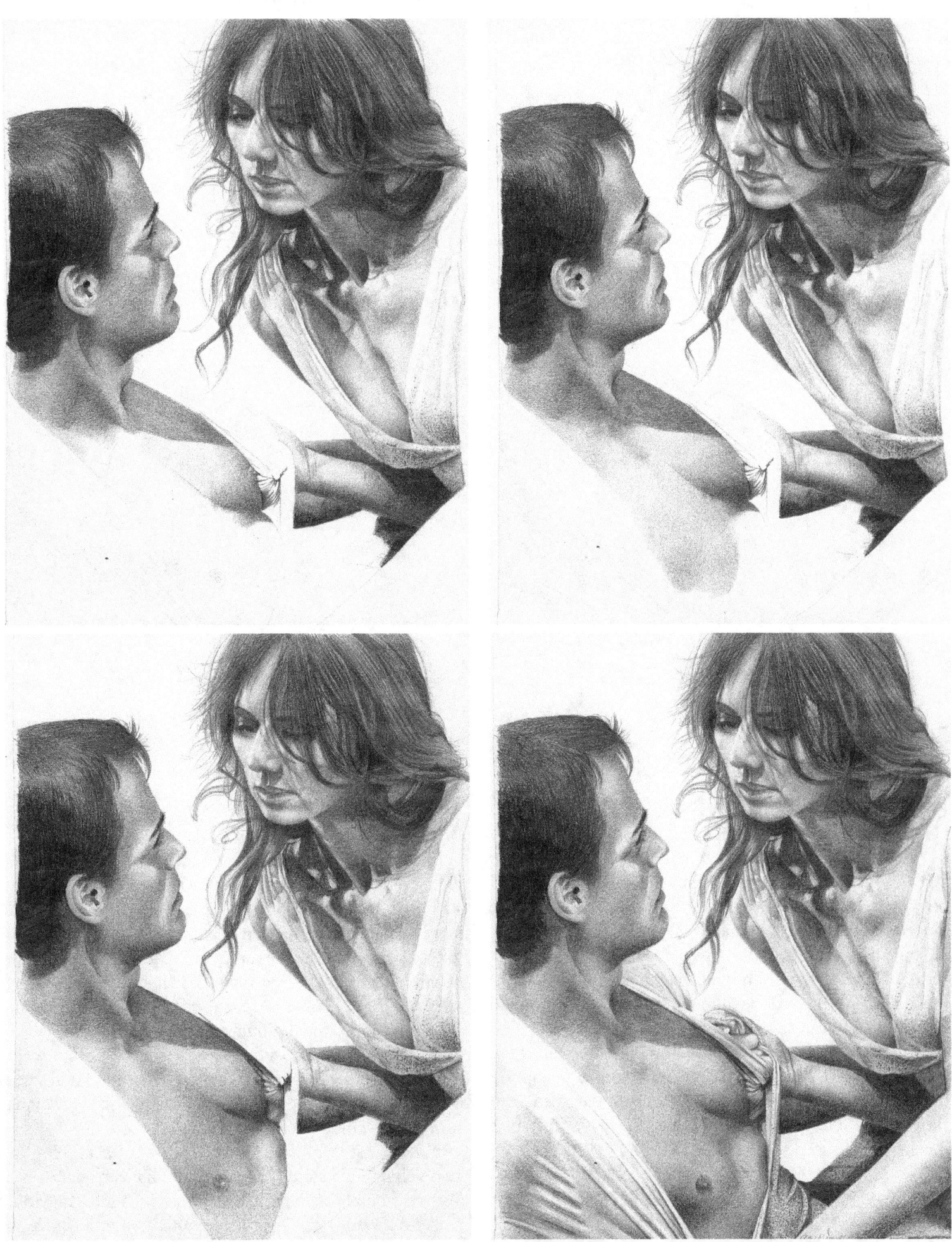

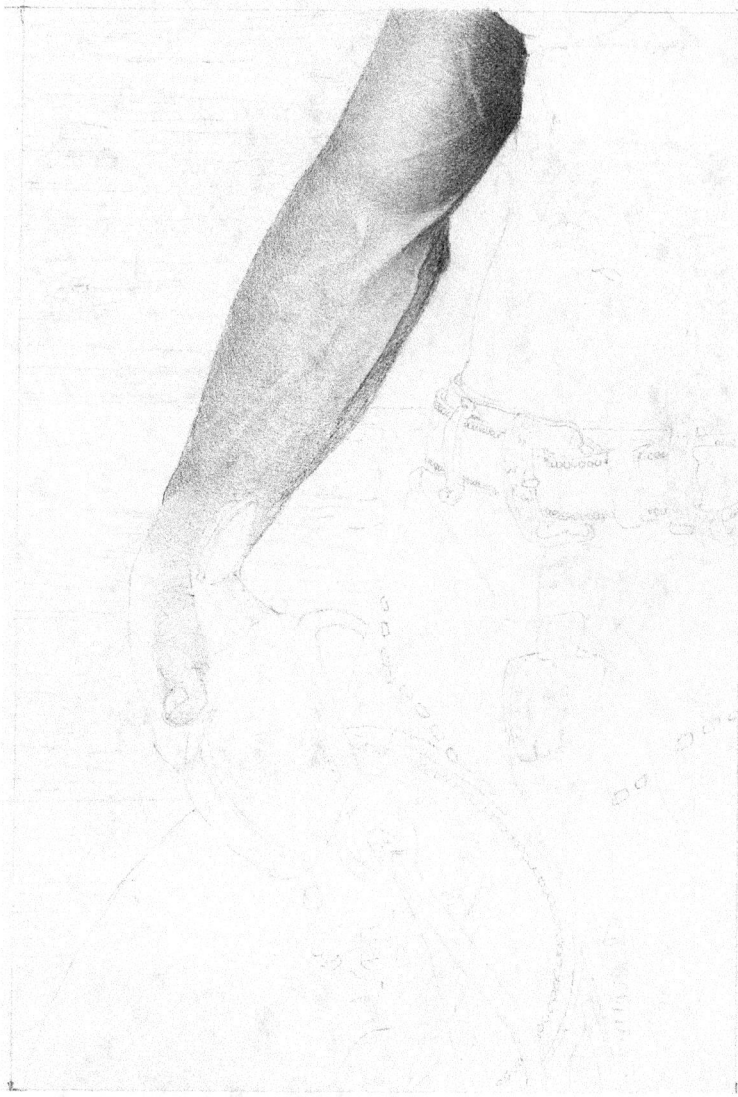

Step One:
After sketching he majority of the subject on the paper, find the main focal point and make that the start of your drawing.

Step Two:
Following the contour and shade to each muscle, with a sharp pencil, using curved pencil stroke, set each line in place.

her breast and her hand takes hold of his wet shirt.

The flesh on Gordon's chest is far darker than Nancy's skin (as in the original photograph) so I had to make sure I didn't get carried away and make him so dark as to lose the muscles in his chest. No matter the ethnic background of the model this rule applies to who ever you are drawings. Without shadows your drawing becomes flat and lifeless.

In the case of Gordon without a tan his wet shirt would not have stood out as well.

Creative freedom is given to any artist no matter the subject they are working on. For me I choose to capture the chemistry between the two and just enough sand to show they were at the beach even though the beach is nowhere to be seen.

Felix.
When it comes to selecting models, photos, or poses to create figure drawings from, it is not always important to include the entire body or face. For a more dramatic drawing, focusing on an area, as seen in this drawing of Felix which is a perfect example of that. In this art piece the strength from holding the saddle and the detail in the rancher's arm become the focal point leaving the saddle as the secondary focal point.

For any artist who is serious about capturing every detail in his work it is important to get up close and view every part of the model's body. This is where drawing from photos comes in handy.

Whether it's the shape and shadow of a nipple, the deep veins in his arms, or the fold in his jeans detail is a must when drawing a realistic portrait or figure drawing.

As with this drawing you see that you don't have to

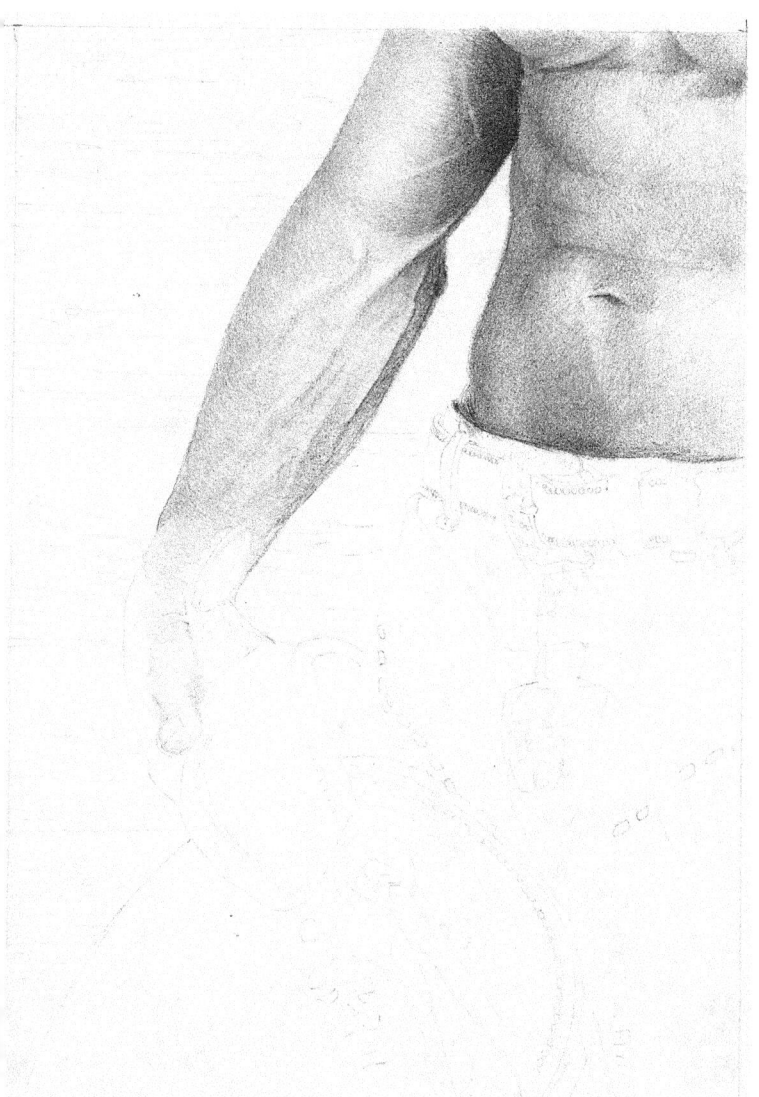

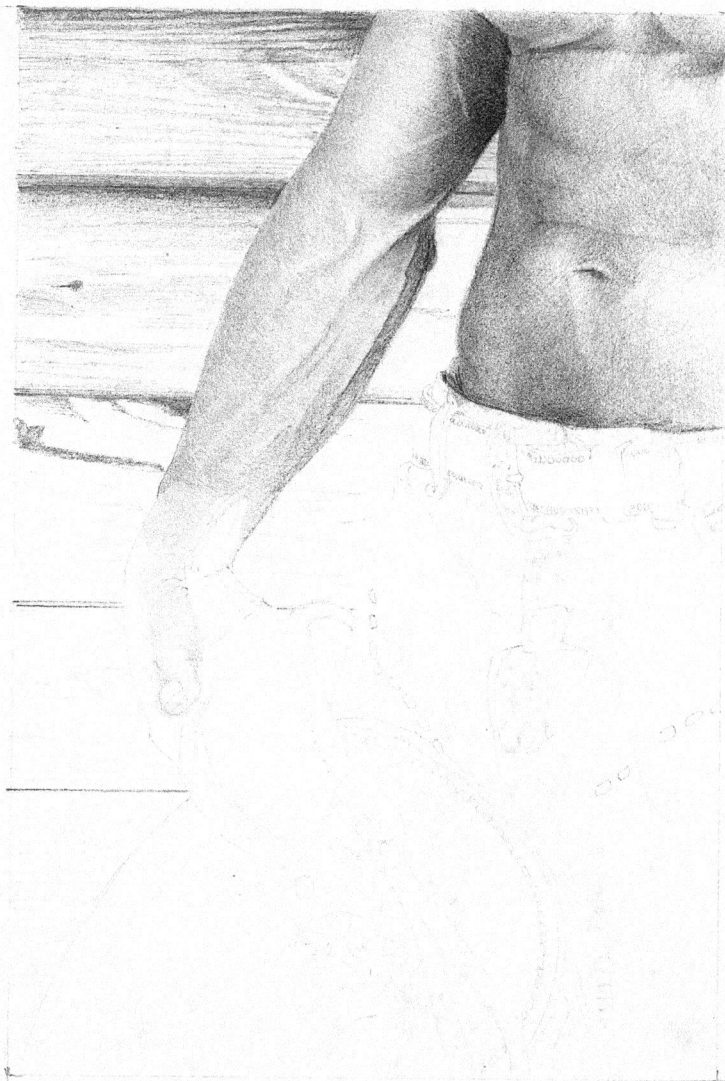

Step Three:
Keeping the pencil lines lighter when you start out, gradually darken the strokes where the shadow comes into play. Such as the veins in his arm, or the underside closest to his torso.

Step Four:
With a kneaded rubber eraser bring out the highlights by gently lifting the graphite off the paper. Then using a 2H pencil place the lines back on the drawing, as you blend over the dark graphite.

draw everything in the photo! Often focusing on an area of interest makes for a more dramatic pencil drawing as you can see here of Felix holding the saddle.

A professional firefighter, rancher, and model Felix was one of the first models I approached who jumped at a chance to be drawn for this book project. A man in his 40's his poses offer more than some of the more youthful friends I have drawn in the past.

It's important to capture the tightness of his abs and the deep veins in his arm as he holds the saddle since that's the main focal point here. Again, if you follow the contour of the body, your drawing will have a realistic 3-D feel about it.

Since there are no eyes for me to start on this drawing I chose his arm pit to be the center of the drawing. Here is where the darkest shadows spread out across his arm and allows his veins to come alive.

That same shadow travels down his chest and abs until it disappears under the top of his jeans.

Drawing veins is fairly easy but time consuming compared to the rest of this small 4.25" x 6.25" drawing.

Use your lighter pencils to shape his upper arm muscles and add the shadow so you don't have any stopping points on the arm. It's extremely important in a small drawing such as this to get ever detail right.

With a larger drawing you don't have to worry about detail such as veins or the nail of his finger but its these fine details that make up this small drawing so you have no choice but to get it right the first time.

Several layers will be placed on his arm as the veins start to jump off the page. Using darker pencils up against a highlighted areas they slowly start to appear before your eyes.

As you have realized by now your lighter blending

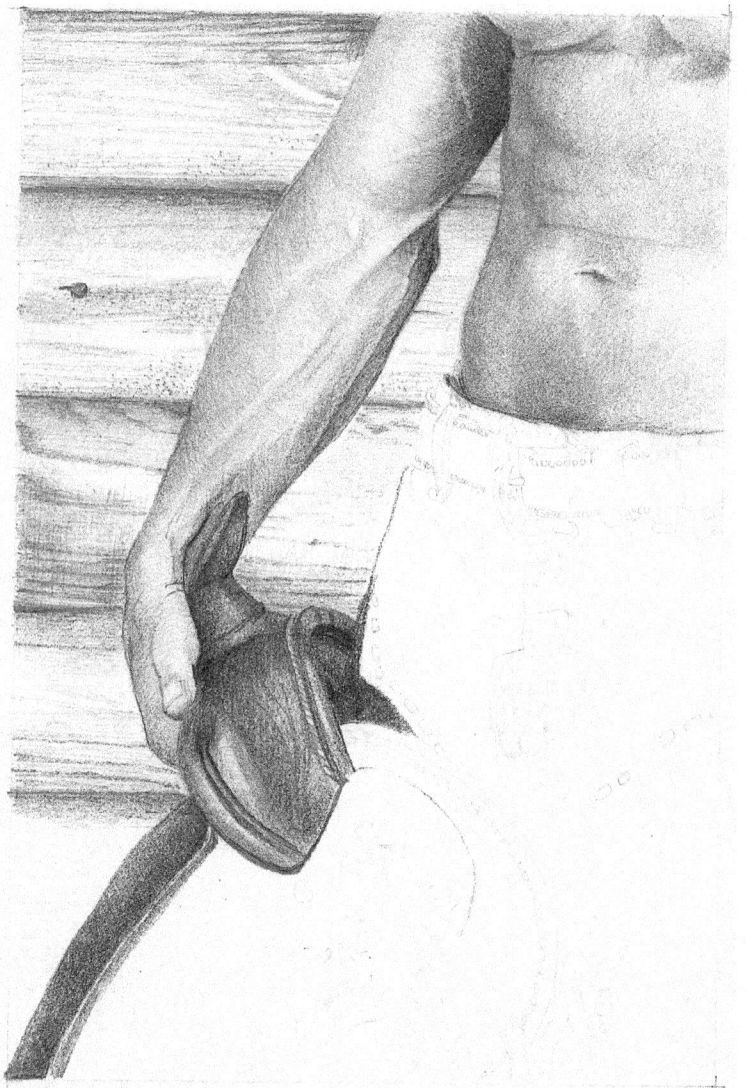

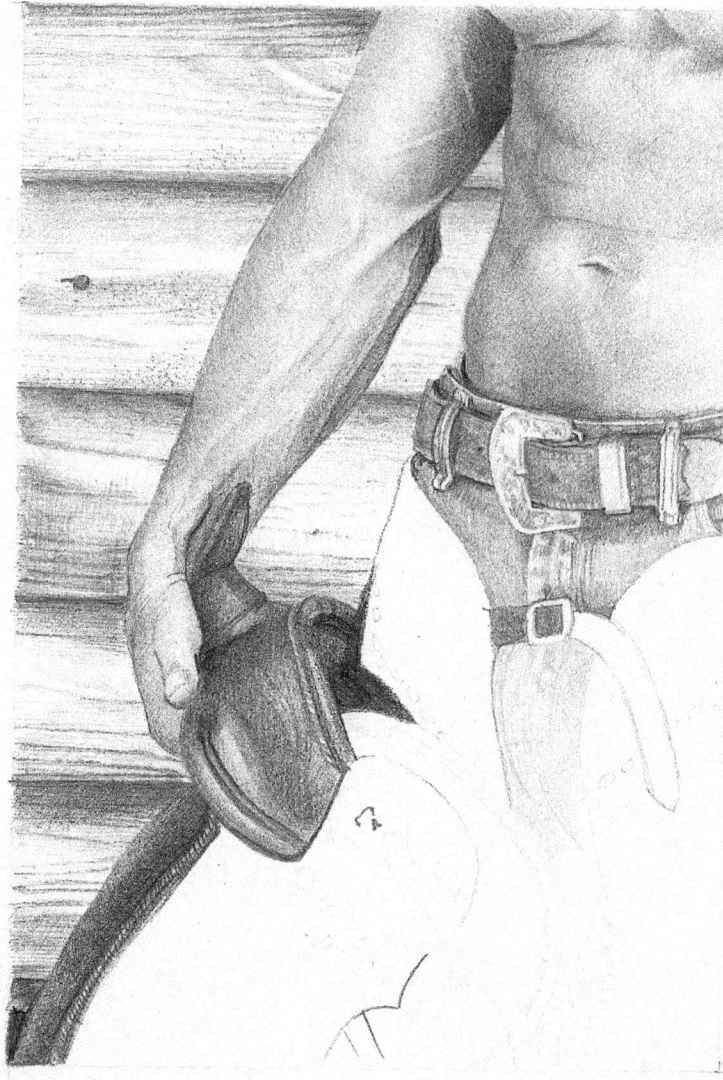

Step Five:
When drawing different textures and surfaces, be sure to take your time and draw each object as seen. Wood grain, leather and skin will have its own look, and still be drawn with lines.

Step Six:
The slightest detail can easily be overlooked by the viewer. However, as an artist, be sure to draw every detail, no matter how small. Yes, even the weaved leather in his belt.

pencil (2H and 4H), as well as your kneaded rubber eraser, have become your best friend.

The eraser is easily formed to the shape you want to lift from the drawing. Such as a 'C' shape or fine point to be pressed against the paper to make your highlight appears.

Crosshatching comes into play here, even for his abs and stomach, as shadows slowly lighten up to reveal his deep rich tan.

If there were body hair (which this model had none) you would use a medium range pencil to bring out each hair. This time we are safe to say this drawing works well without the body hair.

If you look close under his navel you will see two veins. One in the center of his flat stomach and a smaller one just barely seen to the side of the navel. Details such as this are very important, especially when drawing a fit,

athletically built individual.

When creating a background it's very important that it doesn't over power the image in the foreground but rather help showcase it.

Using lighter pencils for the background is a good idea when the object is up against the person such as seen in this illustration.

To keep the natural grain of the wood simply follow the shading with both the tip of a sharp pencil as well as the edge of the pencil. The tip makes for a sharp strong detail in the wood and the softer side helps to blend the grays and shadows where the planks over lay each other.

Using the same pencil for the side of the barn and the man's arm can be a challenge if you aren't familiar with how lighting effects an object.

Go ahead and use the same gray tones but be sure they don't blend into each other. Dark hairs on his arm

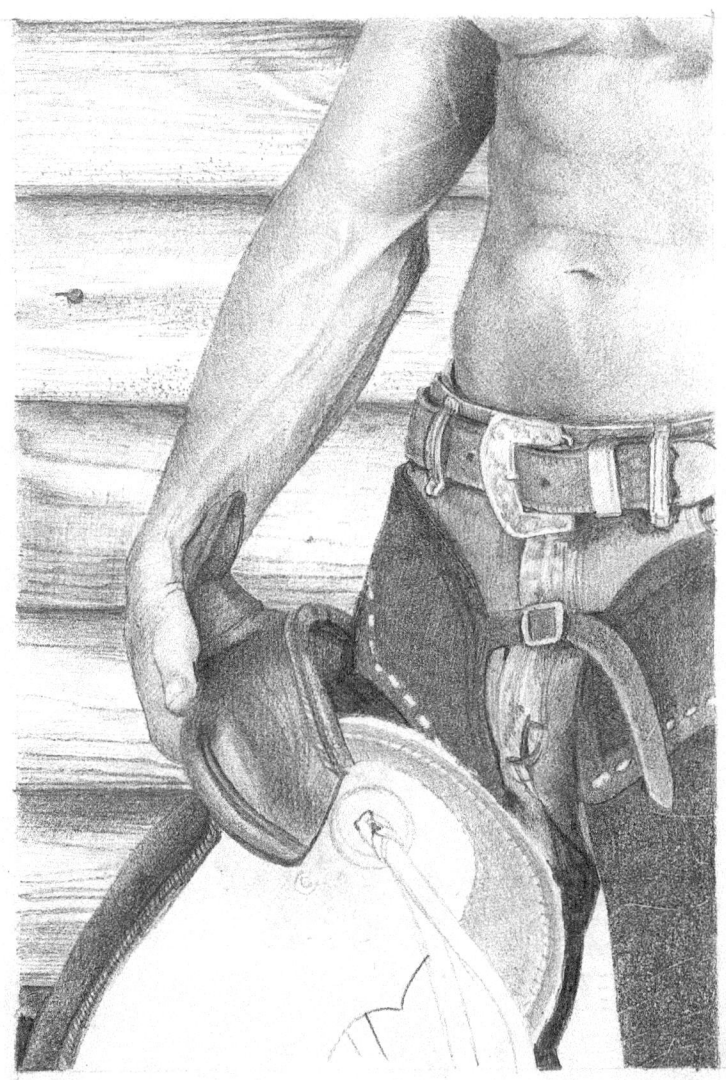

Step Seven:
The difference between leather and jeans? The lines in the jeans follow the weave in the fabric, as well as the folds following his body. Leather in the saddle is created using circular lines.

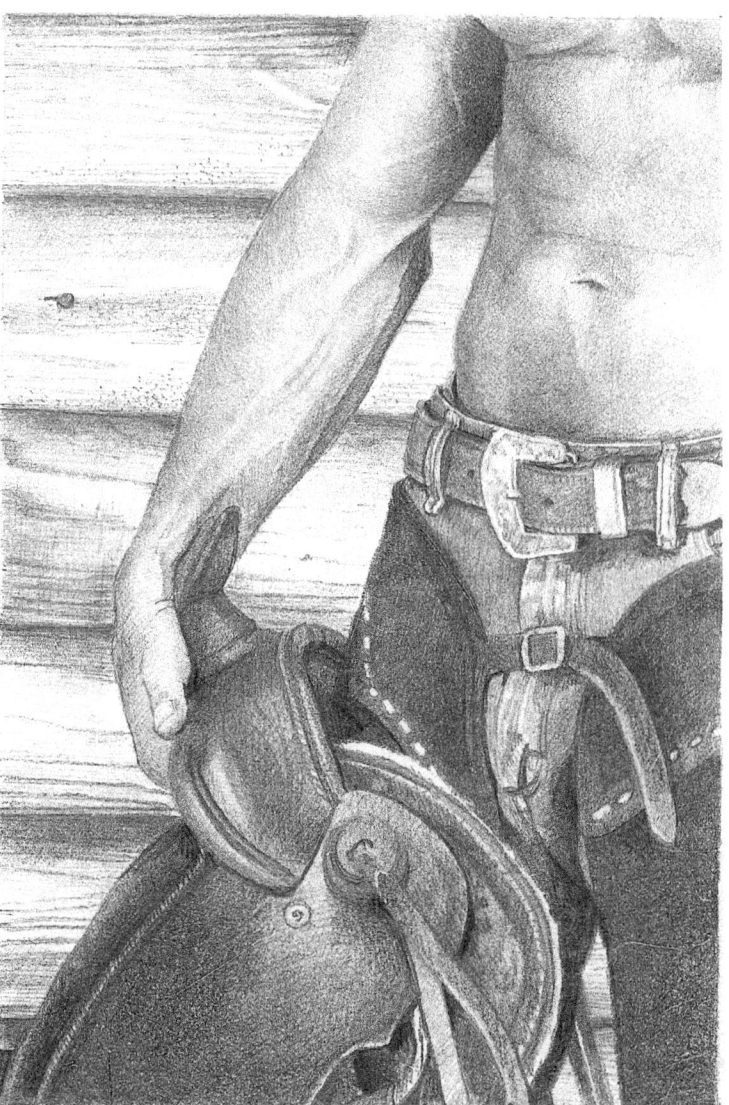

Step Eight:
A strong contract between light and dark will make the best pencil drawings. And at often times it will give the drawing a 3-D appearance, as if it can jump off the page.

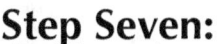

help to separate the lighter grays in his arm that match the wooden slats.

The best part about drawing wood is you don't have to worry about making it perfect. But you do need to make it look like wood. Each grain is different due to the growth of the tree and the cut from the saw.

Leather chaps and the saddle also have fine lines and crosshatching. Crosshatching to set in the first layer and then lines to follow the grain of the leather and the cut of the pattern found decorating the leather.

You may find yourself attempting several layers of gray before you reach the gray needed to create the brown leather saddle so be patient. After all this is a small drawing.

The belt attached to Felix's jeans have both leather and metal to draw. The leather belt strap has a pattern so be careful you don't shade over the design or it will turn

out to be just another strap.

The carving in the belt buckle is captured in the photo with the aide of shadows and reflected light. When lighting of an object is too bright, and prevents you from seeing the detail, you need to decided how much of the object will you draw. Based on what you see, or do, fill in areas you know would be there? A choice only the artist can make.

By now you are asking, just how detail can this guy get into a small drawing, and my answer is a lot! If you keep the pencils sharp.

Notice how the side of the barn, the leather chaps, the saddle, jeans and even the texture of his skin are all different. Another important detail that, if not otherwise there, people would notice what is missing from the drawing rather seeing what is in the drawing.

Yes, people are that odd and picky.

A little history on evolution.

One thing I have noticed - and the reason behind this second edition - is that the drawings completed in 2012 and those from 2008 appear to be from two different artist as my style continued to evolve.

All as if I have no control of how I draw.

Quite scary and yet interesting at the same time.

Granted, we should strive to improve with each piece we create, making it better than the last. But we seldom think a drawing will take us further than what was possible a few years back. Let alone a few drawings back.

Prior to 2000 my drawings took on a softer, smoother appearance, to the point they were nearly flat and lost on the paper, as seen of the "Untitled Woman" (page 85) that I drew in my senior year of high school in 1979.

Using a single #2 writing pencil, the drawing had no choice but to be flat and one dimensional compared to the other two drawings show here. These two drawings were the result of a college instruction introducing me to drawing pencils a year after she was drawn.

The use of various pencils in a single drawing brought a completely different look to my projects I would never have achieved with a single writing pencil. Instantly the eyes came to life and the shadows brought depth as well as allowing the contrast of light to reflect off the paper. (Tom R. -1985, and Joanne -1990).

With the drawings in 1985 (top right) I was still blending the graphite with a blending stump. By 1990 (bottom right) I started to pull away from that style and use more lines that were visible in the finished drawing.

In early 1990 my first step towards becoming a professional artist occurred during an interview for a drafting assistant position. The woman doing the interview asked if I could draw a straight line. After showing her my portfolio she asked if I would draw her daughter.

I told her to hire me and I would only charge her $200.

It was a temporary on-call job but it lasted until I found a job closer to home.

Home at that point had been established in Kingsburg, California. A small community alongside highway 99. In the middle of California between Fresno and Visalia which is right in the middle of no where!

My wife and I look back now and see it as God's way of teaching use to rely on Him as well as each other.

It was also a time I was able to use my drawing skills to supplement my income and provide a little more for my young family since the job I had at the local lumberyard wasn't enough to survive on.

Again the Lord's way of showing the importance of

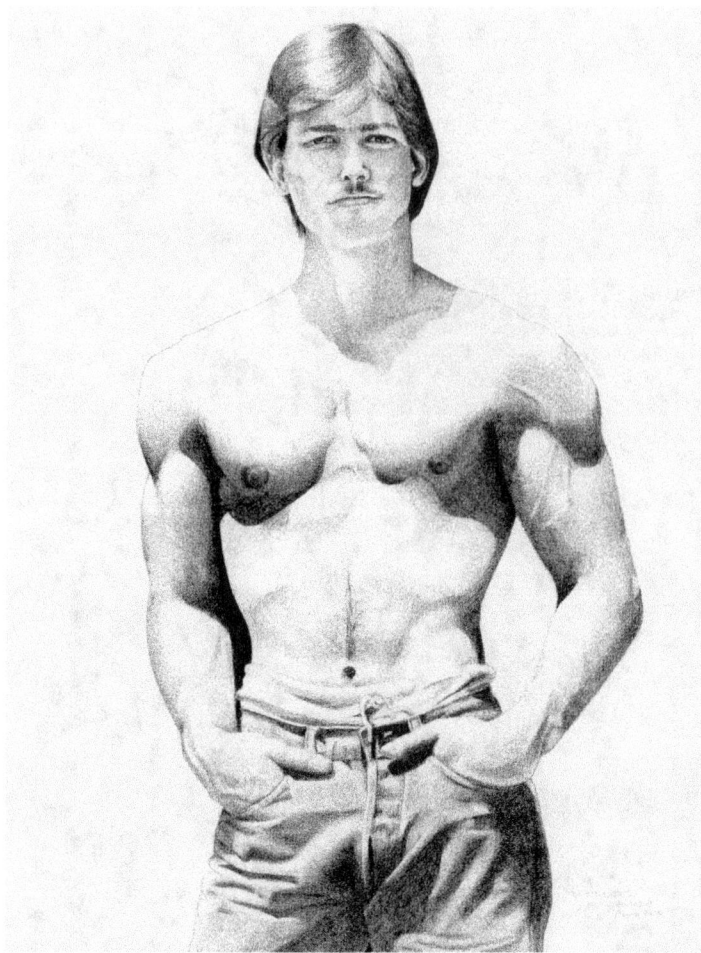

Tom R. - 8.5" x 11" graphite pencil drawing on paper

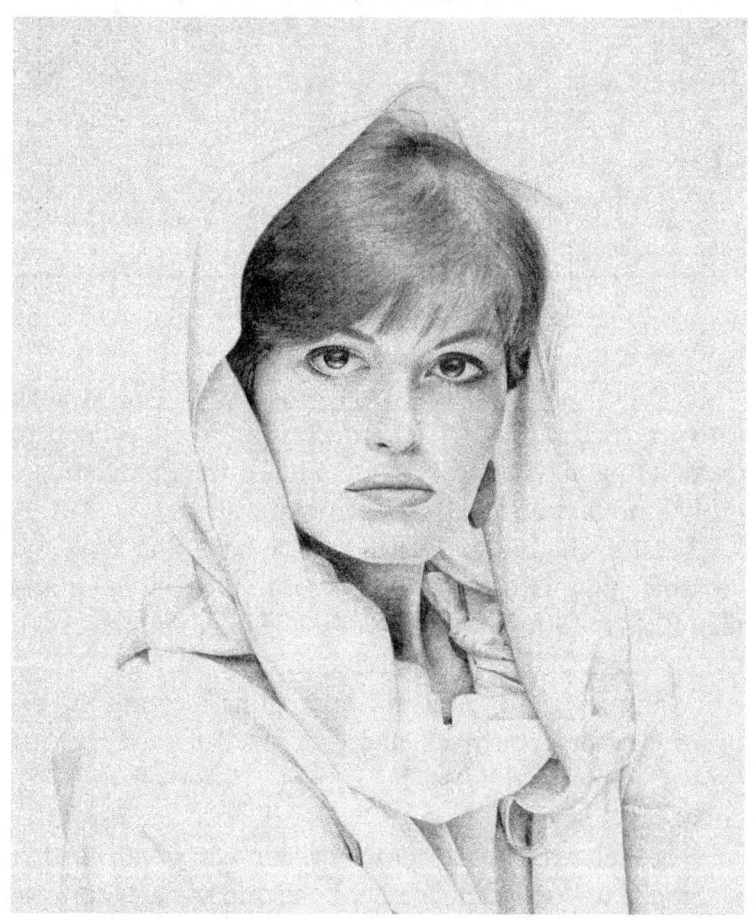

Joanne- 11" x 15" graphite pencil drawing on paper

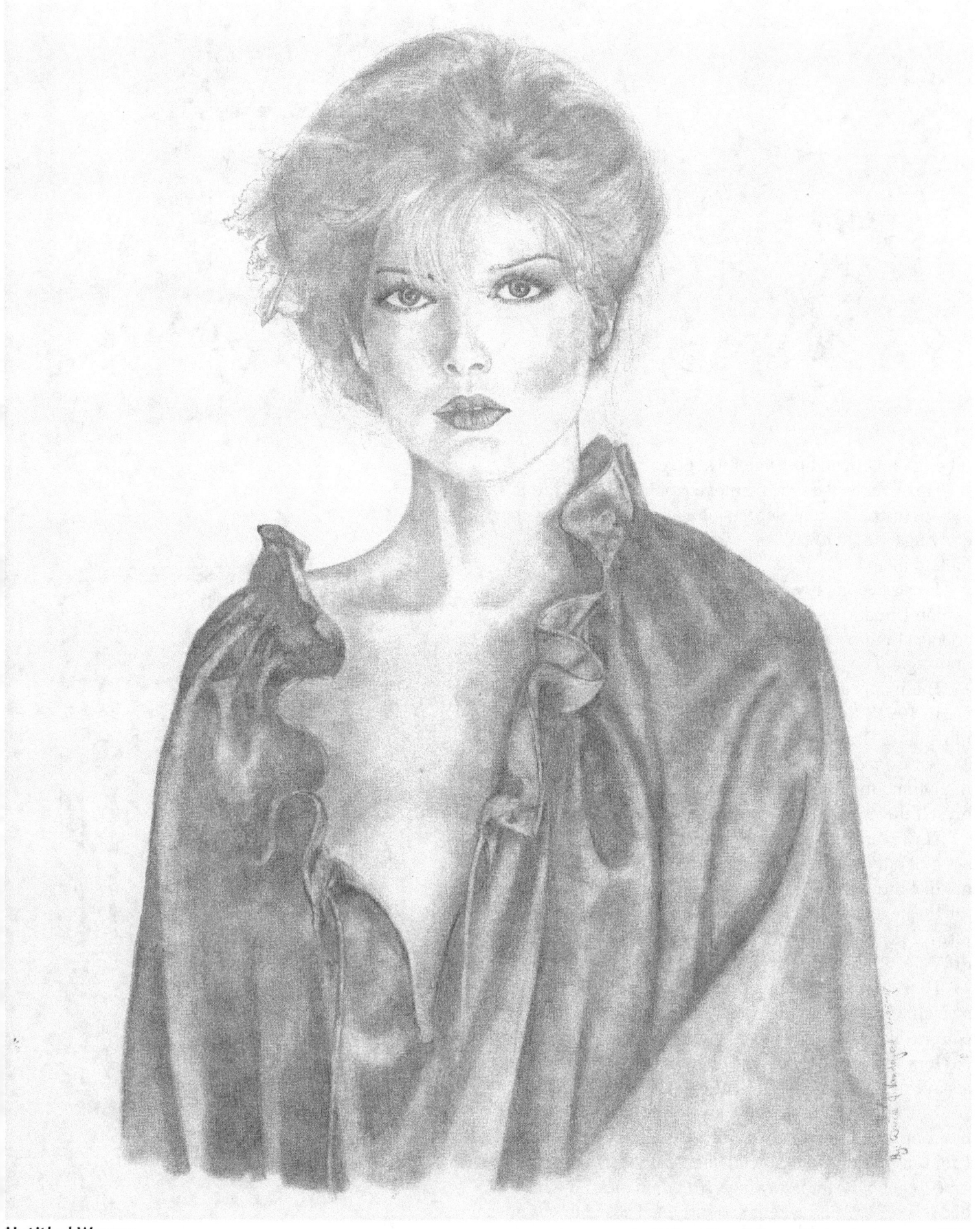

Untitled Woman

8.5" x 11" graphite pencil drawing on paper. 1979

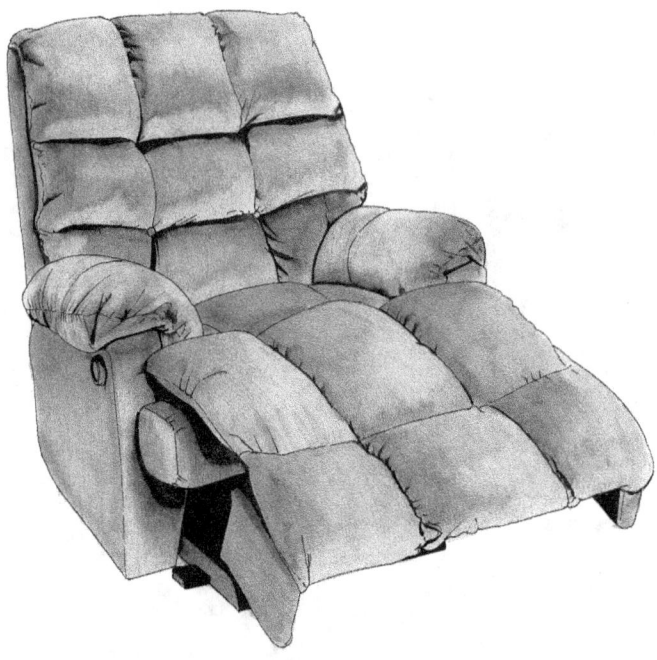

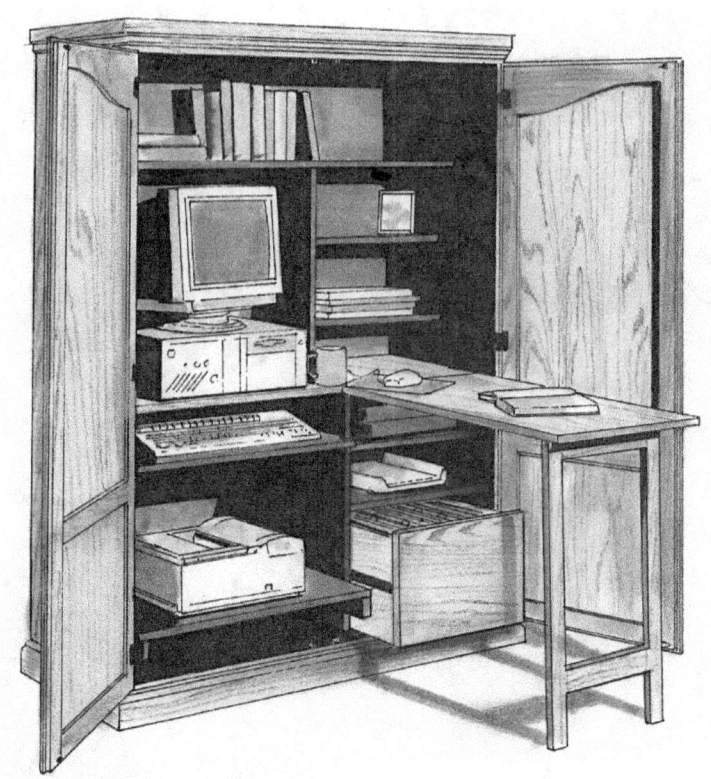

relying on Him and the talent He gives to each of us.

However by the time we moved to Bakersfield, around 1993, frustration and depression sat in to the point my drawings started to take on a darker, rougher, and harsher look to them.

Frustrated in myself, my drawings, and the fact I couldn't find a decent art supply store anywhere in this county, I put away my drawings and promised to never draw again.

But it appears that giving up wasn't an option.

In 1994 I took my first full time job as a professional illustrator. Drawing furniture of all things!

Far from drawing portraits but it was good money and it gave me the opportunity to stay after hours and teach myself the needed programs to become a graphic artist.

However the frustration was still there.

Not only was I working at a job where the owner did not like me. Every day I was in fear that I may not have a job the next day This is when I realized I missed drawing just for me but I didn't know how to pick up where I left off.

Don't get me wrong. I was enjoying the job I had and all I was able to learn from it. However to draw commercially is not the same as drawing for ones self. No longer was there passion in my art and I had become a slave to what was required of me.

It wouldn't be until 2000, and a few years after being hired on at the local newspaper as a graphic artist, that I told my wife (more so convincing myself) that it was time to get back into drawing. If I could pick up where I had left off I would take it seriously and strive to get my work out in the world to be seen.

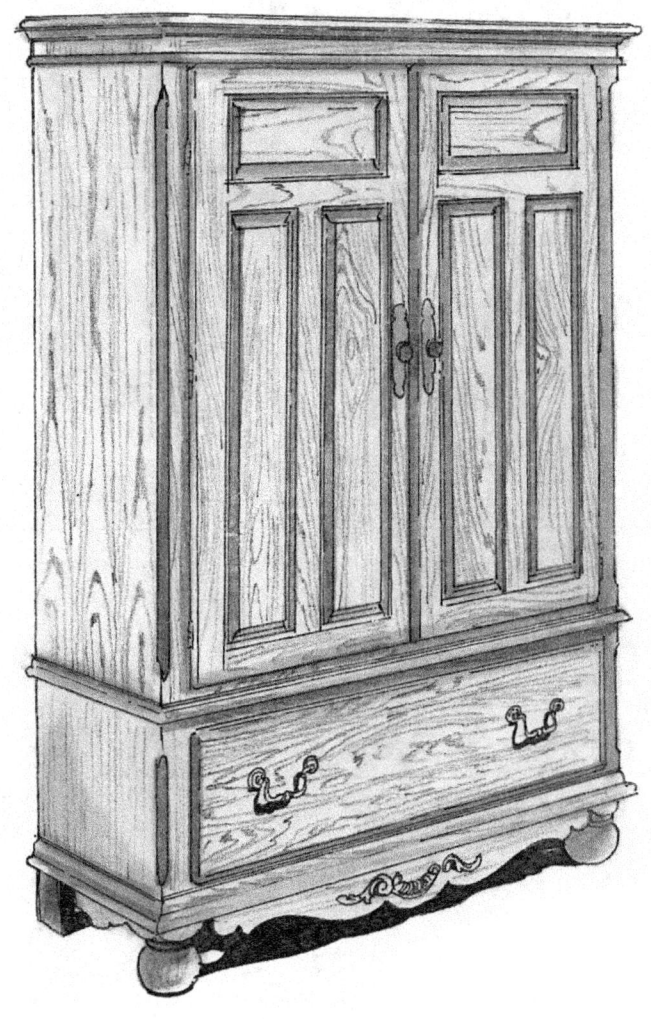

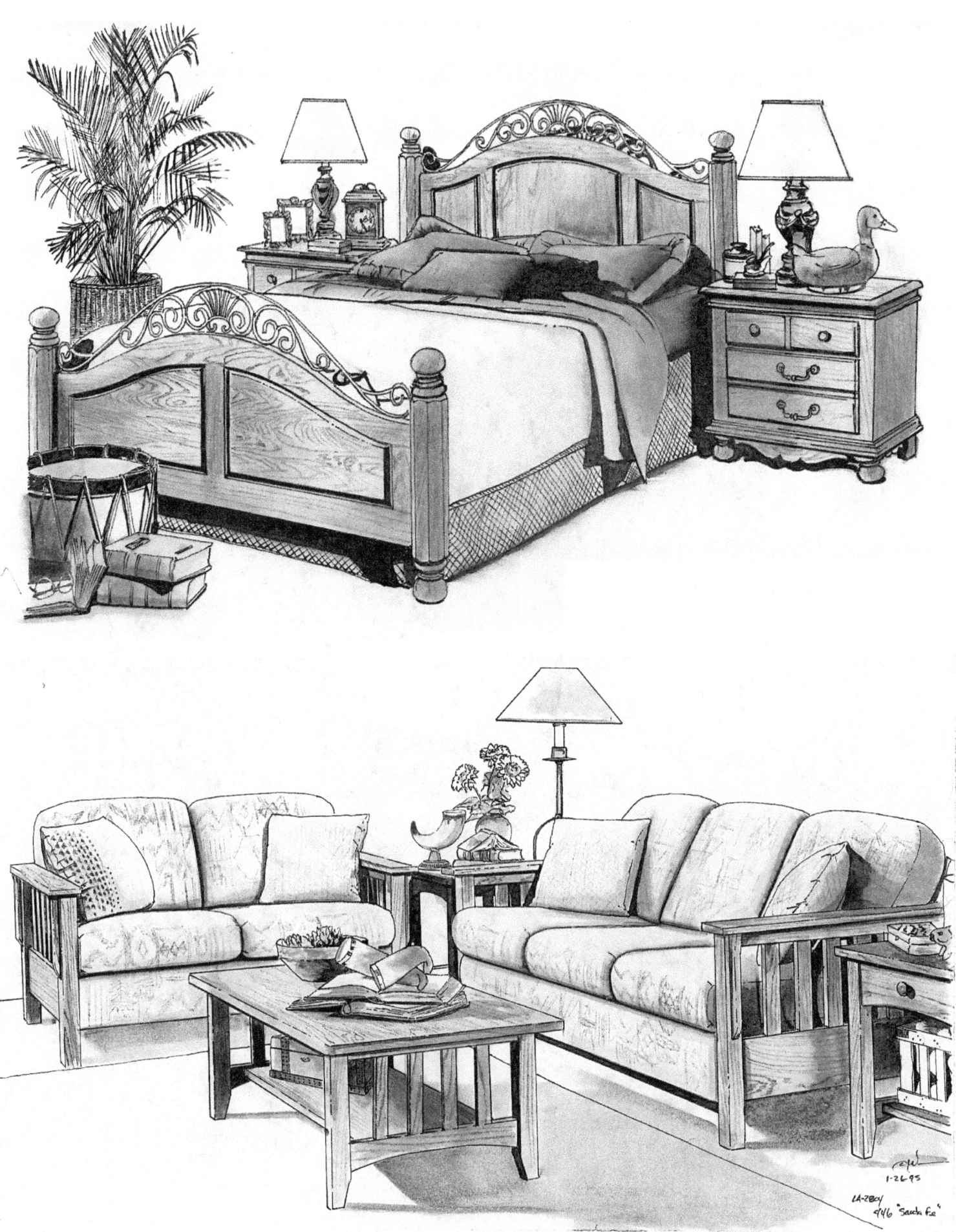

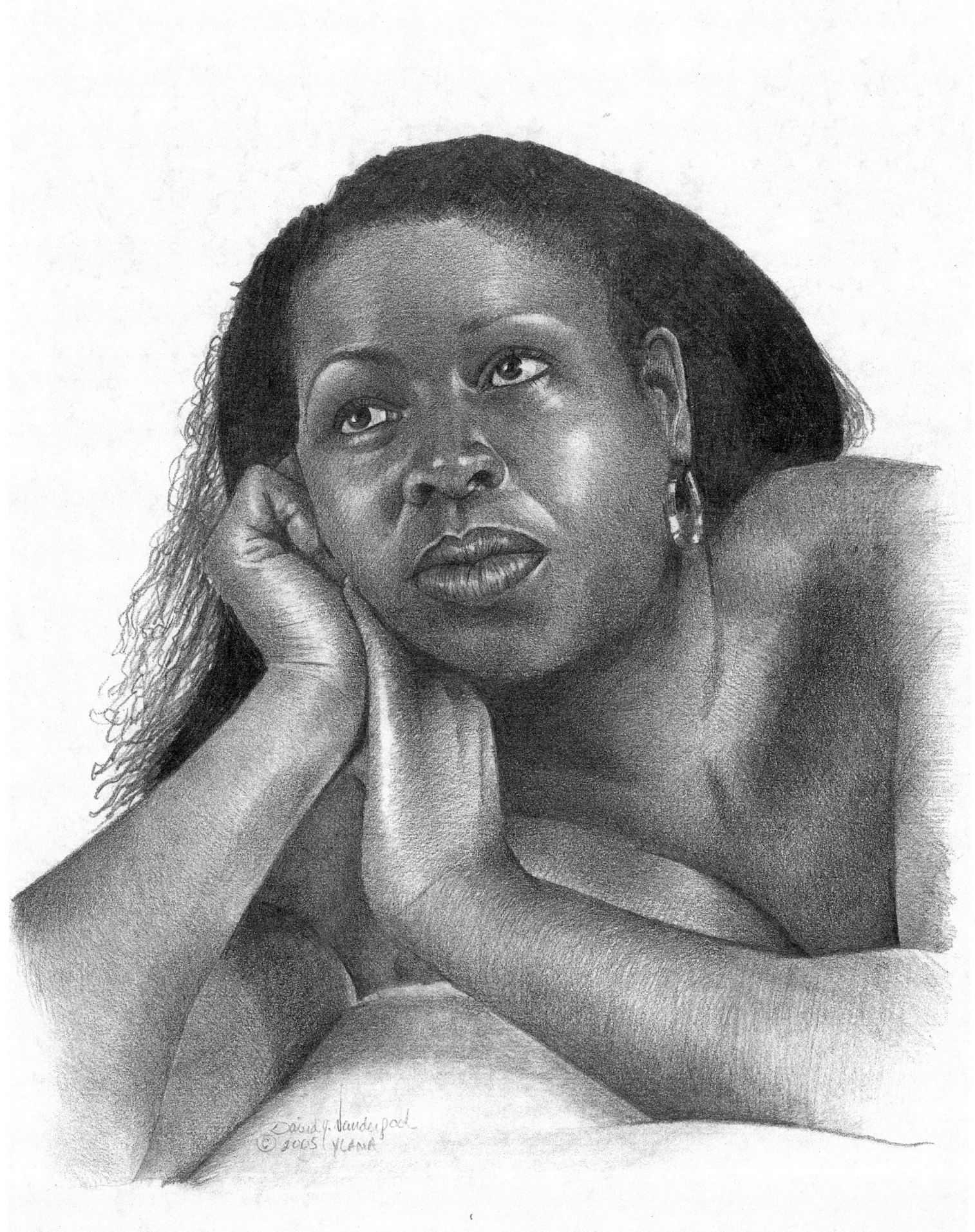

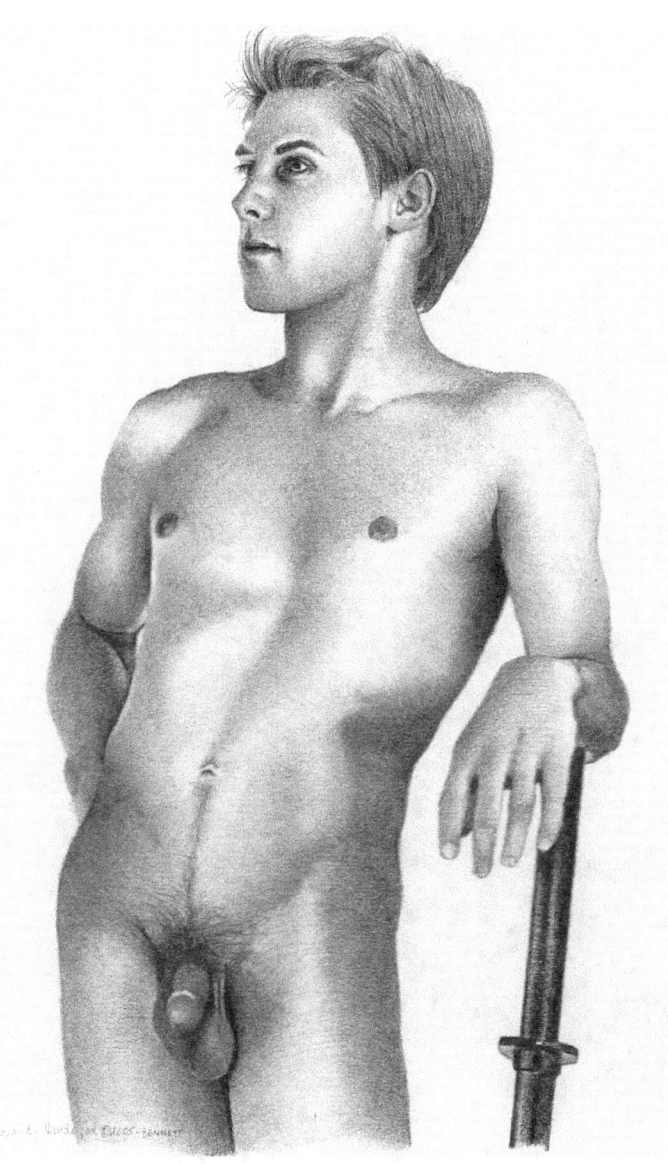

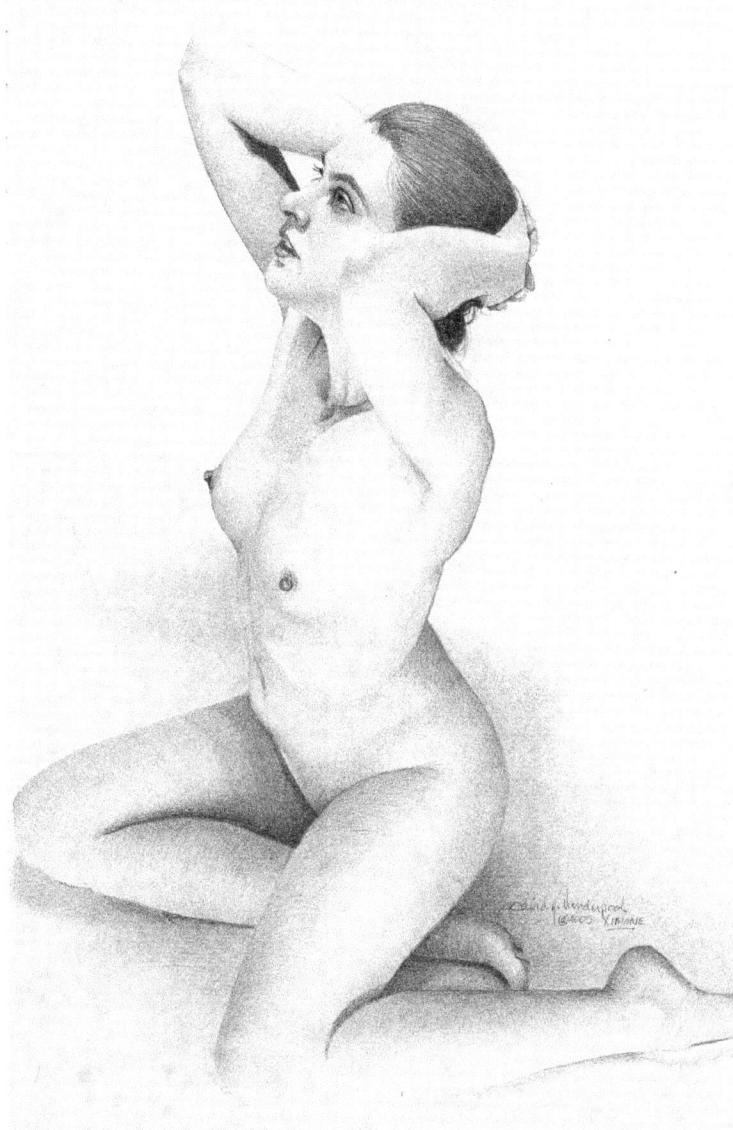

Back to pencil drawings.

By 2004 I was well on my way of establishing myself as a professional artist as my commissioned drawings started to pick up, prints were selling globally, and art galleries started to take an interest in my work. It was around this time I started to see that there was an audience out there I had never expected. Artists were asking me how did I draw.

Approached by authors Maureen and Douglas Johnson who were putting together their second book on "Life Nudes Art Models", they expresses a liking to my style of drawing and asked if I would be willing to draw a few of the models to be featured in their book. No payment but it did promise me some good exposure.

Taking on the challenge, I presented them several drawings, and the three show here were selected for the book. The latter drawing, of Ylana (seen left of here), was completed a few weeks before the book was published.

Giving the artists who participated in the project freedom to select whoever they wanted to draw I was

shocked to learn no one had selected her.

Keeping in touch for a brief period, with the male model who went by the name of Bennett, I finally told him that as much as I enjoyed completing the figure drawings of him, I would really like to draw a simple portrait. An opportunity to see if I could draw the way I used to.

Yes, I had noticed my drawings were taking on a darker appearance then and I was starting to worry.

Sending me a photo to draw from and I had no idea that it would be the last drawing I would ever complete that was of the style I was once know for. Leaving much of the paper untouched and drawing just enough of the model to bring out the more recognized features. (See page 90)

It was around this period I took advantage of networking with other artists, models, and photographers and began combining our talents. Of course I obtained permission and respected the legal rights for each photo that attracted me, or rather inspired me to draw.

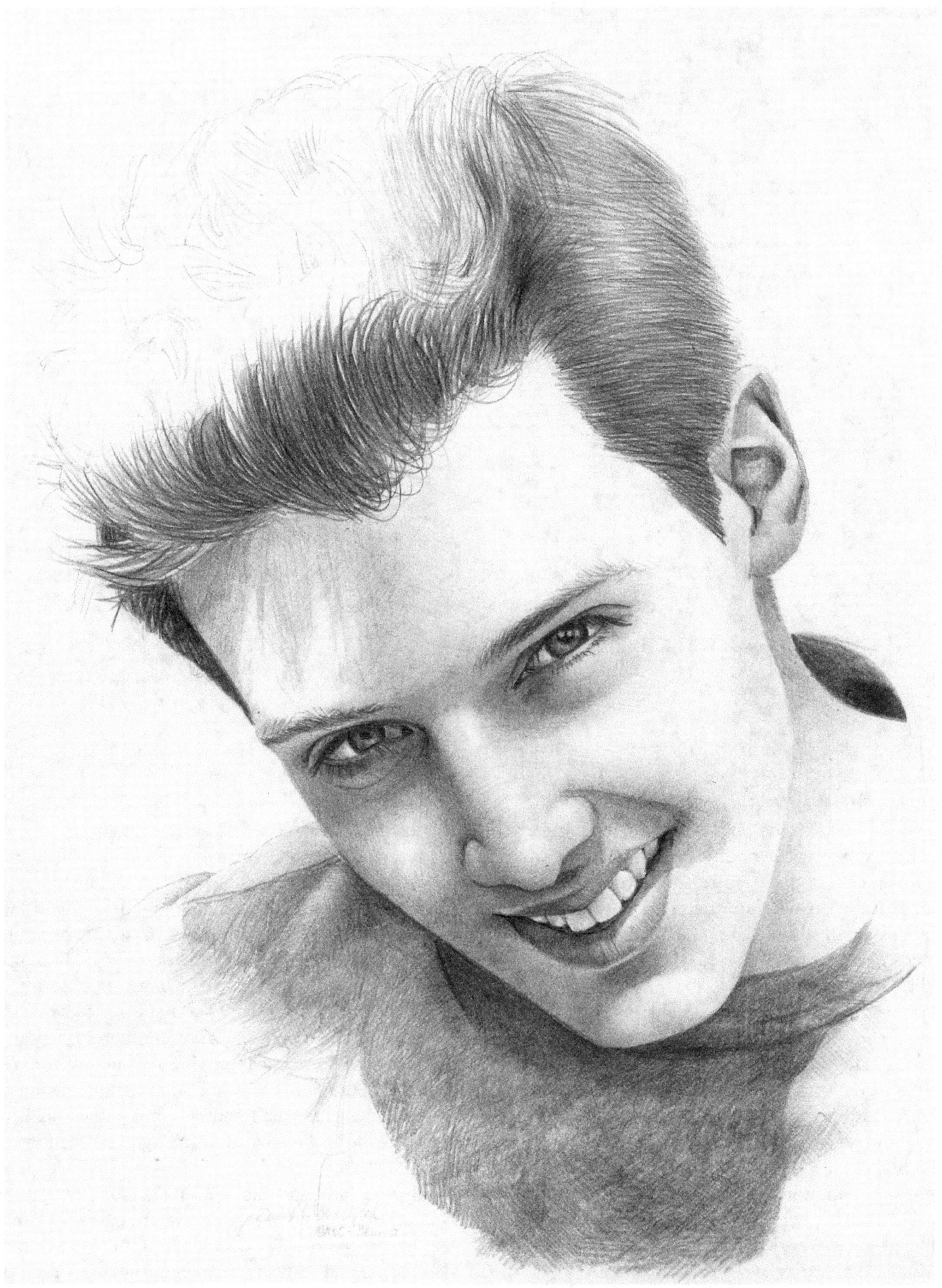

Bennett

8.5" x 11" graphite pencil drawing on paper. 2006

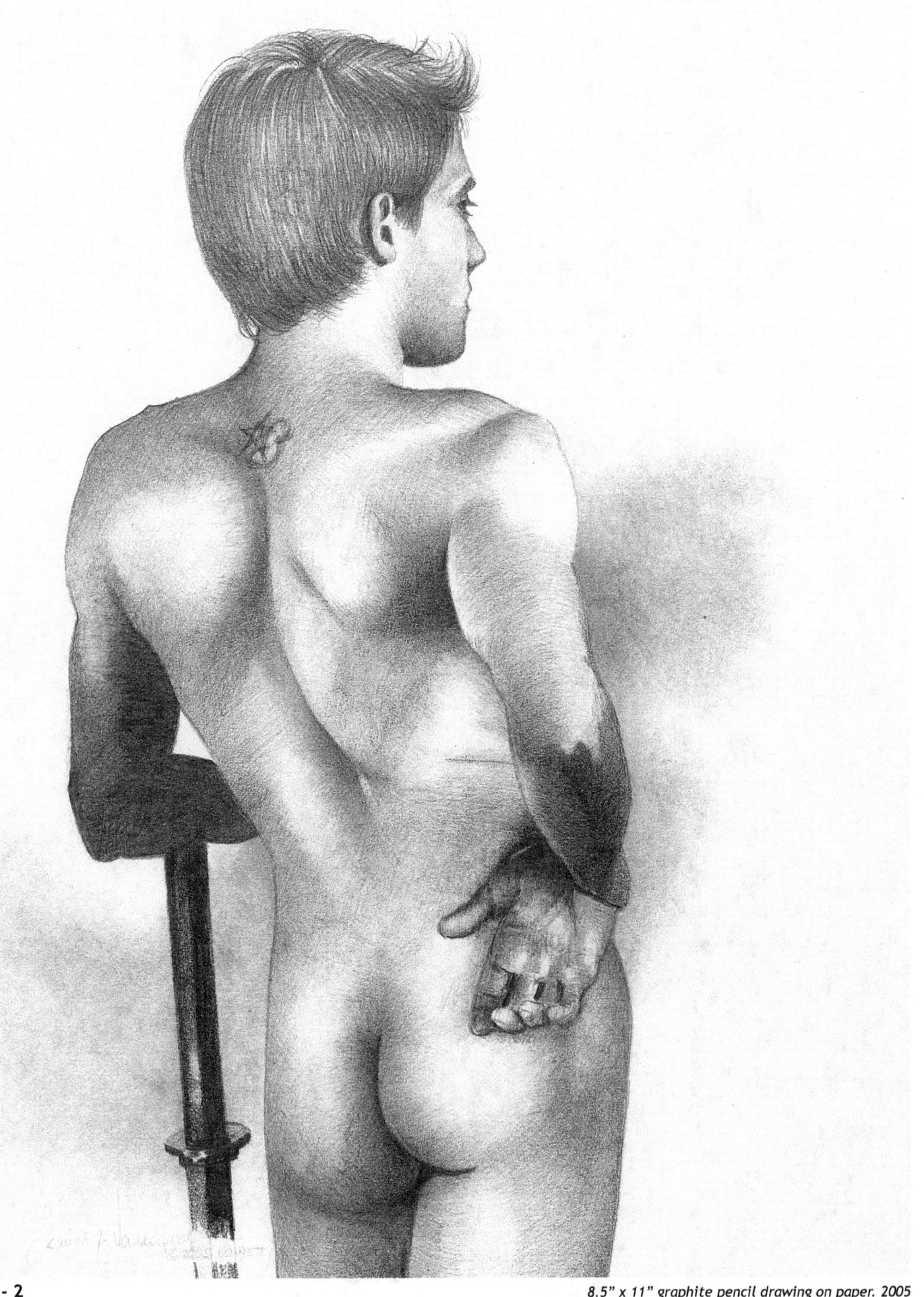

Live Model - 2

8.5" x 11" graphite pencil drawing on paper. 2005

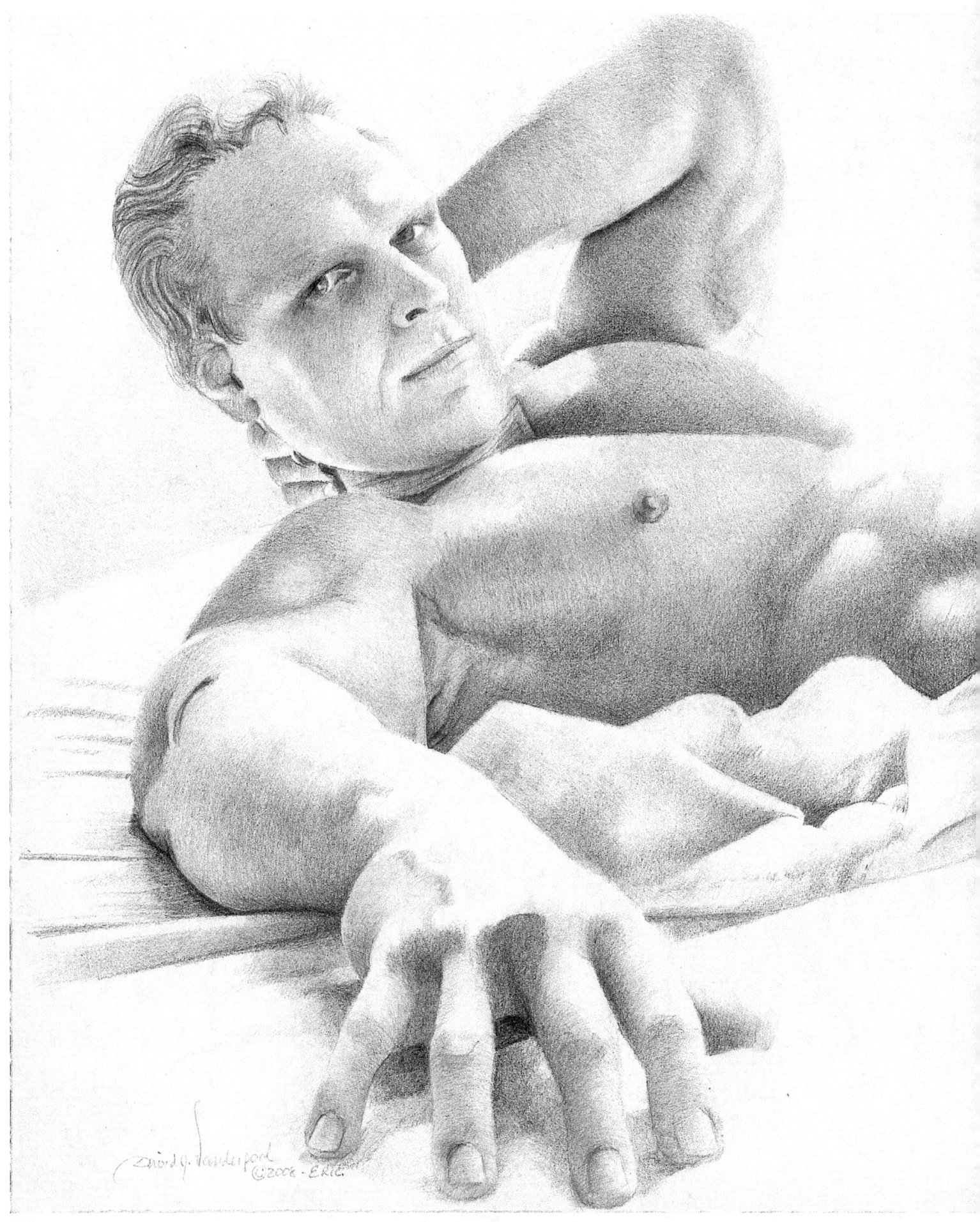

Eric

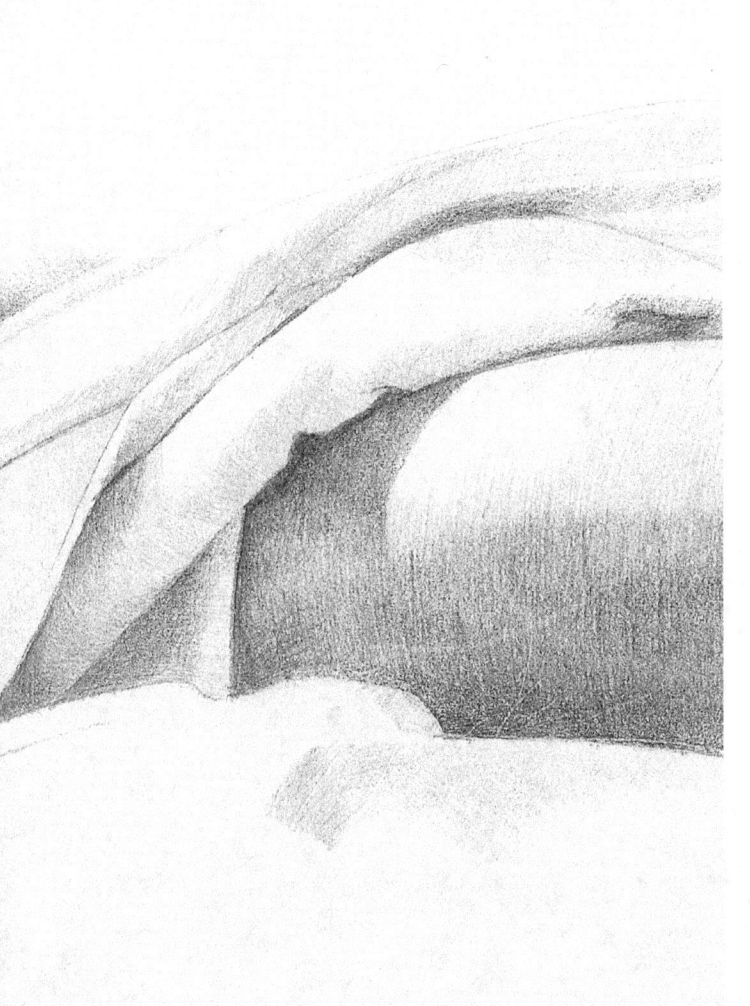

11" x 8.5" graphite pencil drawing on paper. 2006

Eric.

Yes, not all nudes have to be as revealing as what we saw in the drawing of "Kevin-Repose" or "Stephen" - nor should they!

Eric Krauss was a young man from the Midwest who had moved to New York to develop his acting skills and his body. Working out daily to get in to the best physical shape he possible could, and taking acting classes to get that perfect role someday.

Taking on this drawing, prior to 2008, I still struggled with drawings that focused on hands. It was still one of my weaker areas I needed to develop. Therefore, I made an effort to look for models that would challenge me.

After all - what challenge is there if we keep it safe and continue at the level we have already achieved?

The photo this drawing was taken from was in front of a large window somewhere overlooking New York City.

Which was perfect for allowing the light to reflect off of his stomach, hips, and hand. Leaving just his face, chest and fingers showing any real detail.

Before settling on a pose to draw Eric and I went through several photos. We were in search of the best one that would benefit the two of us.

He wanted a drawing that showed off his upper body development and I just wanted a simple portrait. Frustrating since neither one of us could agree on the same pose.

Keeping with the drawing style I had developed by this time I knew the bright light reflecting off of his body was perfect for creating an unfinished drawing. Leaving little doubt to where I was going to leave off.

As with any figure or portrait that represents the person who is going to view the drawing it's important to get a likeness you both will be pleased with. A challenge when working on small drawings such at this one. Too small of a portrait, and the detail can become blurry and unrecognizable.

Therefore, before even starting a drawing, one must decided where the focus will be. Because of the paper size selected for this drawing of Eric, do I focus on his hand and upper torso, or should I use larger paper as in the drawing of "Kevin-Repose"? A drawing which would not have been as effective and powerful if on smaller paper.

Since his fingers are the closest objects to the viewer it was obvious the photographer had already established the focal point for the photograph. Therefore, I simply set out to draw what was before me as if he was modeling for me personally.

Elongated poses can be a challenge and yet rewarding once it starts to fall into place. The pencil lines used to create his arms and chest must be kept clear and sharp. The lines used on his fingers and face show less detail to give the appearance of being out of focus - or in the case of his face - at a distance.

It's easy for the mind to want to draw what it thinks should be seen as apposed to what is actually there so be careful you don't draw what isn't there.

Case in point: When dealing with white glare across his body as a result of the light source coming in from the window directly behind the model - you know there is skin, muscle and bones in under that glare, but it doesn't mean you have to draw it. Fact is you really shouldn't!

When drawing a blonde haired individual I pretty much kept to the same lighter shades of gray I use for his skin and hair. Reserving the darkest pencils for his eye lashes, the pupil of the eyes, and some of the deep shadows within his combed hair.

The highlights against his body were left untouched so the natural color of the paper could be seen. No shading from my 2H or 4H over the highlighted areas as was done on most of the other drawings in this collection.

By keeping the majority of the drawing light due to the light source that is behind him (and in front of you) the medium range graphite pencils were enough to pull out the detail establish by the shadows. They were used to lay most of the foundation to his upper torso as well.

Eric's chest, arms, and abs are well defined and the best way to capture them on paper is to make sure the shadows gradually blend into the medium shades already in place.

To achieve this - use a 2H pencil to blend the darker graphite into the medium shades and then gradually place the pencil strokes lighter on the paper as you approach the highlighted area.

Making sure to follow the contour of each muscle. The wrong angle will flatten the drawing and prevent you from achieving the look of that muscle you are drawing.

To avoid flattening a drawing. Never - ever - use a blending stump or tool on a graphite pencil drawing!

Surprisingly the clearest spot of the drawing

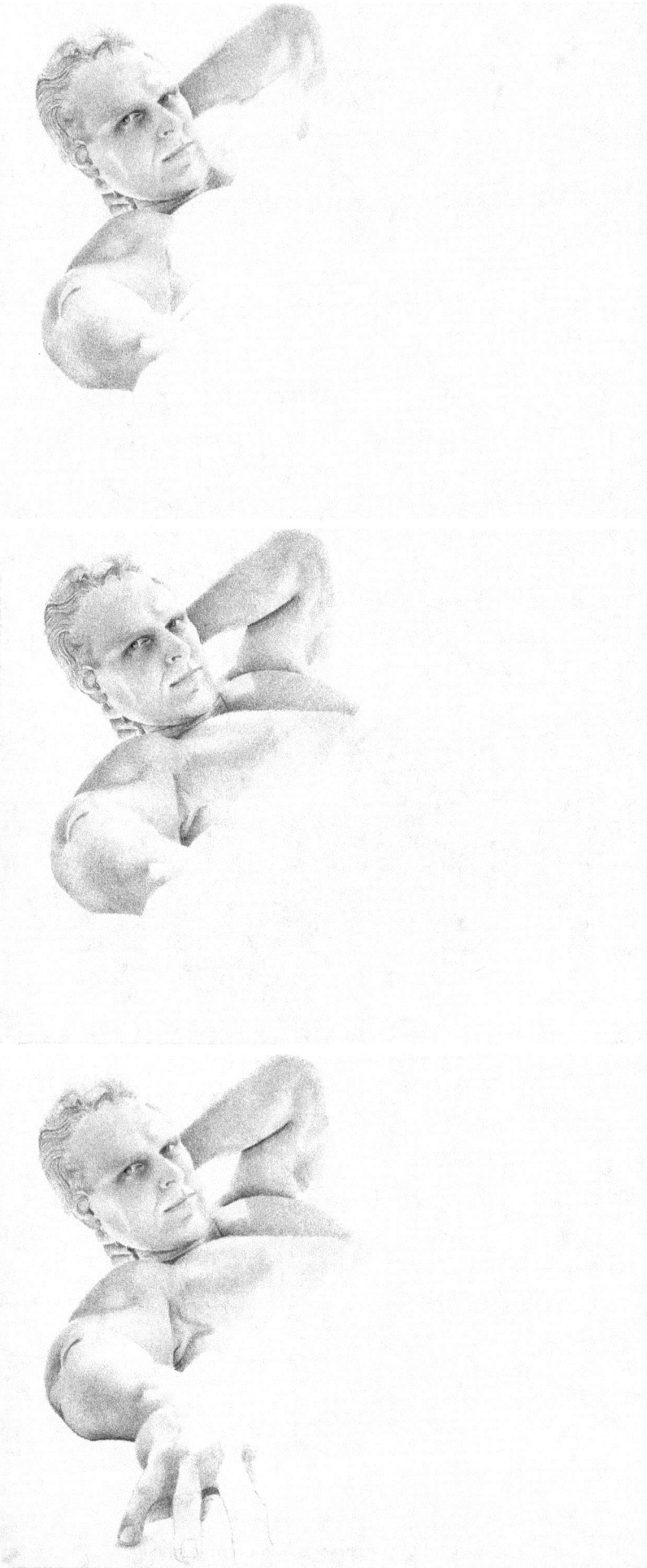

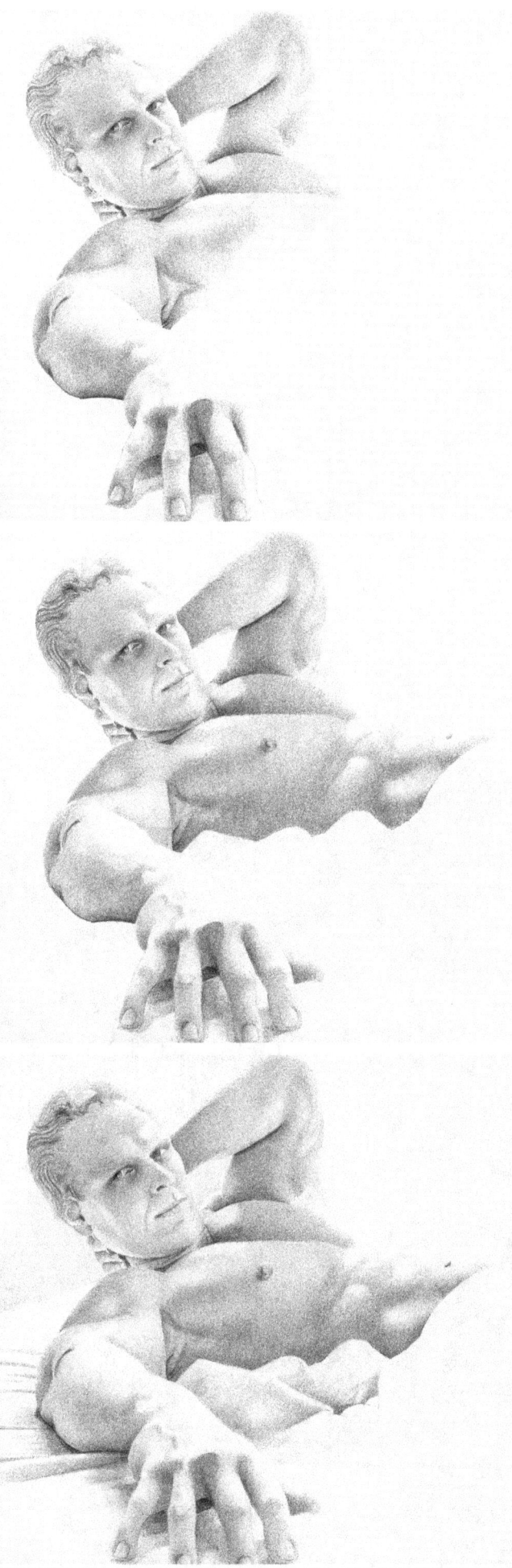

(photograph) is the center of the image.

From the left of the drawing, starting under his chin, across his right breast plate and nipple, and on to his abs and right leg, the pencils used to place each line just need to be sharp and clear. This requires the need to stop and re-sharpen the pencil before going any further.

Every other part of his body is slightly out of focus. Giving the figure a soft look throughout the entire drawing.

To try and draw the fingers clearer, using the same amount of detail seen in his chest and neck, would have been a mistake. We know he has all his fingers in place so all that was needed was to make them look believable. Even if they were meant to be blurry.

His abs, as a result of the light source being so bright, are left incomplete.

Using the kneaded rubber eraser to keep the paper clean from any graphite that might have transferred while touching the paper, also helps to make the highlights their brightest. Simply press the eraser and lift repeating until the desired effect is achieved.

Don't be afraid to allow the natural color of the paper to blend into his torso and hand. A sold line isn't needed to establish an edge. Your mind will tell you where the figure ends and where the bright light takes over.

Even though the original photo shows a window and part of a wall behind his head I choose to leave that out.

Granted to have completed this drawing may have made a more powerful impact. But due to the size of the paper, and the detail it would have required, everything left out of the drawing helps focus on his hand, then lets the viewer eyes look up and into his.

Callaway.

As seen in the drawing of Felix it was deliberately cropped to focus on him holding the saddle. An elongated figure can be cropped into a portrait as seen here of Eric. It is not necessary to draw everything you see in a reference photo.

Not only does it help establish a style and mood of the drawing. It can intentionally leave the viewer wanting for more as seen in this next drawing I have titled "Callaway".

This tastefully posed nude drawing took some

convincing to do, on my part, in regards to getting this friend to let me draw him nude. Not wanting to reveal his face, let alone more than what most would see in a given week, we both agreed that a full frontal nude of this firefighter would not be shared within these pages.

Giving my word as a gentleman and artist, I promised that the world will only see just enough to wish they could see more. I couldn't think of a better way to do this than a pose such as this!?

Having never drawn a man in a shower I opted out drawing the drops of water on his arm, shoulder, and chest which could clearly be seen the photograph. What I did keep was the sensual look he held and the lighting the tiled wall reflected against his body.

Using the white from the paper, I left his shoulder and upper chest alone, as with part of his lower arm. Unfinished are his leg and the towel he holds to cover himself.

This drawing has several focal points and each person viewing the drawing will most likely see things differently: His chin, because of the deep shadow and how he looks away from the camera; The dark shadow coming from behind his back and slowing clinging into his rib cage; And last the veins in his hands.

All these stand out because the contrast between light and dark. You can not have a powerful drawing without deep rich shadows or a strong light source.

In creating this drawing the body had to be broken up in several sections. Or I should say, one muscle at a time, which made for a lot of time put into this drawing.

This 8.5" x 11" pencil drawing took me two weeks to complete. Drawing a few hours each evening as time allowed.

Keeping in mind that each part of his body is curved or round I had to be sure to follow the muscle just as it was. This was a bit of a challenge due to the highlights that prevented me from seeing some of the muscles. If you were to remove the skin from his body you would see how each muscle wraps around the other and in which direction they pull. That is the direction you must make your pencil strokes and lines follow.

The muscle from his collar bone to his ear wraps around his neck in an upward direction. Depending on the direction his head is turned. This is drawn with a 2H and 4H pencil, and then darker for the shadow at the back of his neck and hair line. This is an area that doesn't have to show much detail but it needs to be drawn to hold up his head.

Being in a shower, his hair is obviously wet, yet combed. Be sure to draw each cluster of wet hair

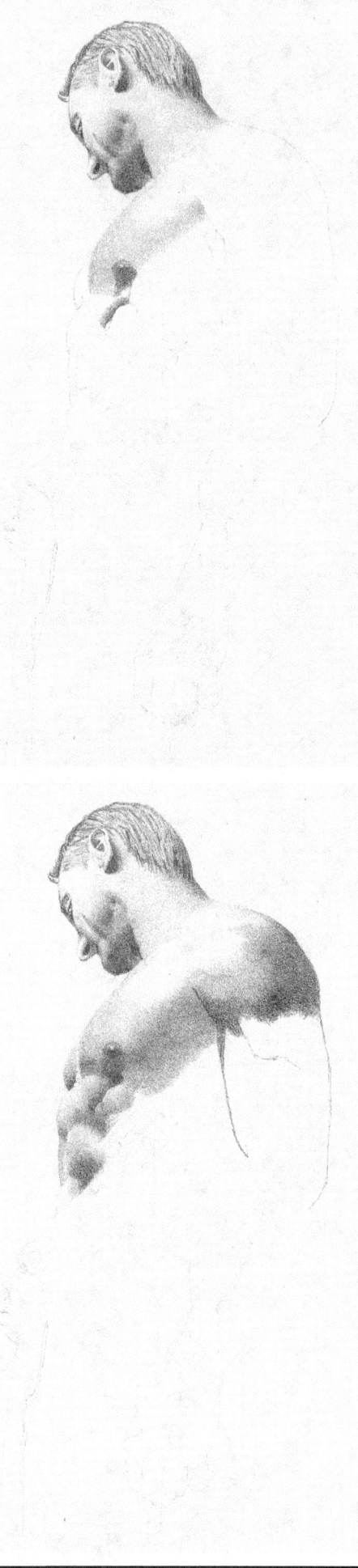

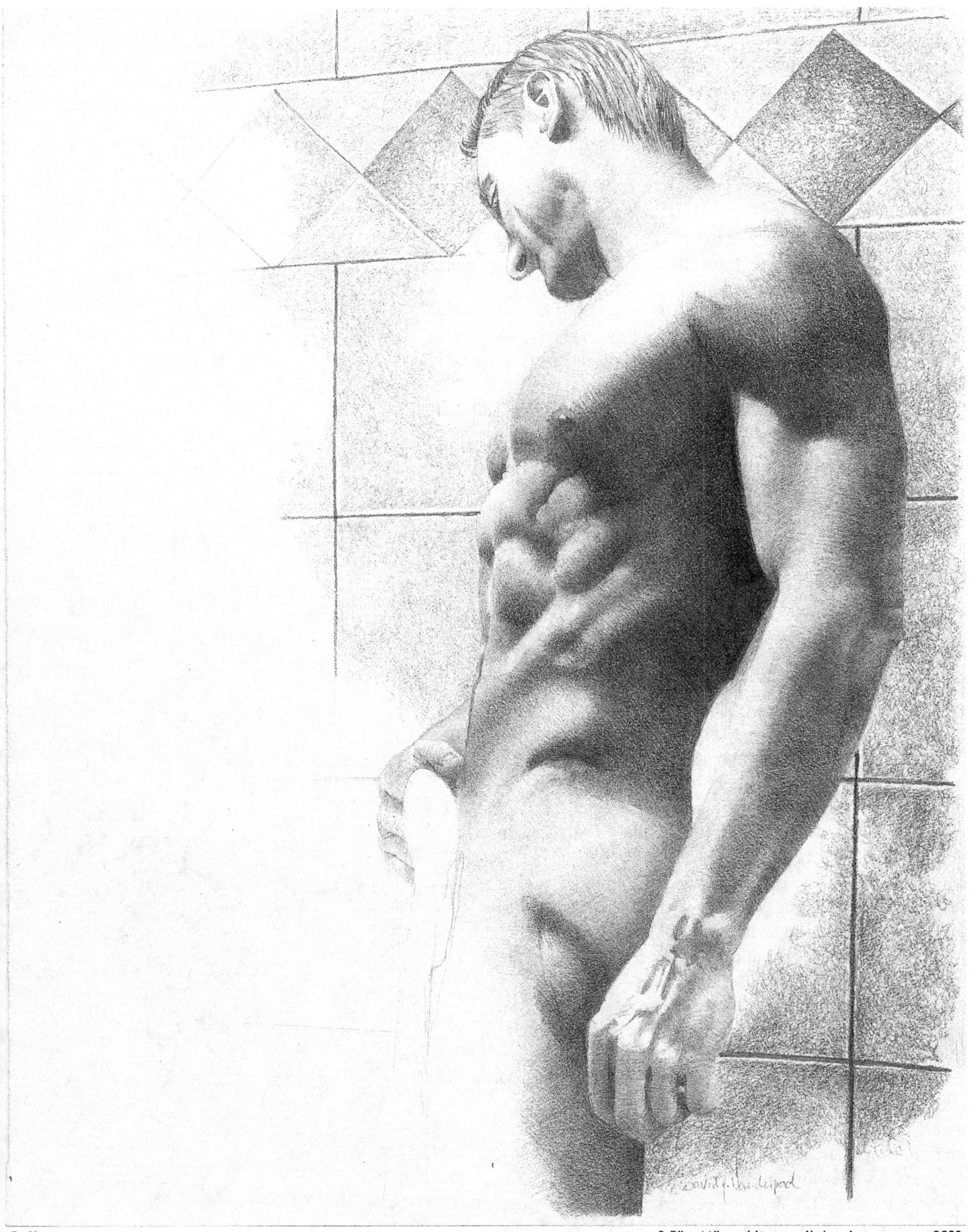

Callaway

8.5" x 11"graphite pencil drawing on paper. 2009

separately, along with its shadows and highlights so his hair doesn't appear to be dry.

When drawing muscles do your best to not have solid lines between each muscle unless it's for a deep shadow. The better built the model is the deeper the shadows. A more rounded model of course wouldn't have all the muscles as seen here with Callaway.

When drawing shadows you still need to follow the contour of each muscle. Don't just darken an area with your Ebony pencil and call it done. That's not acceptable for even a dark pencil will show the contact and direct of the graphite you are drawings.

From your darkest black to an "F" pencil it's best to gradually blend the shades at the same time. This means drawing a dark area, followed by the next lighter shade, and then so on until you have filled the area you are working in. It doesn't matter how big or small the muscle is the process is the same.

What makes this figure drawing appear realistic is the fact the lines of the pencil follow the curves of the muscle. Notice how the breast muscle is rounded off from the white highlights to the pit of his arm, but the darker shadow is perhaps a 4B pencil. That's because the shadow in the pit of his arm is the darkest shade in that area and the Ebony pencil is reserved for that.

Also take notice of his stomach muscles. The pencil strokes start at the top left and move to the bottom right hand side. Not a straight line but in fact lines that curve inwards since there is really fat to be seem on his body.

This is a case where the background is a must when deciding if you should or shouldn't draw what's around him. A naked man standing with a white background is just another naked man. However, with the tiled wall behind him, the viewer is invited to explore Callaway on a more personal level. In the shower with him!

The lines for the tiled wall are lightly placed with a ruler before going over it again with a darker pencil to give it a 'freehand' appearance.

Yes another secret and tool to get the job done right!

The shading to each tile are created with lines, but this time not sharp, and by using the side of the graphite and not the tip. Moving the pencil in a circular motion you can see the texture as well as the gray tones of the tile taking form. Let the white of the paper to show through, where the major source of light bounces off the wall, and on to his chest and shoulder.

Leaving the cloth he is holding to cover this lower region unfinished the drawing puts the focus on the deep shadows that wraps his torso and ribs. Making the drawing

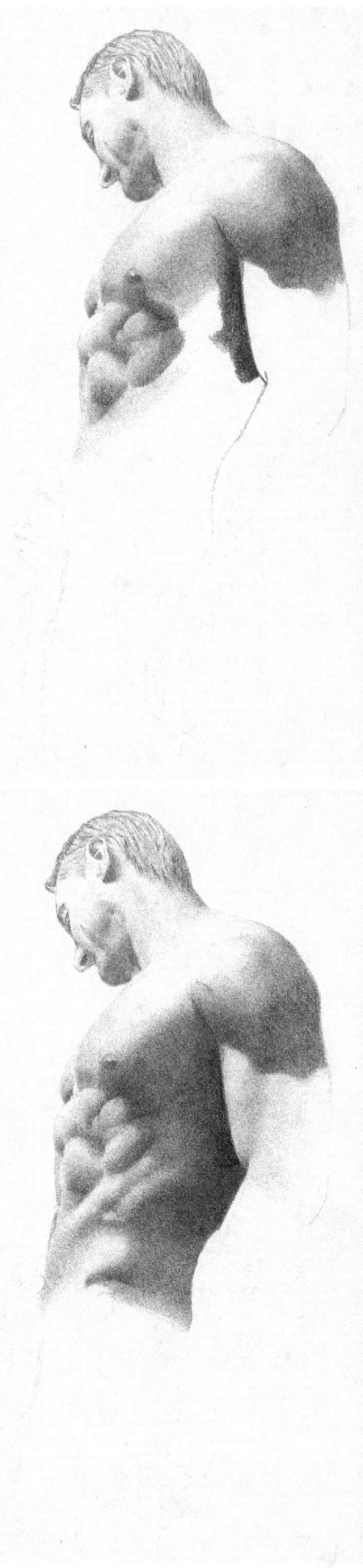

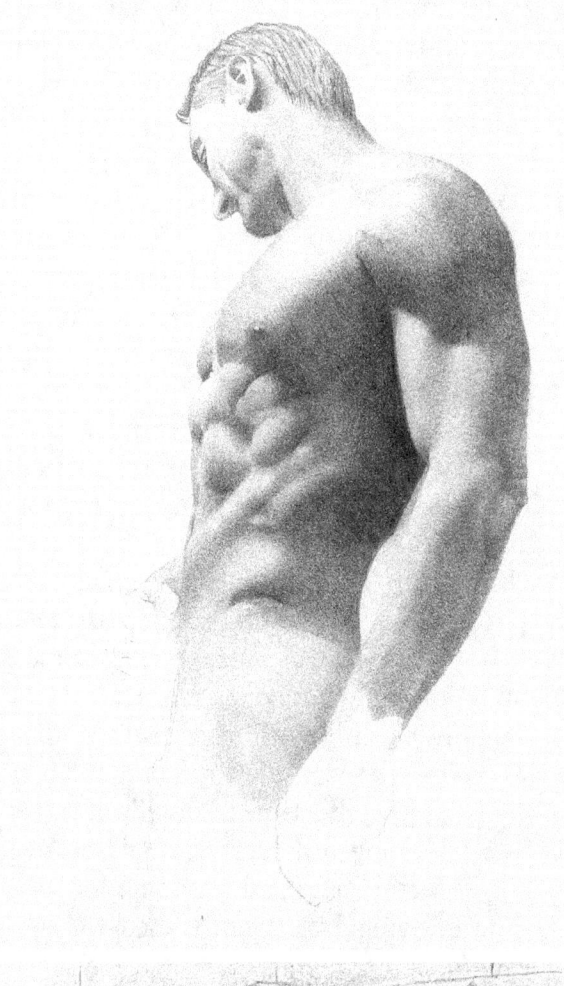

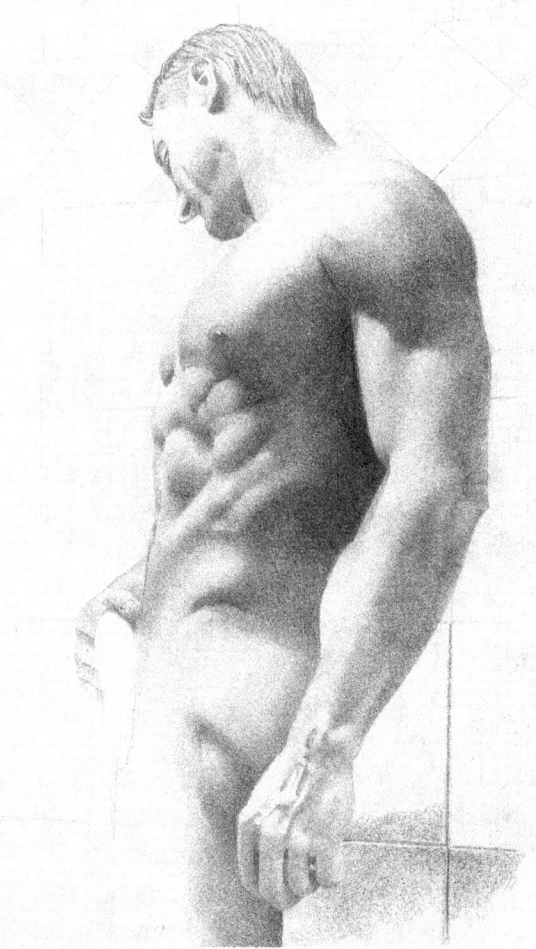

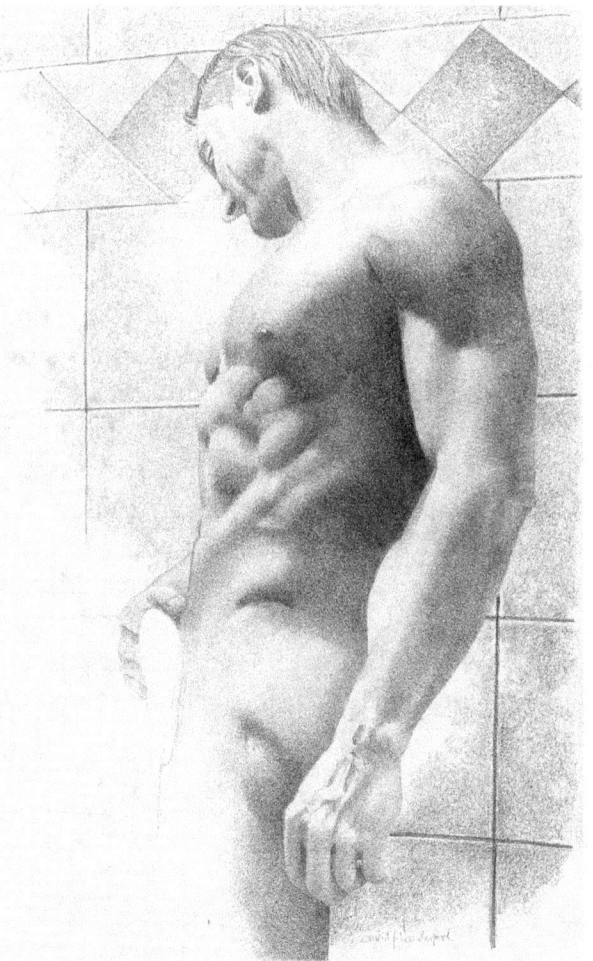

less erotic and another classic study on the human male.

In a world where today's male nudes can take on a sexual overtone and can quite frankly scare the average person if they are not accustom to such art. By carefully selecting a pose that is more classical, or traditional, the viewer can be introduced to the beauty of the model which they might not otherwise be willing to publicly acknowledge - let alone accept.

Nudes.

Taboo still for most and yet accepted by others due to not only education or social acceptance but wether or no the viewer is comfortable within themselves.

Never one to take on a crude, or sexually explicate drawing, that is solely based on my personal belief and the choices I have made, in order to be who I am.

Emotions, faith, social issues, and acceptance of who we are is apart of most of the things we do or don't do in life. Whether that applies to the model, artist or art collector.

We react to what we see and how it makes us feel. I believe it is what we feel as the result of seeing, that directs us to accept, judge, or condemn those who made us think in the first place.

Russell.

Some of the best commissioned drawings are the ones that surprise you the most as I was with this drawing here. A young Christian bodybuilder who was willing to allow me to draw him but just wasn't too sure what pose would work best.

Several of the photos Russ sent me were great poses and the lighting was perfect for a black and white drawing, but without the photographer's permission and better quality copies to draw from, there was no way I could draw him well enough that I'd put my signature on them.

The better of the photos turned out to be this simple pose that surprised me because it was nothing I would thought a young bodybuilder would have had taken of himself. It was simple, not flashy, nor showing of his developed muscles, but rather a relaxed and comfortable pose.

Clean and simple.

This portrait of Russ is a fine example of the importance of keeping your pencils sharp and following the contours of his muscles. The the elongated positioning of his body brings him up close and off the edge of the paper.

Here muscles fold into one another as we see in his shoulder and neck area. His hands are well chiseled as the veins can be seen protruding from under his skin. Even the slightest details of a few freckles can be seen on his face and shoulder.

All details that must be captured using sharp light and medium shade graphite pencils. Which means having to stop ever so often to re-sharpen each pencil. Time consuming, let alone consuming many pencils, the final pieces is well worth the time and investment.

With this drawing it's easy to see several areas of interest or focus. His eyes and his hands were intended to be just that. Yet it's the deep shadows against the whites of his skin that lends your eyes elsewhere throughout the drawing. The shadow under his right arm, his chest against the pillow, and even the slightly round buttocks seen in the distant background of the drawing.

However, with this drawing, it's the soft pillow he is resting upon that makes this young bodybuilder's forbidden portrait a work of art.

Forbidden, since such a drawing will most likely never be displayed or revealed to friends or family. At least until later in years, as his youth fades away and he finds himself looking back at a time, when such beauty as this made it easy to capture him on paper.

Unlike many of the male portraits and figure drawings I have created, where they appear dark in both character and background, it is very important that when taking on a project where the man is younger, surrounded by light rather than darkness, the drawing does not take on a soft appearance. That isn't who the man is or how he wants to be portrayed.

When drawing youthful looking men it's very important to keep them masculine and strong in appearance. Especially if that's who they are in real life. It's far too easy to make them appear soft when they aren't so be very careful that you don't replace a sensual look for a feminine look.

Just how does one make a young man look masculine while laying butt naked on a pillow? Focus on his eyes, hair, and with this drawing making the main focal point his hands.

To do this use the darker pencils for his eyes and deepest shadows. By doing so the artist leads the viewers eyes to look in various areas, one after the other, and not spend to long in just one set place.

Again - starting with his eyes, lips, that deep shadow between his chest muscles, down to his hand which casts another shadow, this time along his arm, the viewer finds him self looking all over without realizing this young man is in fact nude. A nude and no longer a portrait.

The drawing is left unfinished for the sole purpose of giving it the appearance of a classic pencil sketch. Intentional left unfinished to add mystery to the piece that may or may not be real. For what is reality but perception based not on fact but by sight? Sight that triggers ones imagination.

Imagine having to created in secret and on borrowed time. Here is a man in the prime of his youth who desires passionately to be captured by an artist. Yet he fears being caught by those who would not understand and therefore mock him. He finds himself slowly allowing social doubts to enter his mind.

Worried and scared - the fear that entered his head becomes panic in his heart, and just as quickly he was willing to strip and pose for the artist he leaves before the drawing could be completed.

Leaving everyone to wonder what this pencil drawing could have become if he had not run off.

Leaving the artist to never see the young man again.

Leaving the artist to seek his own 'Dorian Grey' elsewhere.

If any of that was true.

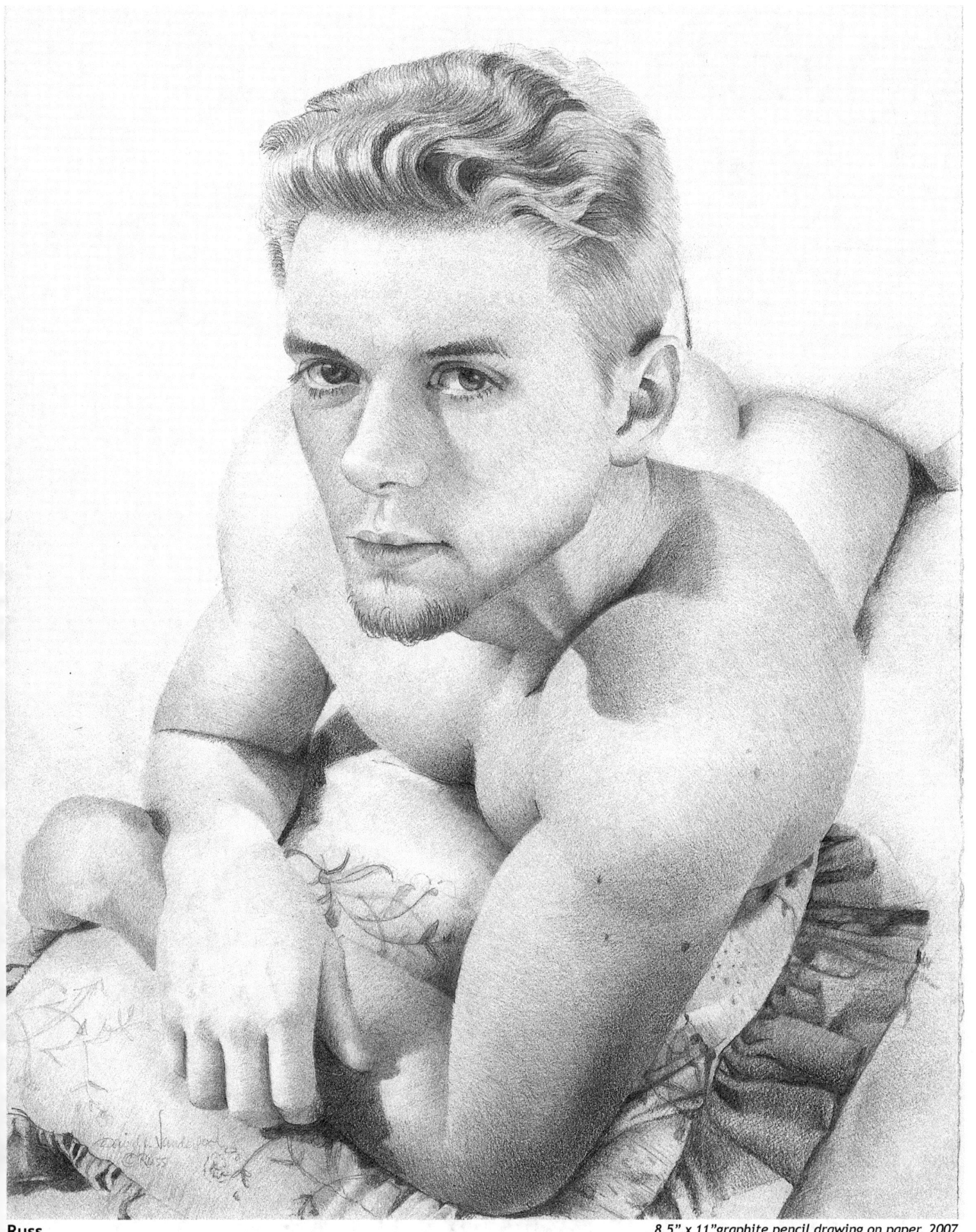

Russ

8.5" x 11" graphite pencil drawing on paper. 2007

A look into the art of David J. **Vanderpool**

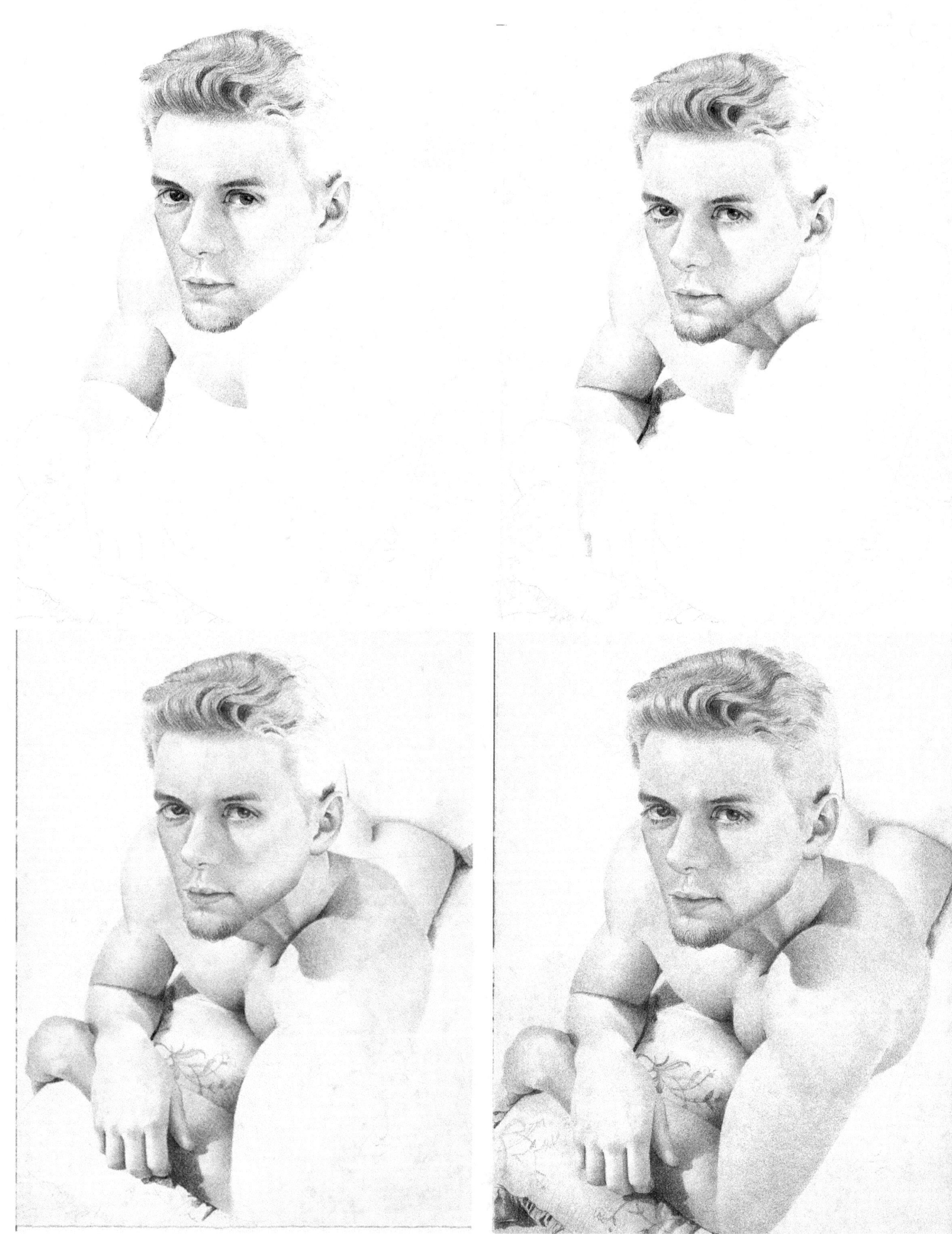

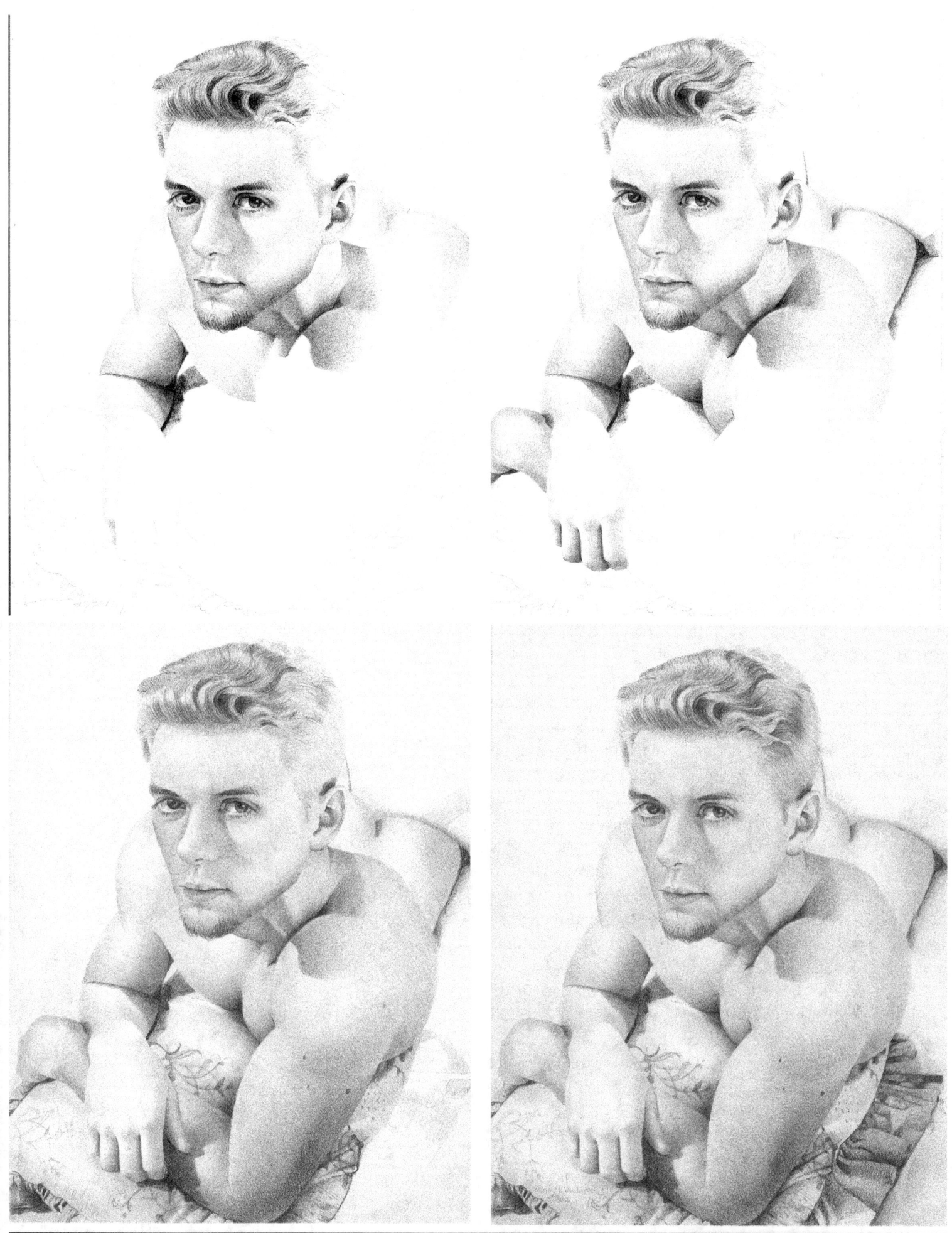

Lantern Keeper.

When drawing from a photograph, you as the artist, have the right to capture what you feel is the strongest feature within that image. You also have the right to alter it in any way when it's not a commissioned drawing requested by someone in advance.

Not to say that creating the model exactly as seen is wrong it's just not necessary when making the drawing your own piece once it's done.

I came across this photo taken by Russian photographer, Andrei Vishnyakov, shortly after posting several of my drawings on www.redbubble.com for print sale (http://paper2pencil.redbubble.com) and instantly I knew I had to add this to my collection of drawings!

The young photographer was quick to e-mail me several of his photos but this one was my top choice because of the lantern the man was holding. The idea of having the light shine out from the glass and reflect onto his face was something I had never done and I instantly wanted the challenge.

By this time my drawings had started to take on a darker feel to them. More and more of the portraits had dark background allowing the model to emerge out of the darkness. So what better than to draw a man holding a lantern producing the light source from in front of him?

However there was one thing I wanted to change. He was too pretty so I made him slightly older and added facial hair.

A few years later Andrei would inform me the young man eventually grew to become the man in the drawing.

Knowing in advance that this drawing had the potential to be very dark and easy to smear I made the effort to use the lightest pencils I had for his face. Keeping the darker pencils for the pupil of his eyes and eye lashes.

His eyes turned out to be perfect for what I was looking for. They had to reflect the light that was right in front of him.

A 6B graphite pencil was used for the shadow across this face and the deepest lines on his lips, however, an 8B was used for the eye hidden in the shadow of his face.

Drawing the darkest shadows is never an easy task. Graphite will only get so dark and the darker the pencil the softer the graphite is so the effect you want may be a challenge. Therefore, this is where various pencils comes into play and using different technics other than crosshatching.

Just how does one make a dark graphite pencil darker? Use a lighter harder pencil over it.

Doing so will clean and sharpen the edges. Which is perfect when drawing the pupil of his eyes, the edge of

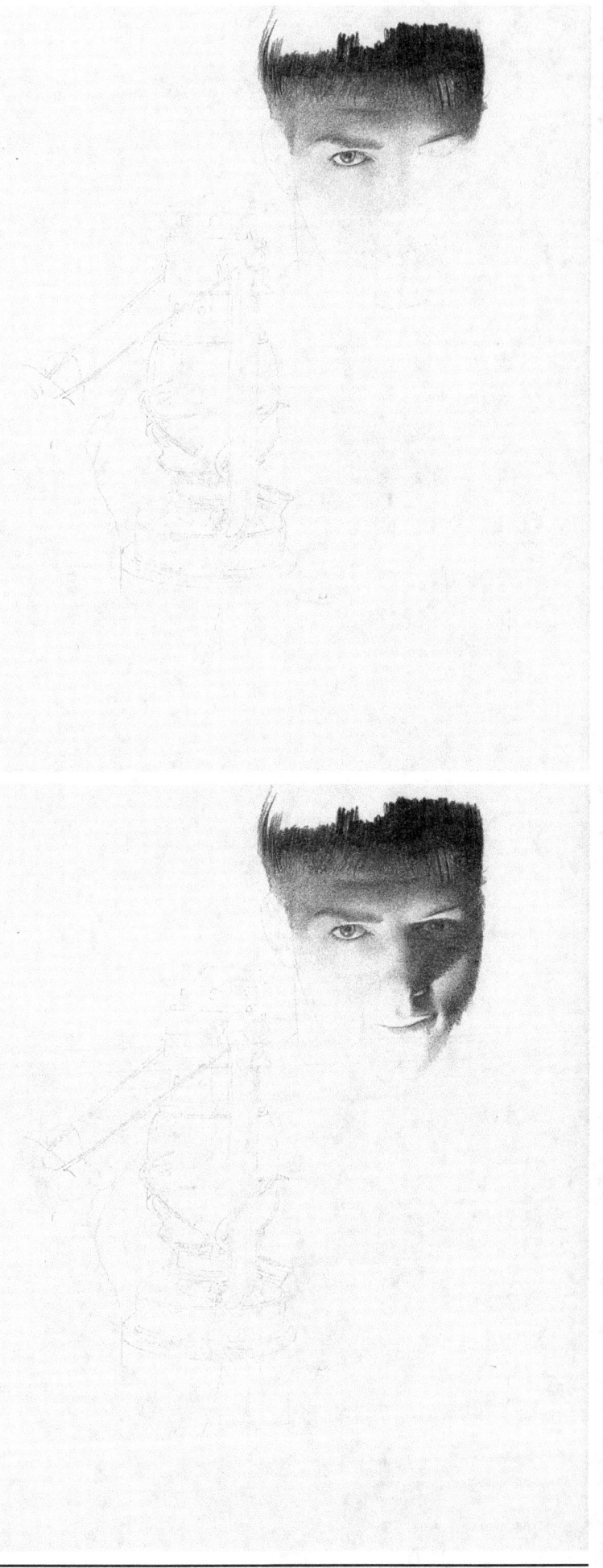

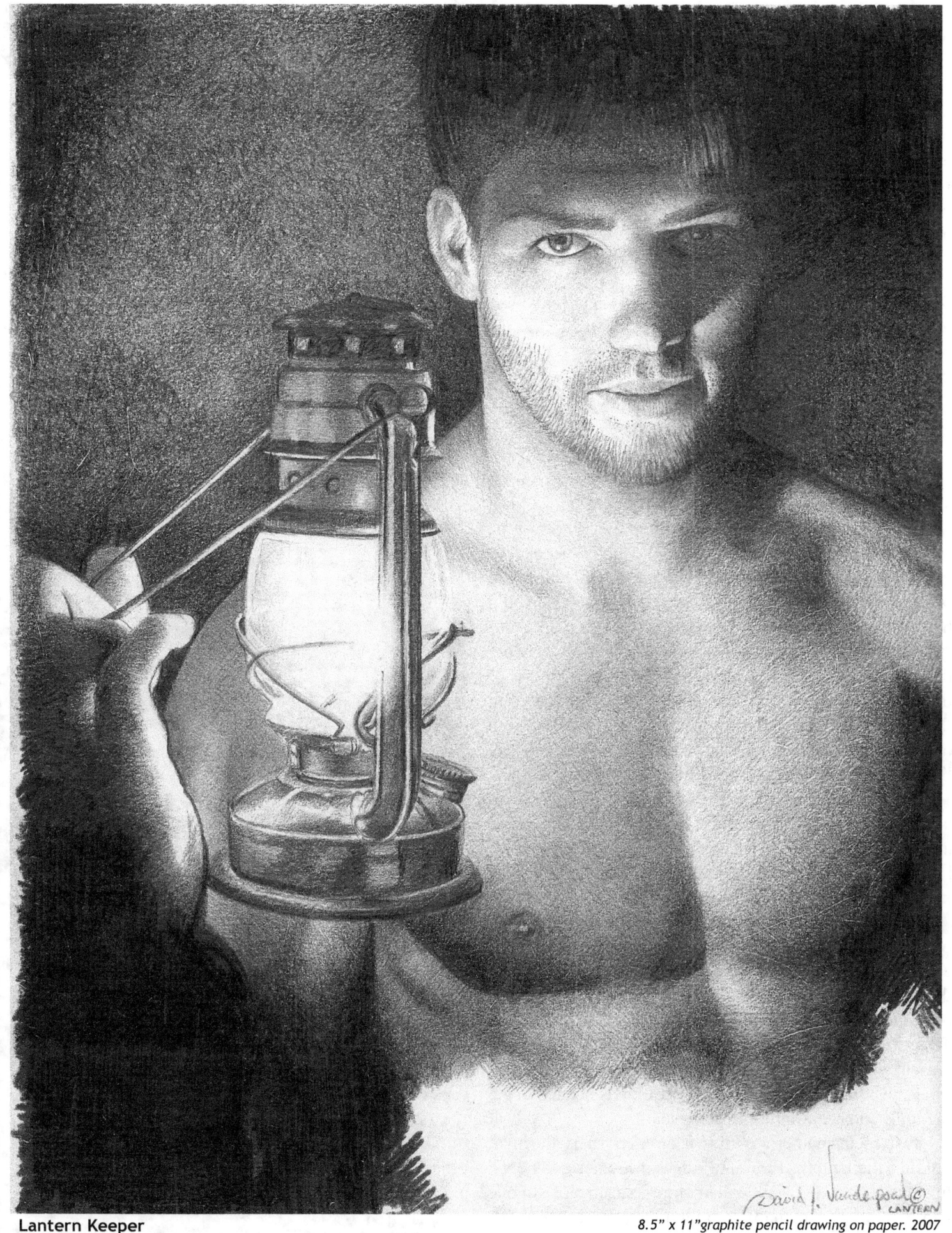

Lantern Keeper

8.5" x 11" graphite pencil drawing on paper. 2007

his lips, and when merging the deepest shadows from the out edges of the drawing where the light can not reach.

The background shown over his shoulder had to reflect the light and appear to bounce off whatever may be in the distance behind him. To create this effect I used several pencils and kept them dull. Then I used a circular motion until I achieved the look I wanted. Once the entire surface was covered in the first layer of graphite, I used a 4B as my blending tool and went over the entire background as my second layer. This time using lines and keeping the lines all going in the same direction.

Usually I would never use a darker pencil as a blending tool but since this was a dark background it made sense. After all, the lighter pencils used in the circular pattern in the first layer were harder pencils and left an impression under the layers to follow. I just had to make sure that those layers weren't so dark as to cover the textured look on the wall behind him.

I used the same Strathmore brand that I used for the portrait of Darko. You can see by the darker appearance shown in the grayscale images used in the book. The Strathmore drawing paper had a slight cream color tone to it. I choose this paper since the body needed to appear darker, and should I need to use a white pencil to bring out the illuminated glow from the lantern, I would have the option of going that route.

When drawing objects along with a portrait drawing the lines placed need to appear different than those of the human skin. Be it jeans and saddle as illustrated in the drawing of Felix or here with the lantern. Drawing objects is the same as with drawing skin and muscle the lines placed by the pencil must follow the object.

As seen in the top half of the lantern the lines wrap around the metal from left to right. This gives it the appearance that the object is circular. To place the line in an upward to downward stroke would have flatten the lantern.

Mid-range pencils would later be used for the wire brackets that holds the lantern's glass in place. And once again the kneaded rubber eraser is used to pull the light that shines from the glass. Observe how the light plays over the brackets, across his chest and towards his face. This effect is achieved by gently pressing the kneaded eraser over the area needed to lighten the desired areas.

Repeating this process as many times as needed to get the look you are wanting to achieve.

Just as the lantern is drawn circular so is the man holding the lantern. From the ridge of his nose, his ears, lips, his fingers and neck - all are lines placed close to one another follow the shape in a circular manner. To use a

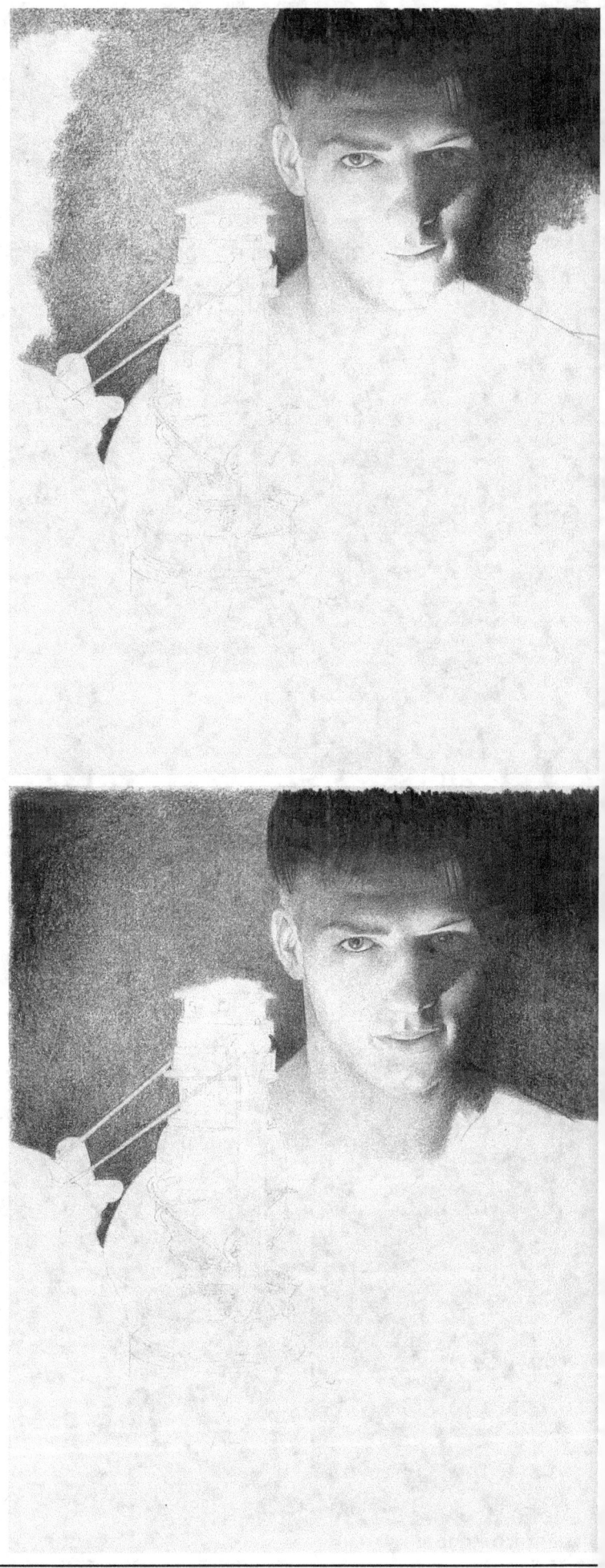

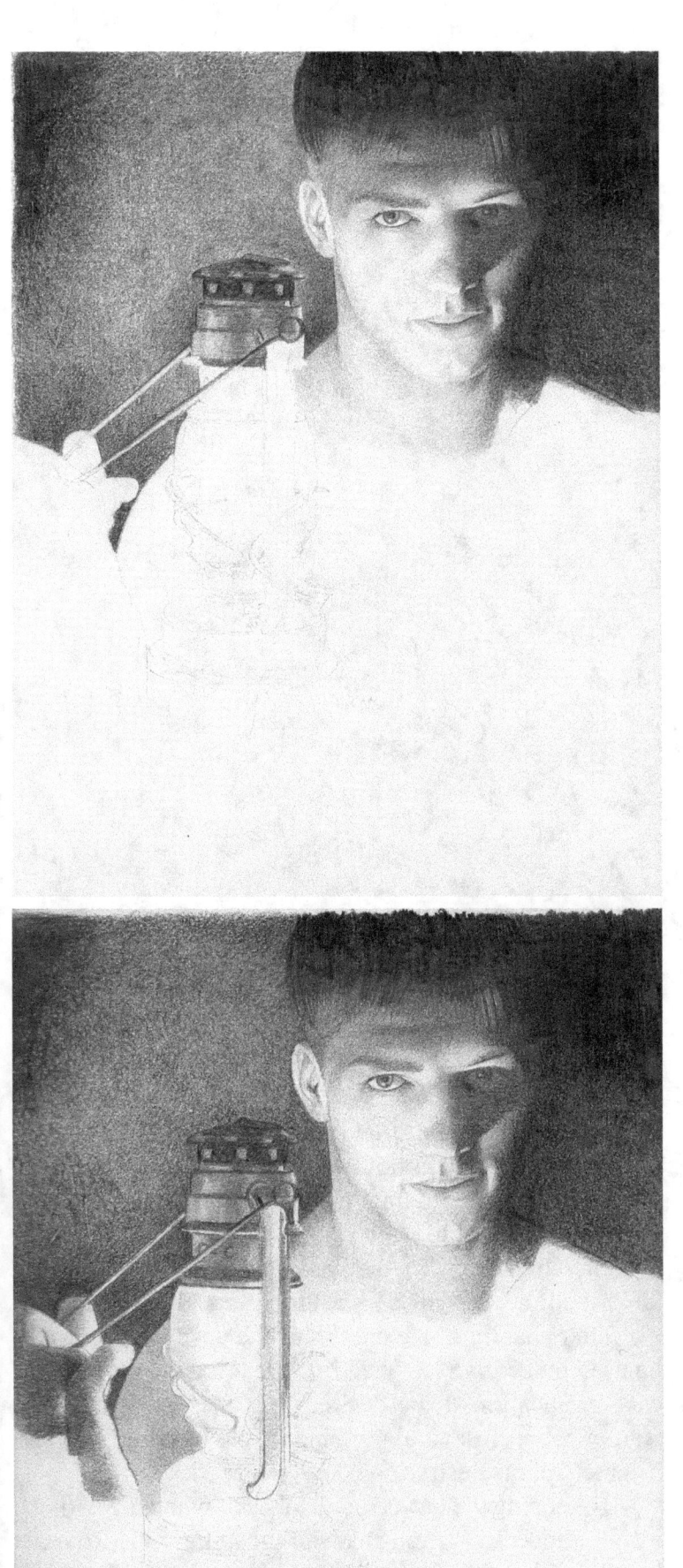

flat or straight line would have flattened the drawing.

Flat or straight lines were reserved for his chest.

Normally I would not have covered the lighter tones of the man's chest with anything more than a 4H pencil. In this situation in order for the light to give off a glow from the lantern it was required to start off with an "F" graphite pencil.

Starting off with a "F" pencil I established a layer that wrapped across each chest muscles. Allowing the lines to be seen going from top left to the bottom right of the chest seen on the left of the drawing. Then I drew top right to the bottom left for the chest shown on the right side of the drawing always keeping with the natural pull of each muscle.

By using both, a 2H and 4H, pencils over the layer established with the "F" pencil, a lightly darker yet still soft shadow started to take place. This is what gives the soft blurry shade that shows through the glass.

At the risk of possibly over working the drawing and making it too dark his chest needed to be carefully drawn out. Making sure that the shape of his chest reveals a strong youthful appearance several layers of crosshatching was required. Starting off with the lighter pencils and working towards the darker ones until the desire effect had been achieved.

Only then using a 2H pencil as a blending tool and going over the entire chest muscles once again. And then again, if needed, until the lighting and shadow was blended evenly.

To bring out the glow reflecting off his upper chest and the side of his face a darker shade of graphite needed to be applied to the rest of the drawing. Remember; the darker the graphite the softer the pencil; the softer the pencil the blurrier the image becomes. That is why a 2H pencil was used to blend the layers already set in place while keeping the lines sharp, clear, and close to one another for a smooth over all appearance.

The closer the lines are together the smoother the drawing will be. Further apart, as seen in the drawing of Daniel (see next page) the rougher the drawing will be. A piece I was working on at the same time I was drawing this one.

Two drawings, same paper and pencils, yet two different styles.

All depending on the desired effect, as well as the time the artist is willing to put into their projects.

Halfway through drawing "Lantern Keeper" I realized I wanted him to have some facial hair. This clean shaven young man was just too pretty for the final look I wanted in this drawing. Nothing against the youthfulness of the

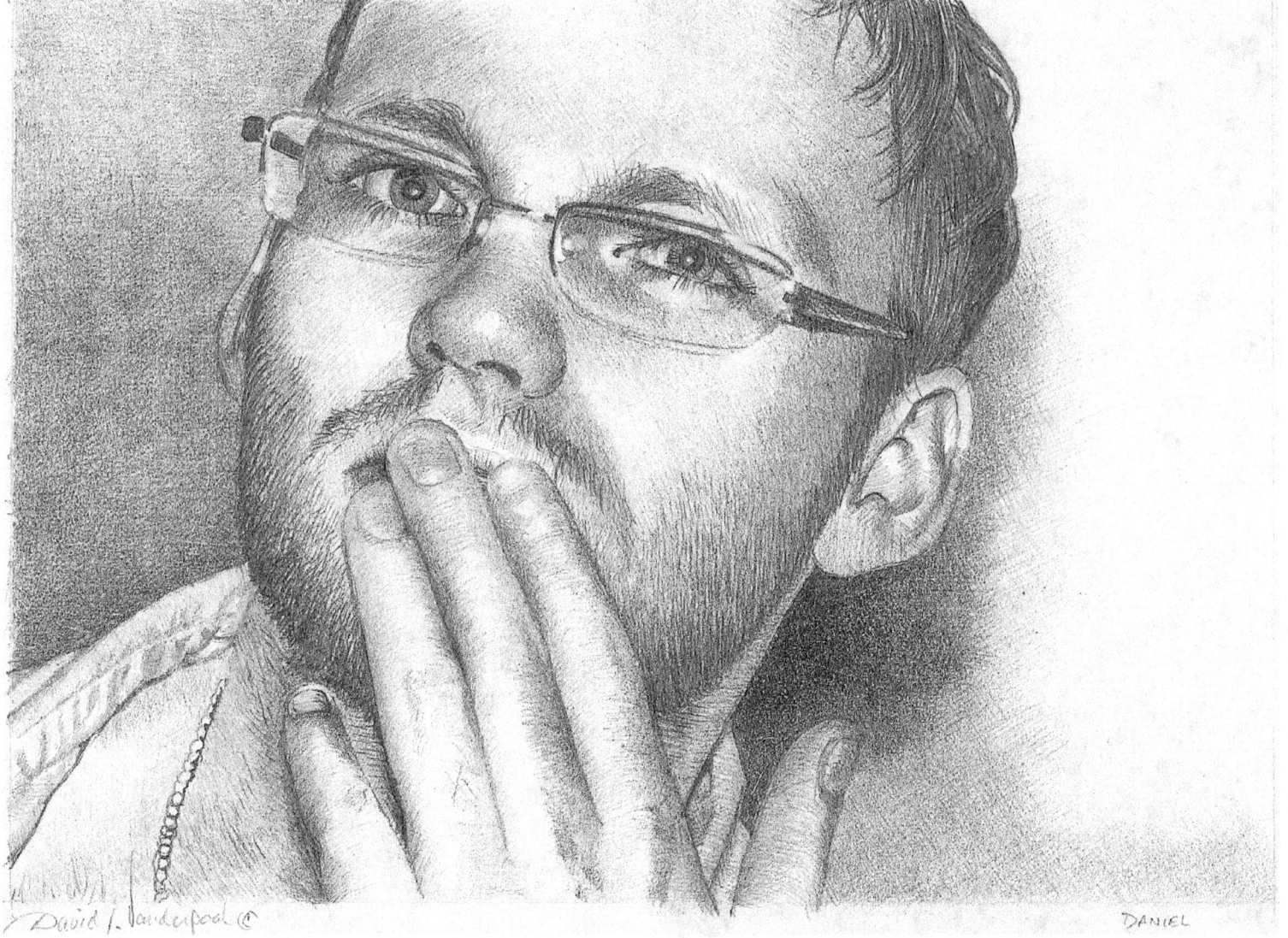

Daniel

Graphite pencil drawing on paper, shown actual size, 2007

model but as the artist I get to choose the overall look I want to drawing to have.

As mention with an earlier drawing; each whisker needs to be drawn one at a time.

The length to each whisker, it's placement, and how close or far apart they hairs are, will be determined by the style of his beard. Be it a full beard, a new one just started, or one trimmed and well groomed. Each whisker still needs to be drawing one at a time. You start with a sharp pencil and draw from the surface of the skin and draw outward. Just as real whiskers grown on a man's face.

With this drawing of "Lantern Keeper" you can see that I changed the appearance of his beard three times before I got it the way I wanted it to be. A risky attempt since the slightest mistake would have destroyed the drawing.

And since you can't erase the sharp line each whisker makes so you have no choice but to take a new beard and make it a full beard if needed to correct any errors.

The final stage to any drawing is taking the kneaded rubber eraser and cleaning up any areas that may have become smeared. Use the same technique to bring out any highlights that need to be stronger and or brighter.

After shaping the eraser to fit the desired area it will be used on gently press and lift. Cleaning the eraser after each application if the desired brightness is needed, or wait in between several pressing before cleaning, if a less brighter spot is desired.

By keeping the background to the drawing the darkest, his face and chest a mid shade of gray, the shine from the lantern will stand out. The desired effect will illuminate across the side of his face, the side of his nose, his neck and chest, and the sides of his fingers closest to the glass. This allows the natural color of the paper to be the light from the lantern.

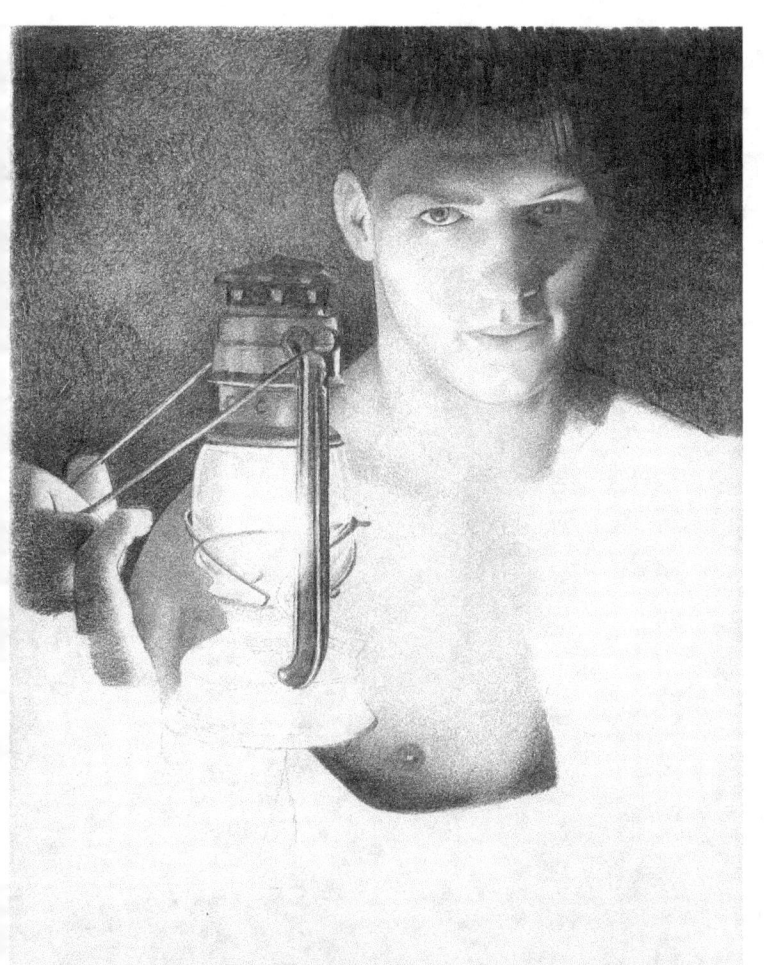
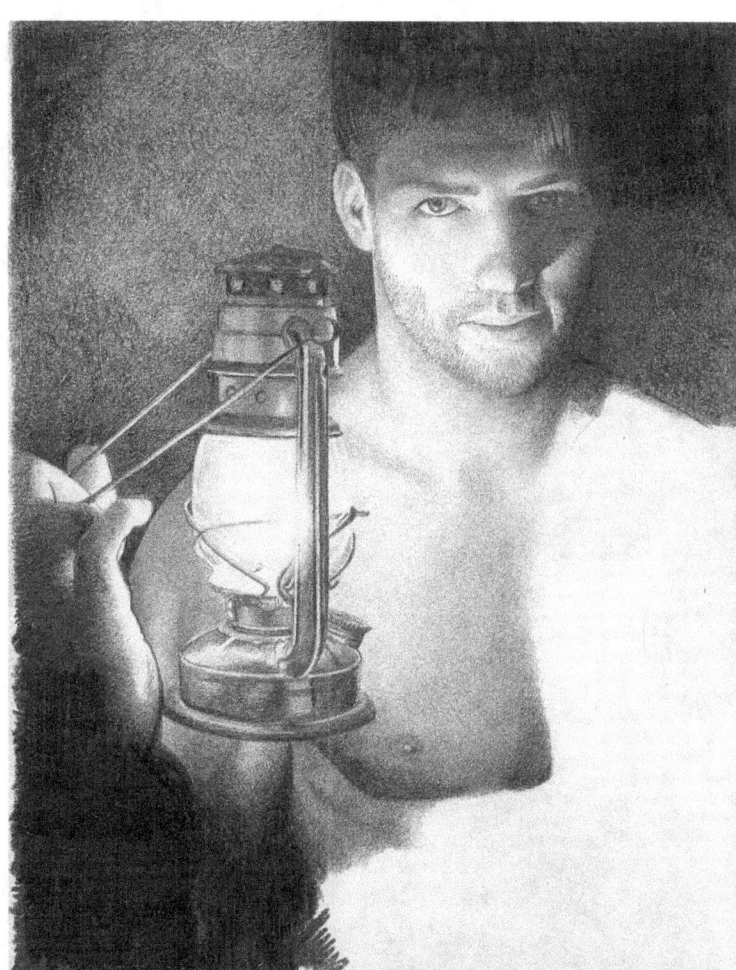
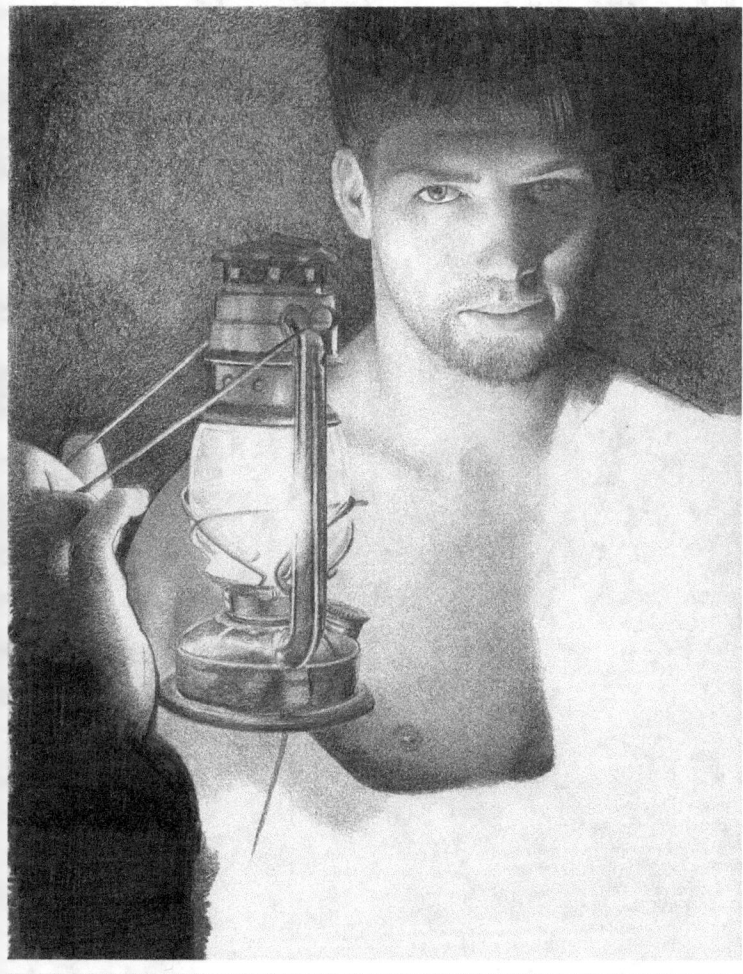
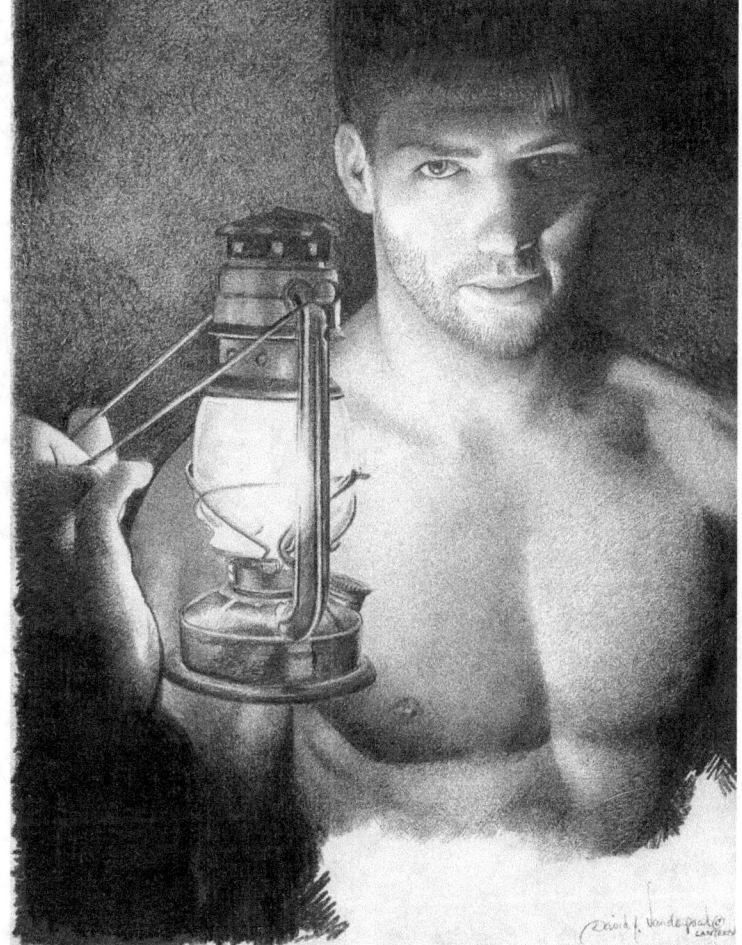

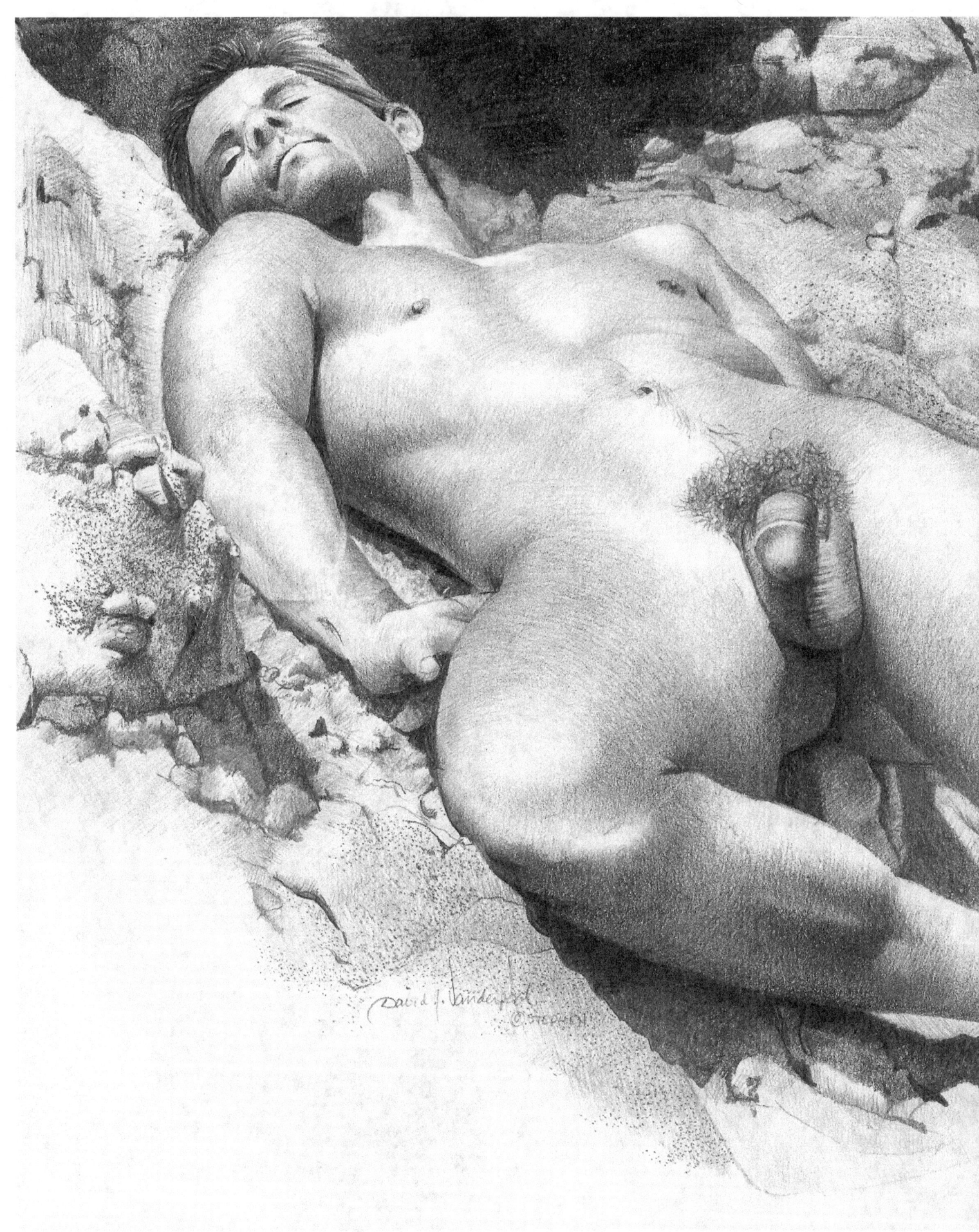

Stephen *(nude in desert)*

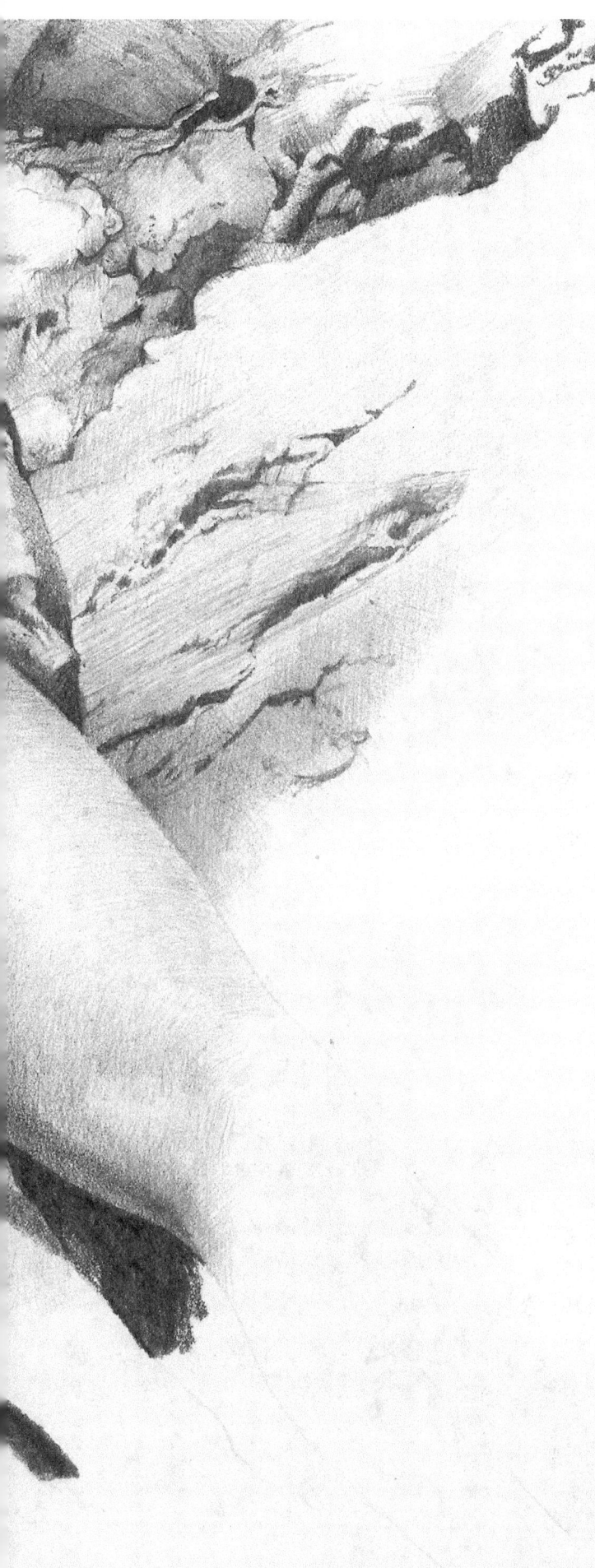

11" x 8.5" graphite pencil drawing on paper. 2007

Stephen.

Drawing a nude male is still seen as a taboo in the art world by many in America even though it's one of the first things an artist must study.

Art courses in colleges and universities throughout the country offer courses in drawing the human figure but good luck getting a drawing such as this in an art gallery or show. All in fear of offending someone, or worse, the artist being labeled for what the viewer perceives based on what is displayed before them!

Thinking back I have to admit I really shouldn't have been surprised of what was to come.

When I first started to take my drawings serious, as a teenager, I was told by my mother that I couldn't draw nudes.

However, rather than take this as a restriction, I took it as a challenge.

Art books on Michelangelo and other great Masters were collected. As well as live model books and even men's fashion and grooming.

Later in college it was required to draw self portraits. Even though I modeled for the class when the paid model wouldn't show up I found it odd drawing myself.

Not because I wasn't attractive - in the contrary I was told I was one of the better models they had in years. I just didn't I see myself as I did with other models I would eventually draw.

Was I good at drawing the human figure? Of course not - but being self taught I knew it was going to be a long hard process as mistakes would surely be made.

Most of my earlier mistakes were when it came to drawing women. As a shy young man one works with who they knew and who they feel they can approach.

It didn't take long before I discovered that there were double meanings when it came to asking people to pose for you!

Where I saw it as art and having the desire to capture beauty on paper. Most, women as well as men, saw it as a proposition with a sexual overtone to it.

I was very naïve!

And yet by the mid 1980's I found myself drawing some of the most beauty people I had known personally. Portraits of coworkers, those I had met in college, and even a few childhood friendships that still kept in touch.

All allowing me to develop a skill I knew I needed to improve on if anyone was going to take me serious. If I was going to take me serious!

This figure drawing of Stephen was a risk from the very start. Simply because it's a full frontal nude male. Not my first full frontal nude drawing, but the first I was willing to share with others.

Stepping out of one's 'comfort-zone' can be difficult. If one thinks too hard about it the opportunity can cause reasoning to become blurry. I've discovered at time it's best not to think of what others might say and just do it!

If the drawing was of a woman the comments and perception of me as an artist would have been much different and a lot easier for me to deal with.

Yes - this male nude drawing revealed an ugly side to the art scene I had not excepted.

Mixed reviews, judgment, second guesses, as well as people pulling away, ending any friendship that may have been there.

Heaven forbid that a Christian, married man, draw other man, especially nude!

HEY - It wasn't I that I was confused with who I am. But it sure confused those around me.

At least those who didn't know me personally.

First of all let me start off by saying a naked man can be seen as art when presented in the right pose. As seen here of Stephen

Relaxed against the side of a cliff in one of the deserts in southern California, this drawing removes it's self from being a naked man, to presenting a nude male, resting in the sun.

Granted, some things aren't always "in your face" as we have here with this drawing, but assuming we are all adults, lets take a serious approach to drawing the male figure.

So what makes a naked man a classic nude? You the viewer and your ability to accept the artist's interpretation of the piece rather than your own perception.

Yes - not all art is open for interpretation. Sometimes it's for the sole purpose of duplicating the beauty God has graced this planet with plus the opportunity to enjoy. At least not this artist.

Whether an artist is drawing the model's eyes, an arm, a leg, or a more private region on his body, an artist must focus on the detail within that area he is working on and not the complete image he is looking at. That is why I keep saying that drawing from photos comes in very handy at this point!

To help see the drawing in a whole different level rotate the paper as you draw.

Drawing the model upside down and

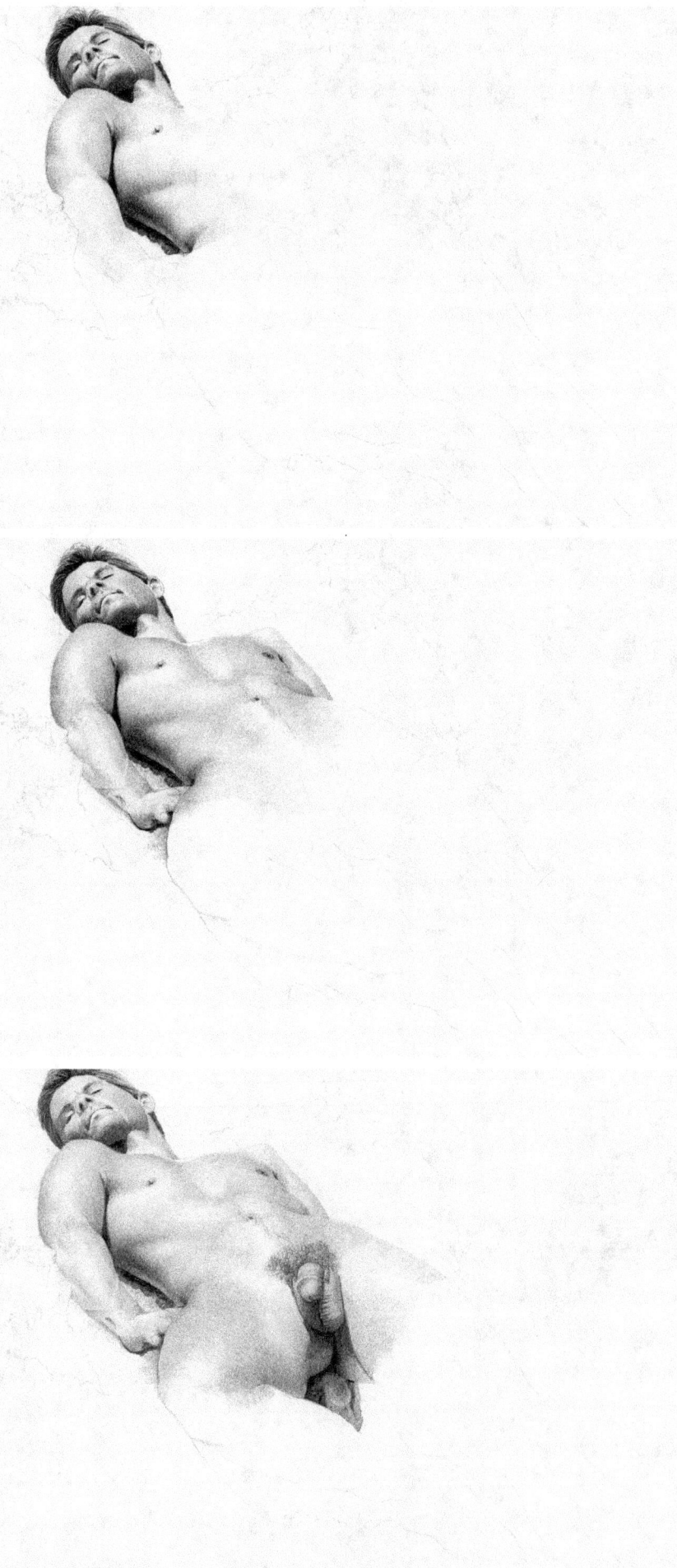

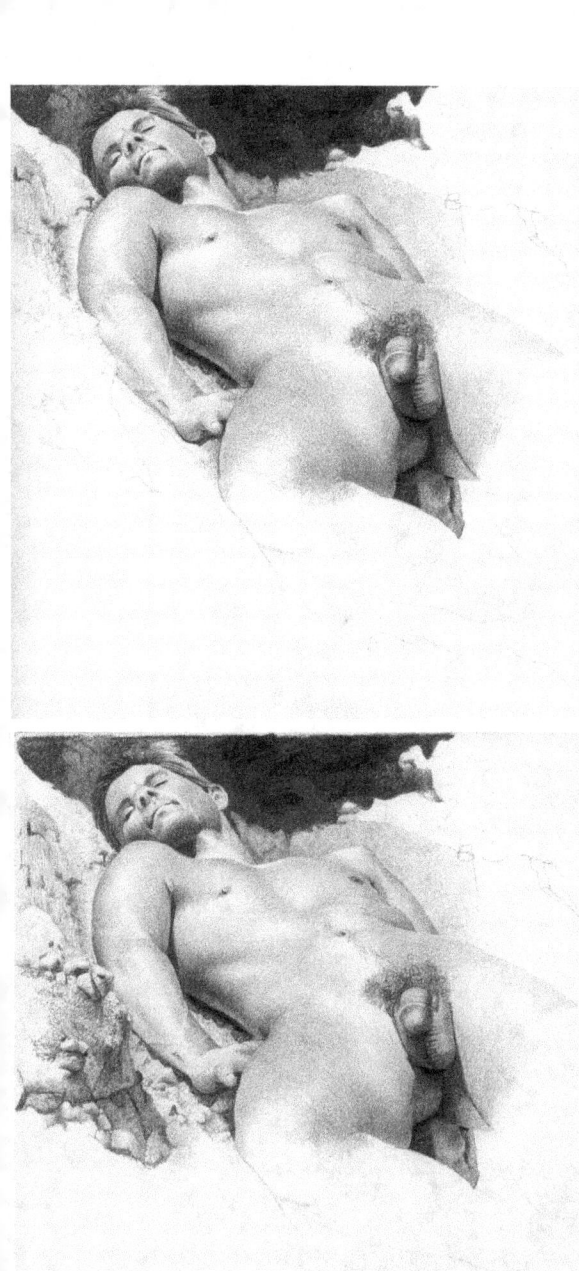

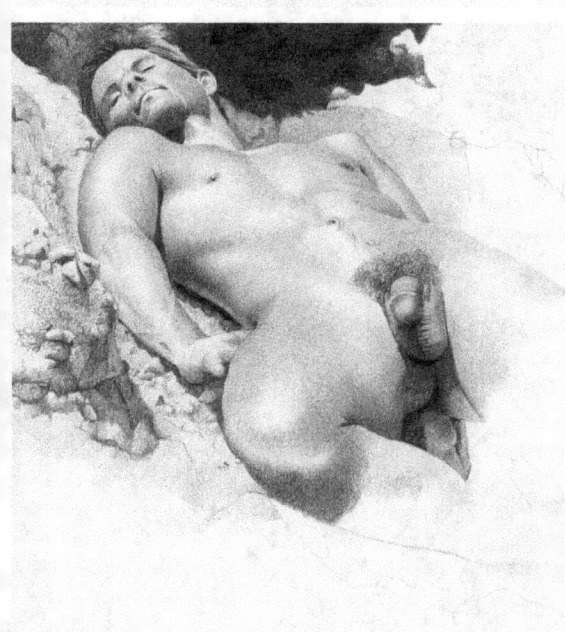

sideways as you focus on the area you are working on, rather than the entire figure, will train your brain to see in a different perspective, than how one would see the drawing if it was framed.

Rather than your mind seeing a photo of something it knows, it allows you mind to focus only on shapes, shadows, and highlights hopefully revealing errors you can easily correct before going any further.

Only by turning the drawing upright can you use lighter blending pencils to smooth out the drawing and see the drawing for what it which is a figure drawing transformed into a portrait.

When drawing on a 11" x 8.5" paper one needs to take into consideration how small the face will be and how much if any detail can be captured.

With the elongated pose here I was able to capture an exact likeness in Stephen. It may have been because his eyes were closed. To draw his eyes open at this size may not have worked as well.

Keeping the pencil sharp at all times, the drawing quickly takes form, and a three dimensional figure starts to appear. Especially as the rocks surrounding him take form and the dark shadows created make the drawing appear three dimensional.

When drawing a elongated pose keep in mind the perspective you are working with and the direction the lines and crosshatching must be placed. Remember curves are a must when drawing any object be it a person or rock.

Granted - when drawing an object that shows a elongated perspective "some things" are going to be in your face, and rightfully so - as this drawing was intended!

No longer a fear or concern on my part of how others may or may not react to this drawing. I knew full well that this pose was best suited for this project. Even though the other photo taken at this time was more impressive and challenging I found this drawing to be my best drawing of Stephen.

When drawing the sexual organs of the human body, male or female, one starts to see things in a different level. After all, not many people get the opportunity to see such intimate details on a daily bases. Or in this case the duration it took to complete the drawing which took over two weeks.

This process goes back to seeing the object you are drawing in sections and focusing on textures and shapes rather than the over all figure that sits before you.

This is especially helpful for people who have had little experience drawing a live or nude model such as this one that has so much detail!

And over whelming it can be!

The background alone took a week to draw.

Again keeping the tip of the graphite pencil sharp each rock and pebble was captured one at a time.

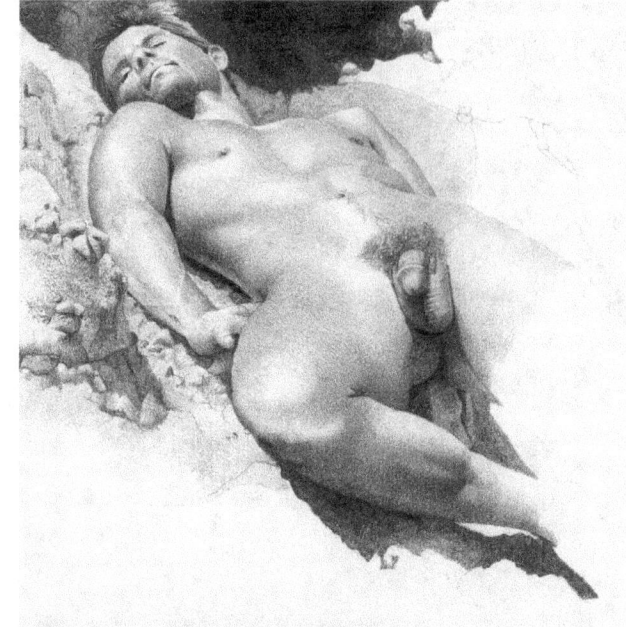

The best part of drawing a natural background is you don't have to draw it exactly as you see it in the photo but you do need to get pretty close. Especially where the body lays up against the hill and where some of the rocks are in front of him while others are seen in back of the model.

Even the smallest detail makes for an interesting pencil drawing. Whether the focus is on the relaxed curve of his penis, or the small pebbles to the left of the drawing, nothing should be left incomplete in the early stages of the drawing.

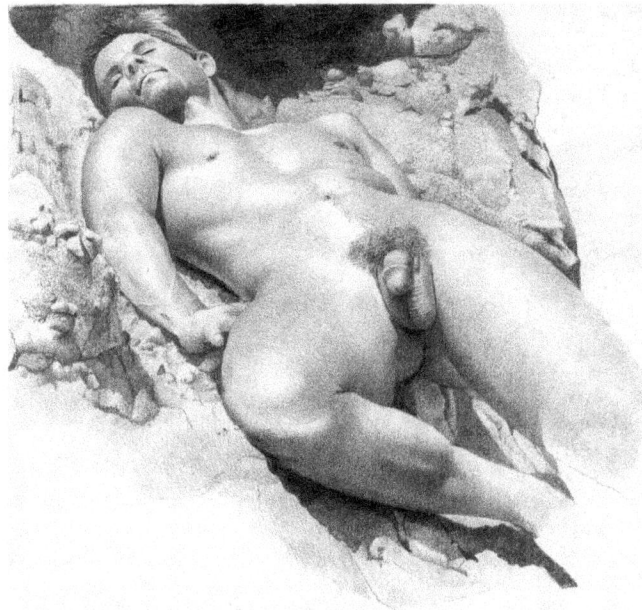

The darkest areas of the drawing took several layers of crosshatching before it was at its blackest black and you couldn't see any separation in the shading. Starting off light and make sure even the smallest pebbles are drawn, then gradually over lay the darker layers one at a time. How dark the shadow is will determine how many layers you place.

The sun is nearly over head so the shadows against his body and the rocks are all directly south of the object the shadows are coming from. Only the deepest areas will have the darkest shadows such as his chin, under his rib cage, and between his back and the rocks he is laying up against, and the protruding rocks to the left side of the drawing. This includes the dead center of the drawing, which appears to focus between his legs, and by all means lets not forget the upper side of the hill, where it appears to be a cave, or crawl space, just above

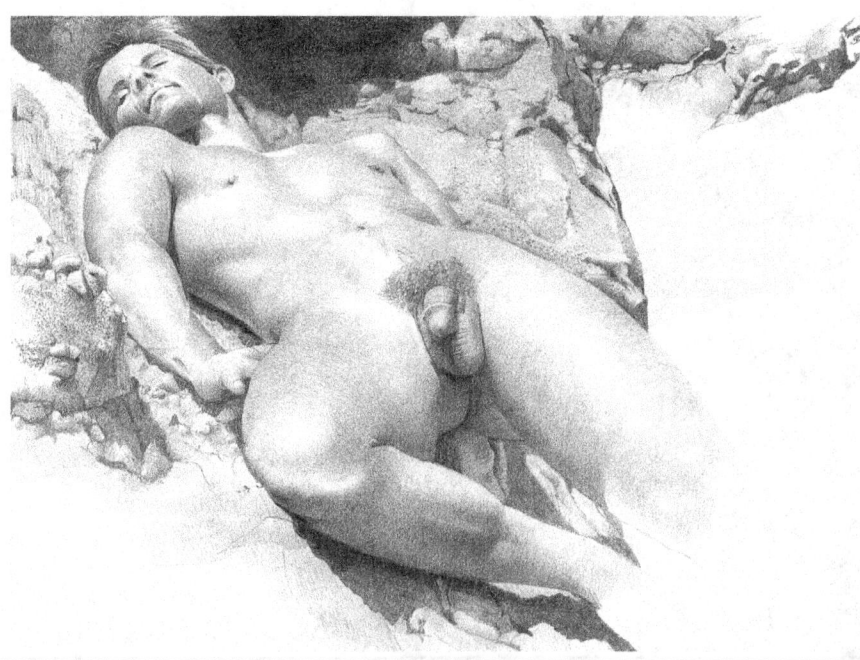

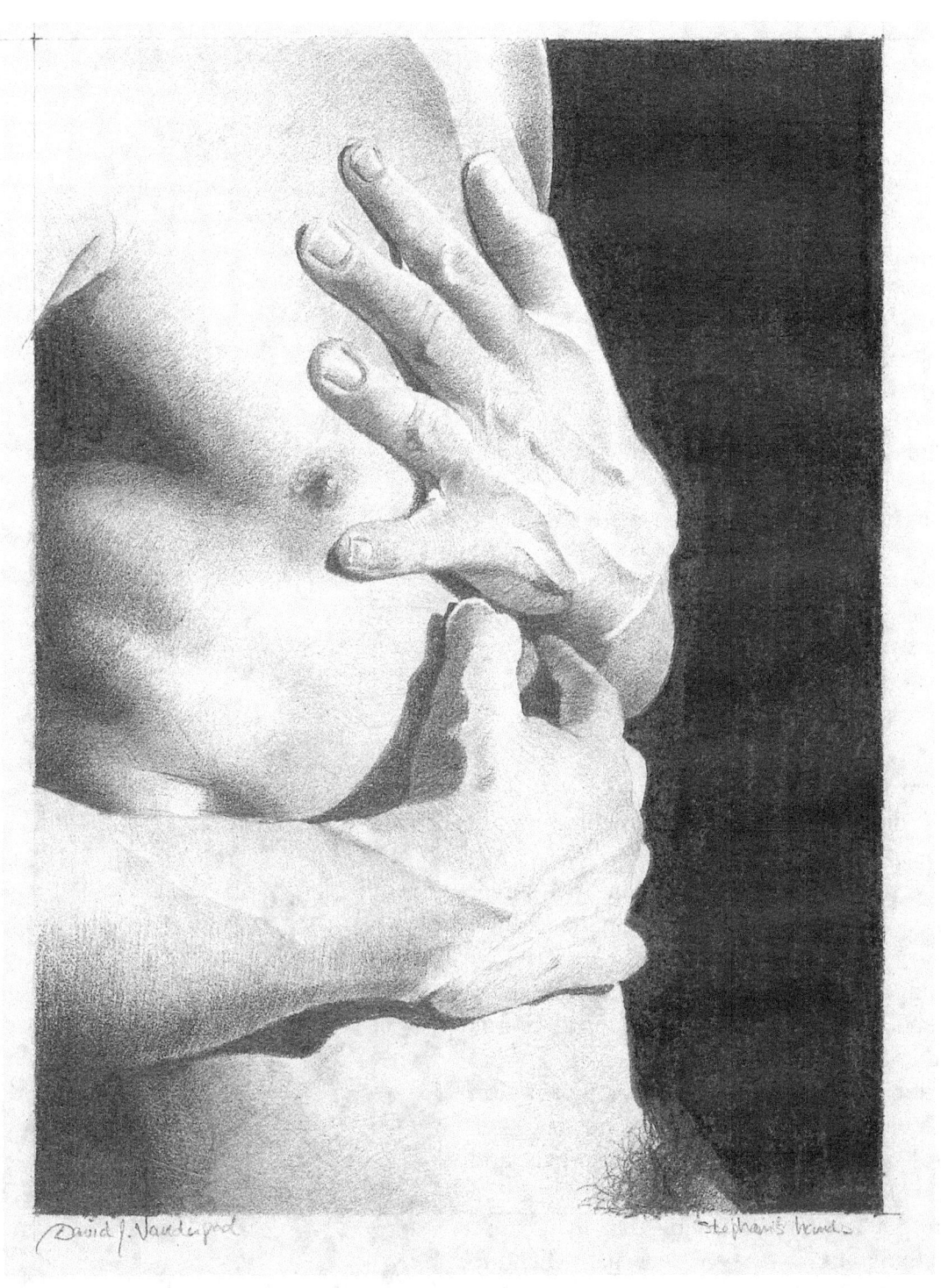

Stephen's Hands

Copyright 2007. David J. Vanderpool

Shown actual size.

Stephen's head.

This unfinished drawing, as it is seen here, is complete. Allowing the man and cliff to take over the paper it is emerging from.

Mikey.

When it comes to selecting a model to draw from, male or female, it is important as an artist to not only draw what they like but to catch the attention and interest of others.

Which brings the question: As an artist do you keep to the morals and standards you have set for your daily life and apply them to your art or do you move away from them for the sake of reaching others?

In doing so does reaching one group of people limit access to others?

For me personally, I draw not only what I find pleasing to see, but I am very selective with whom I draw. And this applies to commissioned drawings that the general public may never see.

Yes - I have turned down drawings that I did not want my name to be associated with. Not to say the challenge would not have been there, or I did not find the model interesting, but rather I was uncomfortable with the pose it's self - and what it represented.

A part of my own maturity? Perhaps.

Besides. What I may have rejected in the past does not mean I won't draw them in the years to come should I decide otherwise.

However, one rule which I have kept and will never change, or alter, is that I refuse to make the nudes I draw crude.

The human figure, no matter the sex, should show a classic form and appearance. Not so much in regards to beauty, for that is perhaps the only thing in art that should be open for interpretation, but rather the emotion the viewer will feel as a result of what they are seeing.

And thankfully networking with fellow artists and photographers has lead to opportunities that an artist like me otherwise might not have. Proving that the phrase "creative minds think alike" is never truer than when the right working relationship develops.

Having drawn Mikey a few times prior to the drawing show here, and received a huge collection of self-portraits from this creative photographer, I found it difficult to select the right drawing for my book project

The first two drawings of him were good but they were far from great. And great is what I was looking for when I was selecting and drawing portraits for *"Pencil Drawings Volume. 2 - a look into drawing men"*.

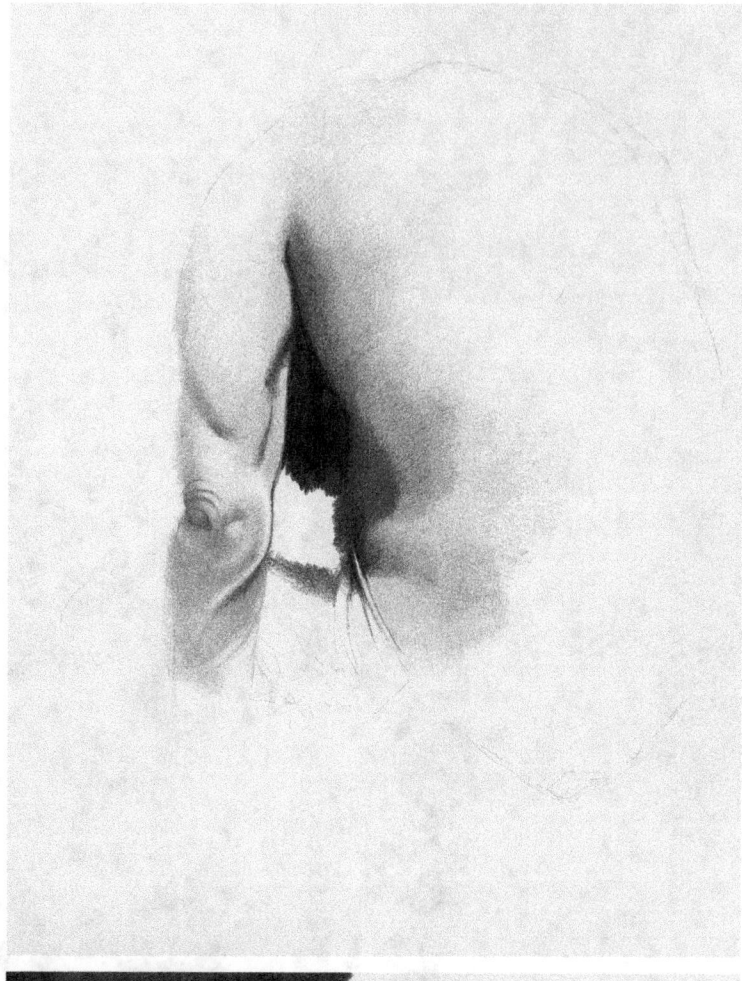

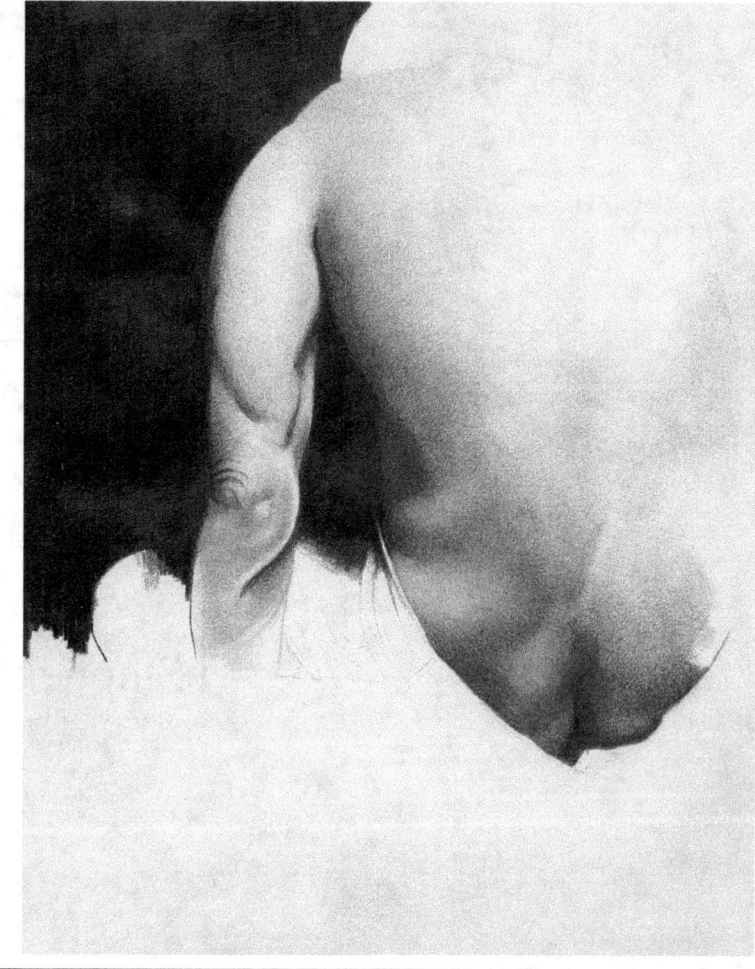

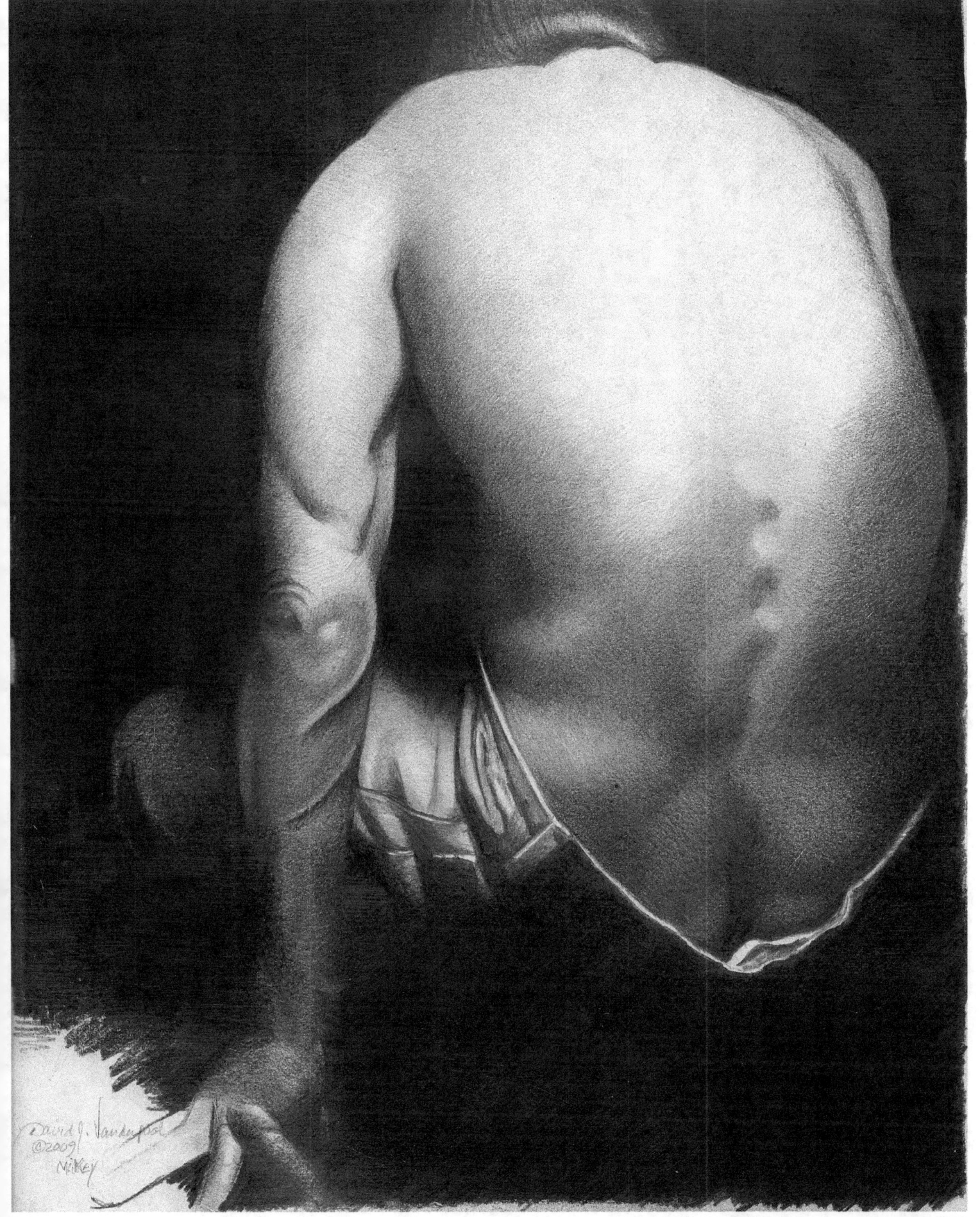

Mikey

8.5" x 11" graphite pencil drawing on paper. 2009

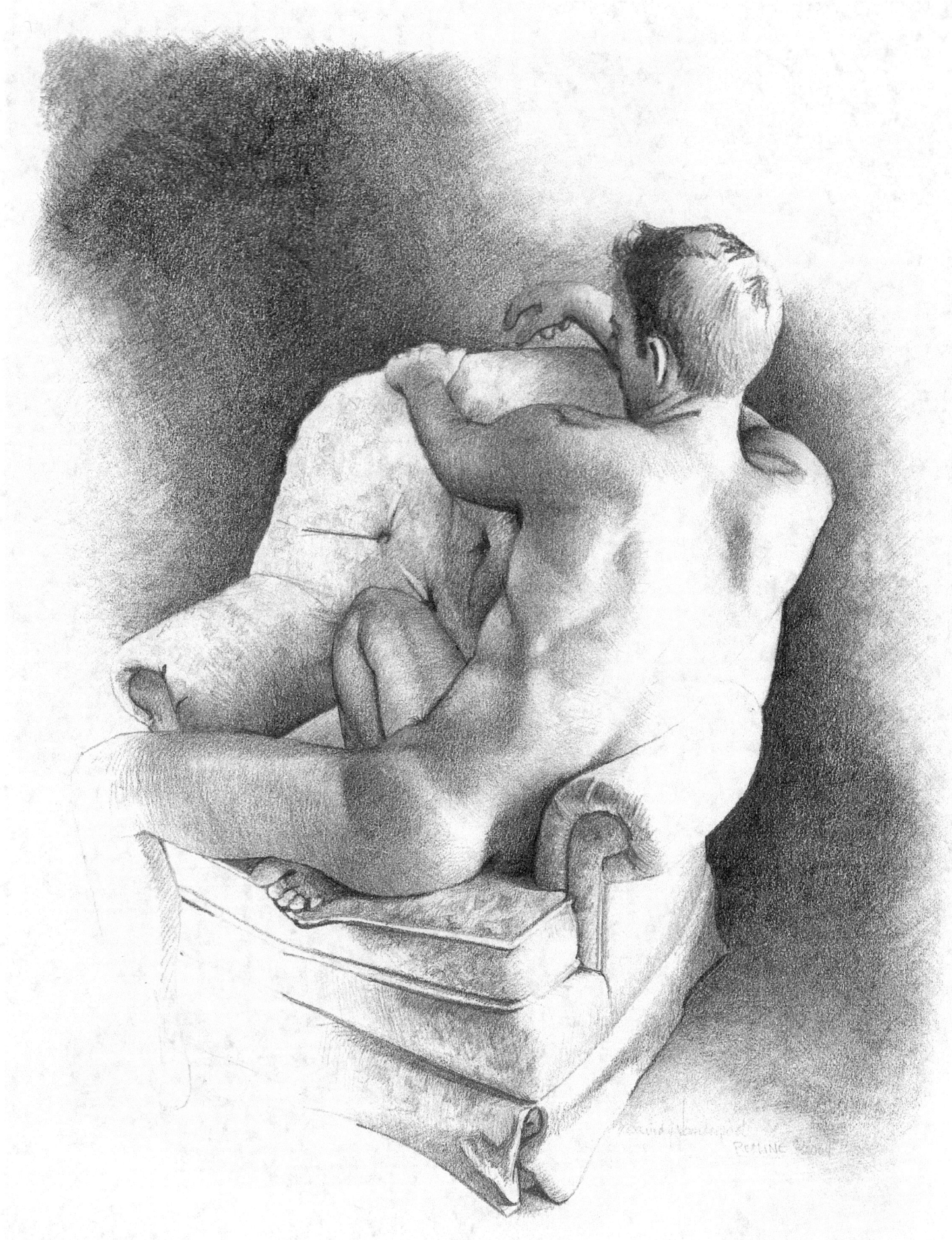

Whatever II

8.5" x 11" graphite pencil drawing on paper. 2006

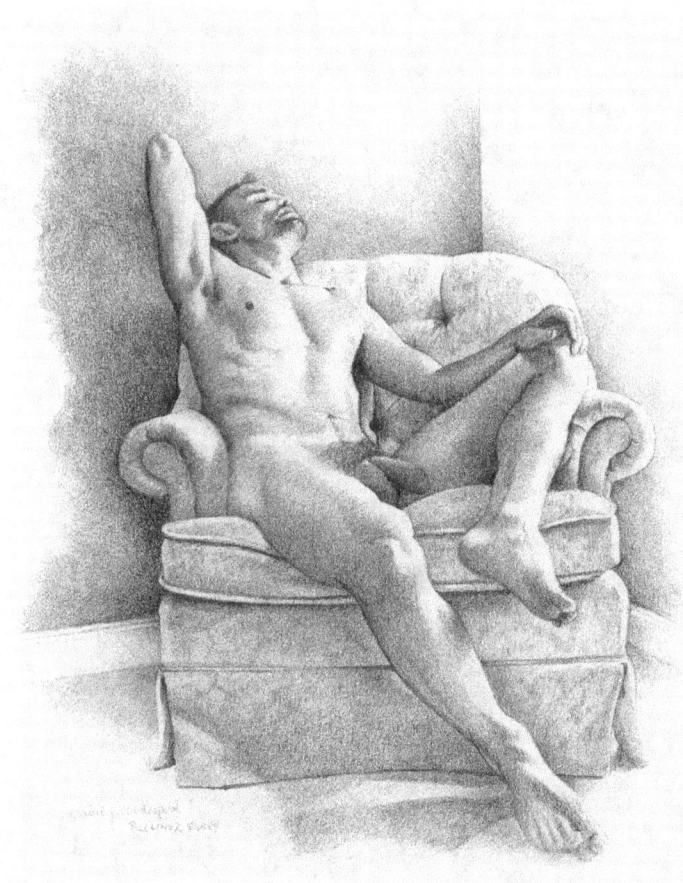

Whatever II - 8.5" x 11" graphite pencil drawing on paper

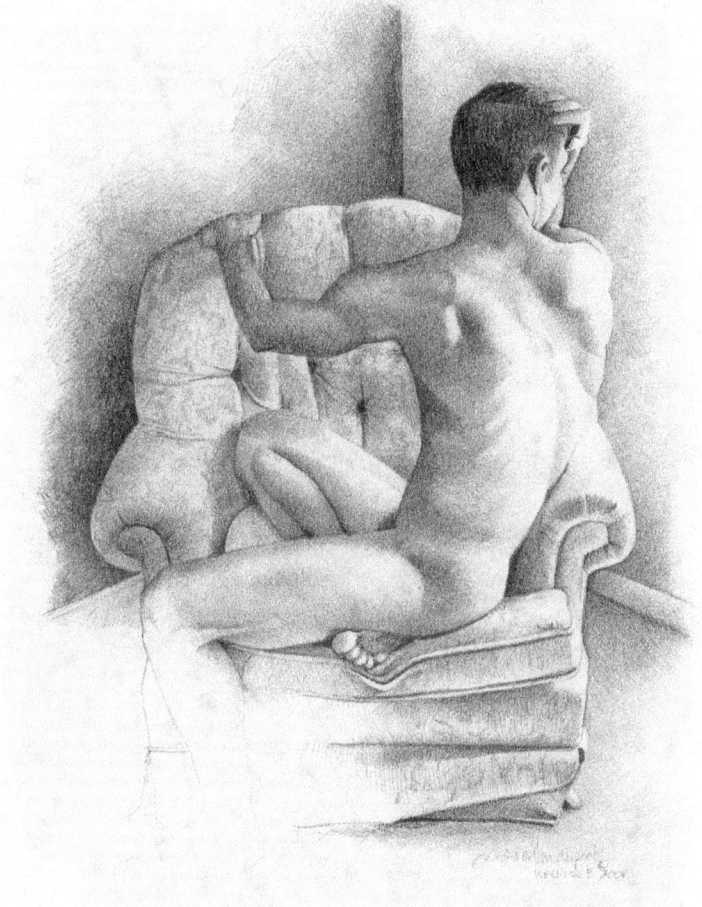

Whatever III - 8.5" x 11" graphite pencil drawing on paper

Knowing what I wanted I could have easily gone to local friends and asked them to pose for me. In fact, I had already done that, but there was still something missing that other's were not able to pull off.

Which is why I was thrilled when Mikey emailed me the photo that inspired this drawing.

Close to what I was looking for, if not better, this was a classic pose in every way imaginable!

From the clean lines starting at the back of his head, which was covered by a knitted cap, down to his loose-fitting jeans. From there this drawing takes the viewer to the left of the figure, along his pant leg, and then back up his arm.

The drawing shows more than just a muscular man in a simple pose it gives the viewer a peek at him while his back was turned.

Perhaps we see a little more than we should have?

No - it's just perfect.

Perfect and yet completely different from the series of the three drawings showing a man sitting in an upholstered chair.

Light, quickly draw, as noticeable by the rougher pencil strokes, this series was completed a few years after getting back into drawing in 2005.

A professional 'white collar and tie' kind of man, who modeled on the side and only for select friends. His only requirement was not to draw his face. Which was frustrating since I wanted to draw a series of him, and these three were what I wanted!

It wasn't until after I drew all three that he gave me permission to show them to the world. Which was a good thing because the third of the series went on display at The Bakersfield Museum of Arts that summer.

People have asked how the series got its name and the title came from an answer he gave me. When I asked what should I titled the series he simply said 'whatever" and so "Whatever I, II, and III" became the series title.

Proving that nudes do not have to be crude.

Mehdi.

When people think of a portrait they generally think of a painting created by an Old Master -- something you would find in a museum. Rarely would they consider a nude a portrait let alone a finished pencil drawing.

When I'm drawing figures I seek a classic pose. I look for one that might well be found in a museum in years to come or in the home of a serious art collector. I want a pose that focuses not so much on the nudity of the model but on the emotion the model is portraying. I believe capturing the emotion of the models pose should be the first thing viewers notice in the drawings they are studying.

In a world where art is limited to what society says is acceptable, the male nude continues to be looked upon as taboo, or even homoerotic, no matter who the artist is. The only way to overcome this is for the artist to go beyond what may or may not be accepted and to create what he or she wants to create. For passion, no matter how it is expressed, should never be denied or prevented from being expressed – as long as the work is done to honor the beauty as God that He Himself has created and blessed us with.

Not to pervert or alter the creation but to honor and respect it. Nor to worship what we see but to admire and recapture what is before us.

Nudity in itself is just a nakedness. But a drawing of a male nude that displays emotion, or makes the viewer wonder who that model is, and question what the model may be thinking, that's art.

As already mentioned - drawing from a photograph allows the artist to take a closer look at the model. Where as doing so with a live model can often be uncomfortable for not only the model but the artist.

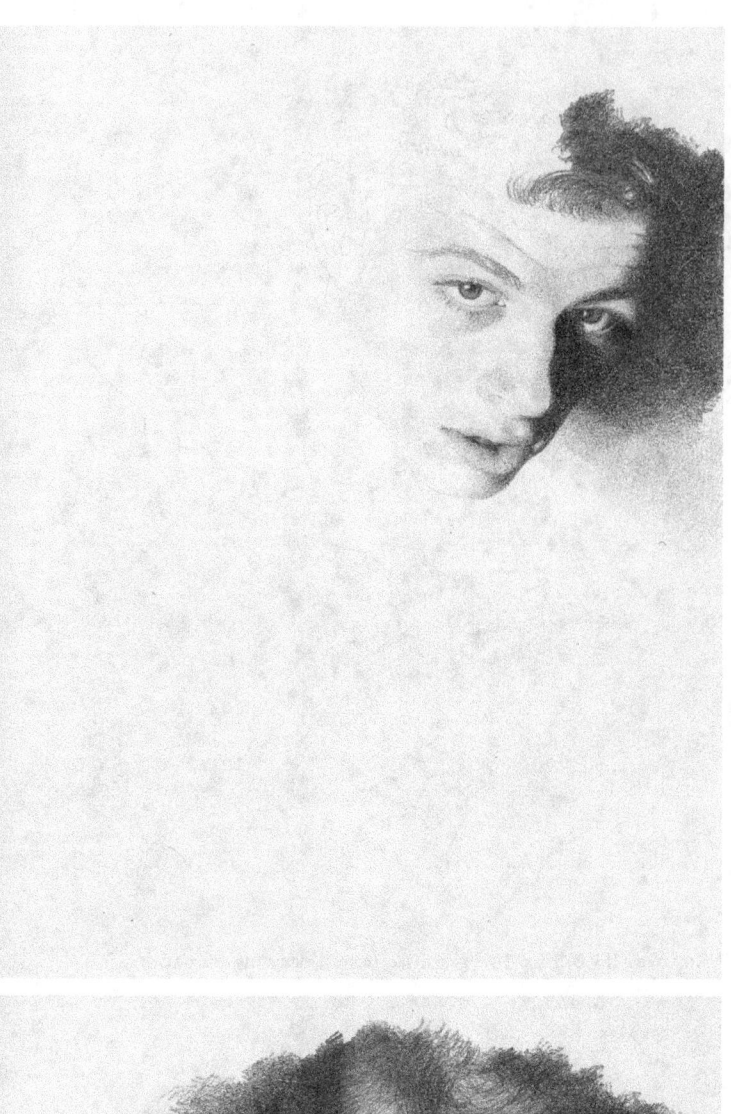

It allows the artist (me) to work with photographers all over the world who have already set the standard for the quality in the models I am able to draw.

Such was the case of Parisian photographer Marc Armytage who specializes in male nudes. He works predominantly in studio settings, in a variety of styles ranging from traditional nudes to more expressive work inspired by theatre and dance, where the model's nudity is of secondary importance.

Since I wanted to draw portraits and figure drawings that showed passion or an expression that allowed the viewer to feel or question what the model was going through, this pose of Mehdi was perfect for what I was looking for!

The drawing shown here is my second attempt at drawing Marc's highly expressive photography. Not because the first attempt didn't turn out right I just felt I would have a better chance at capturing the detail in his face if I cropped the photo above the knees and removed most the background.

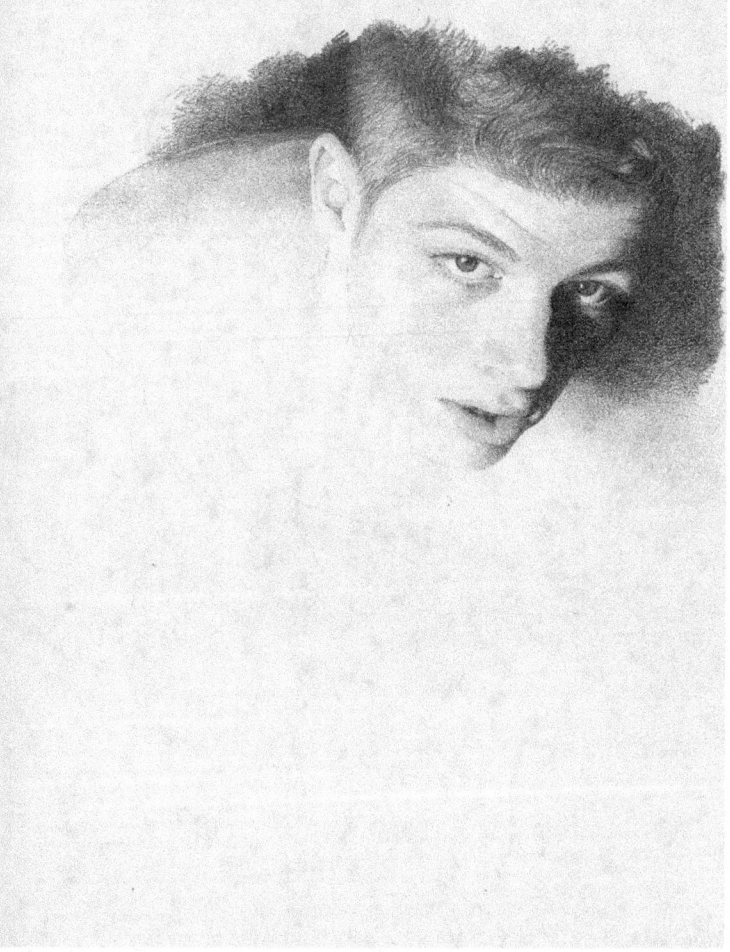

Not to take away from Armytage's excellent work but to make his photograph work with the talent I have. A combined effort if you will.

When it comes to drawing a figure that appear as if it is jumping off the page it is very important that each line be placed on the paper following the curve of each muscle. Never using a straight line and always make the

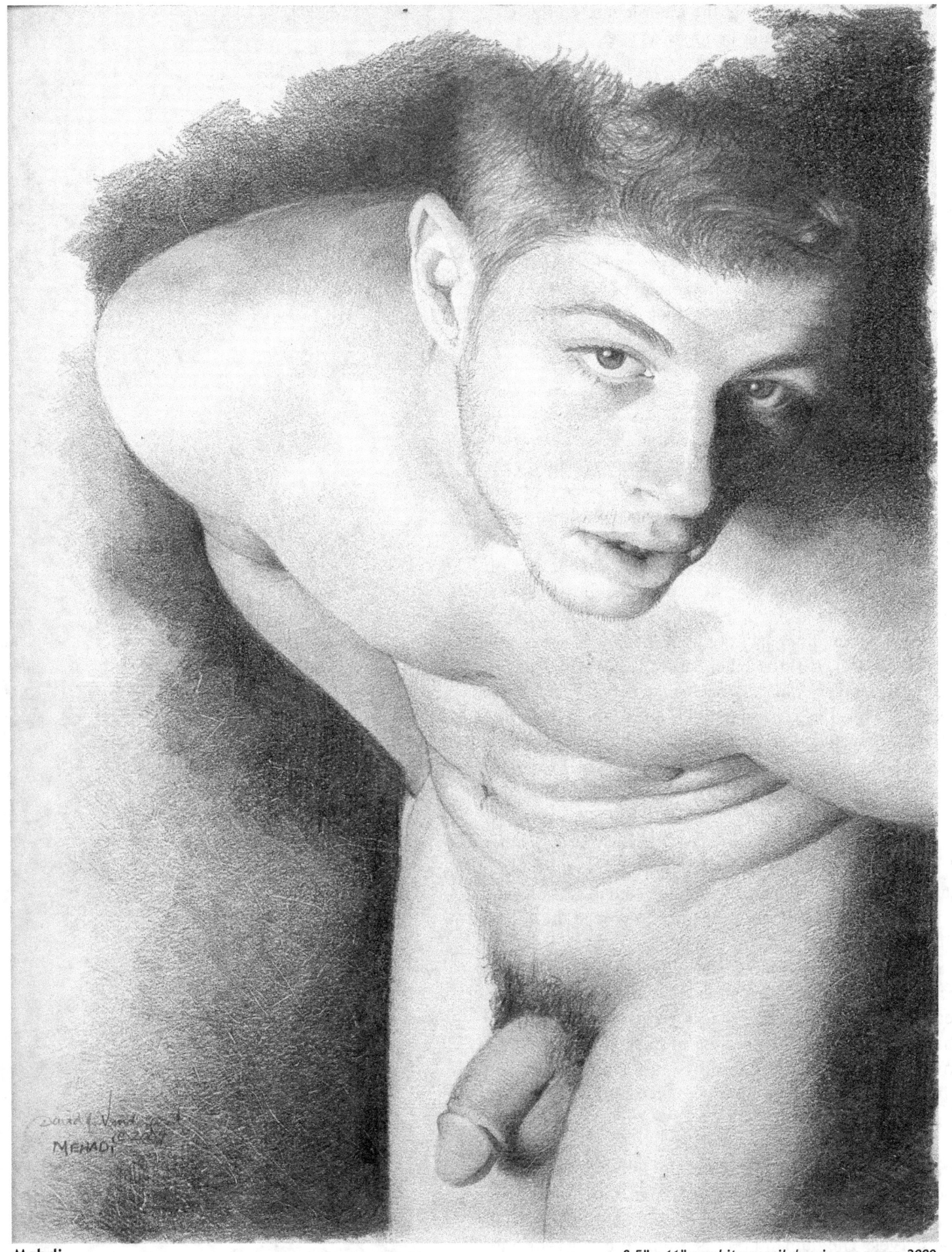

Mehdi

8.5" x 11" graphite pencil drawing on paper. 2009

closet object in the drawing the main focus. In this case it was his nose, lips, and of course his eyes.

Keeping his skin tones light, with just enough grays to allow the highlights to reflect off his nose, forehead and upper lip, the surrounding shadows brought the drawing to life as soon as the first step in the drawing was completed.

Even though this drawing shows a full frontal nude male. The use of the darker pencils makes his mouth and eyes stand out allowing the viewer to focus on the details of his face before sneaking a quick peek elsewhere before looking away and back toward those eyes. Or do as most viewers have already done and look longer at his nude form.

The lines of his shoulders clearly wrap from behind his back and up across his shoulder. They lighten as they start to move down toward his chest. I kept the lines close against one another and made sure that the left side of the drawing stayed clean through a little crosshatching. I did more crosshatching on the right shoulder since that area shows a shadow that takes over that corner of the drawing (In progress step 2 and 3).

In order for Mehdi to appear as if he is coming off the page the background that surrounds him was done in the same style as his hair. Starting at the young man's forehead I drew lines beginning at the hairline and with solid bold strokes, I lifted them upward and off the paper, making sure each stroke matched the way his hair is combed. Then I used the darker 4B and 6B pencils for the darkest strands, and 2B and lighter for the rest of his hair. Crosshatching starts to take over where pencil lines for his hair leave off, keeping to the style already established in this drawing.

I didn't want the background to be blurry as with other drawings in this book. It was important, then, to keep each line to a set pattern, crosshatching small sections at a time, and then alternating the direction seen at the edges. (In progress step 4)

With the unusual angle and positioning of his arms behind him his chest muscles come to a sudden end. This leaves a nearly solid line that is created by the shadow that appears to cut the drawing in half. This makes the lower half of the drawing slowly go out of focus and gives the light blurry effect to the rest of his figure. (In progress step 4).

Continuing with curved lines the folds seen at his midsection and side are set carefully in place. Make sure the illustration of his body is, in fact, bending toward you.

His stomach, though firm and without obvious body fat, curves. The human body is round after all. Not only

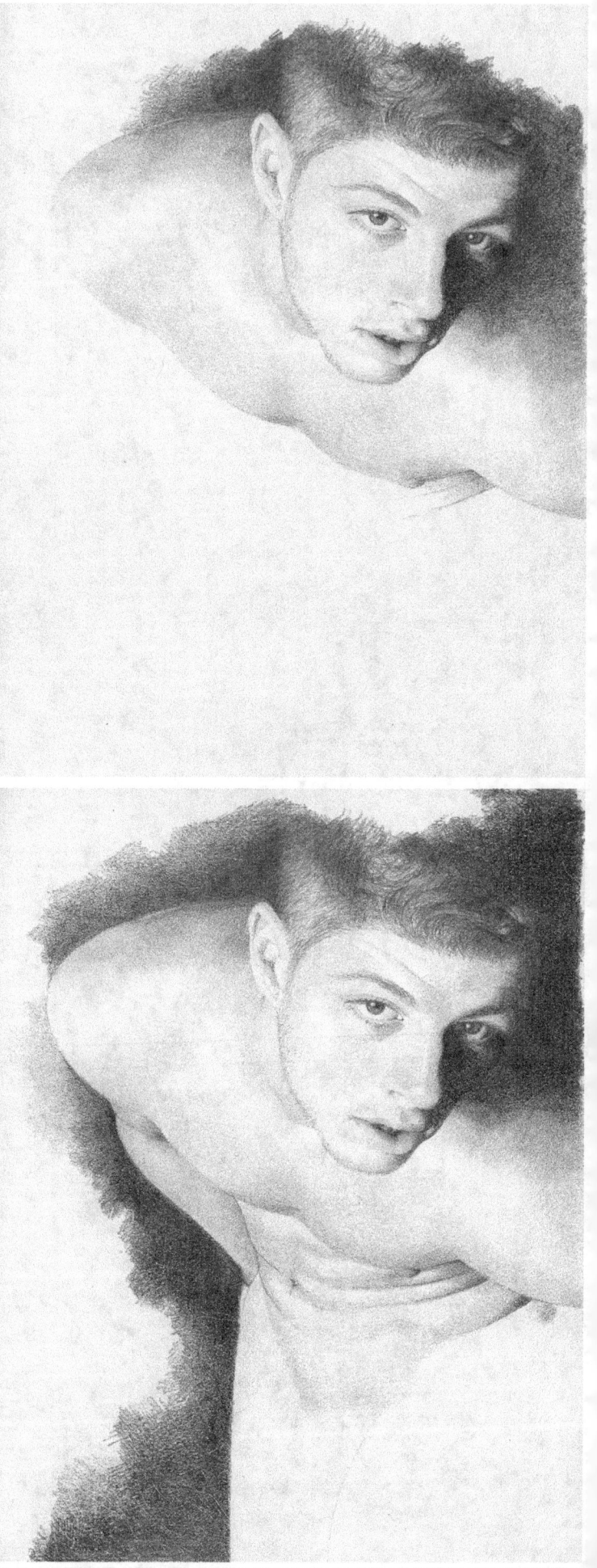

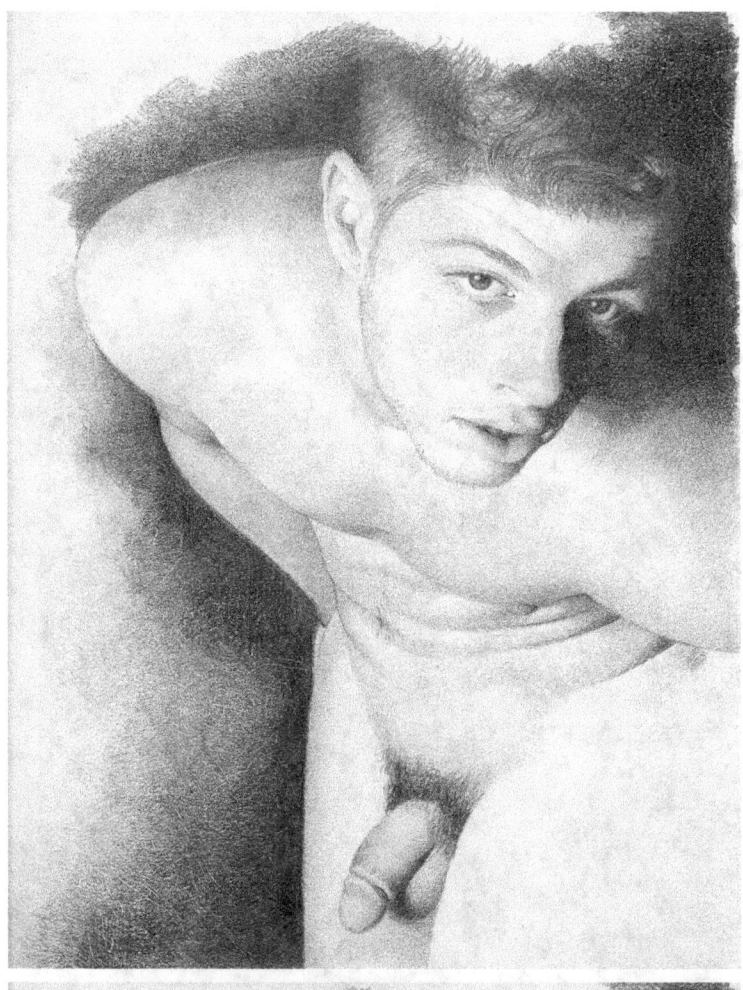

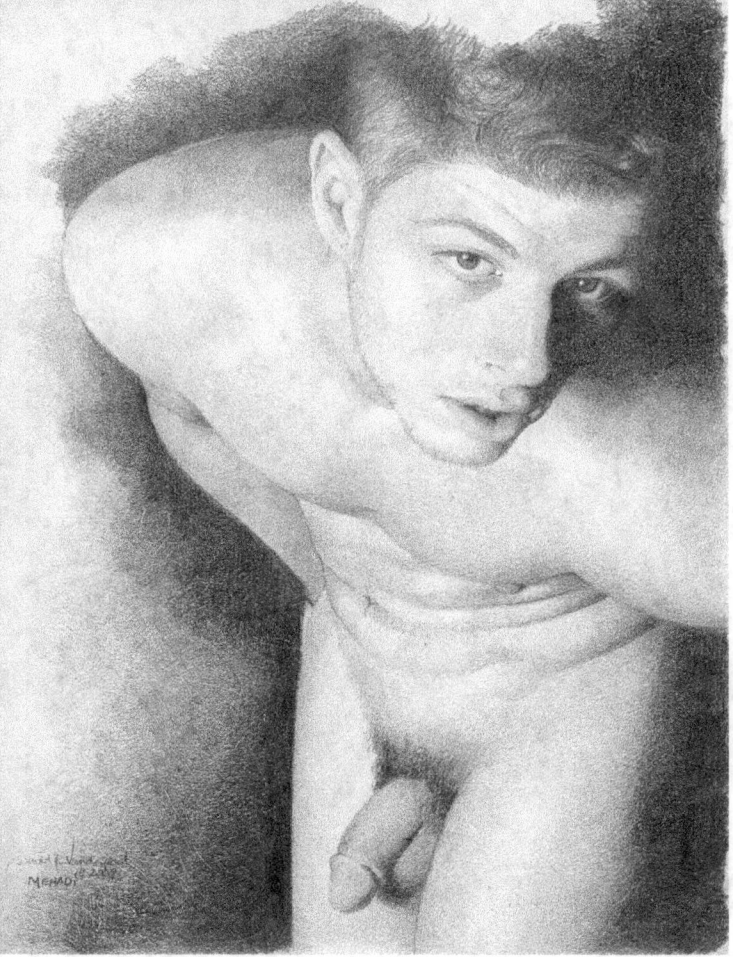

do the lines in this section curve upwards from the base of his penis but they curve around from the right side of his hip to the left.

Drawing his penis and testicles is no different than drawing his nose, lips, or shoulder. As an artist, you focus on the shape of the object and not the object itself. Pay close attention to where the shadows are, where the strongest highlights are, and, of course, where the curves are placed on the paper.

Keep your mind on the section of the model being drawn rather than the object you are drawing. This allows the brain to take over and see the grays needed for the skin tones and where to place the deep shadows. It helps you see where each line and wrinkle should be, as well as understand how much of the object needs to be drawn in full detail. The relatively blurry background gives the drawing a three-dimensional look upon completion.

Rotating the drawing, be it sideways or even upside-down, allows the brain to kick in and override what you think you are seeing and start to draw what you do see.

Before you know it you have nearly finished a true classic male nude. No matter who is viewing the drawing, they can see beauty for what it is, to be admired, respected and understood that beauty is truly the work of God. Only it has been copied on paper by a photographer and then by an artist.

In completing this drawing of Mehdi, the shadow that took over the top right corner of the drawing must take over the lower right corner as well. The shadow that slowly starts to cover the model on the right side of the drawing is at a distance, behind him on the left side.

Mehdi is left in the middle slowly emerging through the darkness as if it were a fog taking over what surrounds him.

Grace

For me .personally drawing women requires the model to be graceful and self respecting. A model that shows true beauty whether it be a portrait or in a pose such as this.

Granted, this strict requirement of mine makes it difficult at times to find the right model or pose. This leads to fewer drawings of women even though the desire to create such beauty is strong. I have discovered over time the final outcome can be well worth the wait.

This is why professional networking with photographers and professional models is necessary when it comes to expanding ones resources. Working with those they may never otherwise get the opportunity to work with.

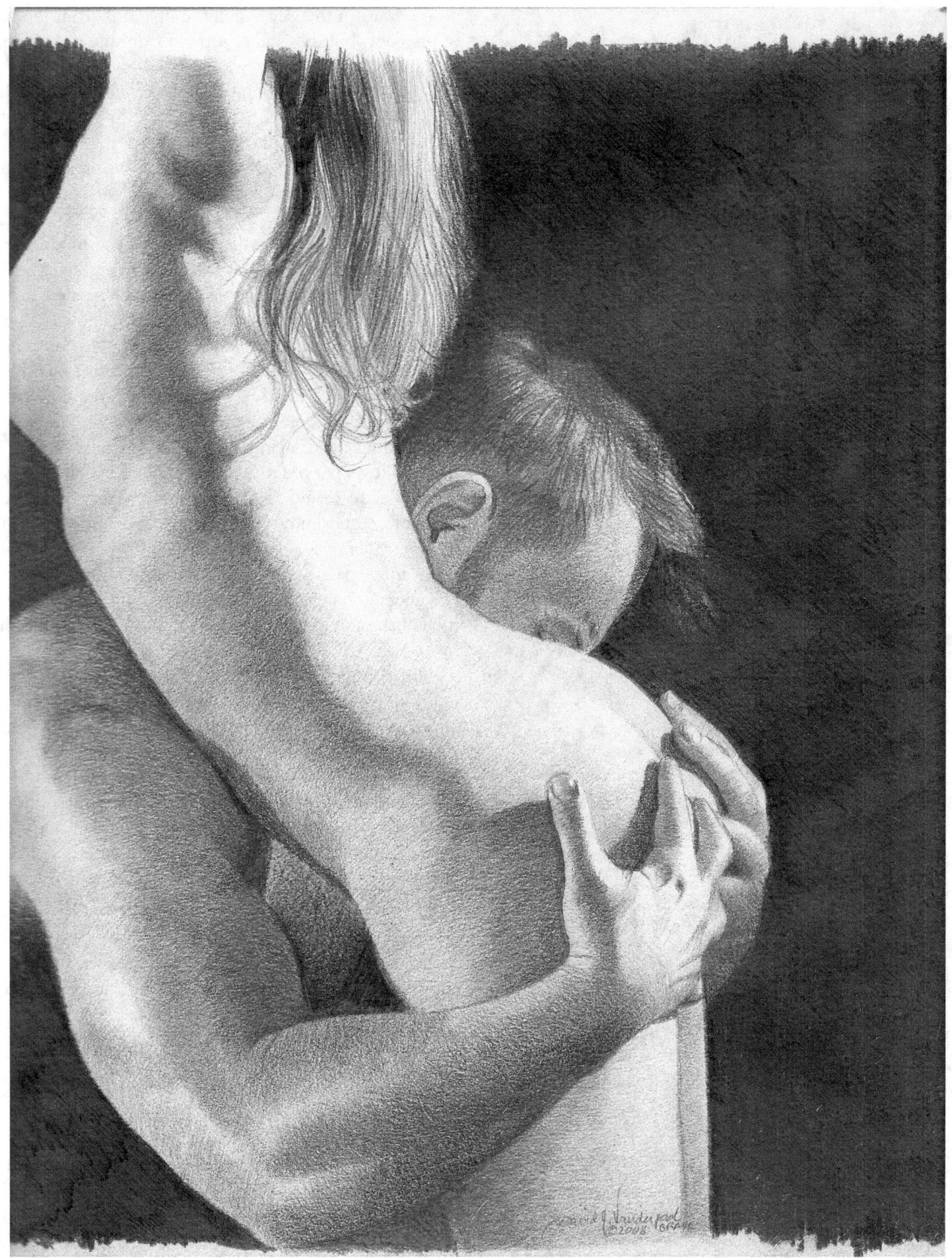

Grace

8.5" x 11" graphite pencil drawing on paper. 2008

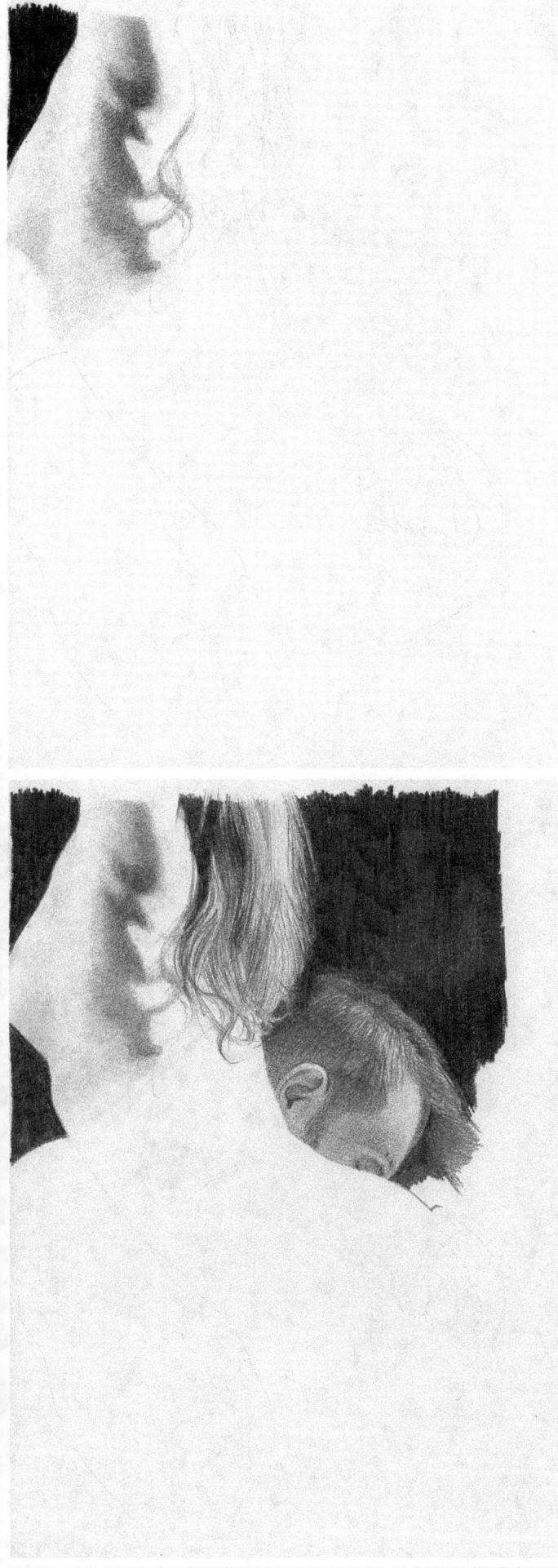

One of the first photographers I started to network was Tony Ryan, from Northcot, Australia, who had photographed and self published a wide range of calendars and posters that has gained great respect and popularity in Australia as well as in the USA, UK and Europe.

However, finding the right pose and photo as a reference is no different than working with a live model. You must not only work with what best suites your style and creative level but offer enough to challenge you as an artist.

Never limit ones ability by sticking to what works best or have already accomplished. Strive to make the next drawing better than the last and if that takes you out of your comfort zone, so be it.

And in this case, I spent a period looking for photos and models that required to me draw hands, before setting on the one that inspired this drawing, that was taken by Tony Ryan.

Drawing hands was something I had feared for the longest time. In fact, I used to avoid them all together, until I made an effort to learn the anatomy of the human hand.

Drawn in 2008, and knowing well in advance my style had taken on a heavy dark appearance to draw just a woman. The image of this couple, which focused on the man's hands, was perfect for my needed transition from drawing men and getting back into drawing women.

Creating the extremely strong features shown his fingers and arms the drawing slowly takes on a softer feel as the woman's figure takes shape.

Granted, one cannot see her arms or face, but her torso is all woman, and therefore had to be soft and feminine.

With no eyes in the drawing to use as my starting point, as I do with a portrait, I started with the top left hand corner since I am right handed. This prevents from smearing the graphite as the drawing starts to take form.

In this drawing, I knew I had to keep her as light as possible, yet bring out just enough of her rib cage and breasts to help make her one of the focal points to this drawing. Using a 2H, 4H and an "F" pencil allowed me to do just that,

Usually I don't bother with the background to a drawing until the main figure is completed. In this instance it was necessary to place the solid black background shown here in order for the light reflecting off her body to stand out.

Crosshatching the background takes time and patience. Keep in mind working in layers by placing the lines in the same direction is important so that reflection from the dark graphite doesn't cause an distracting patterns. Any distracting patterns would take away from the figure in the foreground.

Alternating the direction from layer to layer, makes the graphite dark and should only be applied one layer at a time. Top to bottom the first layer and then left to right for the second. And yes... a third layer can run along the top right corner to the bottom left cover.

The goal here is to prevent any blotches from appearing within the solid background and prevent the darkest graphite from distributing evenly.

Placing as many layers as needed to get the job done is important. Then once more apply one final layer, with a lighter, harder pencil for last time.

The background to this drawing took five layers using an Ebony graphite pencil.

Keeping to the natural curves to her body, each pencil line follows the same direction of each muscle, as it pulls and curves around the figure. Especially when drawing her hips and rib cage.

Her hair was drawn using my lighter pencils, with an exception of a 6B to bring out the deepest shadow, and the deepest shadows were placed first!

Where one would have normally started with a lighter pencils for her body. With her hair it is best to start by filling in the shadows first and then over laying the medium and lighter strands of hair so that the hair blends naturally. Using your lighter pencils are a blending tool.

With hair blending doesn't mean you cross over the lines you have placed with your prior pencils.

Following the direction which hair naturally grows, from the scalp outwards, and using various pencils, the layers of hair eventually takes shape and the cut and style of her hair will quickly fall into place and take on a fuller appearance.

Keeping the pencil lines sharp and up close to one another, visible and not blending flat against the paper, the lines will help the strands of hair stand out and appear more realistic.

Working in layers, it was important to bring out the dimension shown in the model or photograph, and to make sure that the hair did not end up appearing as a flat surface. It was necessary to work the highlights and shadows side by side and allowing light to filter through the lines.

A drawing such as this, or any drawing for that matter, the kneaded rubber eraser continues to be an artist's best friend.

Using an eraser as a tool, rather than to just keep the paper clean, allows the figure to keep a softer appearance, as light reflects off of her. Remove any blotchy pencil

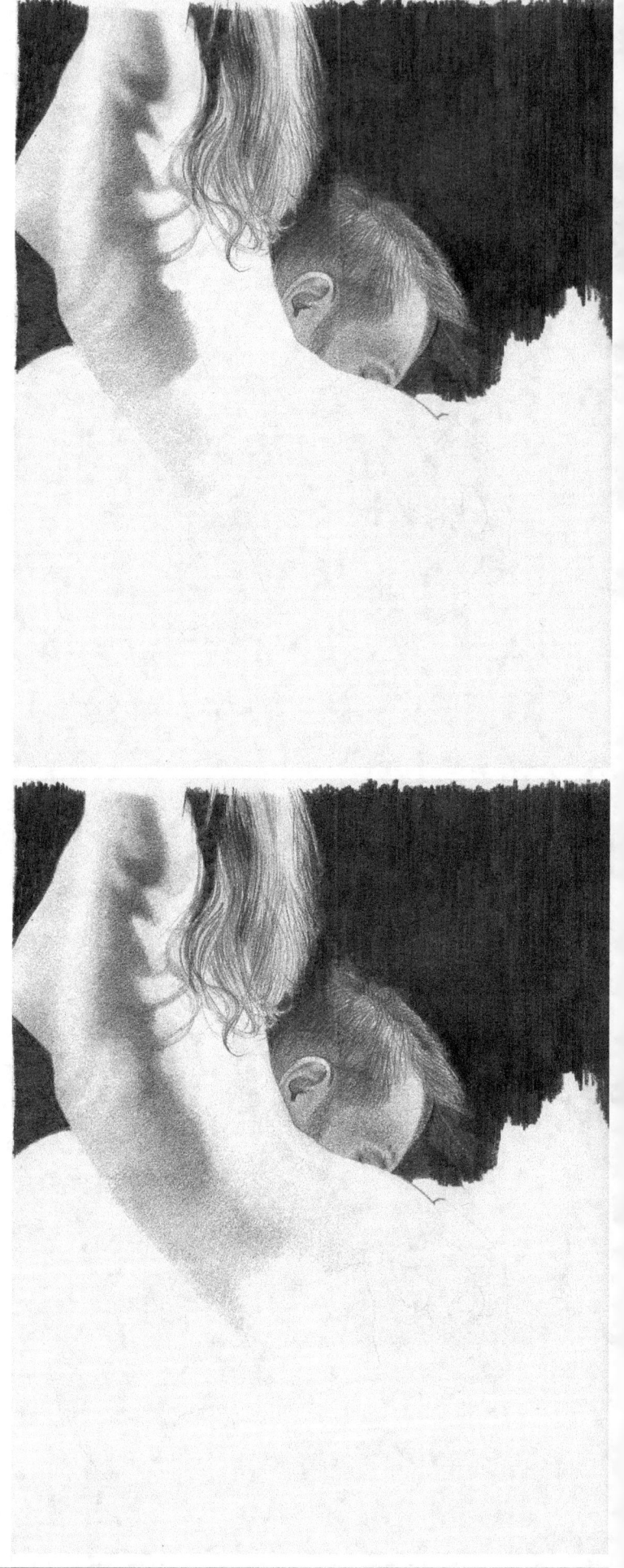

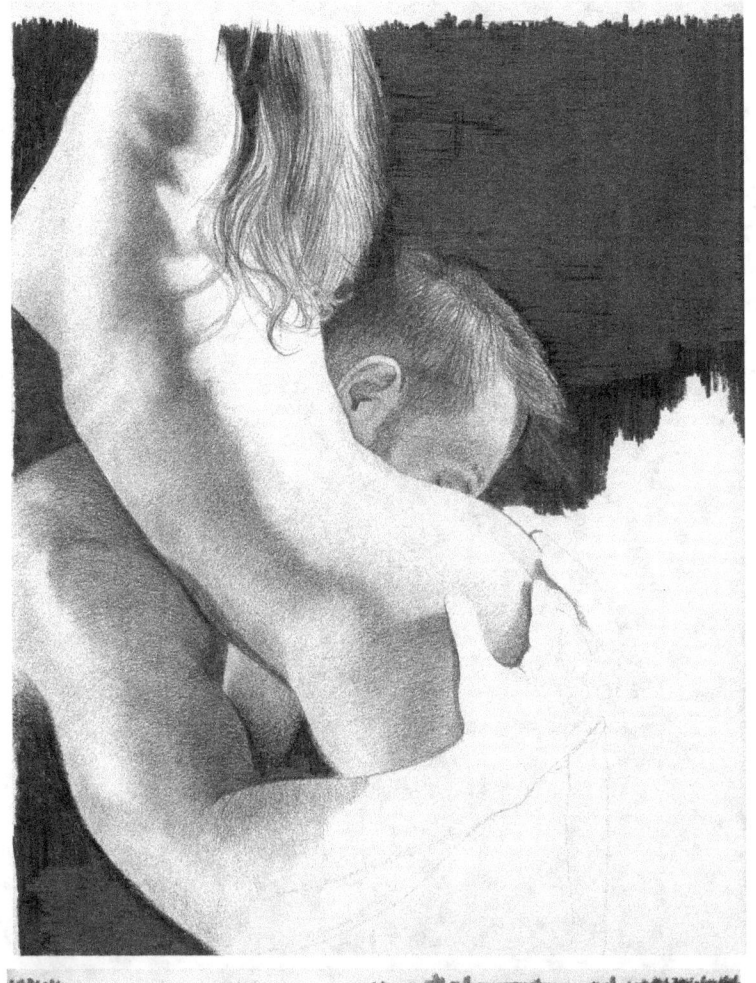

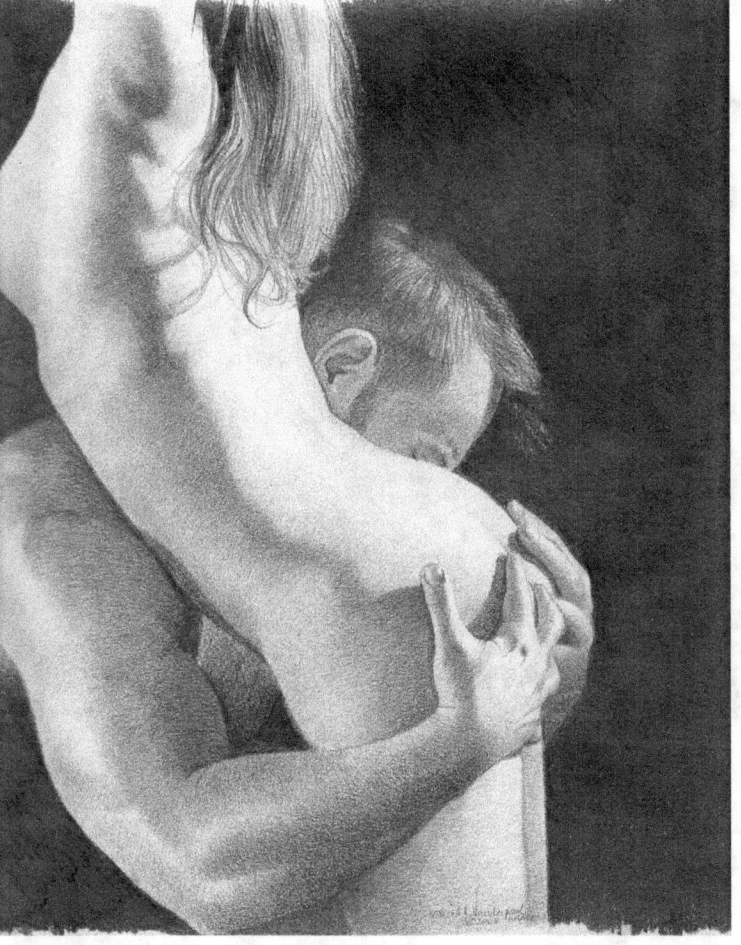

marks that crosshatching or lines tend to leave behind at times.

Without pressing too hard any area can easily be lightened up in order for the highlights to help give shape to her curves. This is a must when dealing with curves and shadows.

Even though the woman is the main focus for this drawing it is just as important to get the man just right. After all, with out him holding her, she is just another naked woman.

His hair is drawn the same as already mentioned but with a little more gray hair in some areas. This allows the man to appear in his mid-to-late forties even though we don't see his face,

The detail in his hair and eyebrow was left slightly blurry than the rest of him so that his hands appeared clear and later the main focus to the drawing.

Making sure that his arm and hands appeared to be strong enough to lift and hold her over his shoulder required using every available graphite pencils I had. From 2H to 8B and then an Ebony for the deepest shadow.

Starting off with a light to medium range pencils each line followed the contour of his muscles.

There are no flat surface here except the one area where his upper arm and lower arm meet. All other muscles curves to take shape and expand as a the result of him taking hold of her in his hands.

His hands were drawn to reveal each finger and vein. Bringing out the deep shadows and the highlights so they jumped off the page and appear believable – that they can in fact hold such beauty gracefully.

The larger highlighted areas were left untouched. Allowing the natural color of the paper to show through as seen with her back and upper arm. This allowed the brightest possible highlights to work with the darkest shadows and adding to the richness to the drawing.

The Sanford Ebony pencil is perfect for the deepest shadows in the drawing. The area between her stomach and his shoulder, the deepest shadows near his arm and her leg, and to help make his hands the strongest feature in the entire drawing, the shadow between his fingers and the flesh of her buttocks.

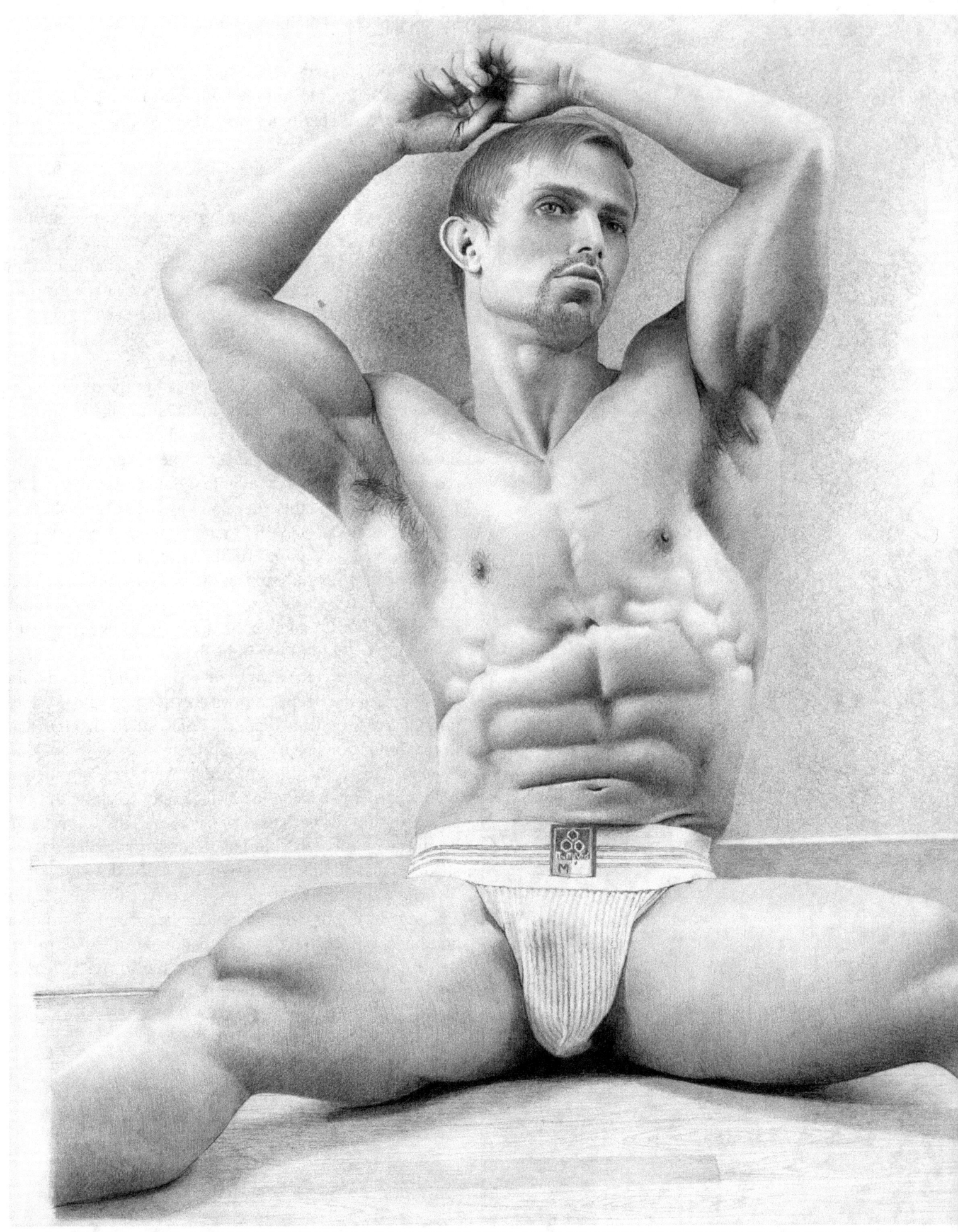

Chapter Four
In Closing - Bigger Is Better!

Looking back on the drawings featured within these pages you would think they were created by two different artist. However I can assure you that is not the case. Just one artist reinventing himself with each drawing he creates.

Definitely the result of challenging myself to make each drawing better than the last? Learning from trial and error, or not knowing how much longer I'll be able to draw, has effected the out come of each project I've taken on?

All options are possible for change.

All are good reason for growth!

By 2010 I knew I had to take my drawings from a rough bold approach and concentrate on making each line smoother, closer together, and sharp in order to achieve the realistic appearance to each drawing.

No longer was just capturing the likeness of a person

acceptable. I had to stop viewers in their tracks and make them question if they were looking at a photograph or a drawing.

To do that I needed to refine each line, each stroke, as I placed them on the paper and that meant taking my time. I had to make sure that each of my lines blended with the other in order to achieve the appearance I was creating in each drawing,

So why the difference in style from one drawing to the other? I'd like to think it's not by choice but in all fairness it was the result of poor choices.

The type of paper an artist uses effects how a drawing will turn out. Size matters when it comes to working with fine detail in a portrait or figure drawing, but the type of paper should be just as important as the model he chooses to work with.

Too rough and the drawing turn out the same.

Too small and you will lose the detail that attracted you to that person in the first place.

Most of the drawings featured in my series of pencil drawing books were created 8.5" x 11". It wasn't until those projects were completed that I was able to draw using much larger paper since I was no longer having to stop and scan the works in the process as I went along.

This is where trial and error continues to teach me to be patient and use what works and not try something new just for the sake of never having tried it before!

Several drawings were started and quickly came to a halt due to the wrong

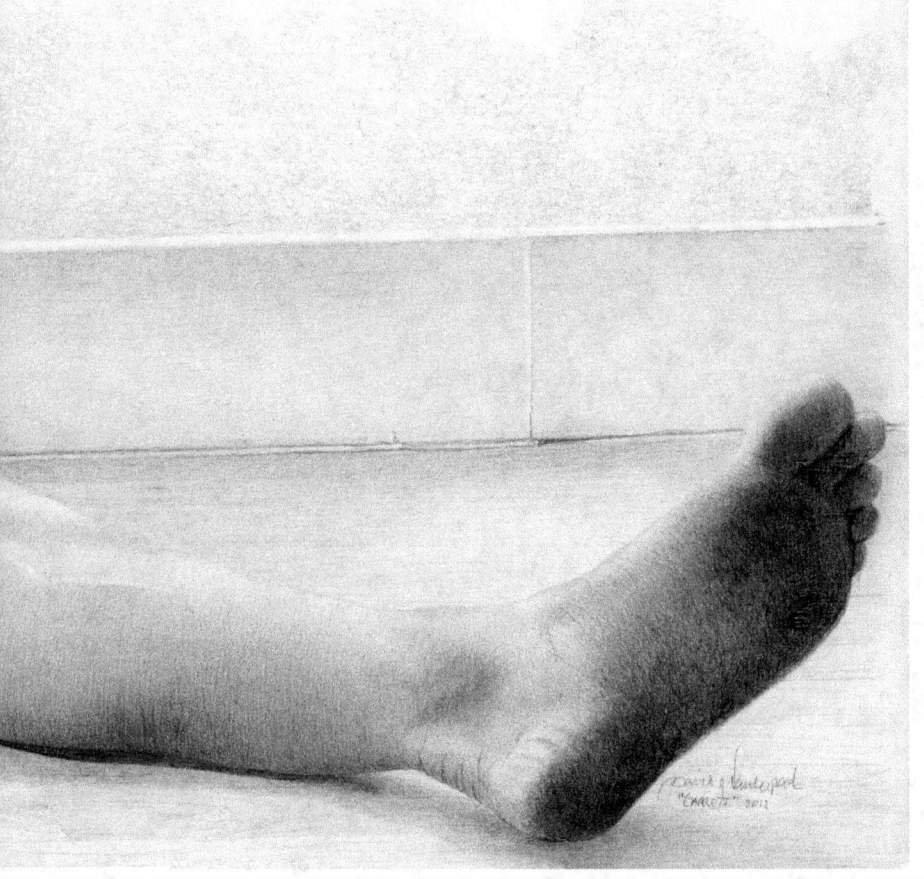

Garrett
25" x 18" graphite pencil drawing on paper
August 2012

selection of paper.

You know the type - over priced drawing paper with the edges uncut. Perfect for art to be displayed floating behind glass. Great paper! Just not right for the detail I need to capture in my drawings.

The first large drawing was "Kevin - Repose" (page 10). A young model friend who wanted me to draw him nude ever since my portrait of him in 2010 (page 12).

Within the first two days of drawing him, I realized the paper I had purchased was wrong for the job. So taking the advice from a fellow artist, I searched the art supply stores for Bristol paper and discovered even Bristol paper came in various thickness and surface textures, but not as rough as the drawing paper I had tried to use.

Purchasing several sheets, not knowing if I'd be able to find the paper in stock when I wanted another piece, I knew I was setting myself up for change when it came to how I and others would see me as a pencil artist.

Thicker, smoother, the Bristol paper allowed the most intimate detail in the drawing to be clear and sharp. Instantly I knew this was going to be an awesome piece of work!

No longer dealing with shadows that were too dark, skin tones too blotchy, and pencil lines could be counted should anyone be foolish enough to attempt.

And most important. The eyes and lips were once again clear, sharp, and the focal point to the drawing.

Needless to say when starting the drawing titled "Courting" (seen here and on page 7), I made no mistake and knew what paper to select and therefore just how it was going to turn out even before I started drawing.

Now that is a sign of a great drawing in the making! When you know what it will be like before a pencil even hits the paper!

Add the fact I wanted to draw my

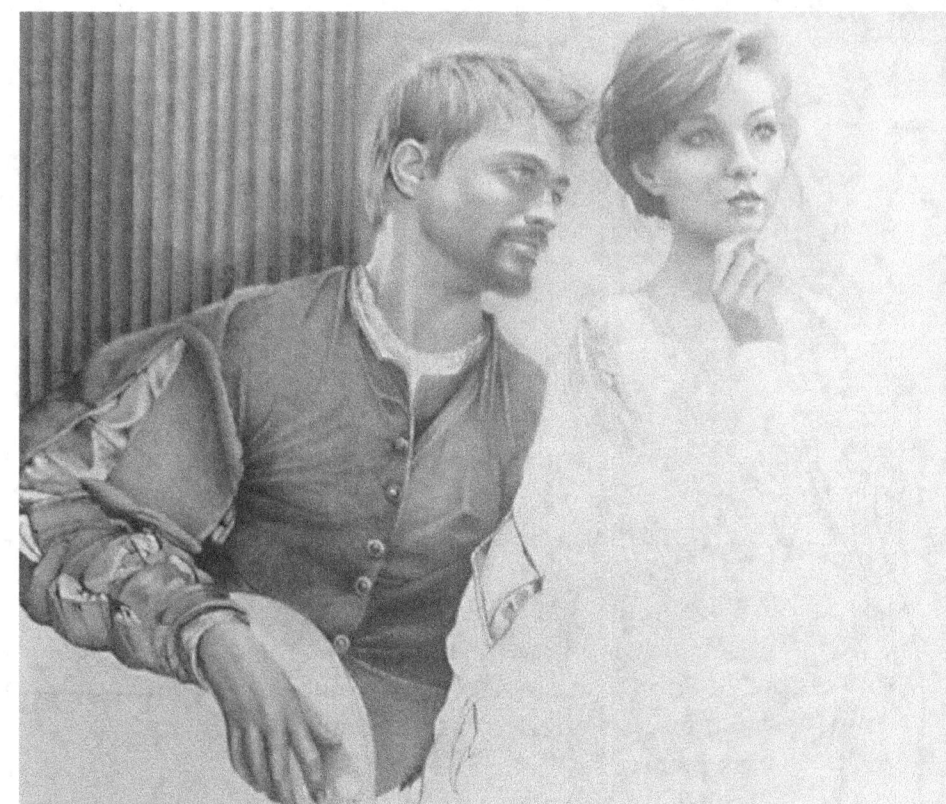

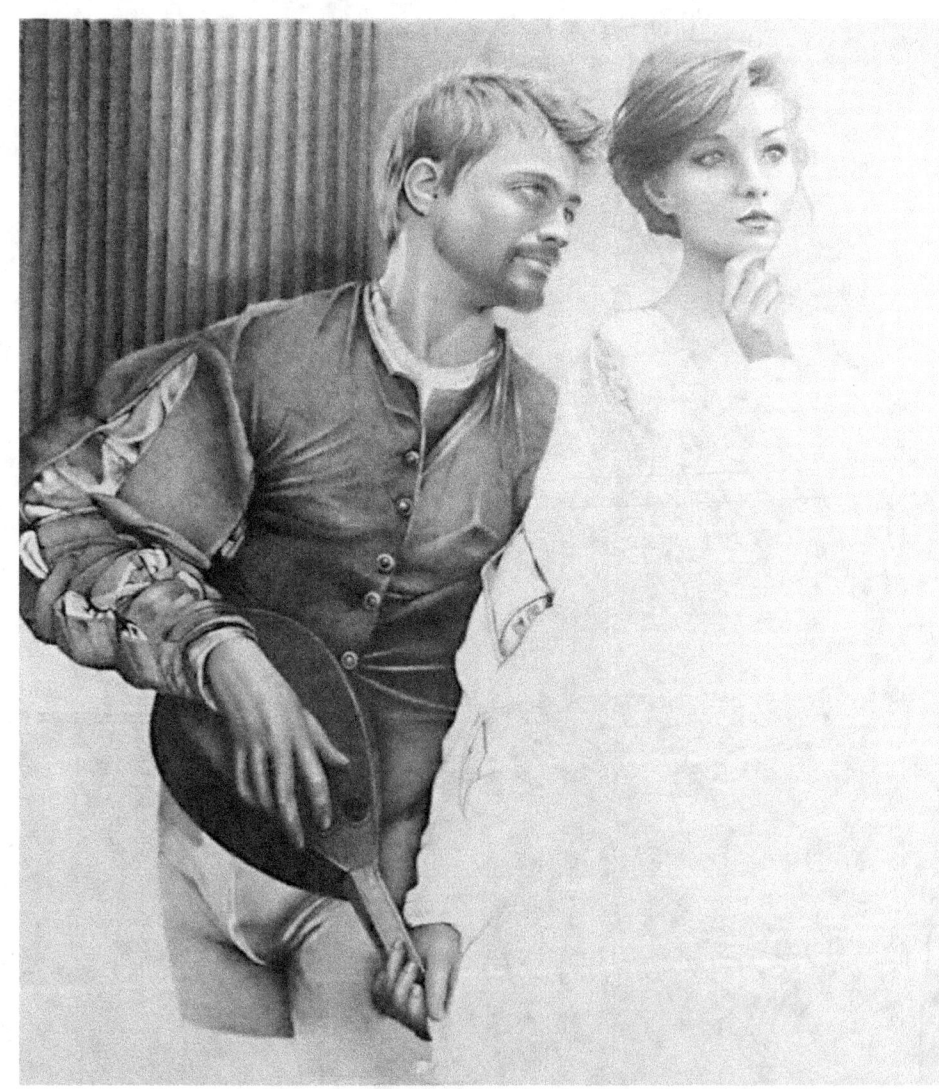

Detail of "Courting" in progress. 2012

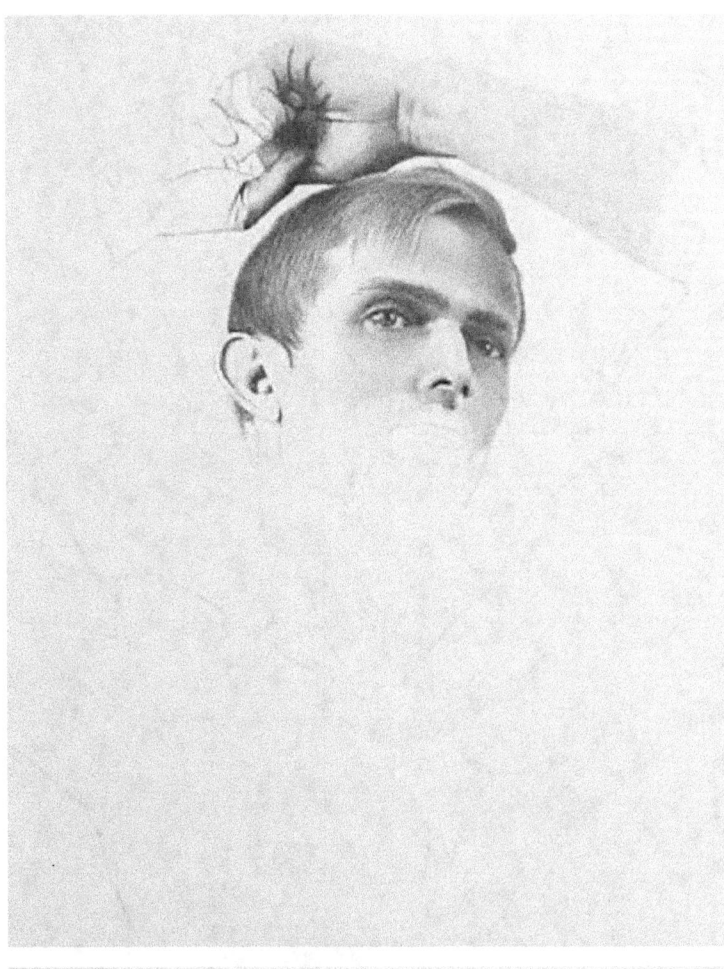

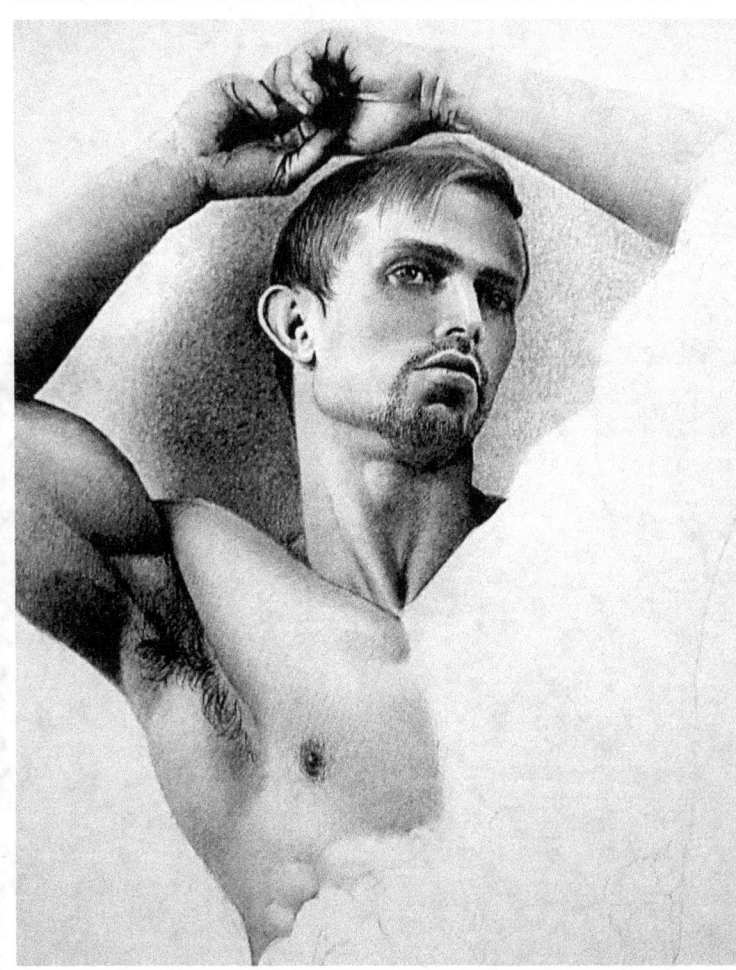

"Garrett" in progress. 2012

these new larger drawings. This would include two large commissioned works giving a total of six new drawings completed in one year.

The lowest productive year in regards to my drawings ever!

Time will tell if these three drawings will become my best. But should no one take notice or care to remember once I can no longer drawing, I can say I did well with "Courting"(page 7), "Garrett" (pages 4 and 128) and "Rodeo" (page 8).

By the summer of 2012, after completing the drawing of "Rodeo", I entered "Rodeo" and "Courting" in the Kern County Fair. I began experiencing pain in my right eye. Pain to the point of effecting my work as a graphic artist at The Bakersfield Californian, and my work as a fine arts graphic pencil artist.

I had known for a year that a cataract had started to develop in my right eye, but cataracts shouldn't hurt, or so that's what I was told!

That summer I accepted the fact that one day I would no longer be able to draw and that I needed to make a choice. Either I stop drawing at a point while I was still at my best - if that point had not already passed - or keep trying until I could no longer create works of art?

Just as the drawing of "Kevin-Repose" was to be my last full frontal male nude, the drawing of "Garrett" was to be my last male figure drawing.

The two drawings were to be the perfect conclusion to my drawing career should my expectations come to be. Each were complete opposites in light and dark and each offered a sensual side of how men can be without trying.

The reference photo of Kevin was taken after a photo shoot, just as he was turning towards the photographer and in an unsolicited pose. Showing the man behind the lens a more candid side to the young man.

The reference photo of Garrett was posed and professional set up making perhaps the most difficult poses look natural.

Where most would see this drawing as erotic, due to not what he wore but rather what he was wearing, I saw a man that celebrated healthy living. A man that took control of his life and worked hard at developing a body that should be admired, appreciated, and in this case - celebrated!

So why end here and not continue to draw what I wanted and respected? Timing.

Drawing men had become a barrier when it came to getting my work accepted and shown in art galleries. People in today's society continued to see men a social taboo when it comes to art - men who draw men do not have a place in the art scene especially if they are not part of the LGBT community. As a result I discovered I really didn't belong anywhere!

Yes - I could rent space at a local art gallery but I still could not display the nudes. Surprised, and offended if I hadn't taken the woman's age into account, I informed her that any nudes in my collection of pencil drawings were a small faction to what I have created through the years.

Tired and frustrated, it was time for a change.

It was time to put together enough drawings and finalize my last attempt at a drawing book. One book would be on drawing women so I could finally complete the last chapter in a project I had started back in 2005.

Agreements were made with the models and photographers. It was frustrating me knowing that I could see well enough to start the project but there was no certainty that I could see well enough to finish it.

I had already disappointed models and friends I was networking with when I wasn't able to draw all the men that wanted to be in the book on drawing men and I did not want to disappoint the ladies too!

In January of 2013 I started to draw a companion piece to go along with the theme and style of "Courting" but it just was not working out. I blamed my choice of paper and insisted that if I chosen the right paper the drawing would have turned out. But deep down I knew it wasn't the paper - it was me and my failing eye sight.

I put the drawing aside and would look at it every night just waiting for the day I could start where I had left left off, but more importantly, the day I could see the detail in my drawings again.

In the mean time I worked on the drawing of Sandra and then later of Cristinia. Two drawings I had intended to start the book on drawing women but I was not pleased with the final results.

I just could not draw as detailed as I used to no matter how hard I tried. I could no longer create the detail needed to draw them realistically. Nor could I draw at the level I like to be when I am creating a piece of art.

As an artist there will be a point in each of our lives where we must face the truth, that inevitable moment, that we know will come some day but do not what it to happen.

The day we can no longer create as we used to.

The day we have to decided to stop doing what we love or find another outlet to release the creative spirit within us.

It hurt knowing that what I found comfort in, what was my way of standing out in a crowd, to be seen and known

Cristina

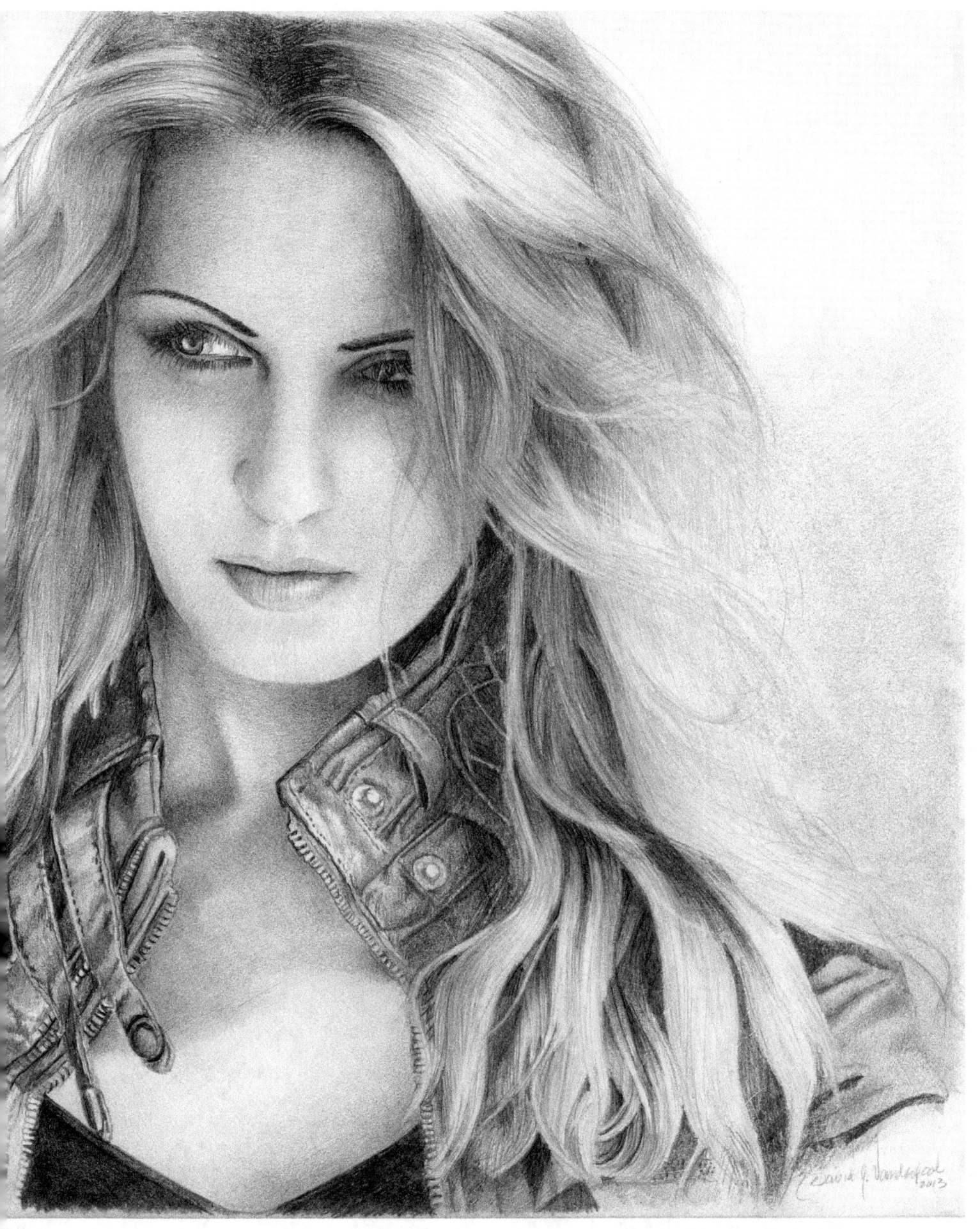

14" x 11" graphite pencil drawing on paper. 2013

A look into the art of David J. **Vanderpool**   133

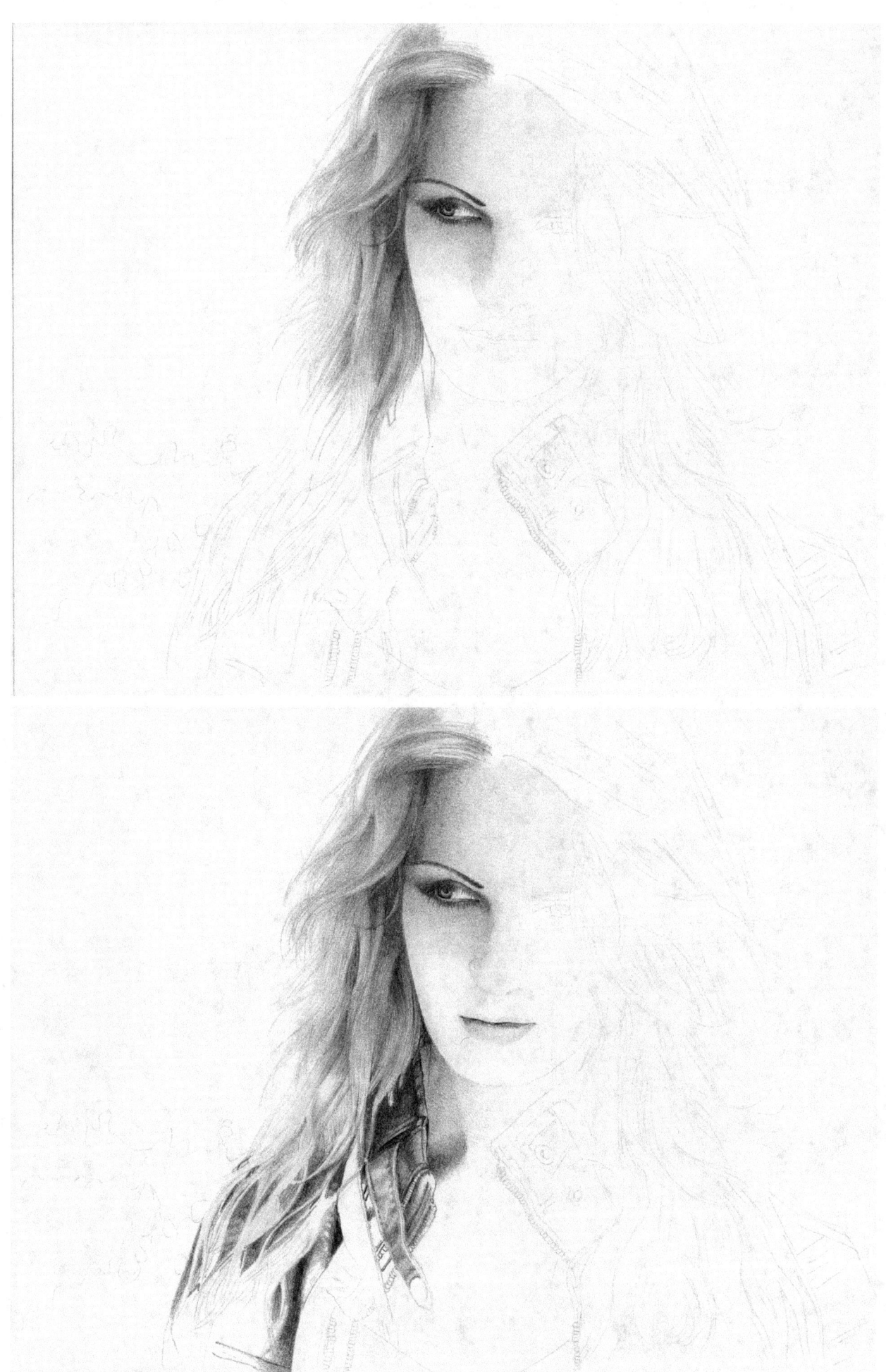

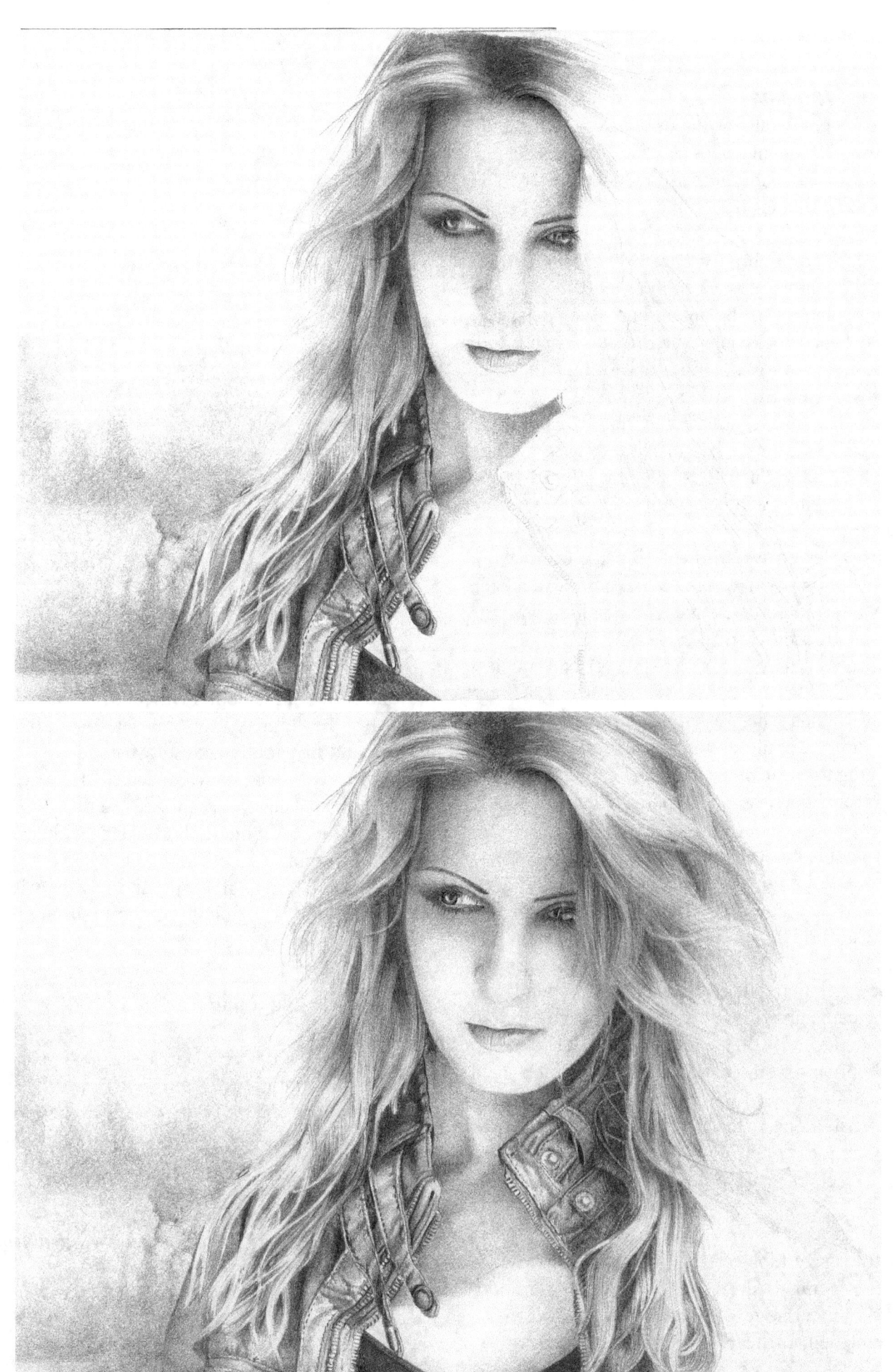

for, was coming to an end.

Eye Street Gallery

Not one to accept what was the obvious — some call it denial — I went to a local drug store and purchased a pair of "cheaters". Those reading glasses for the elderly, so I could finish the drawing of Cristina. The blonde beauty from Romania.

Two days later, on February 1, 2013, I received a call from one of the editors at work who asked if I would be interested in being part of the upcoming "Eye Gallery".

Both pleased and shocked that the Entertainment Editor at work took notice of my drawings and wanted me to be a part of this very selective group, of course I said yes!

Not telling her that I was having trouble seeing was deliberate. I wasn't going to risk my chance at something I had wanted to be a part of for so long. I had found myself silently asking each year why was i being passed over? Why not me?

Each artist selected would create a piece of art work along with a short story about their creation. Then each following artist would create a piece to go along with the theme and include their own short story.

Knowing in advance that the theme was on music I sent
e-mails off to friends who were musicians asking if they might have photos I could use as references. Explaining that I was trying to compile as much as I could so I would have a better chance at being prepared when it became my turn to draw.

Only two people came to my help. Preston Nash who I have drawn a few times, as well as his wife; and Matt Munoz, who worked as the entertainment writer for The Bakersfield Californian. A co-worker I knew of but had yet to meet.

Matt got in touch with a photographer friend and together they came up with a few photos I was offered to draw if I wanted to.

Friday, February 16th, a white binder which held instructions and a copy of the painting that was created by the first artist, along with their 50-80 word story, was delivered to my job.

I was the second artist out of ten to work on this project.

Not sure if I was able to meet the deadline, since other drawings of this size took over a month, I sat down that night and pretty much drew until Tuesday afternoon. Stopping only to rest my eyes about every six hours.

Sleep? Who needed sleep anyhow?

I could catch up what sleep I lost once the drawing was

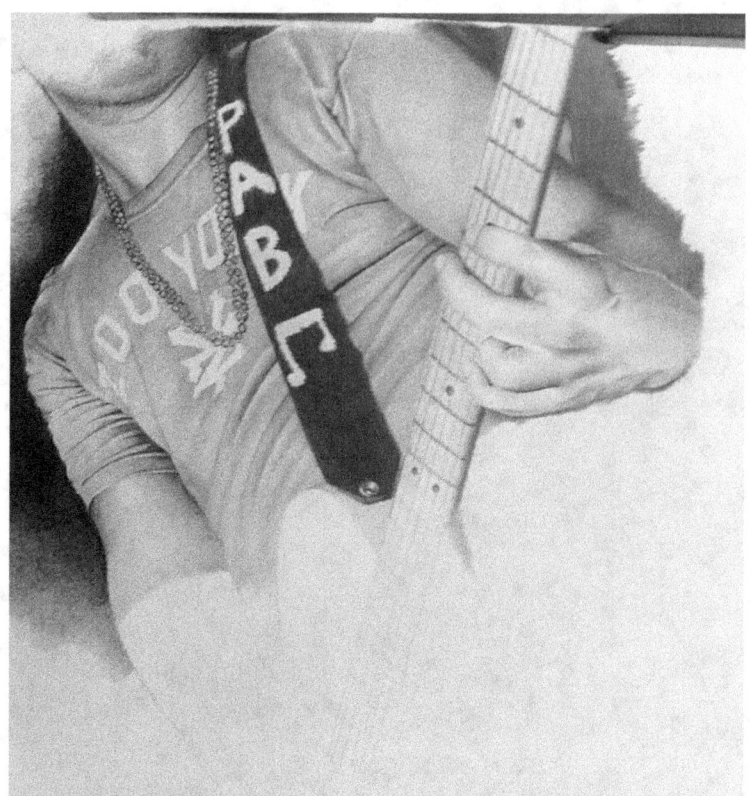

Photographer: Jeremy Gonzalez of No Image Photography, Guitarist: Pablo Alaniz

done couldn't I?

Monday was President's Day and the newspaper was closed for the holiday. I took Tuesday off as a paid vacation and my goal was to draw none stop until I had to deliver the drawing on Wednesday. However, shortly before noon on Tuesday, I realized the drawing was done and just in time. A winter storm was just about to hit our part of California.

The rains started as my wife and I were driving from the museum in Bakersfield to our home in Shafter.

"96 Hours"
A visual narrative collaboration

Although much of our time as artists is spent creating bodies of work that we will show independently, we depend on a community to engage with and support our endeavors. Inspired by a similar collaboration among 27 Bakersfield artists in 2009, "96 Hours" celebrates our community by bringing together the 2013 Eye Gallery artists to collaborate on one momentous art piece in the form of a visual narrative. Every "page" is an individual work of art made by a different artist. One page at a time, each artist contributes a layer to the plot, characters, style, and mood of the narrative. There is neither a mastermind nor preconceived plot, yet, in the end, a story is told.

Overall, the process is simple: Each artist is given a

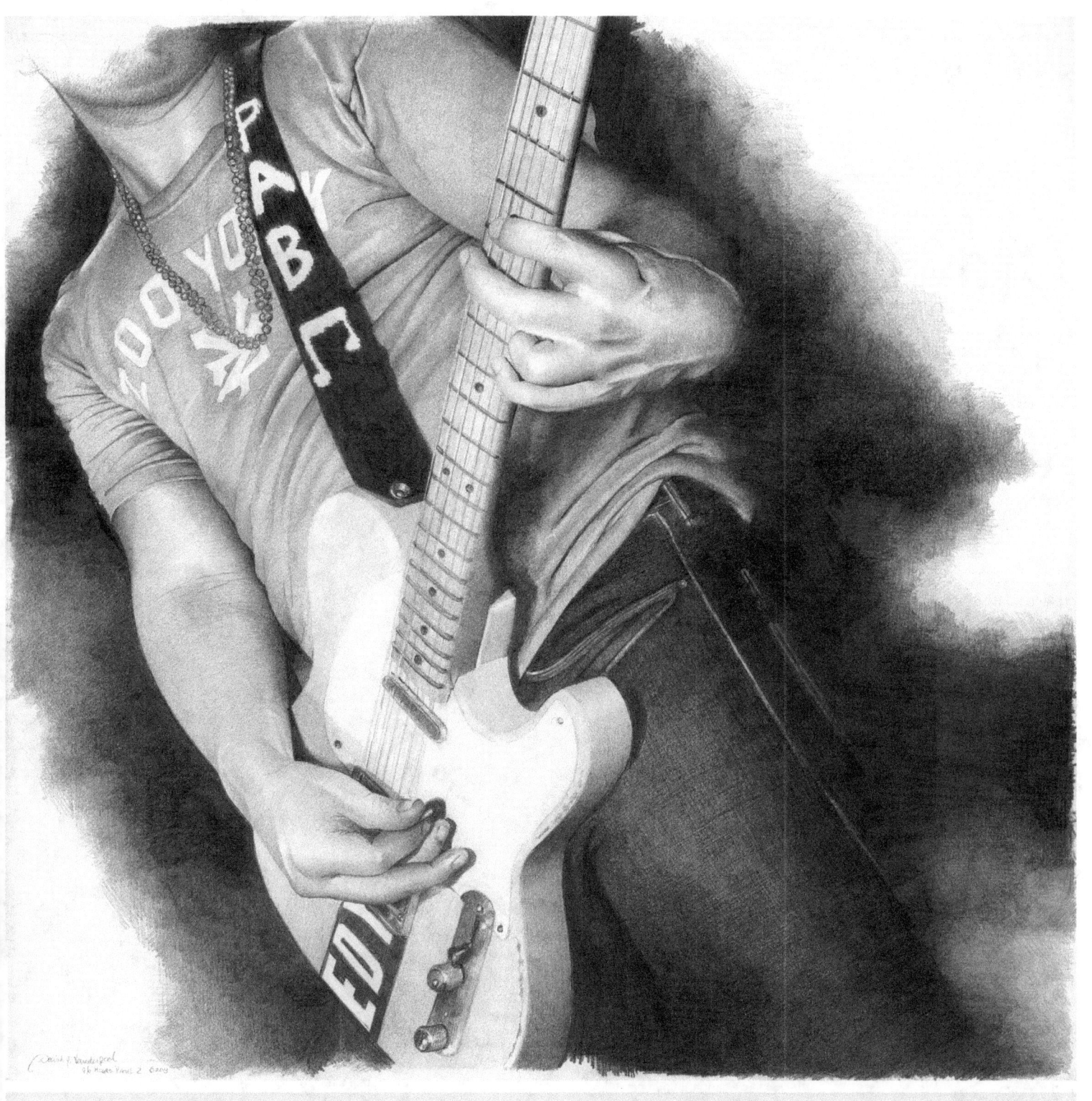

96 Hours - Panel 2

20" x 20" graphite pencil drawing on paper. 2013

"Somewhere between dreaming, and reality, I started to question where was I? I knew the melody that had woken me, I was even familiar with the pain it brought. I just wasn't to sure who the man was standing in the courtyard – or his reason for being there. I did know that I didn't want to relive that longing again. I couldn't. Not if I was to make it through another night like this."

— David J. Vanderpool

A look into the art of David J. **Vanderpool**   137

EYEGALLERY

> "I get art galleries who tell me they love my work and then turn around and ask me, 'What else can you do?' — as if drawing was not an art form."
> — David Vanderpool, artist

Drawing his way around obstacles

Vision, hearing difficulties have not stopped artistic quest

BY MATT MUNOZ
Californian staff writer
mmunoz@bakersfield.com

Artist David J. Vanderpool works in precision. A study of any of his finely detailed, highly realistic drawings — including his piece at left — reveals perceptive eyes and a steady hand.

Actually, make that one perceptive eye.

"The only challenge was making sure the drawing was clear and sharp due to dealing with a cataract," said Vanderpool, 52, who by day works as a graphic artist at The Californian.

"I had to stop every so often and ask my wife if I was getting this right. As for the drawing itself, I wasn't too sure if I could pull this off in the short time given to complete the project. A drawing this size has always taken me a month to complete, with just a few hours a night and weekends to draw."

Vanderpool was referring to the twist thrown at Eye Gallery artists this year: Each was asked to contribute a "chapter" to a larger narrative, which will unfold every Thursday over several weeks. The artists were given reproductions of all the work that had come before and 96 hours to finish the job.

And if the compressed timeframe and cataract weren't enough, Vanderpool has been dealing with limited hearing for years, making it difficult there for a while for the artist to fully appreciate music — the loose theme of this year's project.

"As an artist that was limited to what I was able to hear for so long and only in the last few years able to hear without having to wear a hearing aid, you guys selected an artist that perhaps appreciates sound more than most people in general. I have a whole new interest and appreciation for music. In fact to hear most any sound after the surgery a few years back was a blessing, even the sound of a train in the middle of the night."

But any physical challenges the artist has dealt with have worked to heighten his sensitivity, fully expressed on paper with the help of a graphite drawing pencil.

"It is relaxing, requires little to no thinking and since I was a child, it was my escape. I draw with all lines. I never use traditional blending tools to smear the graphite. I use lighter pencils to blend the darker pencils, keeping the pencils sharp and the lines close to each other as each drawing slowly comes to life on the paper."

For his Eye Gallery subject, Vanderpool chose a black-and-white performance photo taken by photographer Jeremy Gonzalez featuring Bakersfield guitarist Pablo Alaniz and a vintage 1950 Fender Stratocaster guitar.

"Being a portrait artist, I like drawing people I am attracted to, which means

About Eye Gallery
The annual art series is a partnership between The Californian and the Bakersfield Museum of Art whose purpose is to put the work of local artists in the spotlight. This year we asked 10 artists to collaborate on a story, in words and pictures. Each was given 96 hours, a canvas and all the work that had been produced to that point. The story will unfold in Eye Street every Thursday through June 27, when the museum will host a reception for the artists and unveil other exhibitions.

character, charm and who can offer me a challenge, to avoid 'mug shots' when it comes to a drawing, and turn everyday people into a treasure for the generations to follow."

Given the state of your hearing and sight, how did you feel about Eye Gallery revolving around music?

As for my sight, anyone that has dealt with cataract understands how it is a gradual change through time and most chalk it up as old age and get new glasses; however, being an artist I knew it was something more than that when my eyes were hurting. ... I can say I have had cataract surgery in my right eye since this drawing was completed, and so I look forward to seeing what everyone else sees once it's on display.

Explain your process/technique:

I draw from photos, whether they are a local person interested in a drawing or a model from another country. This allows the model to pose once and I can draw at the oddest hours. However I use the photo as a reference and add my style to the drawing that meets the needs to the client's interest. The trick is to focus on one section at a time. Skin tones, eyes, fabric, etc., rather than the overall subject. That way the project doesn't become overwhelming. A grid, mirror or light table can only offer an outline. The skill is taking it to the next level, and that part can't be cheated. You either have it or you don't.

What kind of art speaks to you:

I favor realistic and works from the old masters and Renaissance period. If you have to think too hard, question if the painting was hung upside down, or you left confused looking at what is in front of you, that's not my thing.

When I knew art would be my passion:

When I was told I had to stop drawing as a child, that boys played baseball and football and didn't paint or draw, I took that as a challenge and to prove them wrong and drew everything that sat in front of me. Yes, my way of rebelling!

Work you're proudest of?

"Courting" was last year's Best in Show at the Kern County Fair, and one of my

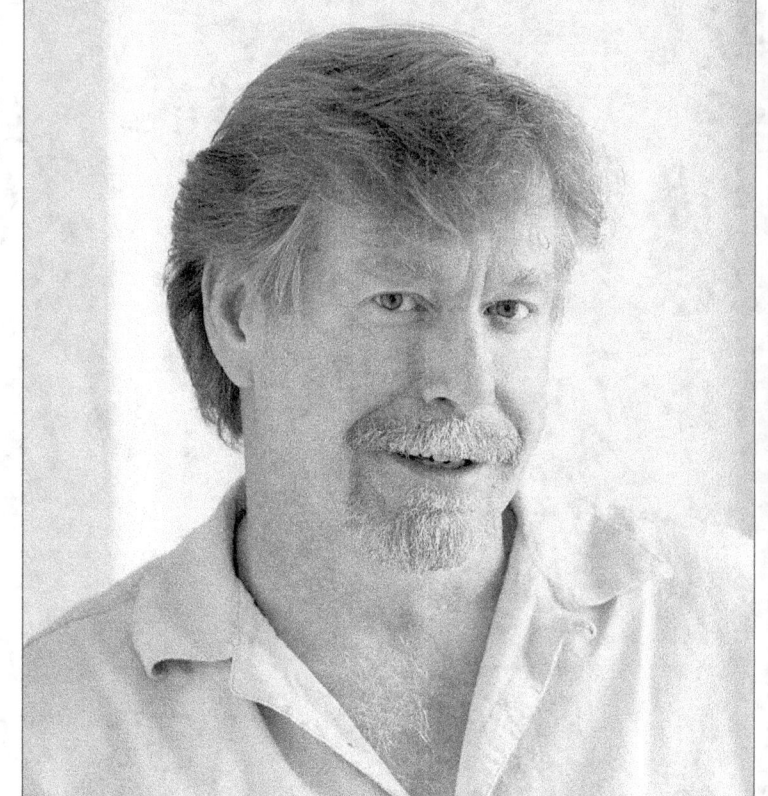

ALEX HORVATH / THE CALIFORNIAN
Artist David Vanderpool works by day as a graphic artist at The Californian.

Next week
Photographer Kristopher Stallworth is drawn to the music that seems to be coming from the mysterious figure, in Chapter Three of our story.

wife's favorite drawings so far. It's not so much being proud of it or it being better than any of my other drawings, but because I did not give up when I was told I had to stop drawing.

Do you get many commissions?

Yes. There are times when I have to turn down commissioned assignments because I have too many to get done, and there are times I turn down assignment because I was not comfortable with the subject matter. I draw portraits and figure drawing, but I have a limit to what I will put my name onto — even commissioned drawings that the world may never get the chance to see.

And yes, there are times when there are no drawing assignments for what seems like ages.

How hard is it to find a place to show your work publicly?

Very hard. I get art galleries who tell me

they love my work and then turn around and ask me, 'What else can you do?' — as if drawing was not an art form. And then there are galleries who will tell me my work is too contemporary while another will say it's not contemporary enough; however I finally had an art gallery in London explain it best. He said that an art gallery cannot profit off a drawing like they can with a painting, because of the time variant between the two.

Memory of the first time you sold a piece of work:

High school. Guys would pay me $20 to draw girls they liked on pin-up bodies.

Who's been your most supportive mentor?

Art teacher from junior high that I also kept in touch with through my high school. He said to create what you have passion for and there will be others who will come to you one day. Never create to meet the public needs, since most have no idea what art is. Create what you desire and introduce yourself to the world through your work.

How to learn more about my work:

paper2pencil.com

blank 20 x 20 inch "canvas" on which to paint, draw, mount, or build his or her piece. Along with this, each artist will be provided with reproductions of the preceding pages and written story line in sequence. By considering the story thus far, the artist will then create the next page in the visual narrative within a ninety-six hour period. He or she may use any medium and may take the plot in any direction. Consequently, each new piece interprets and completes someone else's thoughts and introduces new possibilities for the next. No one knows what will happen beyond this four-day time allotment for his or her page. The story creates itself with its own momentum, each artist reacting and responding to the preceding imagery.

In the end, we have one collaborative work of art that can be examined as a whole, as well as admired for the beauty of each individual page. The viewer is challenged to study each page separately and imagine how it relates to its predecessors. Like any work of art, it must be studied. It must be interpreted. Multiple interpretations are possible and equally valid.

All artwork will be documented, printed at 4"x 6", and hand-bound in chronological order along with an introduction and bios of the contributing artists. A one-time edition of 100 copies of the book will be made. This will form a take-home reproduction of the narrative available for purchase during the exhibit.

Over the course of several weeks, beginning April, 25th, *The Bakersfield Californian* published original artwork created by select local artists along with an interview with the artist.

On June 27, a reception was held at the Bakersfield Museum of Art, where all participating artists's work went on display for several weeks.

Drawing his way around obstacles

Vision, hearing difficulties have not stopped artistic quest

BY MATT MUNOZ
Californian staff writer
mmunoz@bakersfield.com

Artist David J. Vanderpool works in precision. A study of any of his finely detailed, highly realistic drawings —including his piece at left — reveals perceptive eyes and a steady hand.

Actually, make that one perceptive eye.

"The only challenge was making sure the drawing was clear and sharp due to dealing with a cataract," said Vanderpool, 52,who by day works as a graphic artist at The Californian.

"I had to stop every so often and ask my wife if I was getting this right. As for the drawing itself, I wasn't too sure if I could pull this off in the short time given to complete the project. A drawing this size has always taken me a month to complete,with just a few hours a night and week ends to draw."

Vanderpool was referring to the twist thrown at Eye Gallery artists this year: Each was asked to contribute a "chapter" to a larger narrative, which will unfold every Thursday over several weeks. The artists were given reproductions of all the work that had come before and 96 hours to finish the job.

And if the compressed time frame and cataract weren't enough, Vanderpool has been dealing with limited hearing for years, making it difficult there for a while for the artist to fully appreciate music —the loose theme of this year's project.

"As an artist that was limited to what I was able to hear for so long and only in the last few years able to hear without having to wear a hearing aid, you guys selected an artist that perhaps appreciates sound more than most people in general. I have a whole new interest and appreciation for music. In fact to hear most any sound after the surgery a few years back was a blessing, even the sound of a train in the middle of the night."

But any physical challenges the artist has dealt with have worked to heighten his sensitivity, fully expressed on paper with the help of a graphite drawing pencil.

"It is relaxing, requires little to no thinking and since I was a child, it was my escape. I draw with all lines. I never use traditional blending tools to smear the graphite. I use lighter pencils to blend the darker pencils, keeping the pencils sharp and the lines close to each other as each drawing slowly comes to life on the paper."

For his Eye Gallery subject, Vanderpool chose a black-and-white performance photo taken by photographer Jeremy Gonzalez featuring Bakersfield guitarist Pablo Alaniz and a vintage 1950 Fender Stratocaster guitar.

"Being a portrait artist, I like drawing people I am attracted to, which means character, charm and who can offer me a challenge, to avoid 'mug shots' when it comes to a drawing, and turn every day people into a treasure for the generations to follow.

"Given the state of your hearing and sight, how did you feel about Eye Gallery revolving around music?

As for my sight, anyone that has dealt with cataract understands how it is a gradual change through time and most chalk it up as old age and get new glasses; however, being an artist I knew it was something more than that when my eyes were hurting. ... I can say I have had cataract surgery in my right eye since this drawing was completed, and so I look forward to seeing what everyone else sees once it's on display.

Explain your process/technique:

I draw from photos, whether they are a local person interested in a drawing or a model from another country. This allows the model to pose once and I can draw at the oddest hours. However I use the photo as a reference and add my style to the drawing that meets the needs to the client's interest. The trick is to focus on one section at a time. Skin tones, eyes, fabric, etc, rather than the overall subject. That way the project doesn't become overwhelming. A grid, mirror or light table can only offer an outline. The skill is taking it to the next level, and that part can't be cheated. You either have it or you don't.

What kind of art speaks to you:

I favor realistic and works from the old masters and Renaissance period. If you have to think too hard, question if the painting was hung upside down, or you're left confused looking at what is in front of you, that's not my thing.

When I knew art would be my passion:

When I was told I had to stop drawing as a child, that boys played baseball and football and didn't paint or draw, I took that as a challenge and to prove them wrong I drew everything that sat in front of me. Yes, my way of rebelling!

Work you're proudest of?

"Courting" was last year's Best in Show at the Kern County Fair, and one of my wife's favorite drawings so far. It's not so much being proud of it or it being better than any of my other drawings, but because I did not give up when I was told I had to stop drawing.

Do you get many commissions?

Yes. There are times when I have to turndown commissioned assignments because I have too many to get done, and there are times I turn down assignment because I was not comfortable with the subject matter. I draw portraits and figure drawing, but I have a limit to what I will put my name onto — even commissioned drawings that the world may never get the chance to see. And yes, there are times when there are no drawing assignments for what seems like ages.

How hard is it to find a place to show your work publicly?

Very hard. I get art galleries who tell me they love my work and then turn around and ask me, 'What else can you do?' — as if drawing was not an art form. And then there are galleries who will tell me my work is too contemporary while another will say it's not contemporary enough; however I finally had an art gallery in London explain it best. He said that an art gallery cannot profit off a drawing like they can with a painting, because of the time variant between the two.

Memory of the first time you sold apiece of work:

High school. Guys would pay me $20 to draw girls they liked on pin-up bodies.

Who's been your most supportive mentor?

Art teacher from junior high that I also kept in touch with through my high school. He said to create what you have passion for and there will be others who will come to you one day. Never create to meet the public needs, since most have no idea what art is. Create what you desire and introduce yourself to the world through your work.

How to learn more paper2pencil.com

Not ready to give up — just yet!

Too many drawings were started early in the year and each one had the same results — far from my best, and not good enough to show!

The companion piece to "Courting" was not working out for two reason. The theme of the pieces as well as the paper I was attempting to draw on. It wasn't smooth enough.

After further research the first attempt to "Courting II" was abandoned and a new drawing was about to take place - once I could purchase the right paper to work on!

The art supply store had been out for quite some time so I finally went to a craft store to get the paper I was looking for. A little more expensive but it was the only place in this county that sold the paper I was after!

Wanting to use the models I had intended to use on the earlier attempt, I went through their profiles and selected photos I personally favored and that would best fit this new theme I had selected. Taking another Renaissance period painting I wanted to make it my own.

Unlike the reference painting that inspired the first drawing, where the couple may have been just married (a father figure and ring barrier in the back ground in the painting), this second painting showed the man leaning over a wall as he attempts to steal a kiss from a woman at the well.

To tie the two drawings together a rose bush sat in the corner of each drawing.

With no deadline and no one waiting to purchase it,

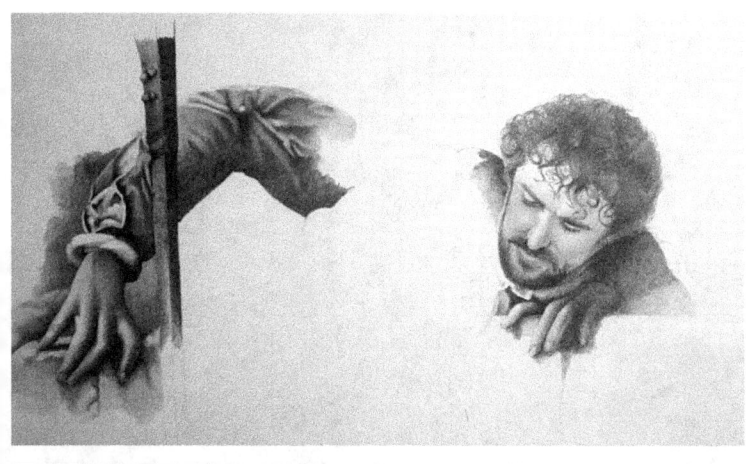

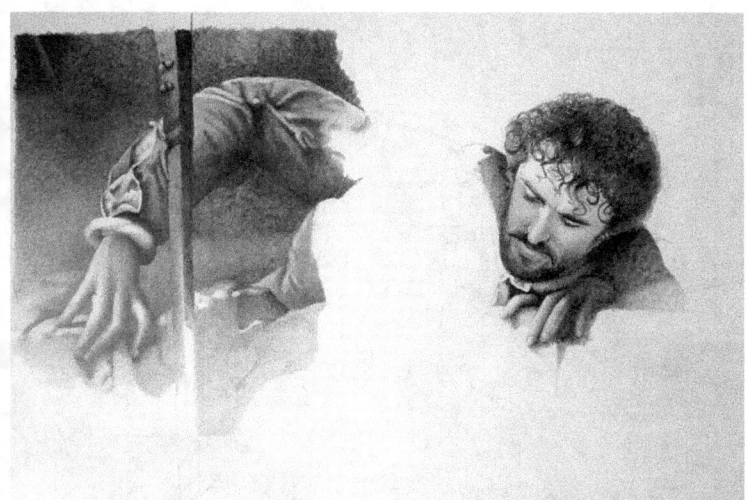

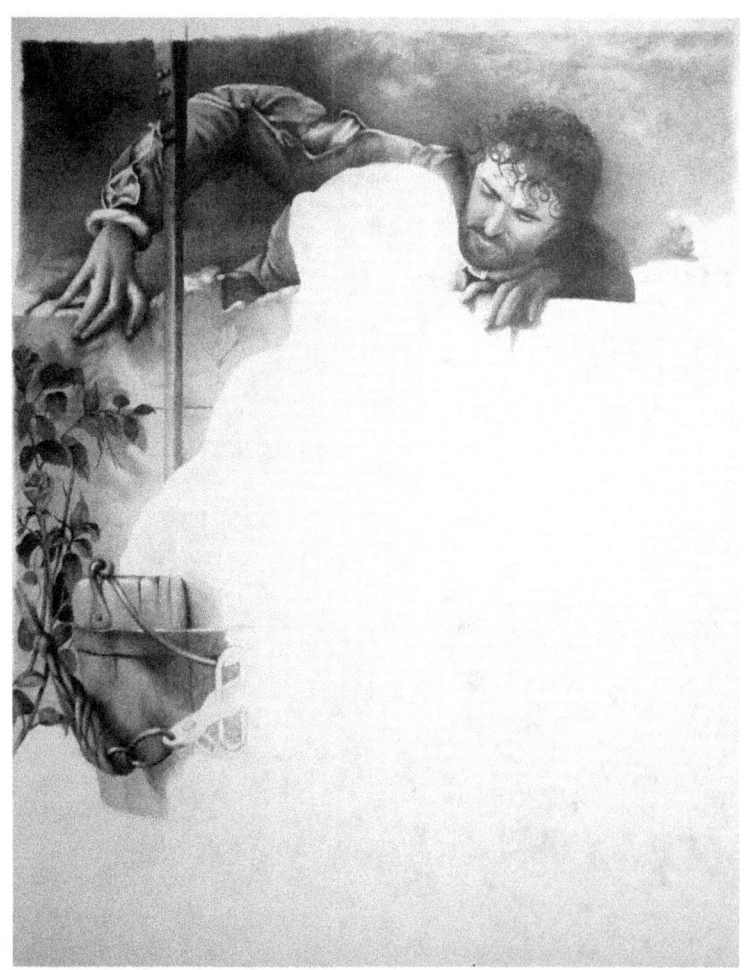

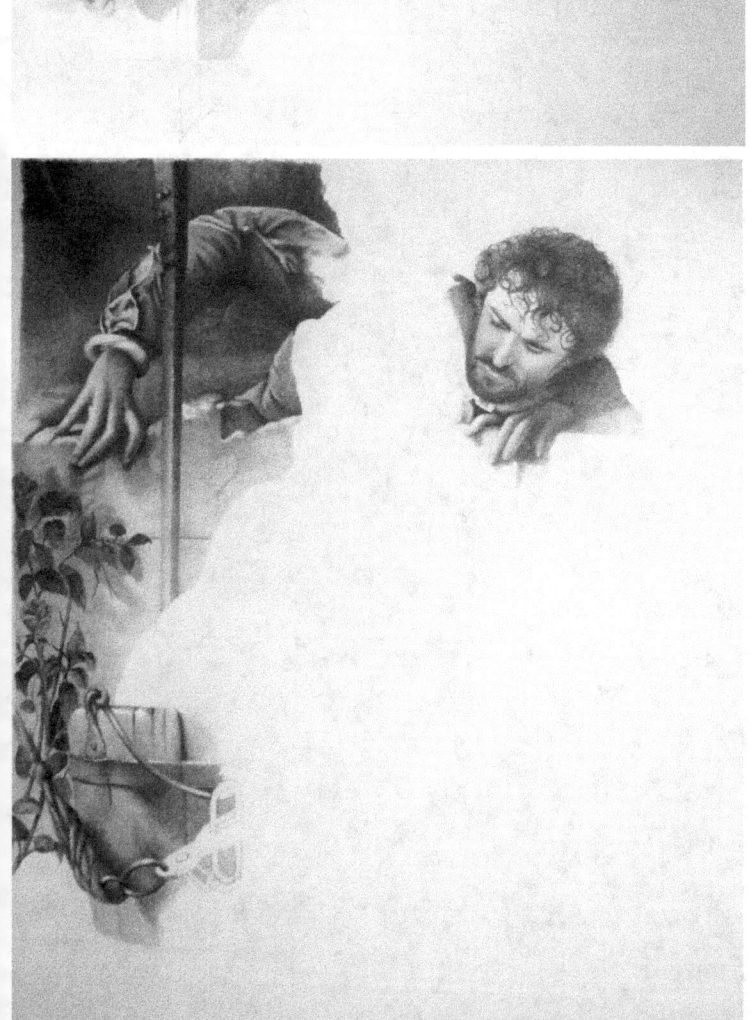

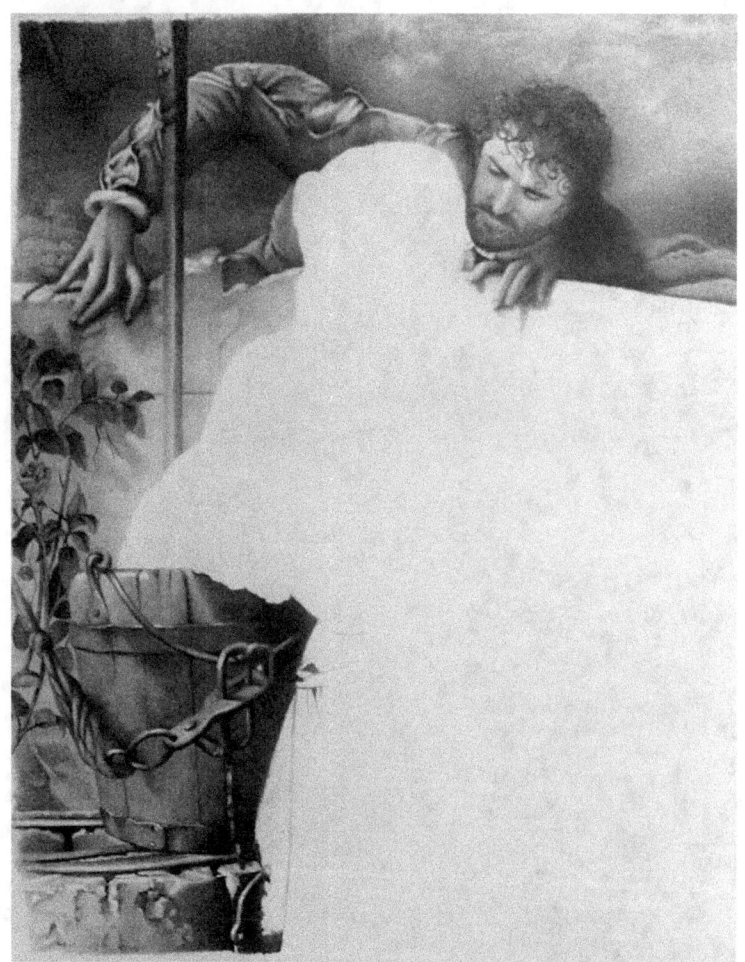

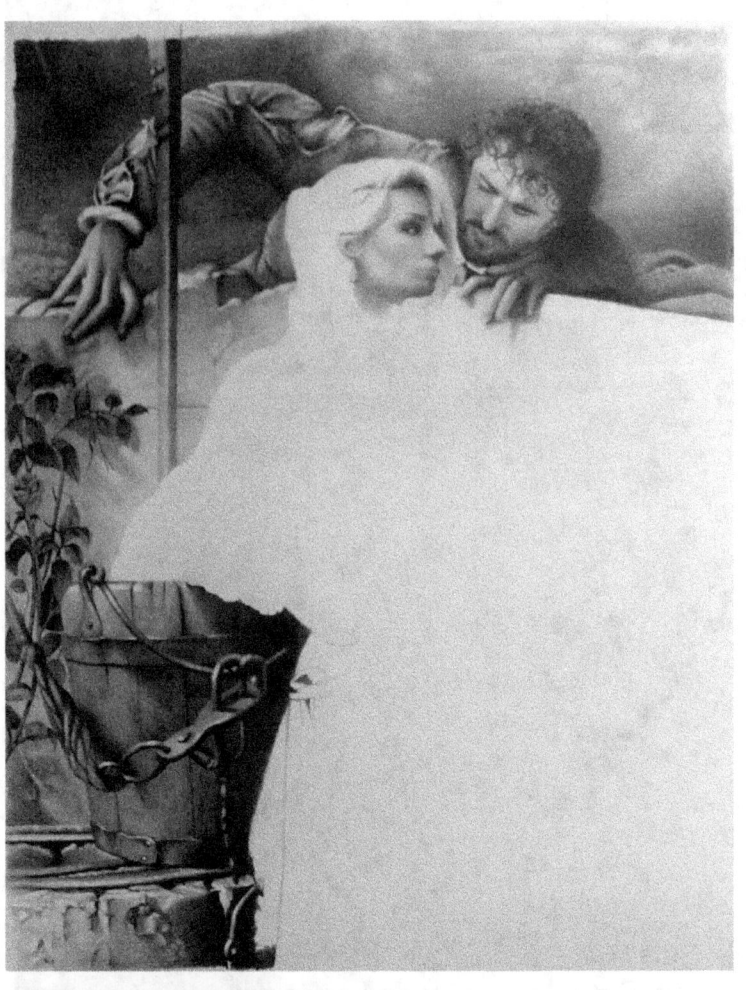
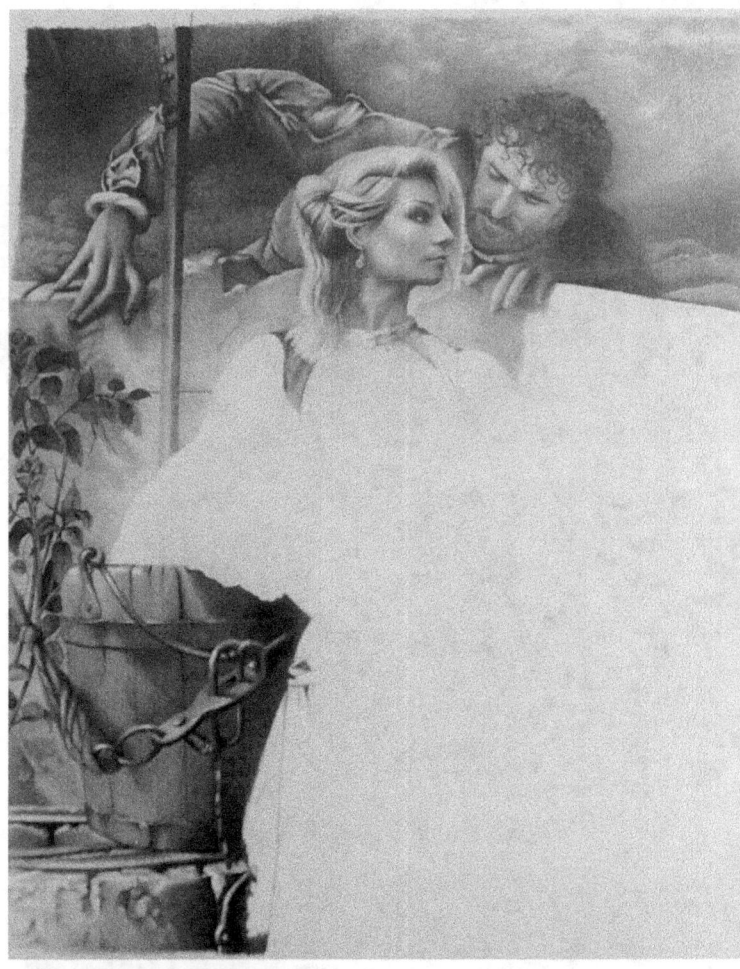
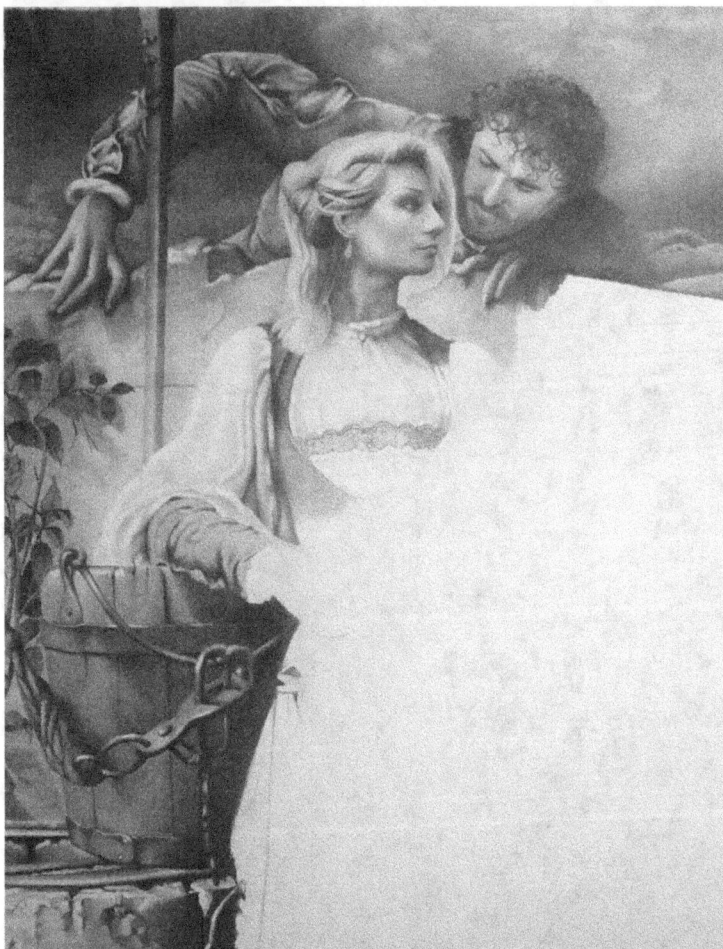
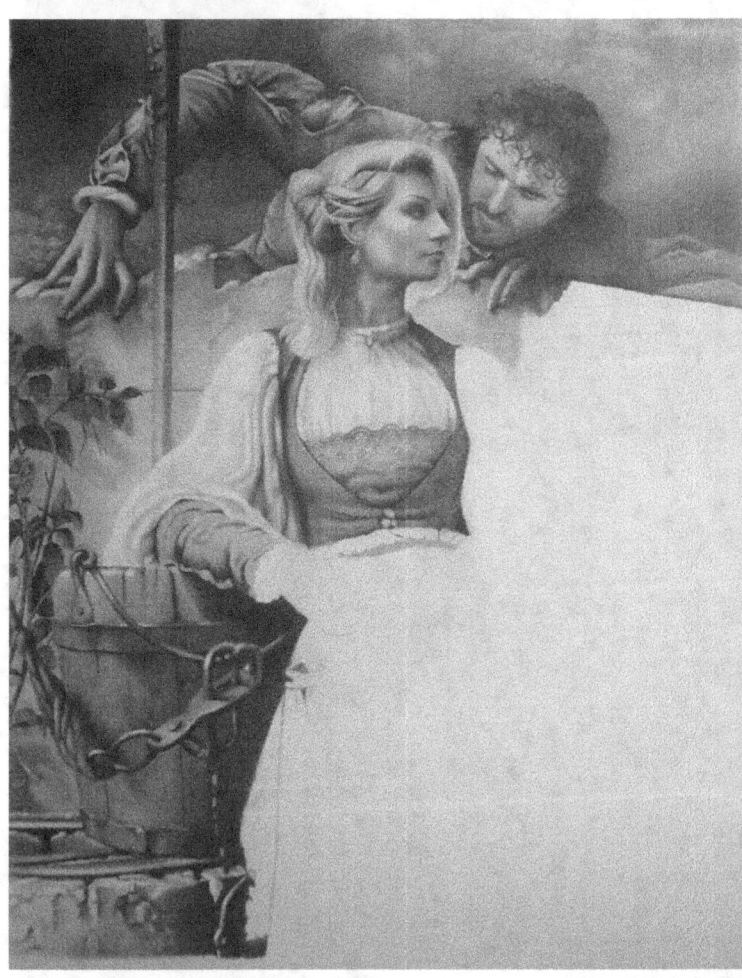

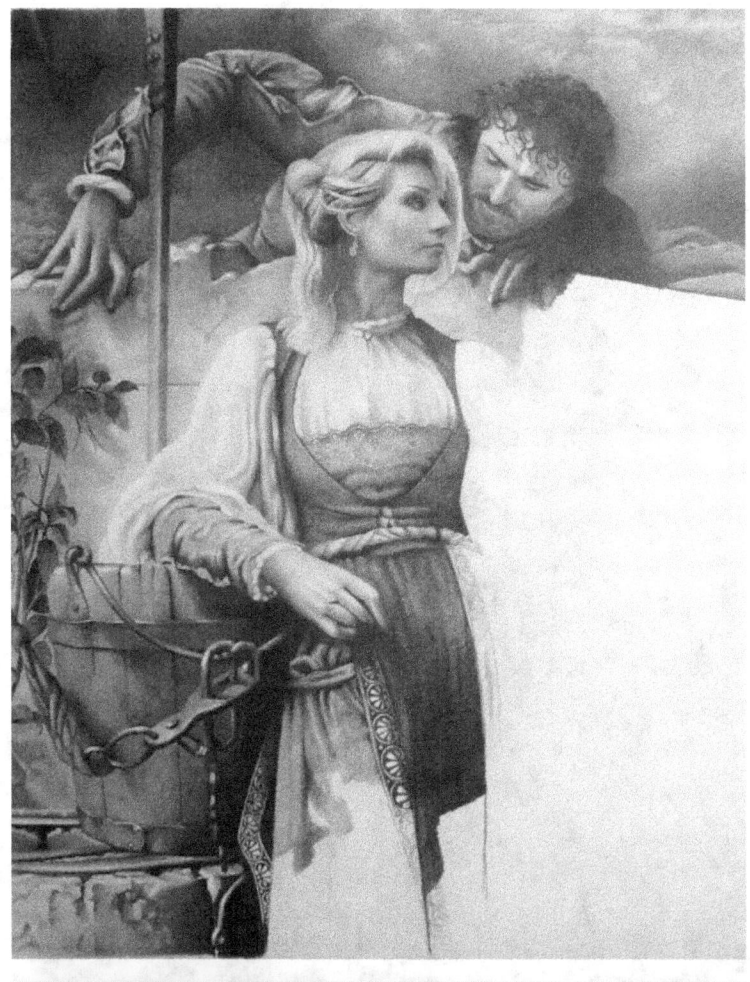

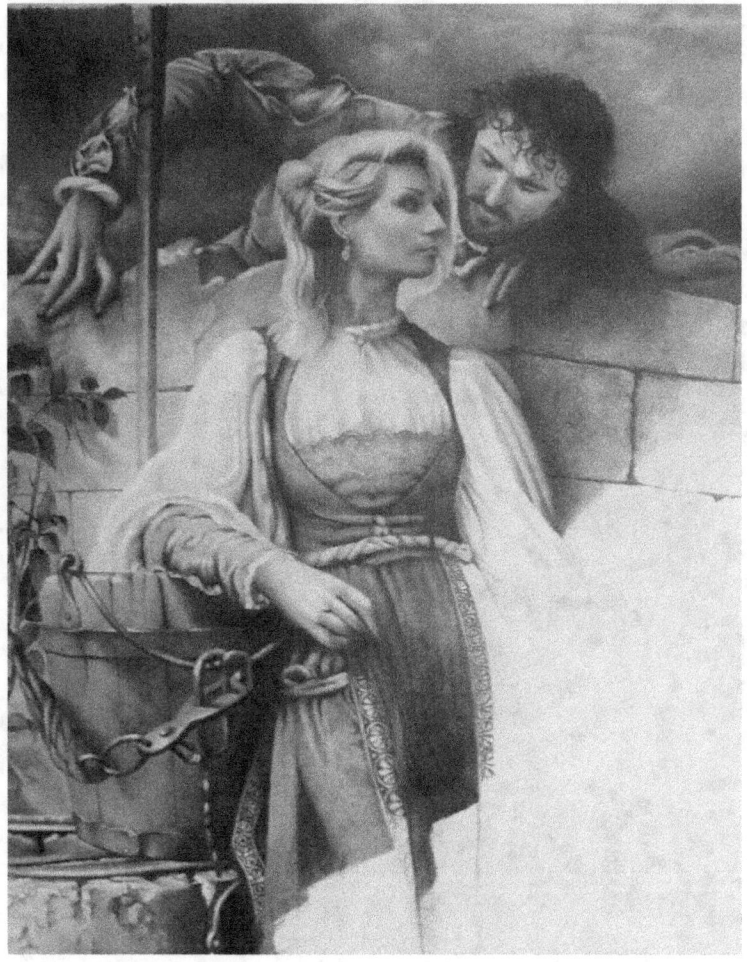

I took my time as I worked on the drawing a few hours a night and on weekends when time allowed. My goal was to at least get as much of the background completed before any corrective eye surgery was to take place. Saving the detail of the women in the drawing for after post-surgery.

I had started to turned down commissioned drawings earlier in the year for fear of no longer doing as well as I used to and disappointing the client. However a few days into this drawing I received an e-mail from a gentleman who had commissioned me to do a portrait of him and his wife back in November of the prior year. He was also patiently waiting for me to have the corrective eye surgery too.

This time I could not turn down the assignment. He wanted five large drawings with no time frame or deadline as to when the drawings were to be completed. He insisted that I take a partial payment that would help remove any worries as to how the co-pay for the surgery was to be funded.

Not willing, nor wanting to delay this drawing, I worked on "Courting II" in between the commissioned drawings. It is not unusual for me to work on several smaller drawings at one time. However, this was my first attempt work on two 20" x 28" drawings at once.

Too large to take to work and draw on my lunch break, and not wanting to put it off in fear of losing interest in it, I had no other choice but to fit it in my drawing routine. Selecting a time when my wife worked on her needle point so we were not taking time away from each other.

Different from my earlier works I started this drawing using my darker shades of grays and used the lighter pencils as my blending tool.

Remembering the difficulty in seeing clear detail while working on "Courting" the year prior, and knowing that I would have gone through cataract surgery in at least my right eye before this drawing would be completed, I intentionally started this drawing making sure that the man climbing the wall to steal a kiss would have a softer, almost blurry appearance, than the woman at the well.

Keeping to the style I had become known for, the pencil lines remained visible even for the blended, blurrier, objects at a distance. Lines are important to keep the shape and depth to the drawing and prevent the subject from being flat and one dimensional. Knowing that blending the drawing can make it become flat I even went over the blurred areas with a 2H and H pencil to show the dimension and shapes to the object.

Except for the far clouded background to the drawing, which required the use of a household cotton swab, the

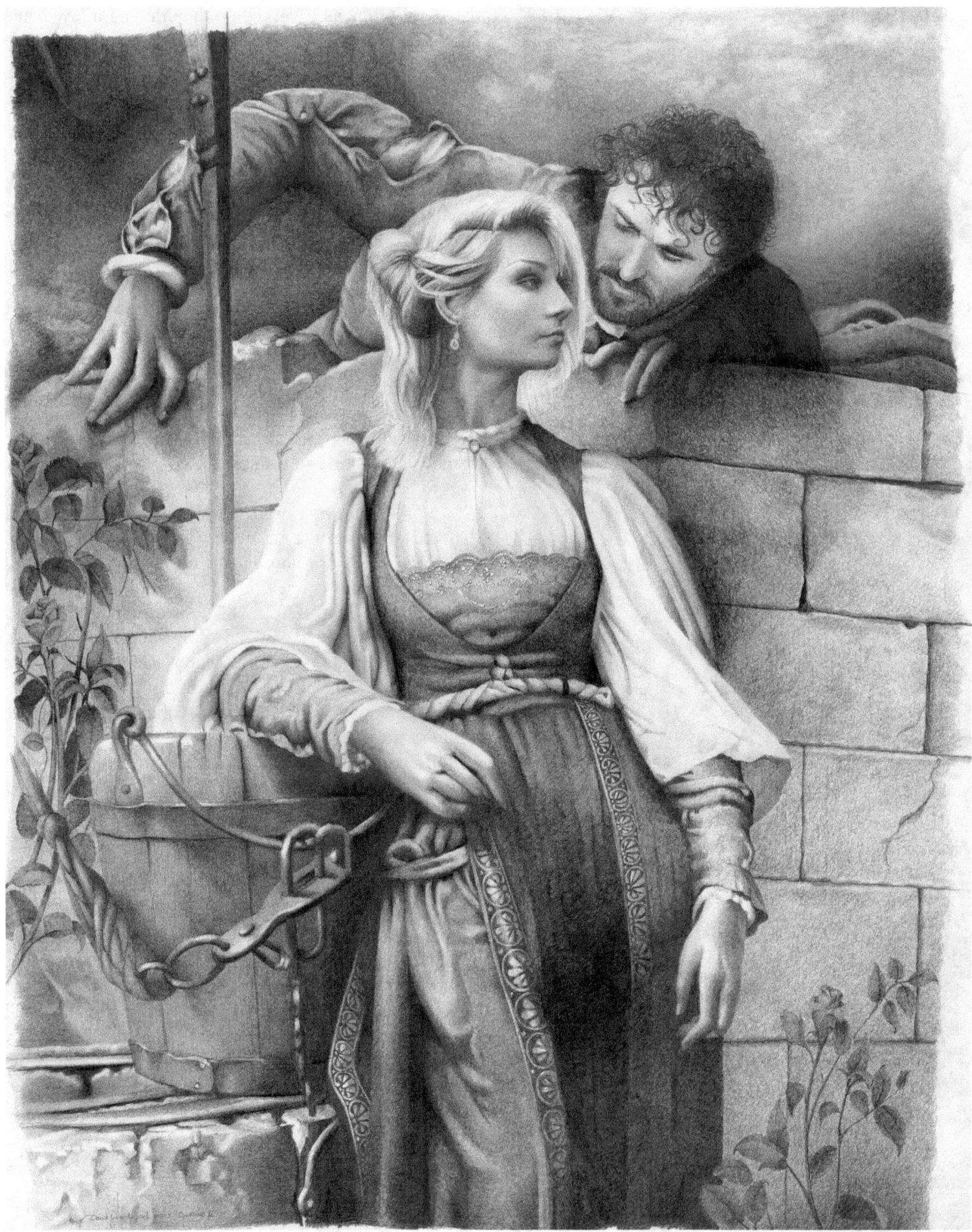

Courting II

22" x 30" graphite pencil drawing on paper. 2013

drawing was made up using all lines.

The man in the drawing was inspired from a follower of my work on facebook, who in fact was the motivation in completing this drawing. It is not the pose he suggested but after some research I felt this concept worked best with the photo references I had to work from.

Starting with his portrait the drawing took on a rough appearance, but through layers of lines created using a 2H and H pencil, the smooth texture of his face came into play. I didn't want him to appear too youthful, or pretty, as in the "Courting" drawing of 2012. The goal here was to capture the feelings and romance of a man that could steal a kiss and not worry about offending the young lady or being rejected.

Once his face was nearly completed, I started to draw his right hand, at the far left side of the drawing, as I worked left to right and top to bottom on the drawing. This prevented any chance of smearing the graphite once it was placed on the bristol paper.

With little detail visible in his hands shadows were used to cover what I was not able to see and then carried into the far background where what appeared to be brush and sky blended into a softer bend of textures.

This turned out perfect since objects at a distance should be blurrier than foreground images in order to keep a proper perspective on the drawing and preventing the subject from becoming flat.

Using nearly every pencil, from 2H to 8B, the far background and the stone wall were drawn using swivel pencil motions. Keeping the graphite sharp for the wall but dull for the brush and clouds.

Only as the wall began to take shape were vertical lines used for each stone that made up the wall. Gently placed over the swivel lines so that the stones make the wall appear solid and strong enough to hold him.

Not found in the original painting this concept came from, a rose bush was added. In fact the same bush that was used in the first "Courting" was redrawn here - with a few minor changes for this drawing.

The other major change made, from the original concept, was the woman looking at the man. The original, she was looking directly at the viewer.

Drawing various textures and object in a drawing can often be over whelming and a challenge, if not taken on one at a time. To do this I focused on the area I was working on rather then the drawing of object.

No longer seeing a rose bush but a leaf. Not seeing a bucket but a piece of wood, and not seeing a metal chain and bar but lights and shadows.

Lights and shadows are what ads depth to a drawing.

Working on this drawing a few hours at a time and as I got further along in the commissioned assignment, I was able to sit back and see the drawing develop and see which areas needs to be worked on next.

One area I wasn't sure about was the edge of the wall he was climbing over. At first thought it appeared he was climbing out of a well but that did not make sense if she was drawing water from the well beside her. Only after drawing the bucket (see top illustration on this page) that I removed what I thought was the wall and made it into the brush behind him.

Whether I got it right or not isn't important. Only that my mind and eyes were agreeing on what I was doing.

The Romanian beauty used for the original "Courting" was again the focus of this drawing as well. This time picking up years later after the fictional couple had been married. The male figure, older, greets his wife for a early morning kiss as he heads off to his travels.

"Courting" and "Courting II" had proven not only to me but to others, that portraits and figure drawings did not have to be confined to what other perceived them to be. That a figure drawing no longer had to be a nude and that a portrait did not have to be a standard sitting pose where the model looked out towards the one viewing the drawing.

Conclusion

Drawing around obstacles has never been truer for this artist! Whether any of this altered the artist I had become may never be clear in our life time.

For when all is said and done and the pencil drawings I once created, with just a few pencils in my hand, have long since faded from the memories of those who had appreciated what I was able to do, the final result is the same for all of us.

It's not how much time we have in this life that matters but what we do with the time that is given to us.

"Create what you have passion for and there will be others who will come to you one day. Never create to meet the public needs since most have no idea what art is. Create what you desire and introduce yourself to the world through your work."

David J. Vanderpool

Chapter Five
In Progress

Some of the newer drawings featured in this Second Edition come from the two books that followed *"Pencil drawings - a look into the art of David J. Vanderpool"*, originally published in 2008.

"Pencil drawings Volume 1- a look into drawing portraits" and *"Pencil drawings Volume 2 - a look into drawing men"* gives the reader an insight to how each drawing was complete. The first book being more like a journal while the second one leans more towards answering questions from readers.

The purpose behind updating this book, by include the newer drawings, was not only to offer a complete look into my drawings, but to share the dramatic changed in those four years.

How working to make each drawing a little better than the last can in fact help a style evolve in such a short period.

Did my style improve after each drawing?

Not with all of them.

But over all, and with right paper, as well as selecting a model or pose that kept my interest, there was a noticeable improvement from not just since 2008, but going back to 2000.

Will I keep improving?

That's hard to say not knowing what the future holds.

The following works in progress are some of drawings that are featured in chapters one and two of this book, that I did not go into detail nor shared the process it took to complete each drawing.

For a more in depth and detailed step-by-step progress of the drawings borrowed from *"Pencil drawings - a look into drawing portraits"* and*"Pencil drawings Volume 2 - a look into drawing men"*, each page will indicate in which of my books the specific drawing can be found.

> " ... if I should stop drawing by the end of this year, my drawings of "Garrett", "Courting", "Rodeo" and "Kevin-Repose" would perhaps be my best. However if I continue, who is to say what I can do?
>
> - David J. Vanderpool
> November 25, 2012

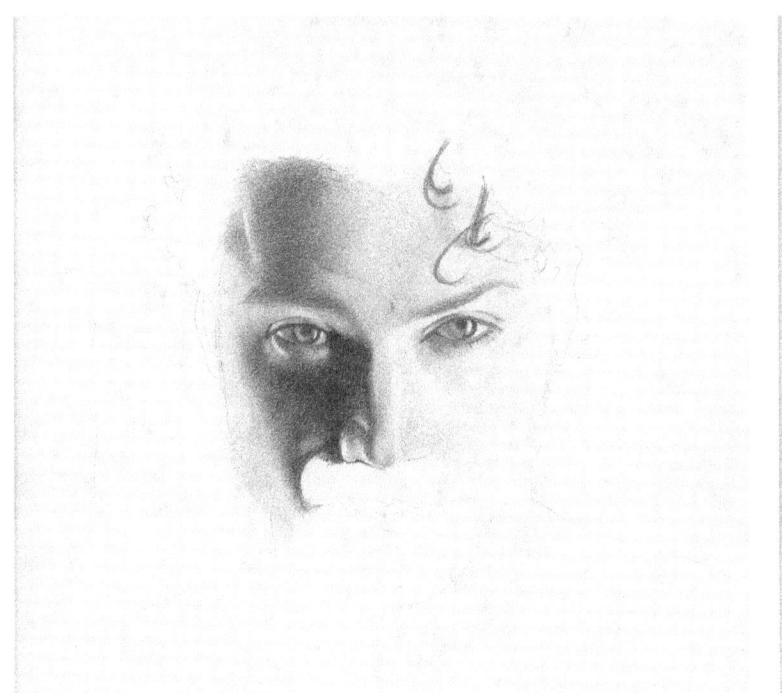
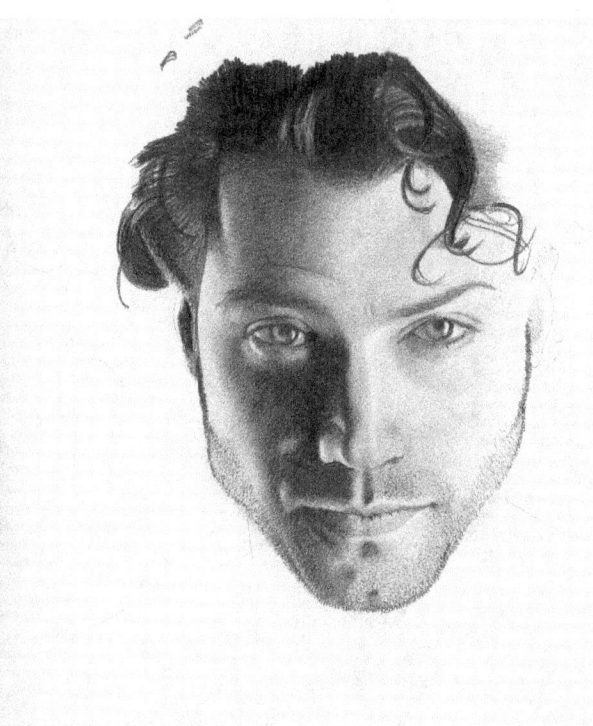
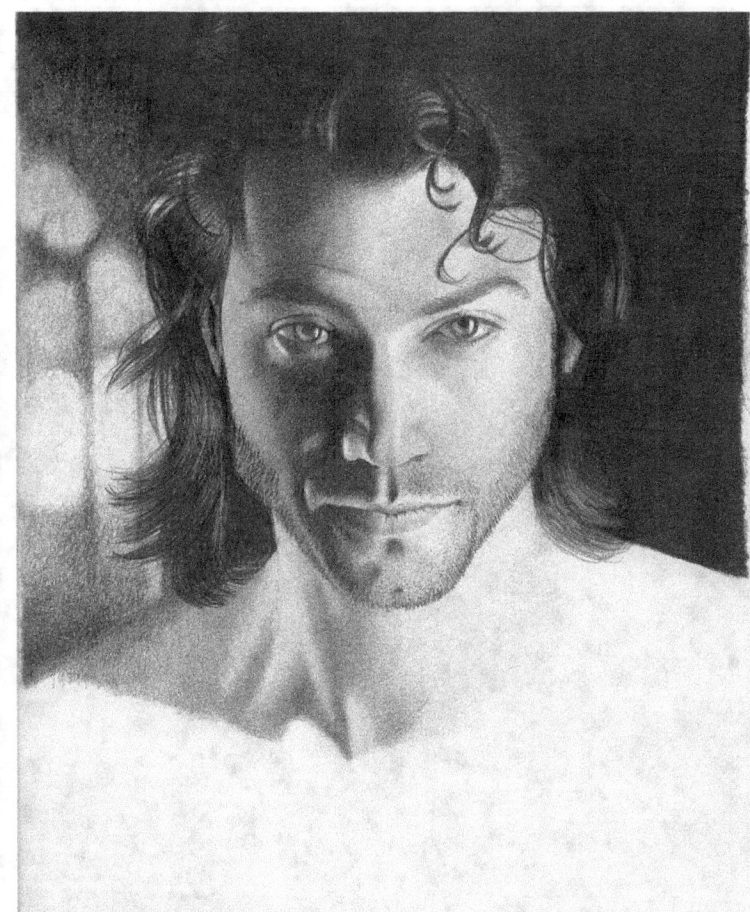
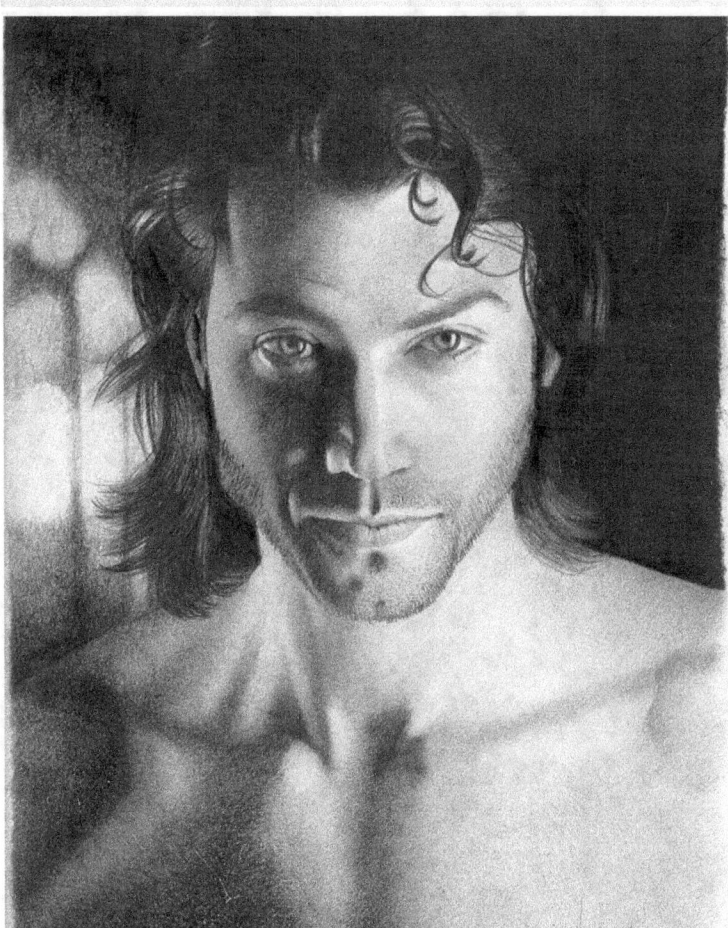

To read more on this drawing of "Ace"
Please see the book:*"Pencil Drawings Volume 2 - a look into drawing men"*

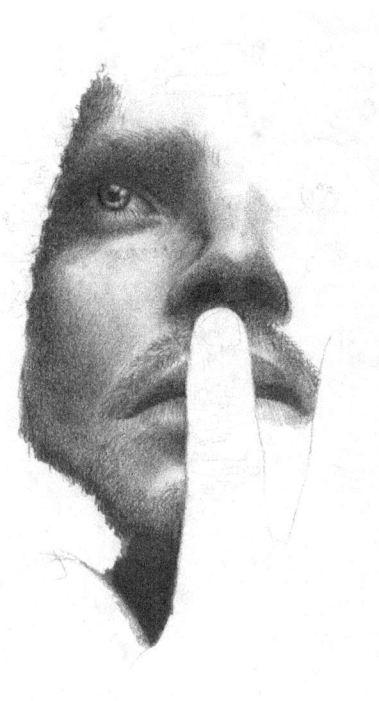
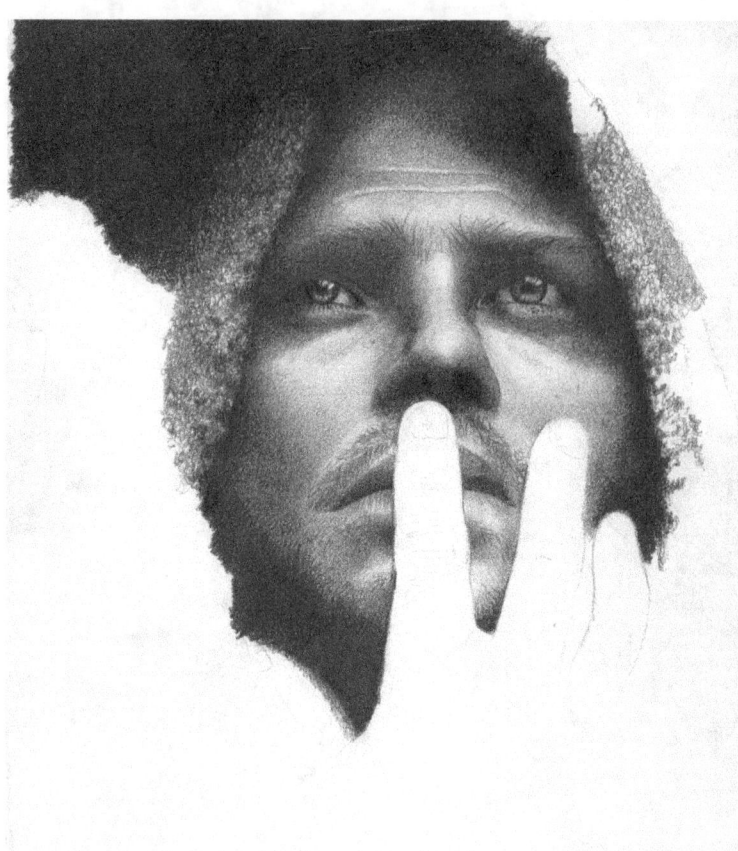
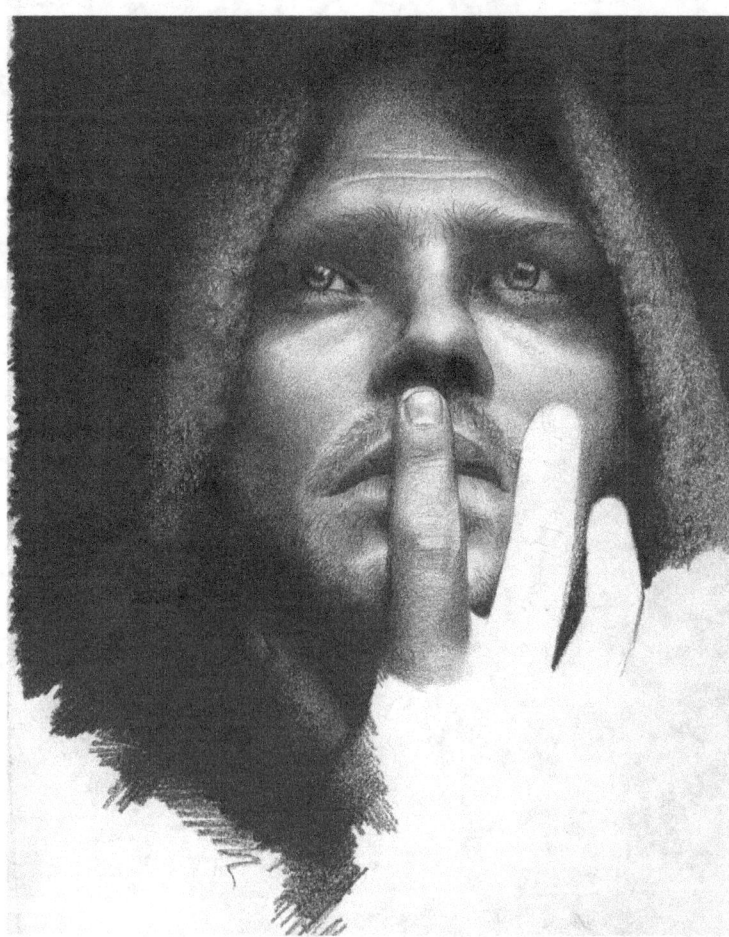
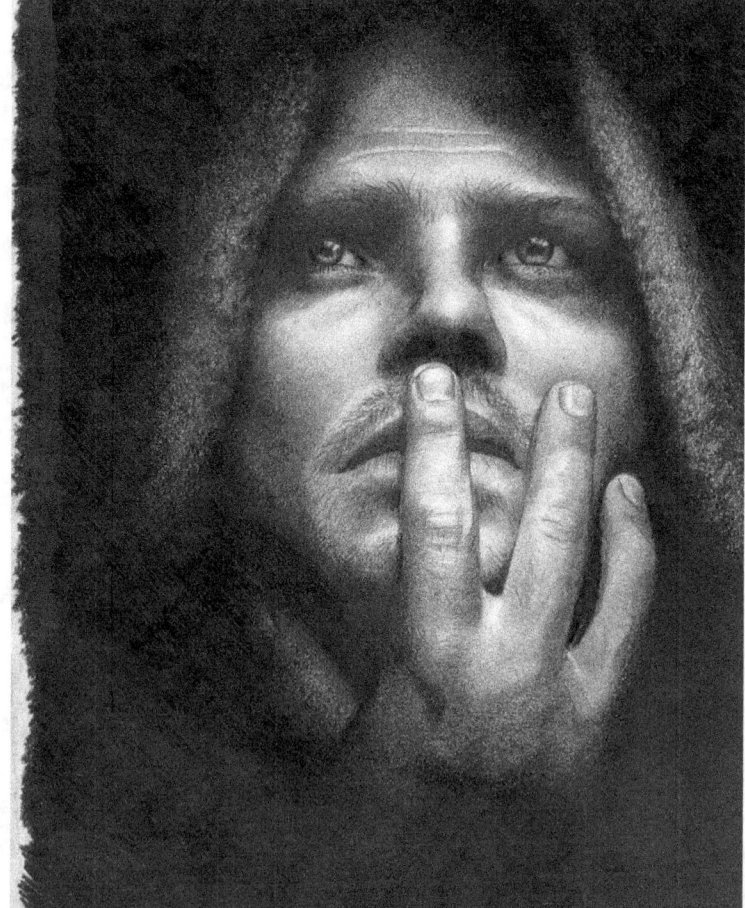

To read more on this drawing of "Aleci II"
Please see the book: *"Pencil Drawings Volume 1 - a look into drawing portraits"*

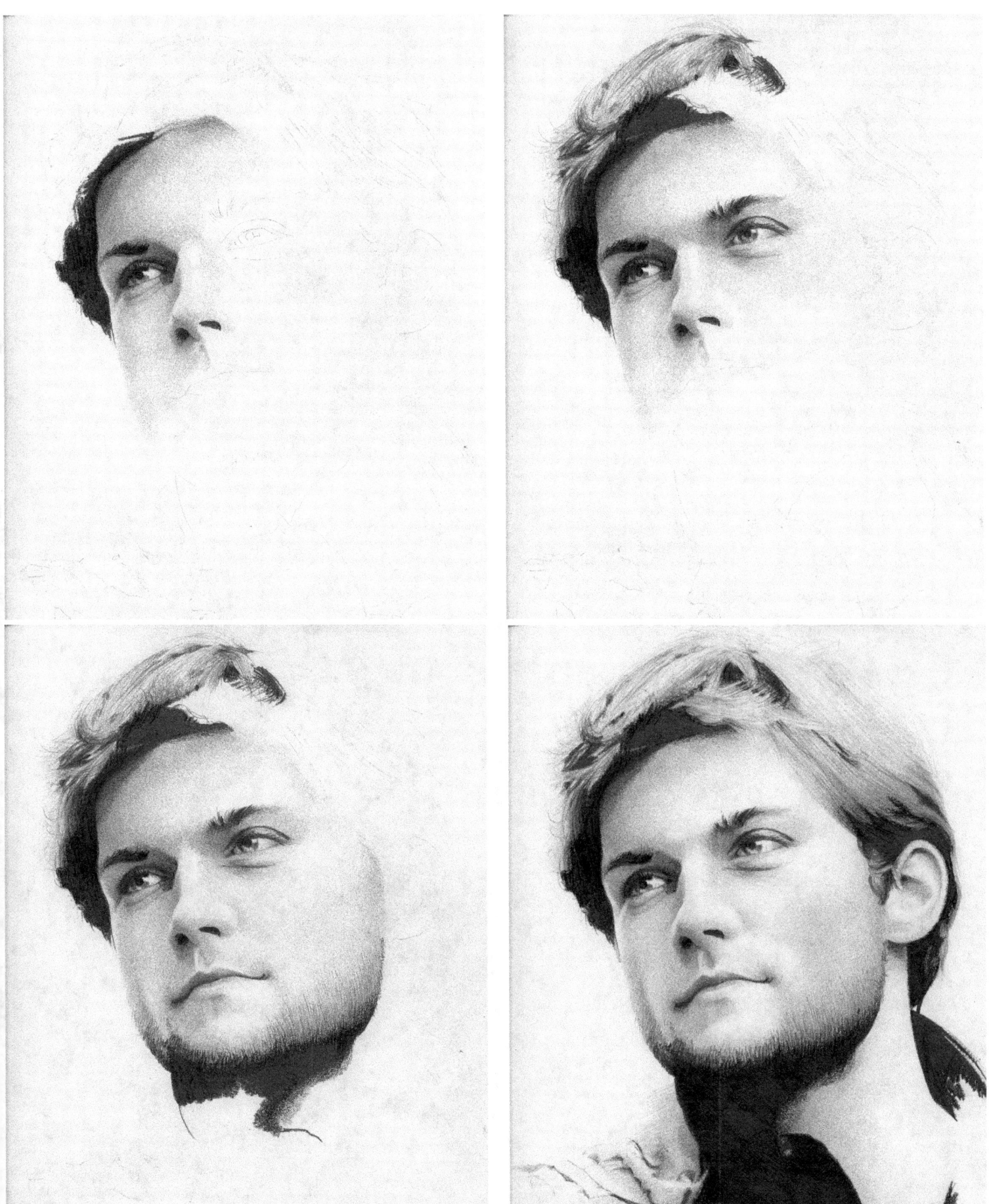

To read more on this drawing of "Allan"
Please see the book: *"Pencil Drawings Volume 1 - a look into drawing portraits"*

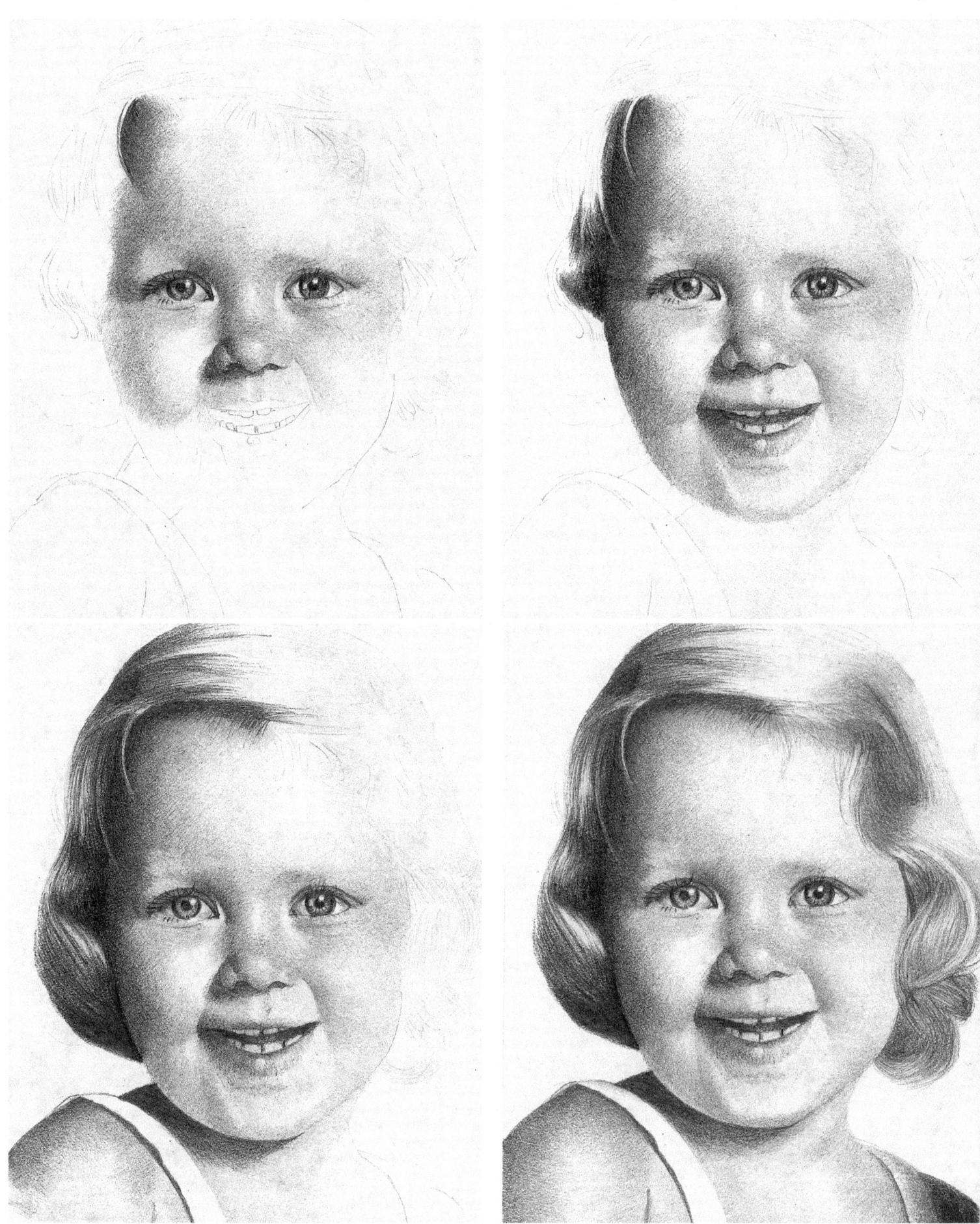

"Amanda"
4.5″ x 6.5″ graphite pencil drawing on paper

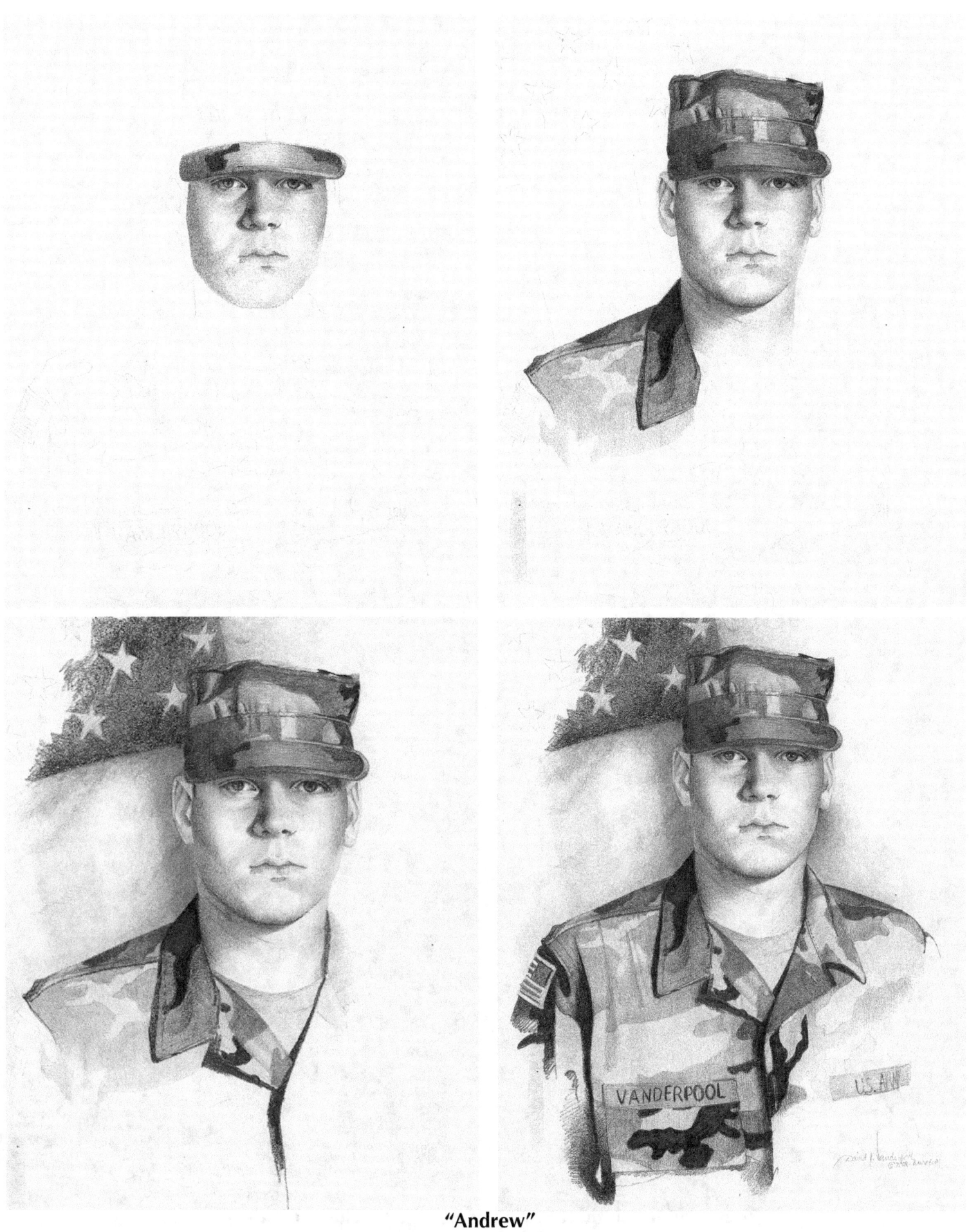

"Andrew"
8.5" x 11" graphite pencil drawing on paper

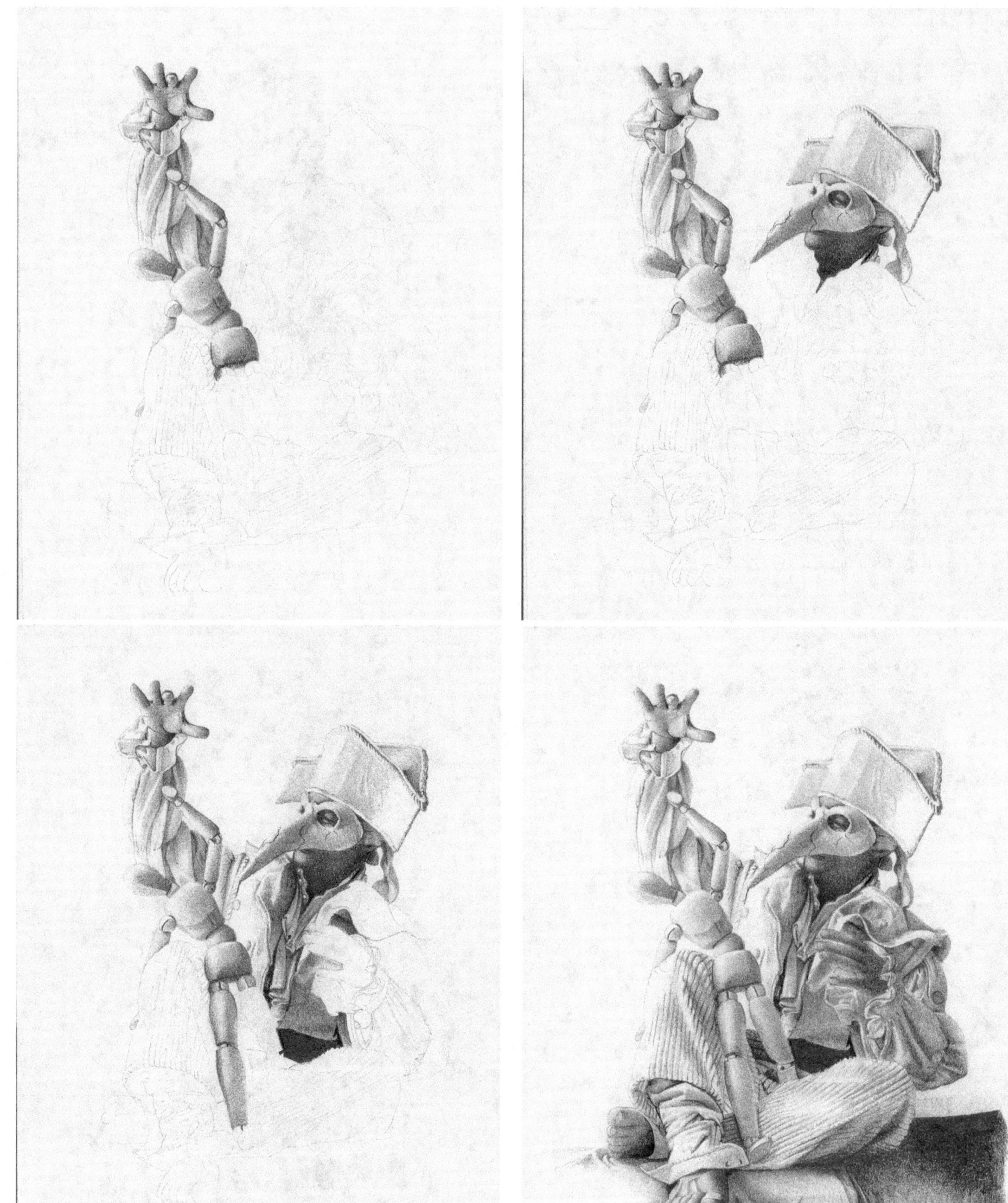

To read more on this drawing of "As The Worlds Fall Down"
Please see the book: *"Pencil Drawings Volume 2 - a look into drawing men"*

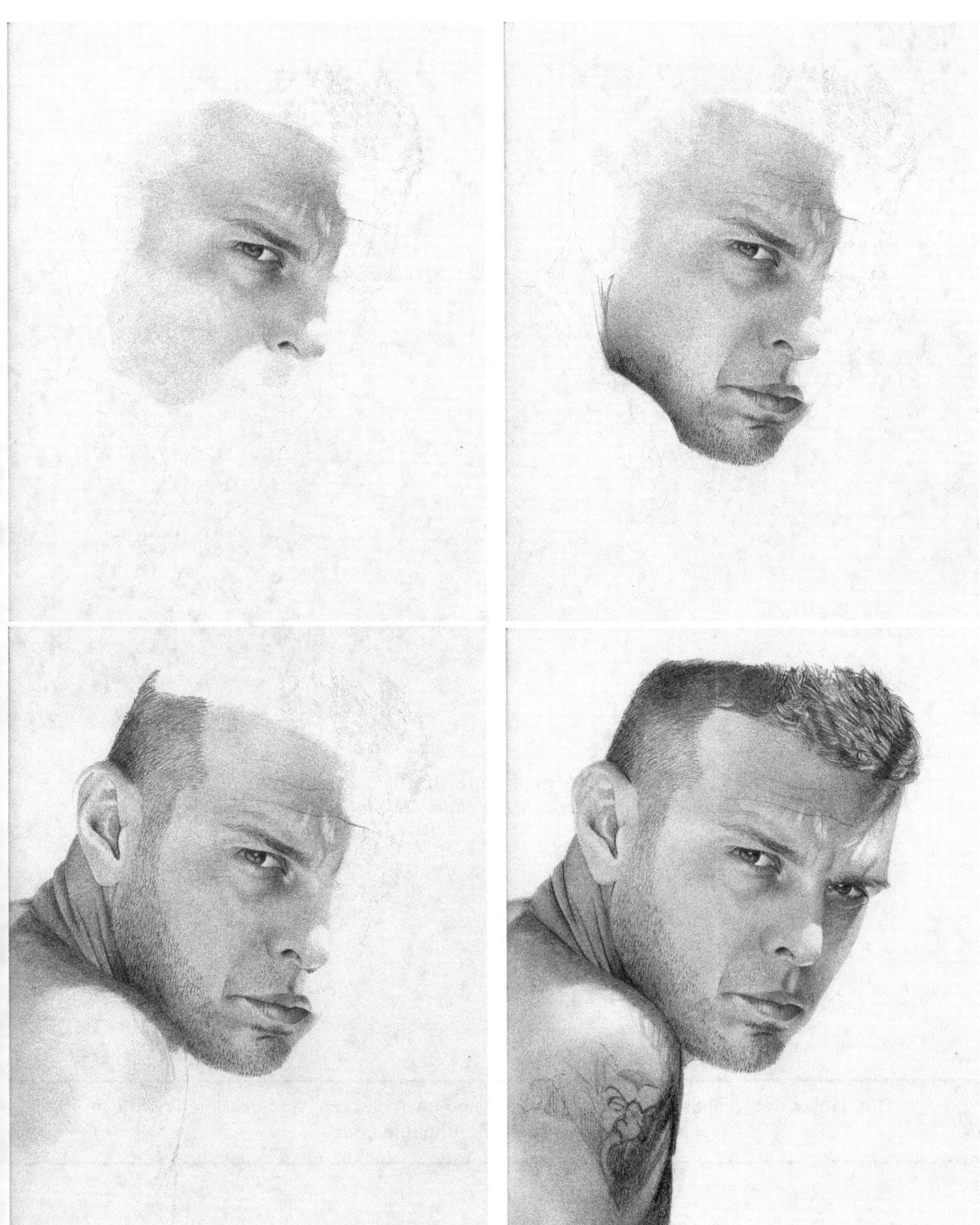

To read more on this drawing of "Augie"
Please see the book: *"Pencil Drawings Volume 2 - a look into drawing men"*

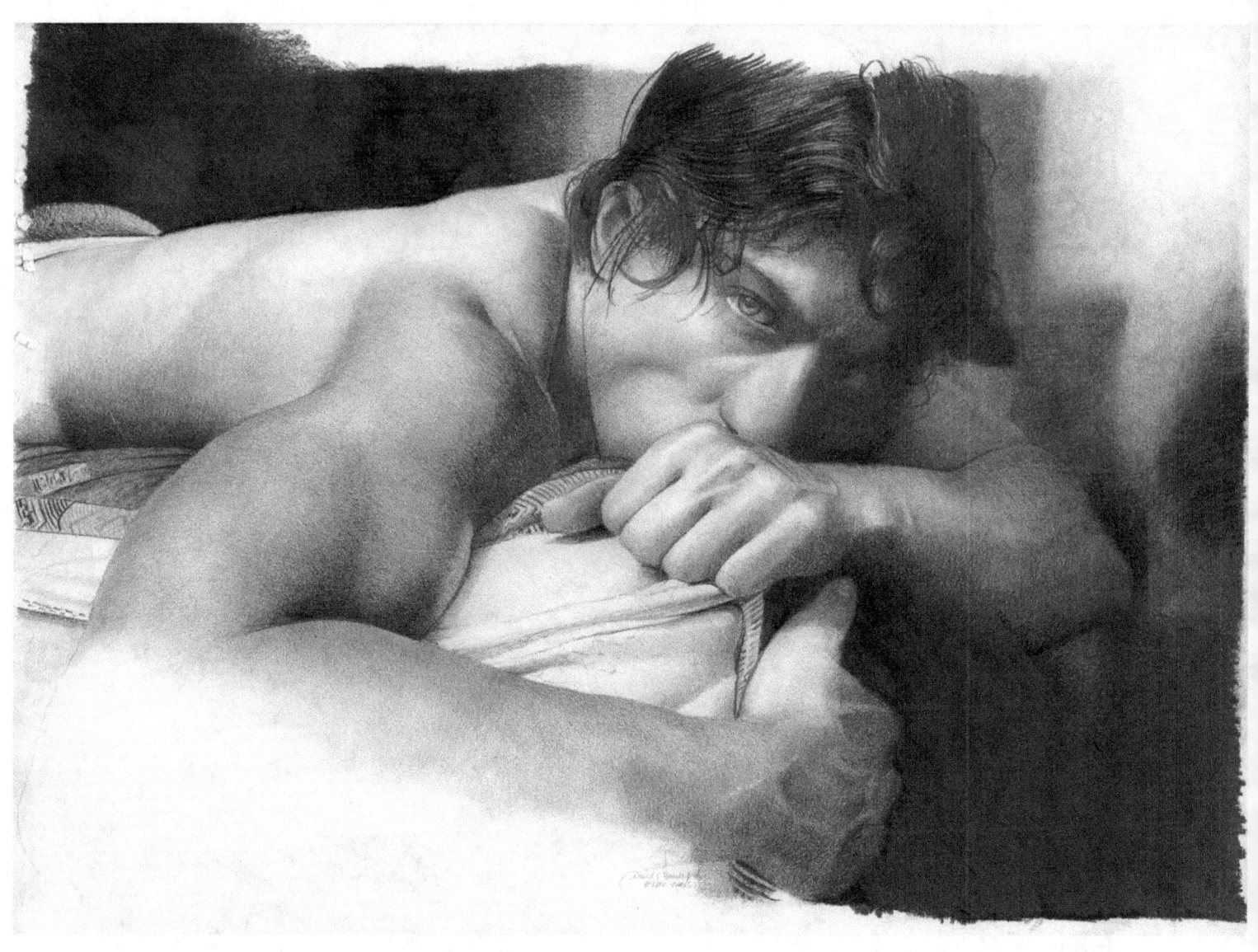

To read more on this drawing of "Chris"
please see the book:*"Pencil Drawings Volume 2- a look into drawing men"*

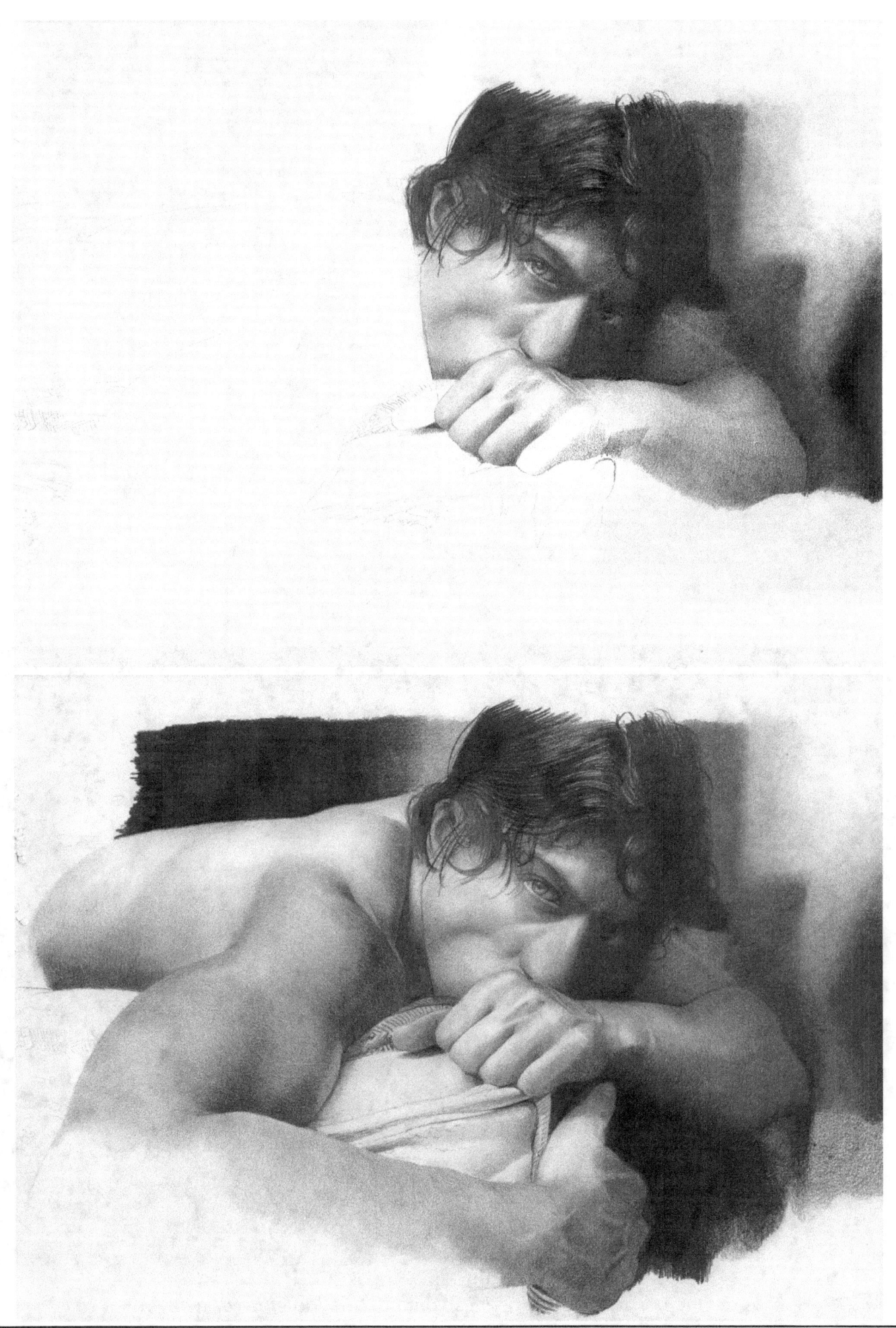

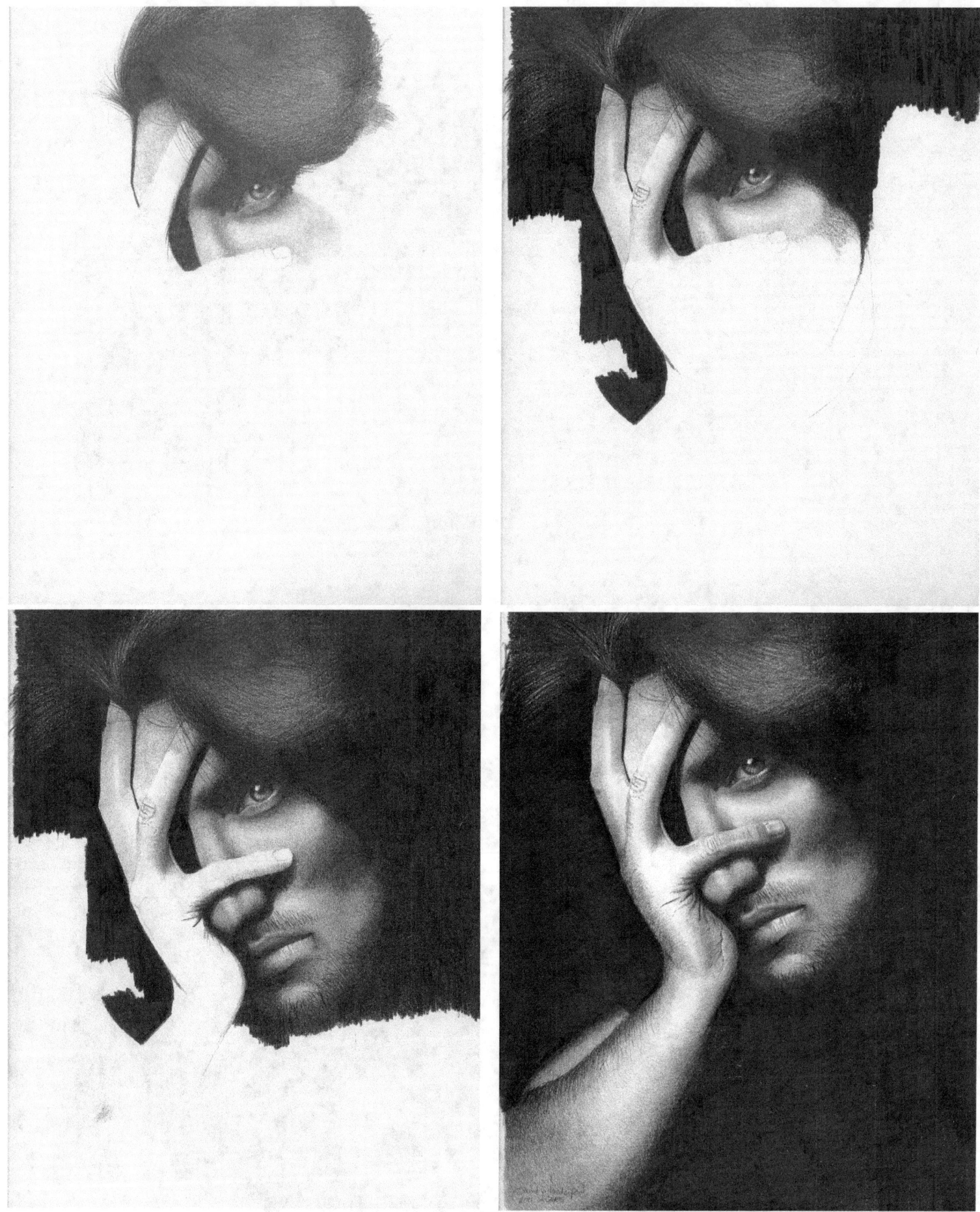

To read more on this drawing of "Chris II"
Please see the book:*"Pencil Drawings Volume 2 - a look into drawing men"*

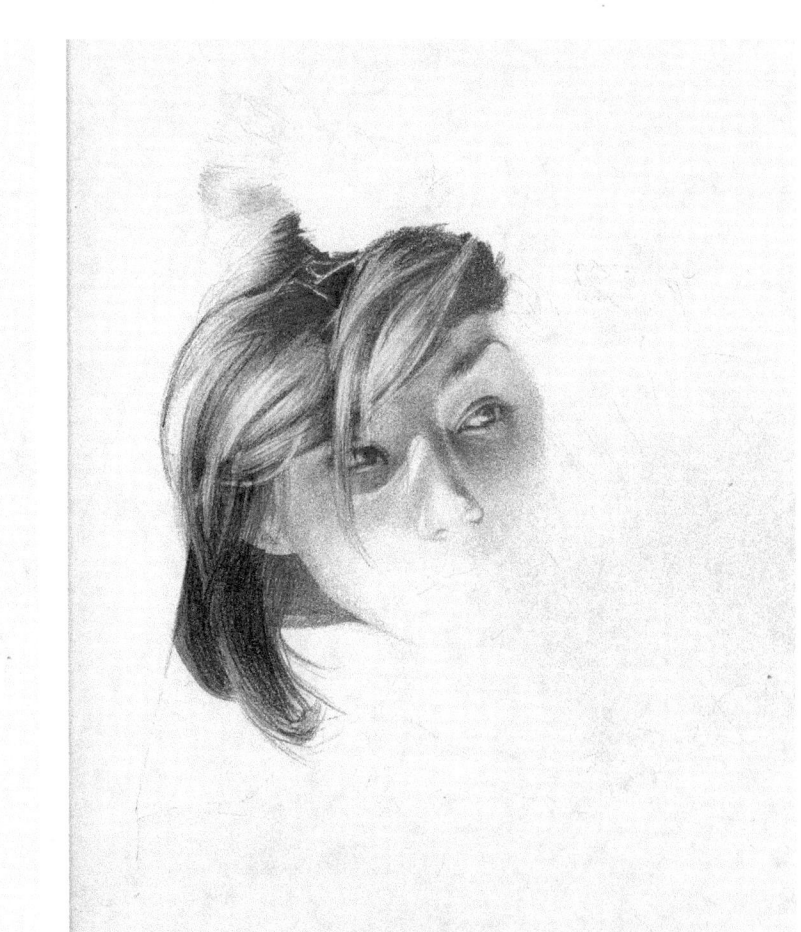

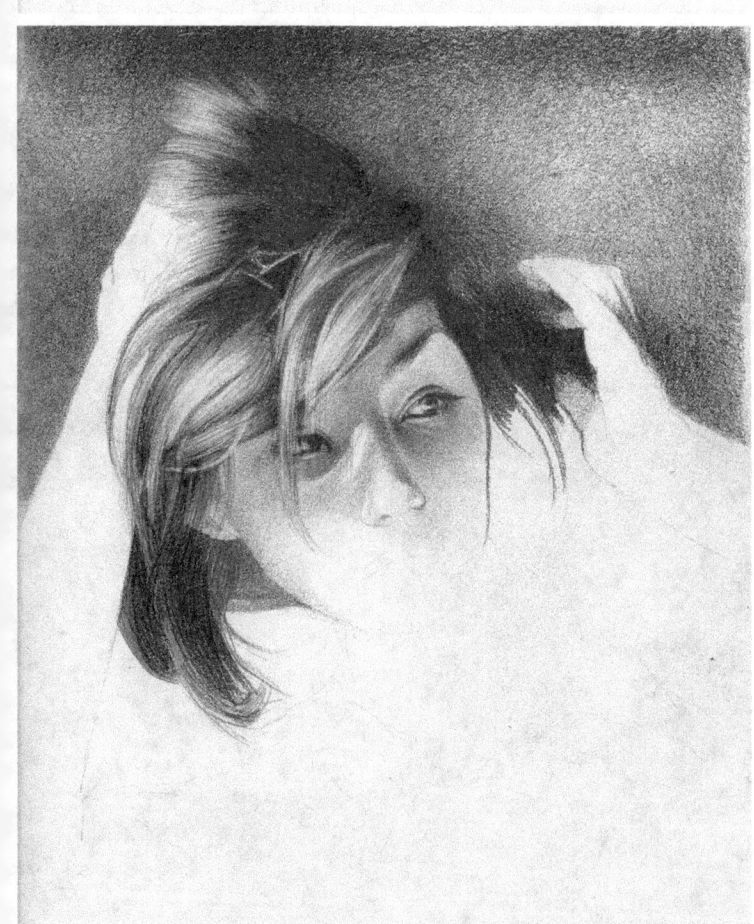

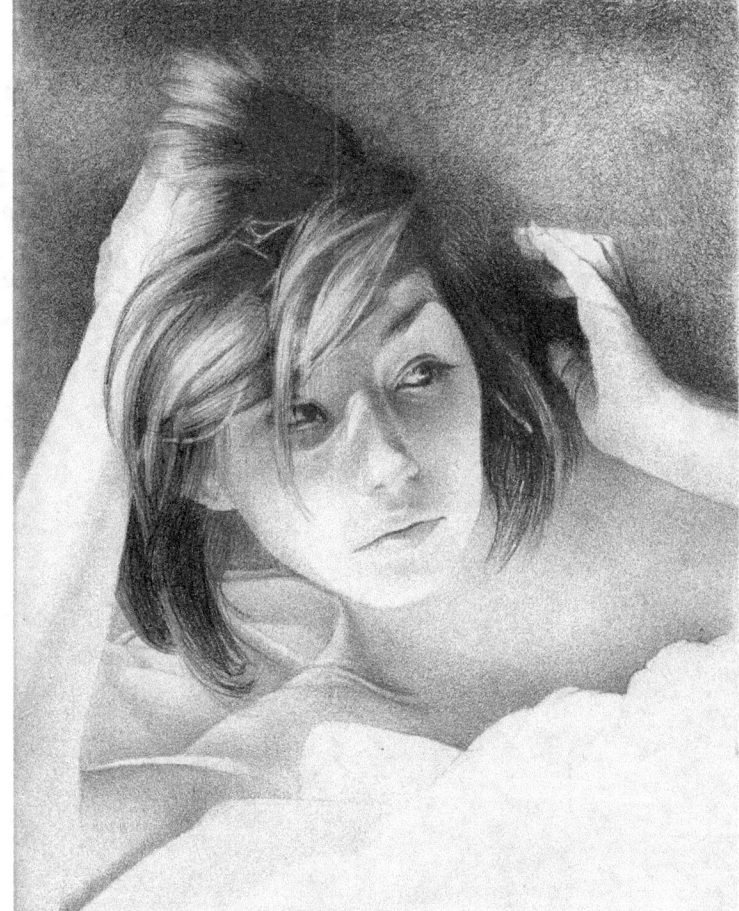

To read more on this drawing of "Christina"
Please see the book:*"Pencil Drawings Volume 1 - a look into drawing portraits"*

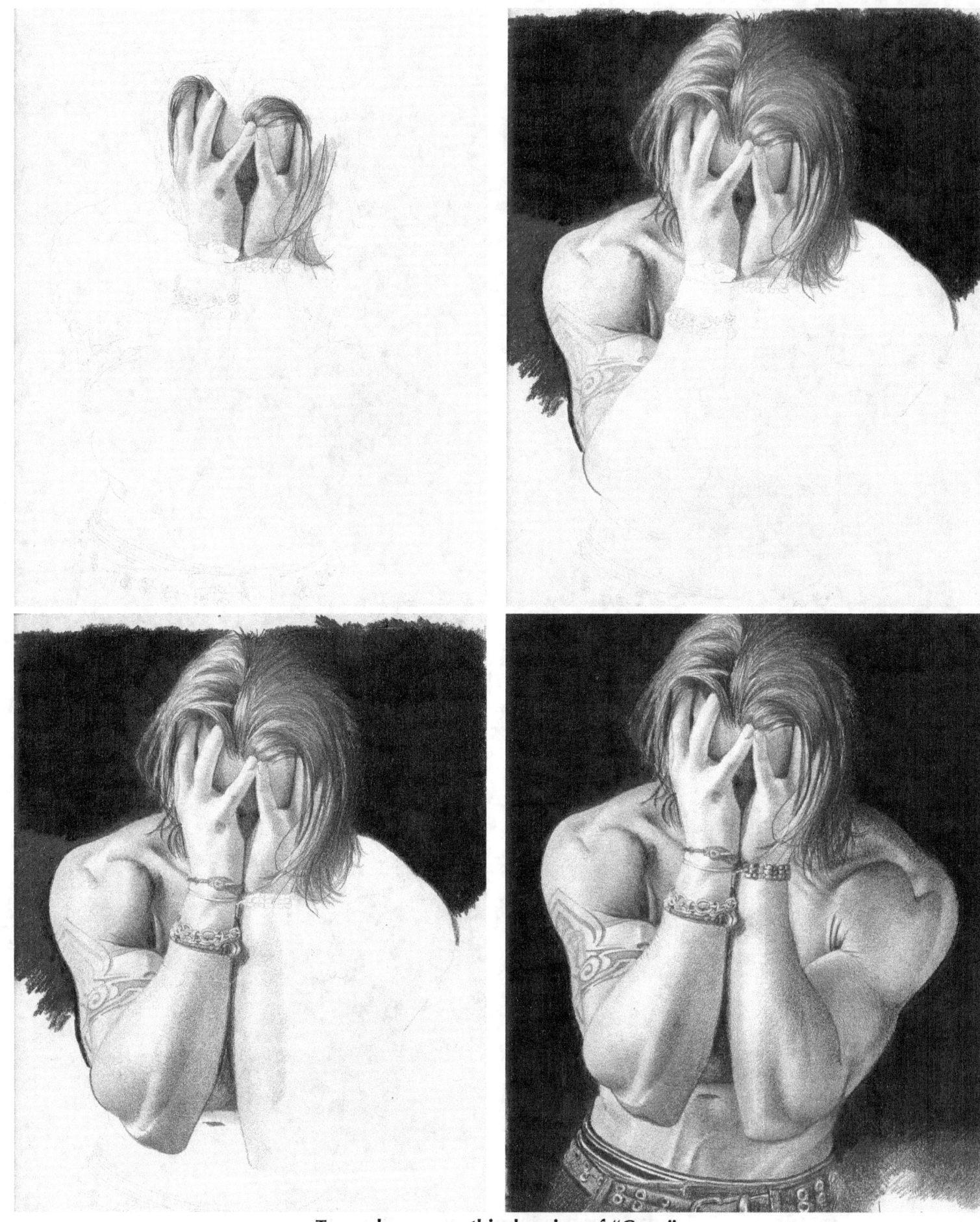

To read more on this drawing of "Cory"
Please see the book: *"Pencil Drawings Volume 2 - a look into drawing men"*

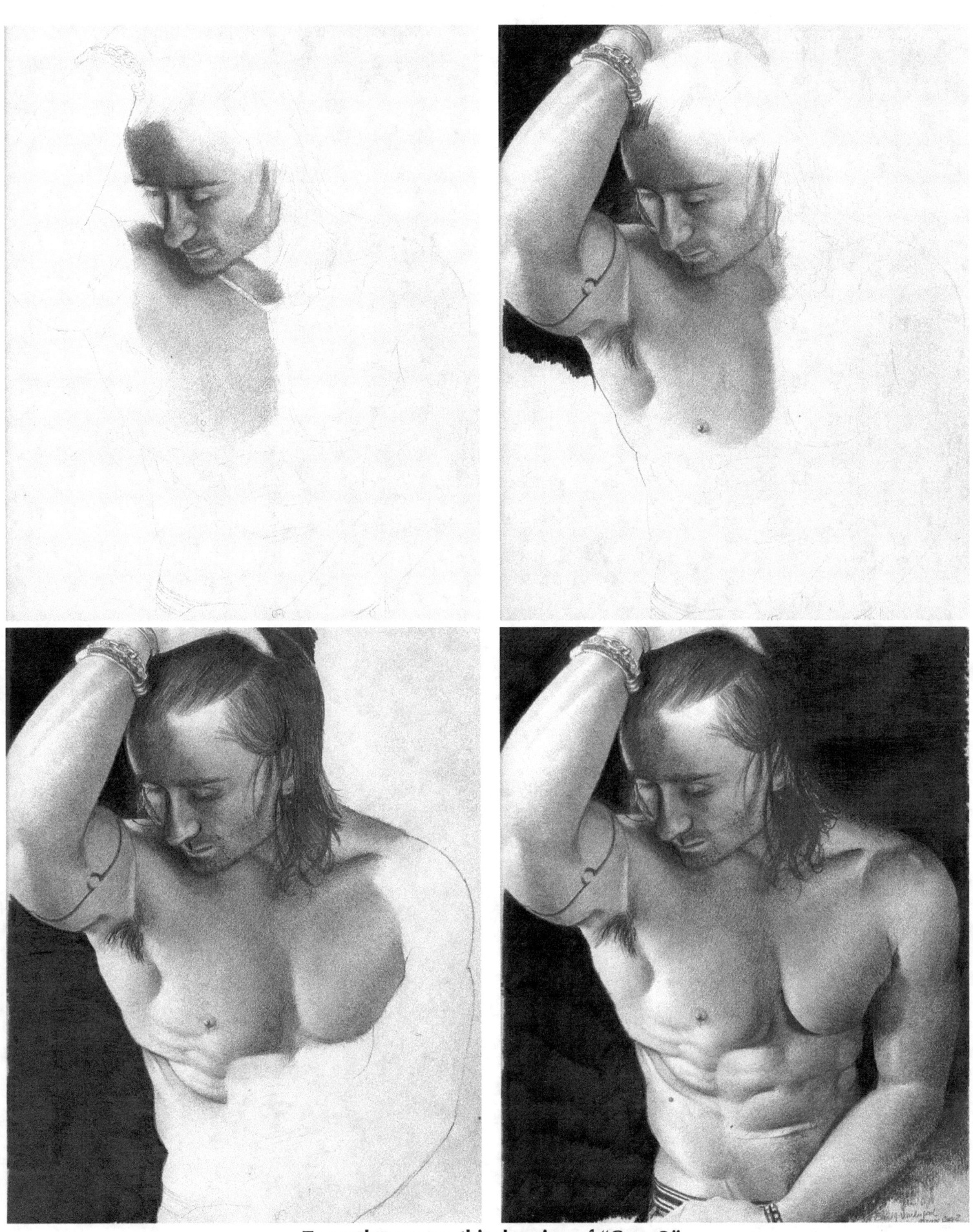

To read more on this drawing of "Cory 2"
Please see the book: *"Pencil Drawings Volume 1 - a look into drawing portraits"*

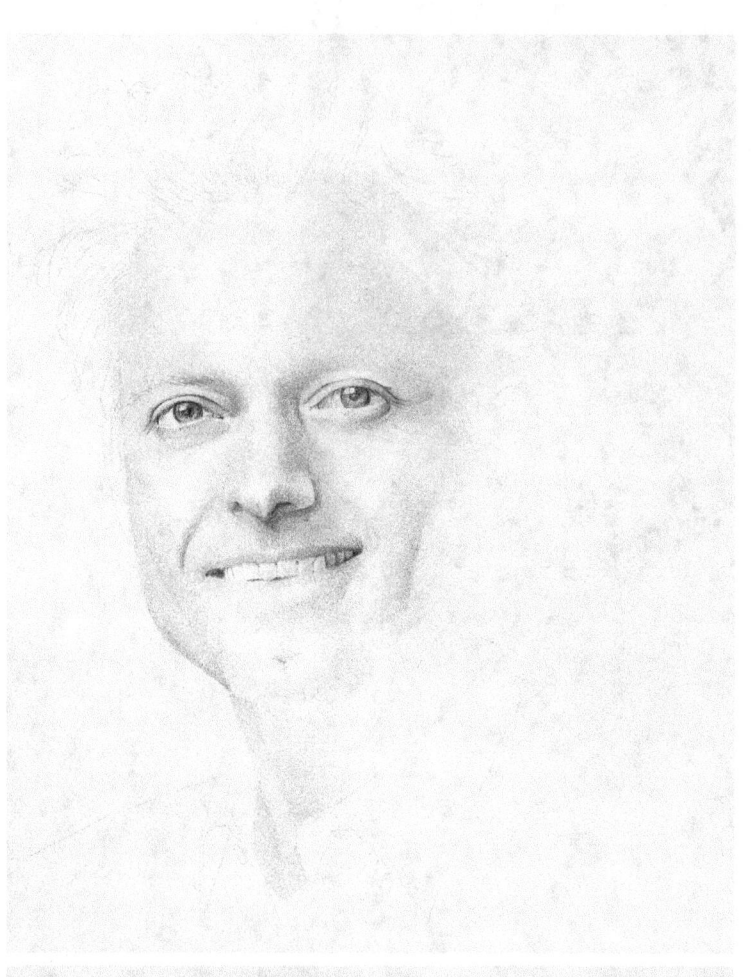
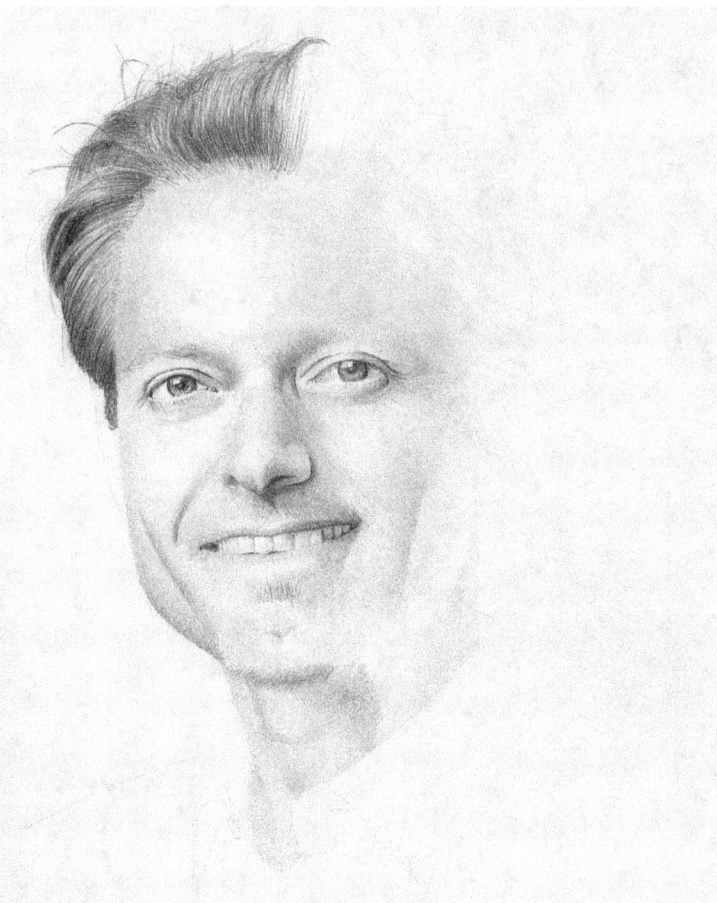
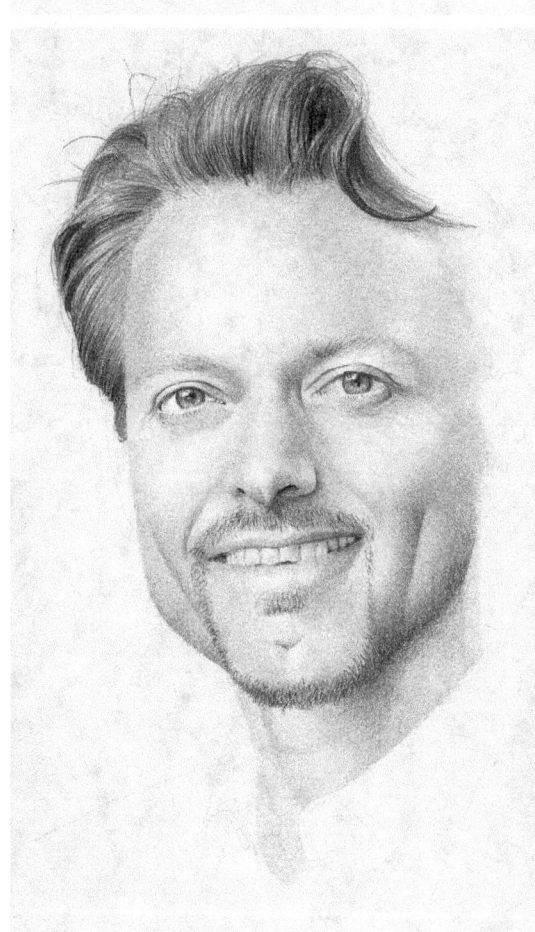
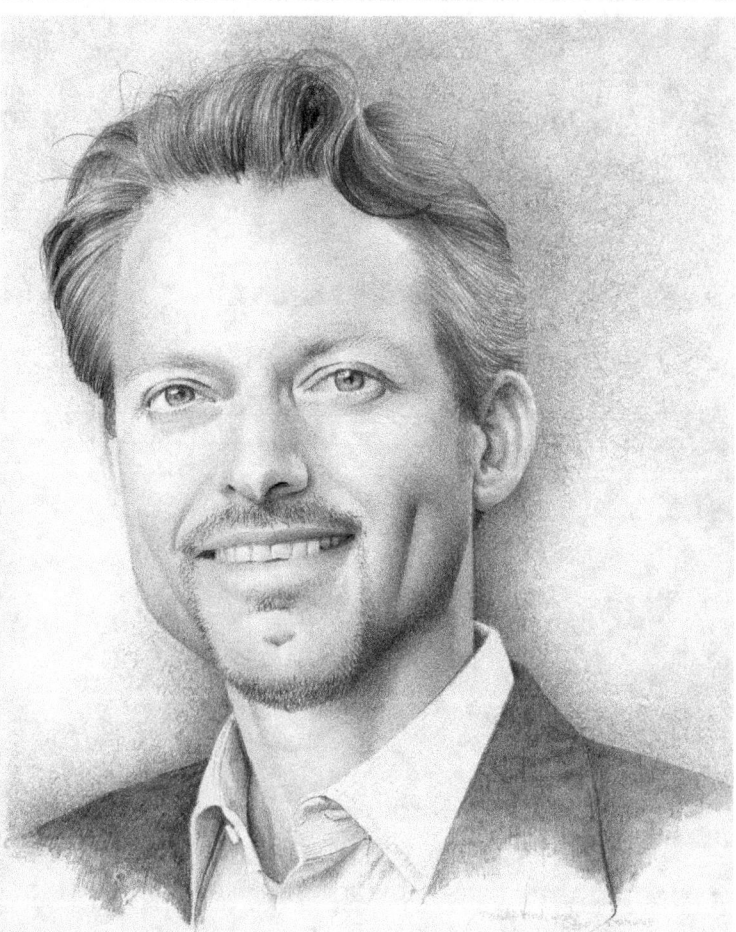

To read more on this drawing of "Edmund"
Please see the book:*"Pencil Drawings Volume 2 - a look into drawing men"*

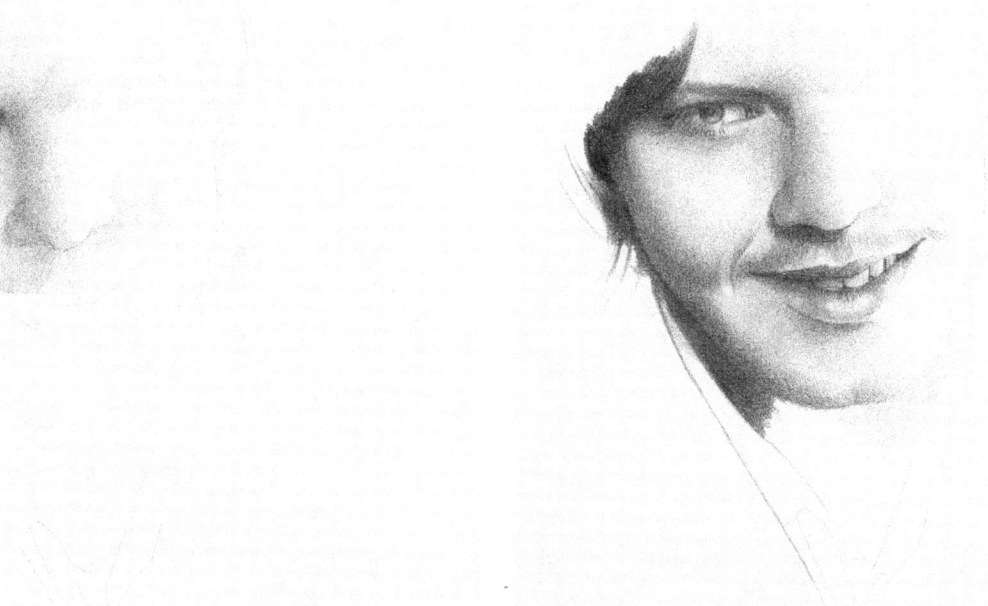

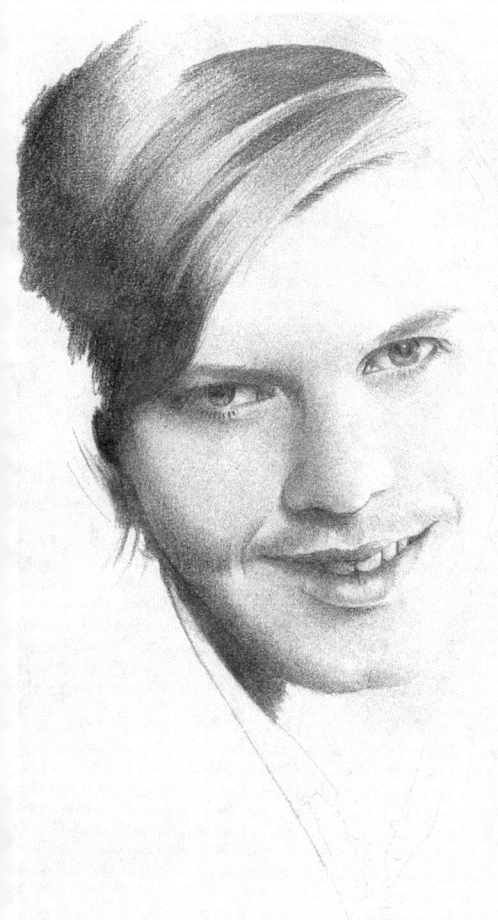

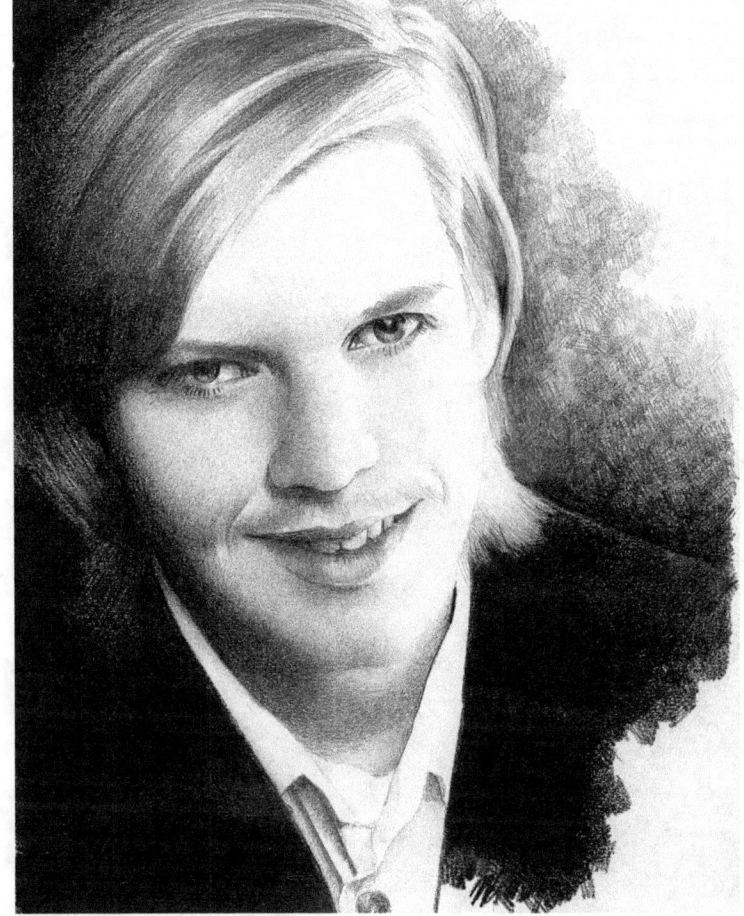

"Jared"
8.5″ x 11 graphite pencil drawing on paper

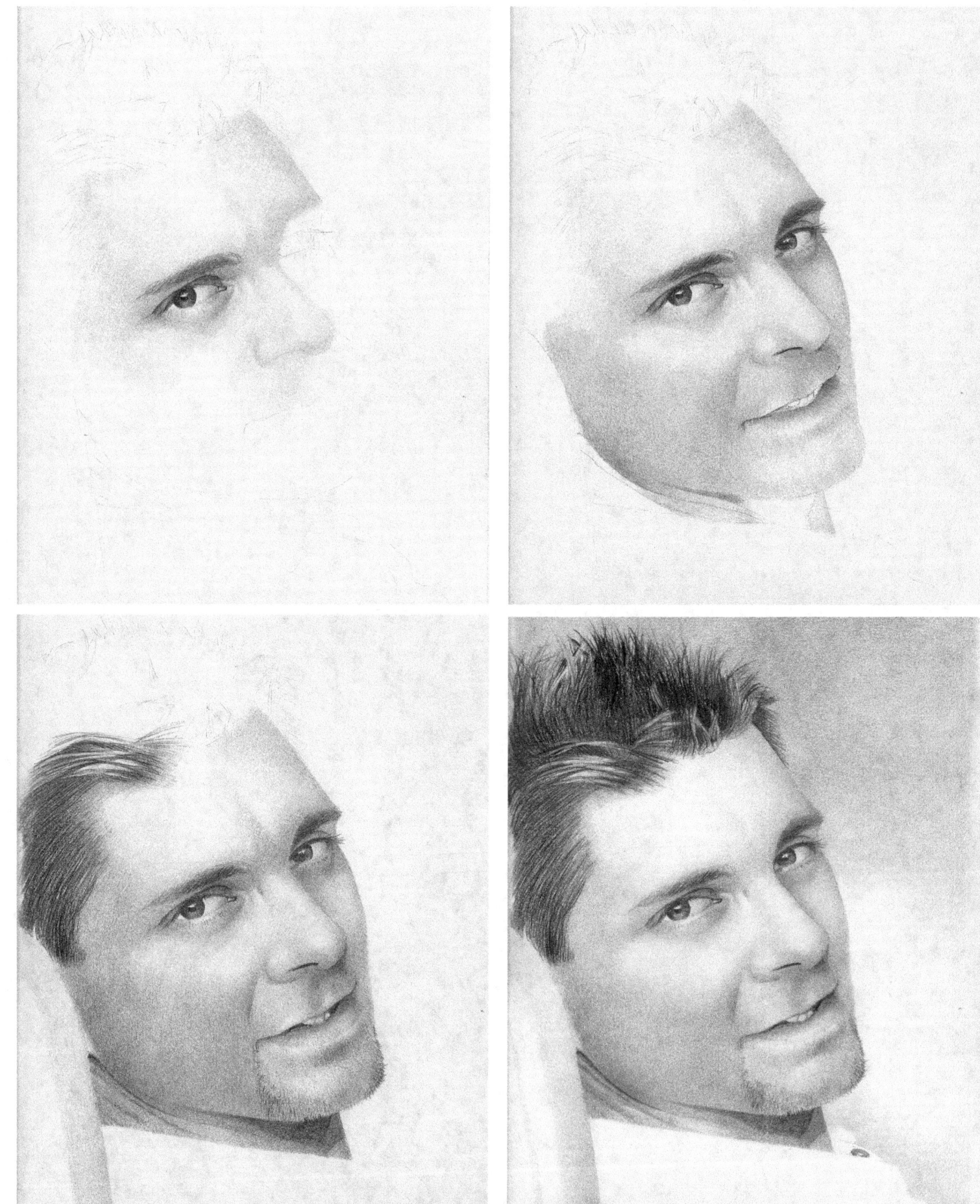

To read more on this drawing of "Jason"
please see the book: *"Pencil Drawings Volume 2 - a look into drawing men"*

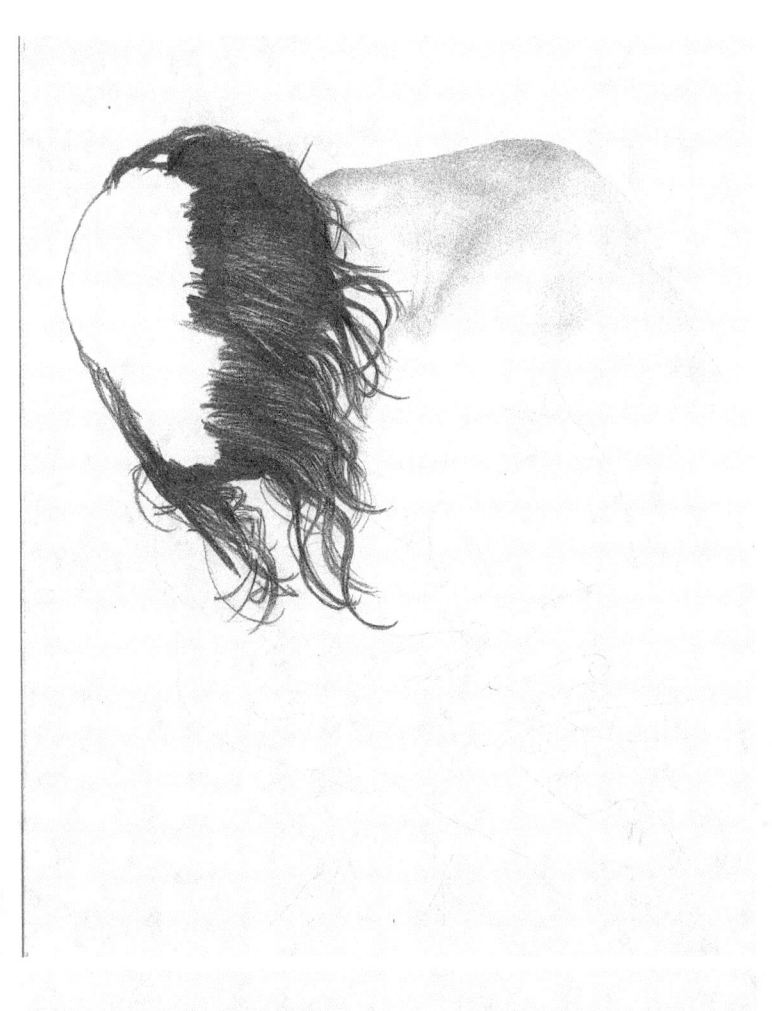
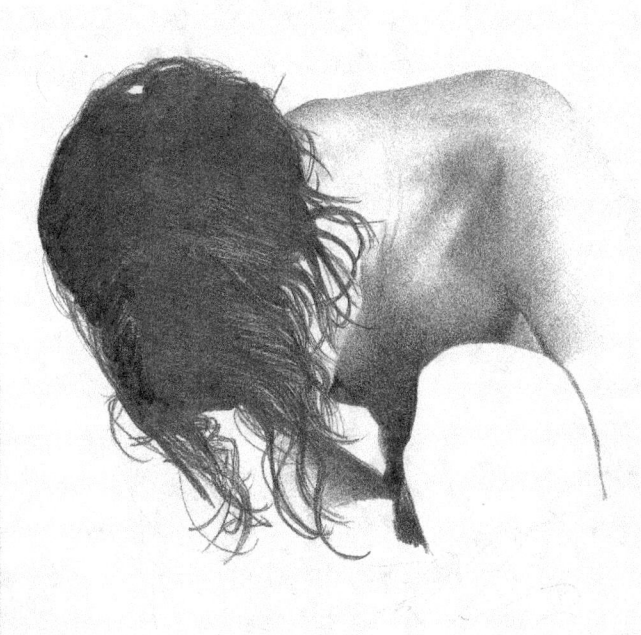
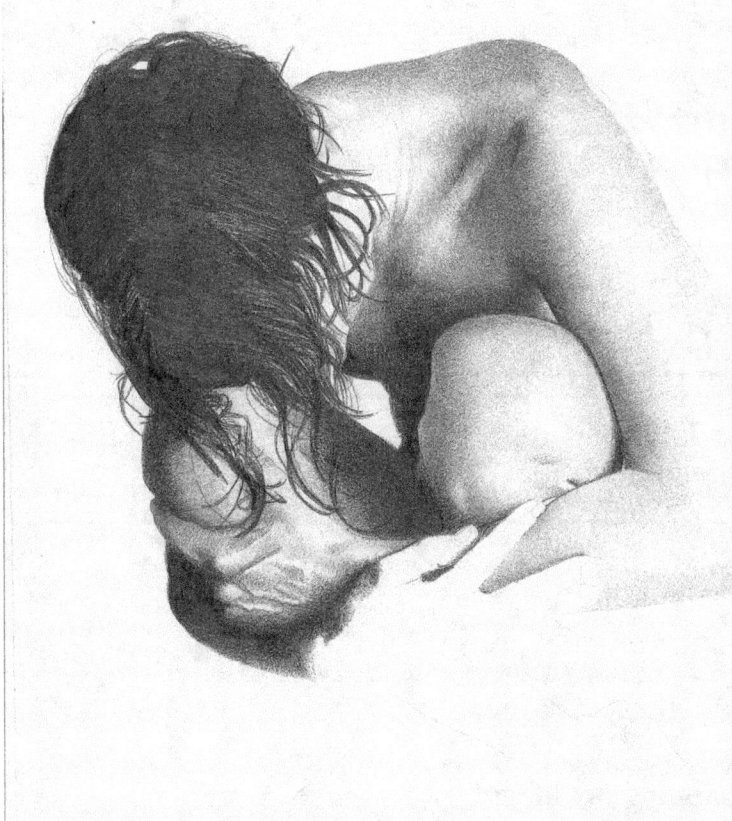
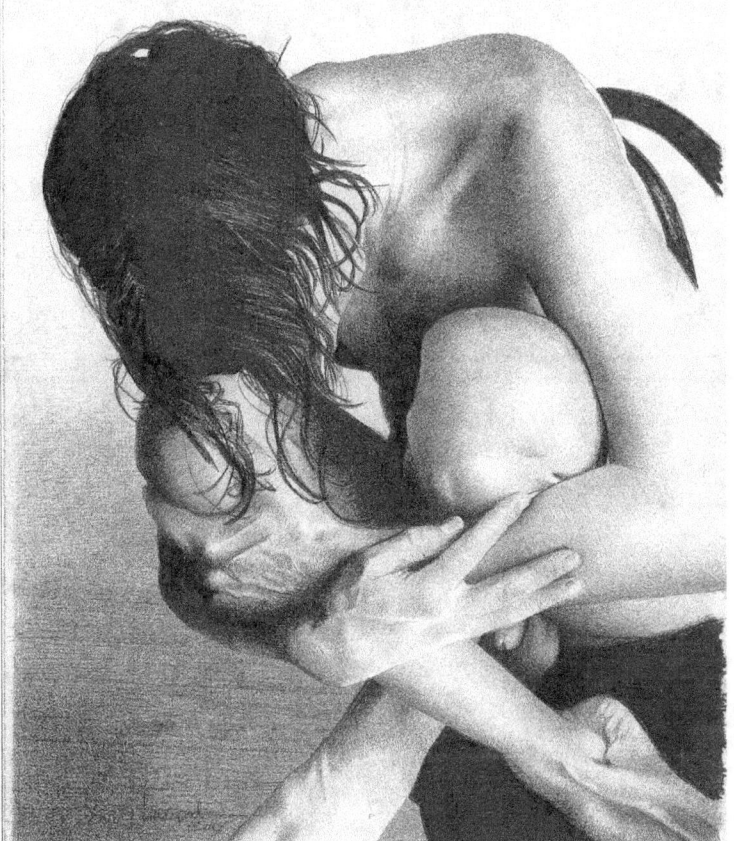

"Josh"
8.5″ x 11 graphite pencil drawing on paper

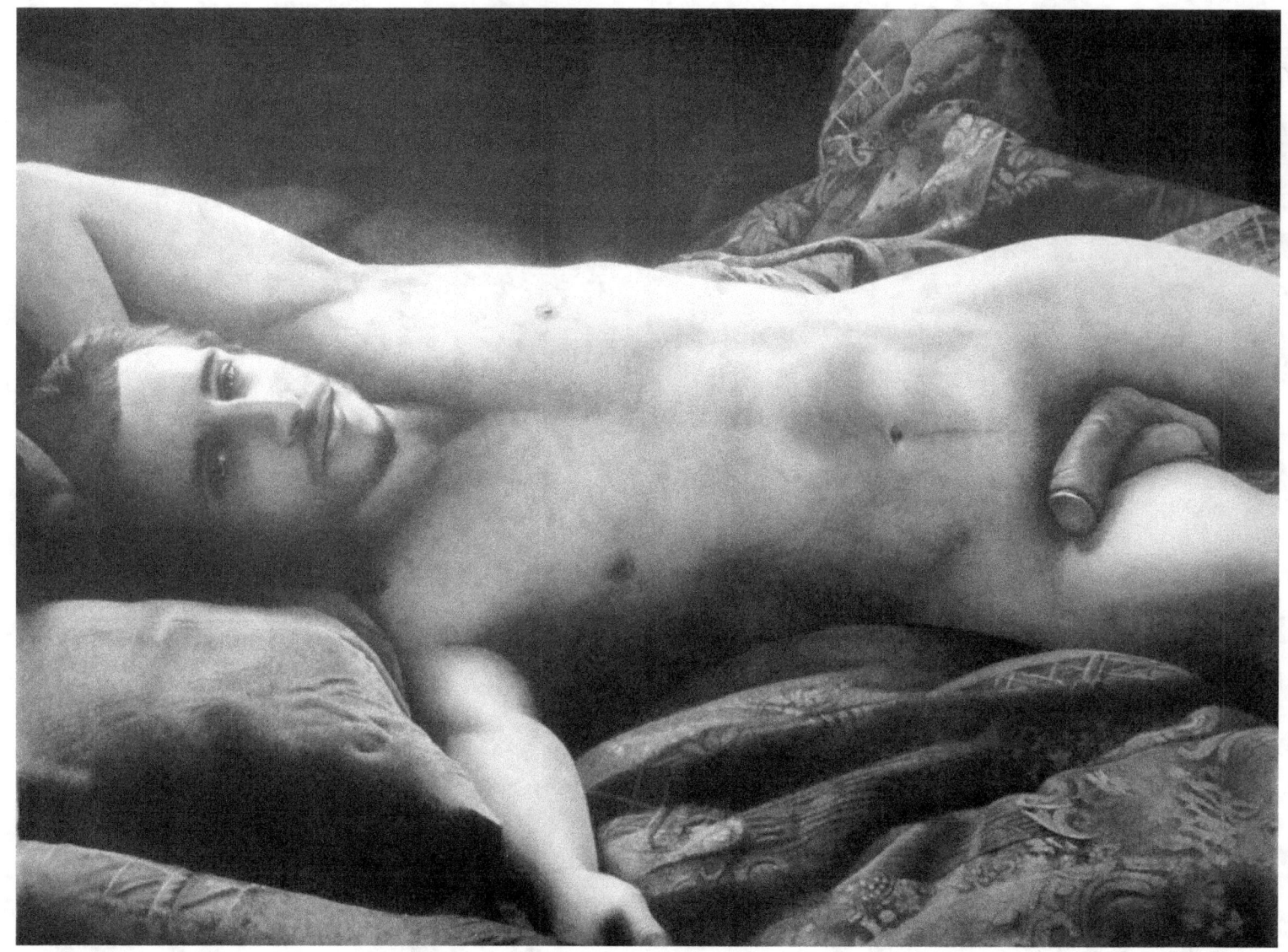

"Kevin - Repose"
28" x 18" graphite pencil drawing on paper

The original drawing of "Kevin - Repose", as well as others seen in this book, can be purchased at
http://www.saatchionline.com/profiles/portfolio/id/3337

Affordable prints of most of the drawings by David J. Vanderpool can be ordered online at
http://paper2pencil.redbubble.com/

Facing page:
To read more on this drawing of "Kevin"
please see the book:*"Pencil Drawings Volume 1 - a look into drawing portraits"*

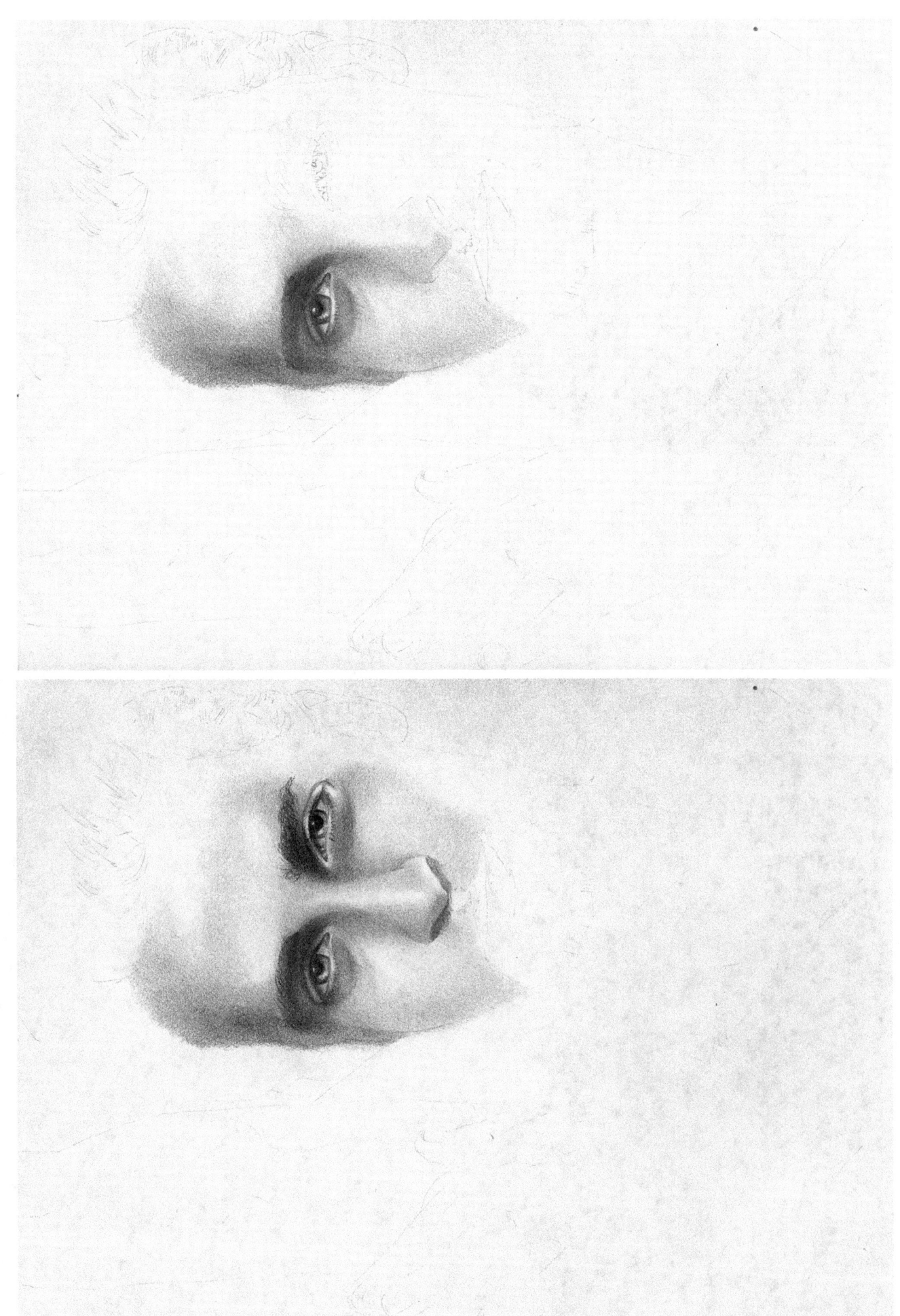

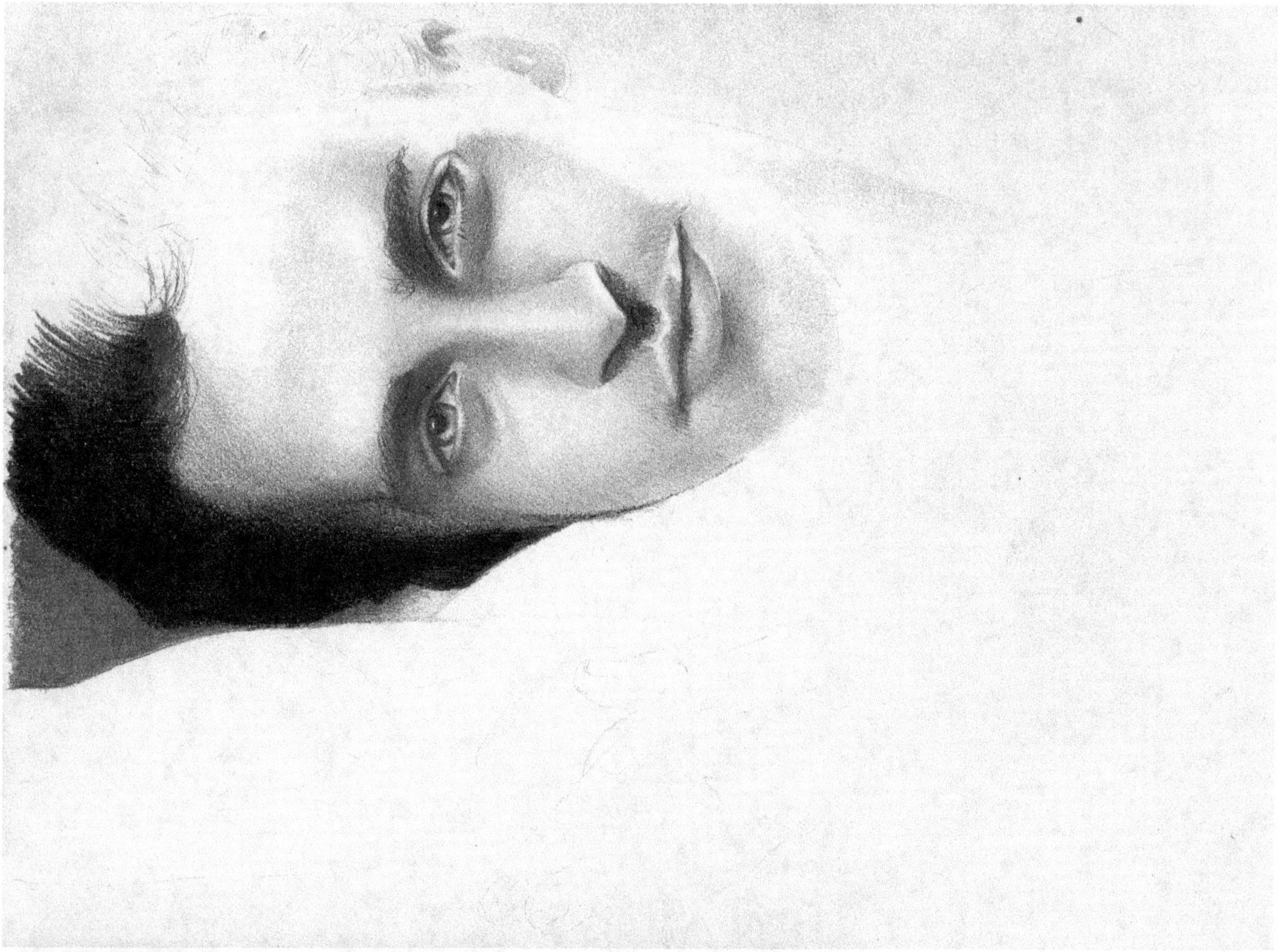

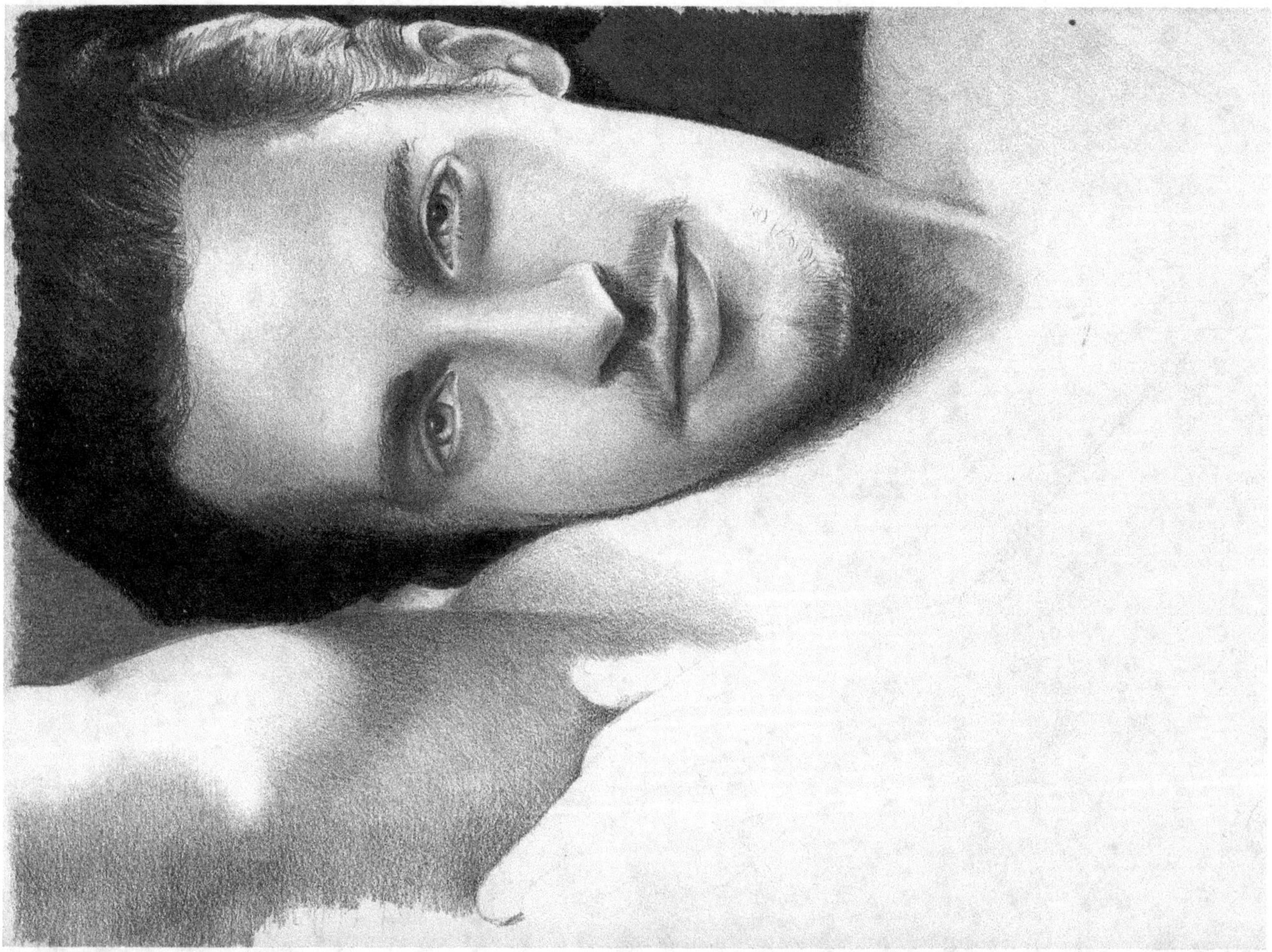

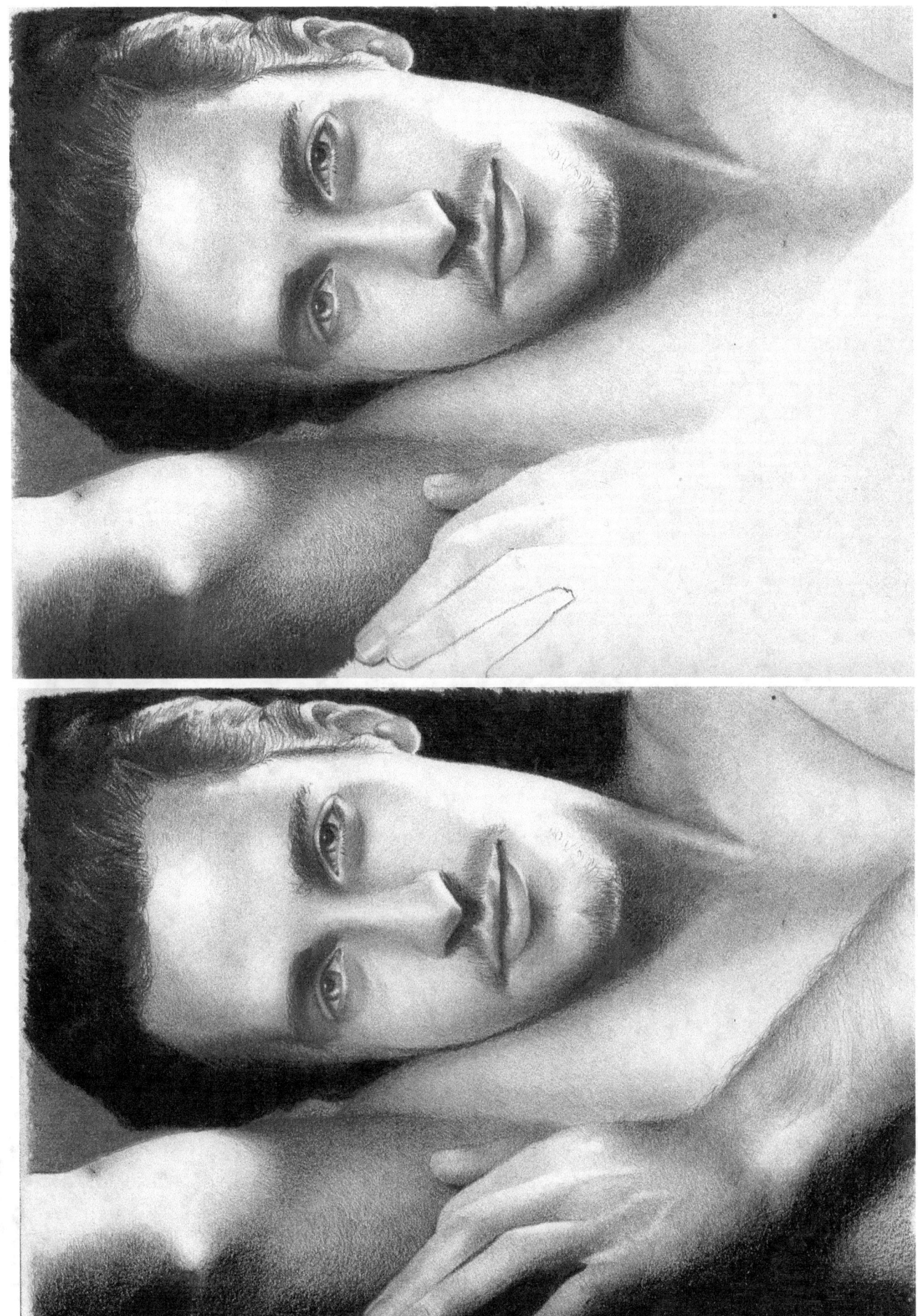

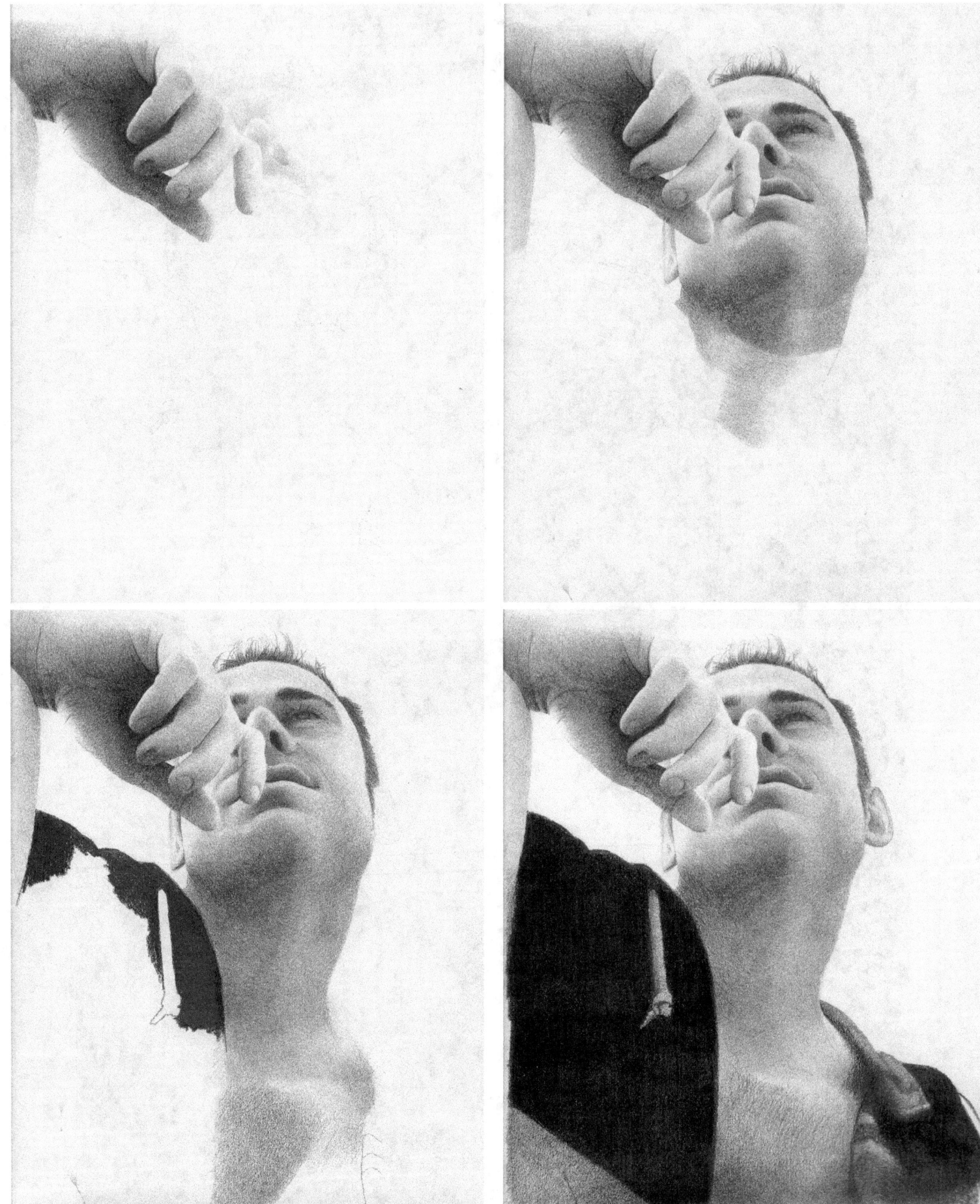

To read more on this drawing of "Riverking"
Please see the book:*"Pencil Drawings Volume 2 - a look into drawing men"*

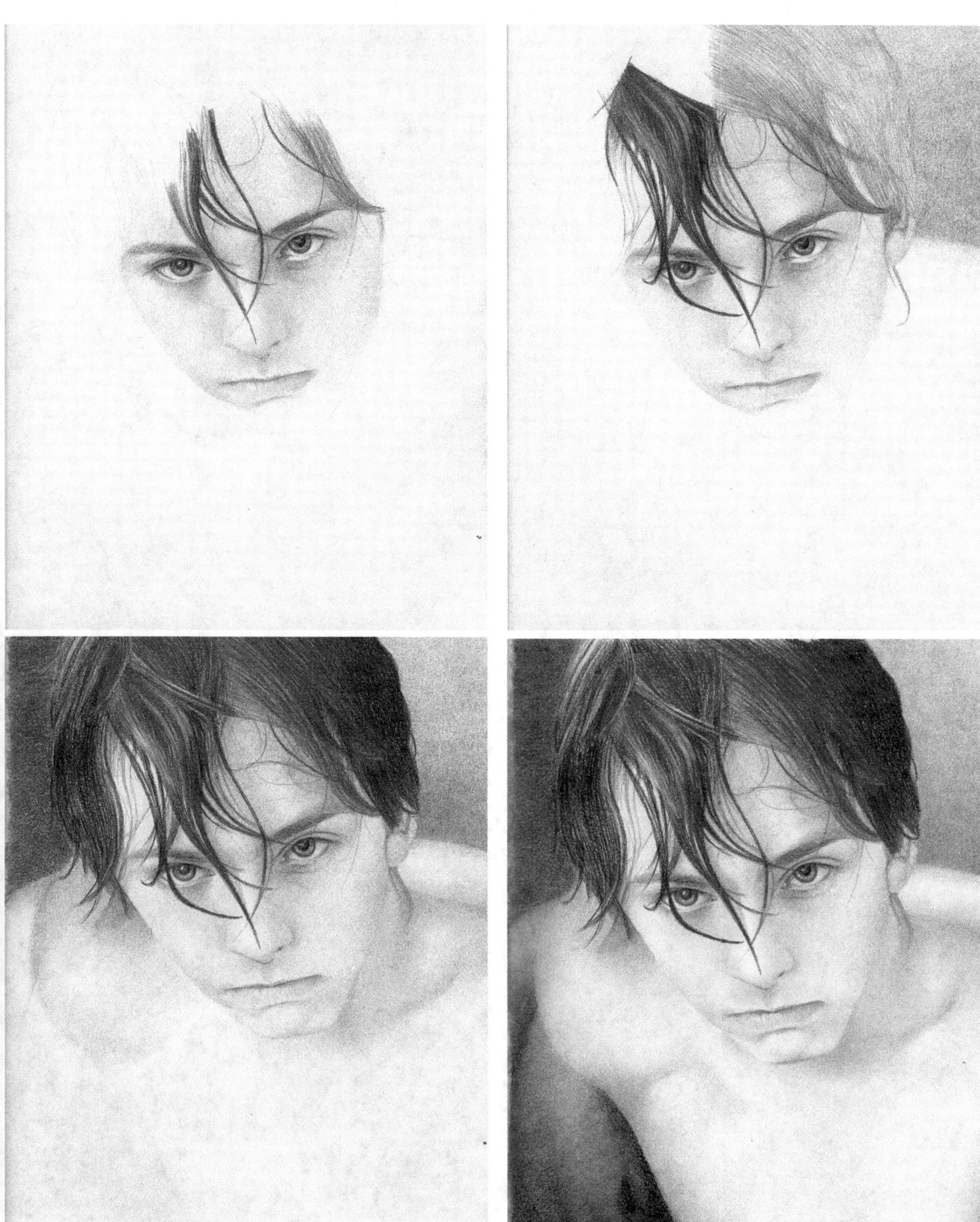

To read more on this drawing of "Matt"
please see the book: *"Pencil Drawings Volume 1 - a look into drawing portraits"*

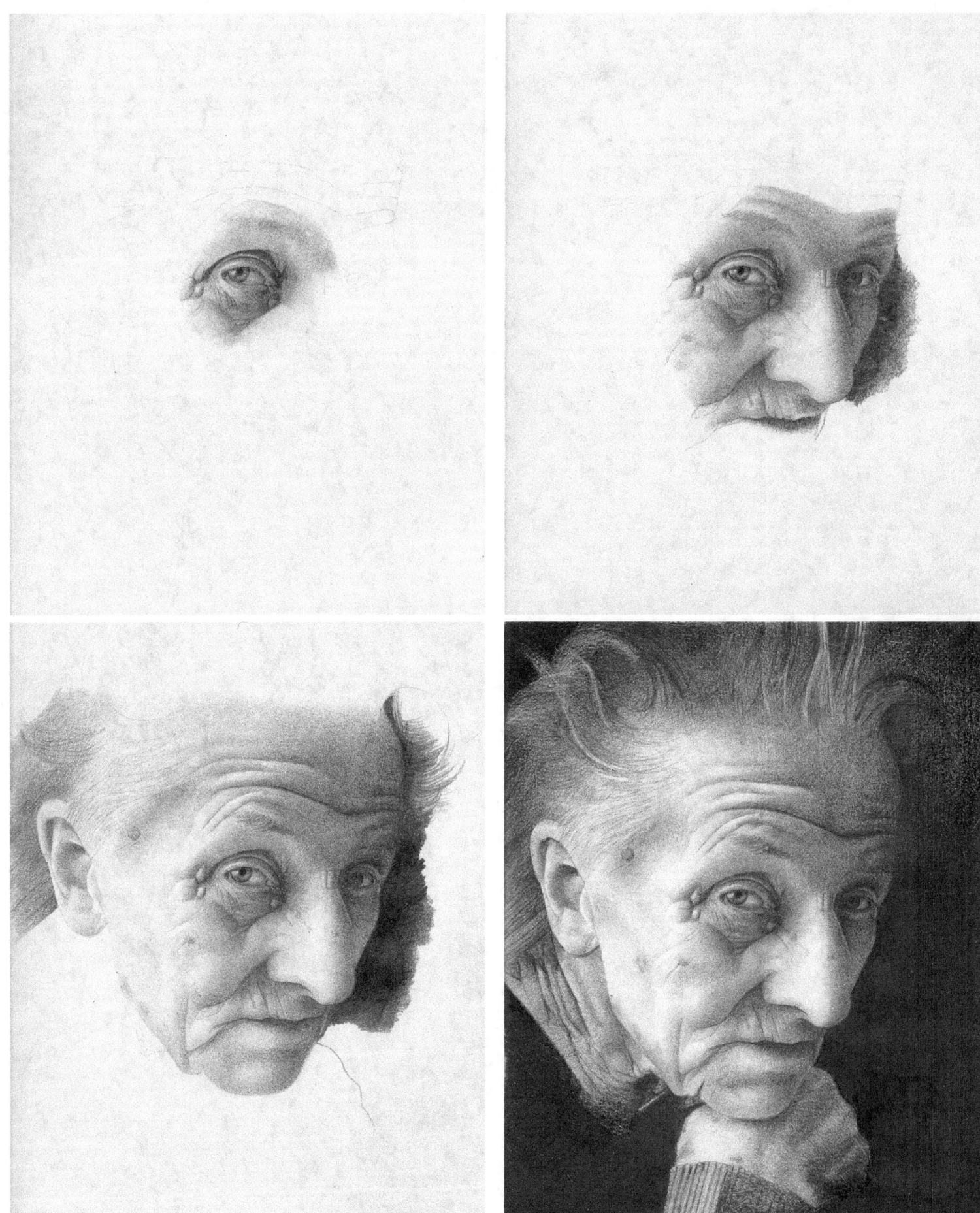

To read more on this drawing of "Nonna"
please see the book: *"Pencil Drawings Volume 1 - a look into drawing portraits"*

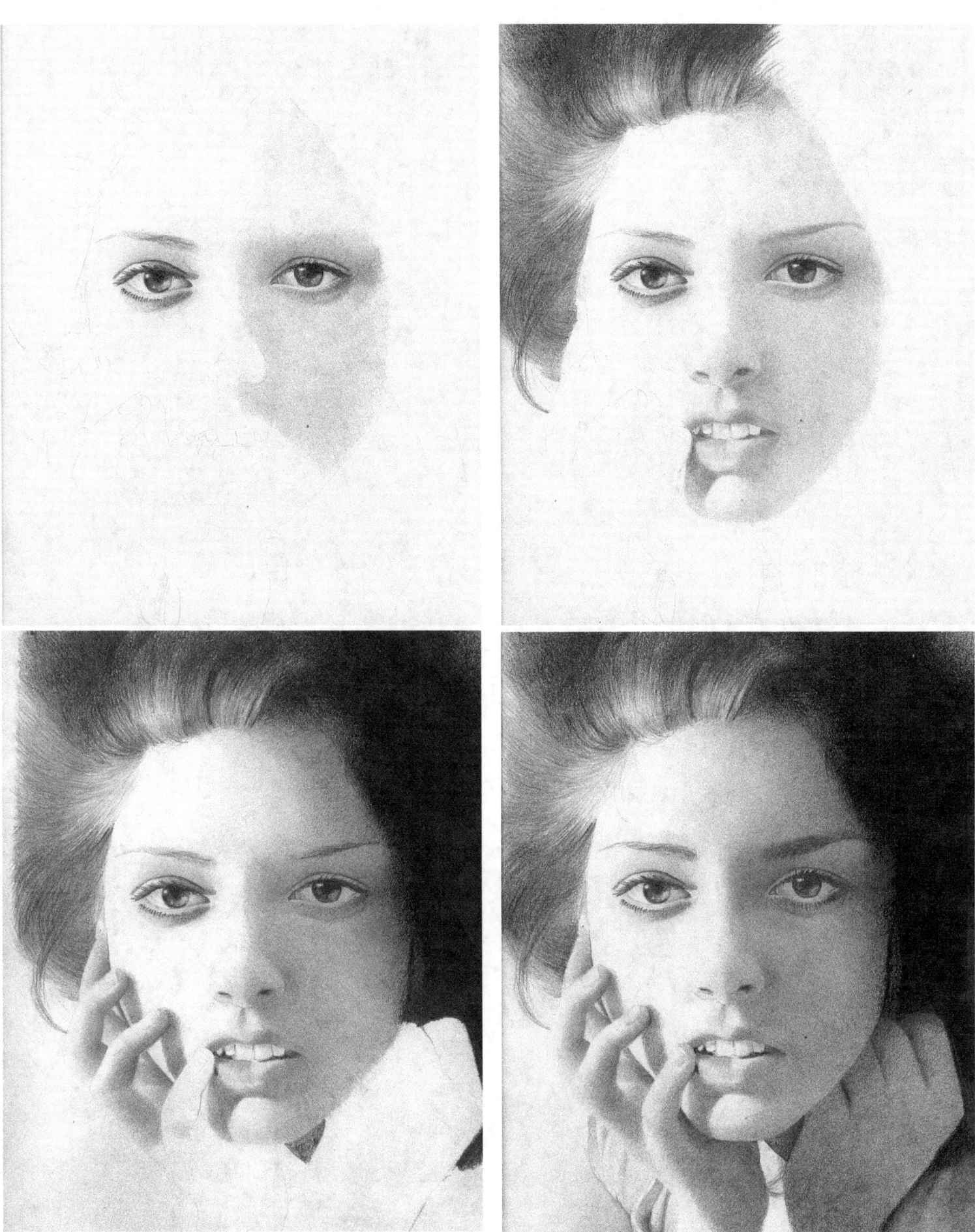

To read more on this drawing of "Odessa"
please see the book: *"Pencil Drawings Volume 1 - a look into drawing portraits"*

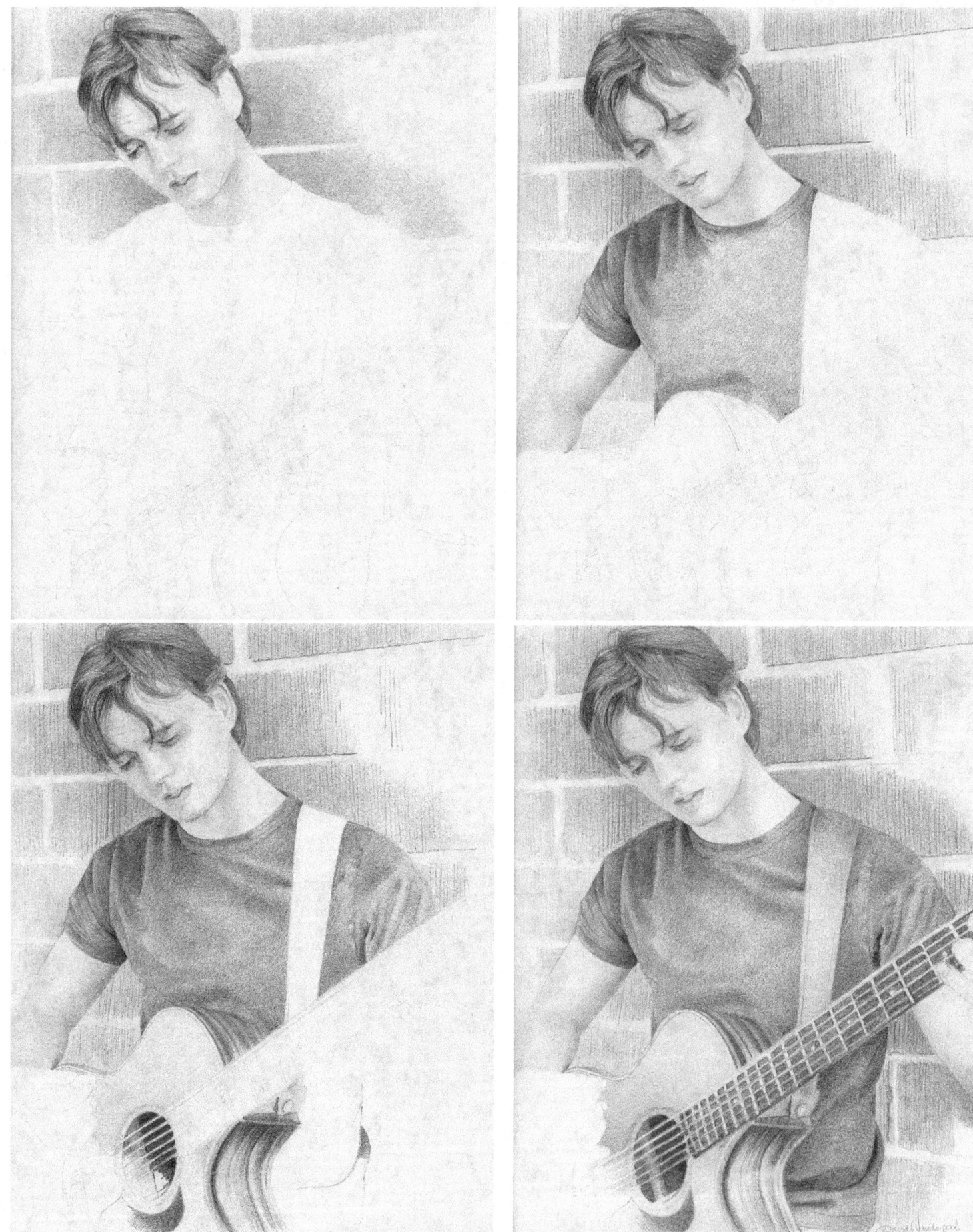

To read more on this drawing of "Peter"
Please see the book: *"Pencil Drawings Volume 1 - a look into drawing portraits"*

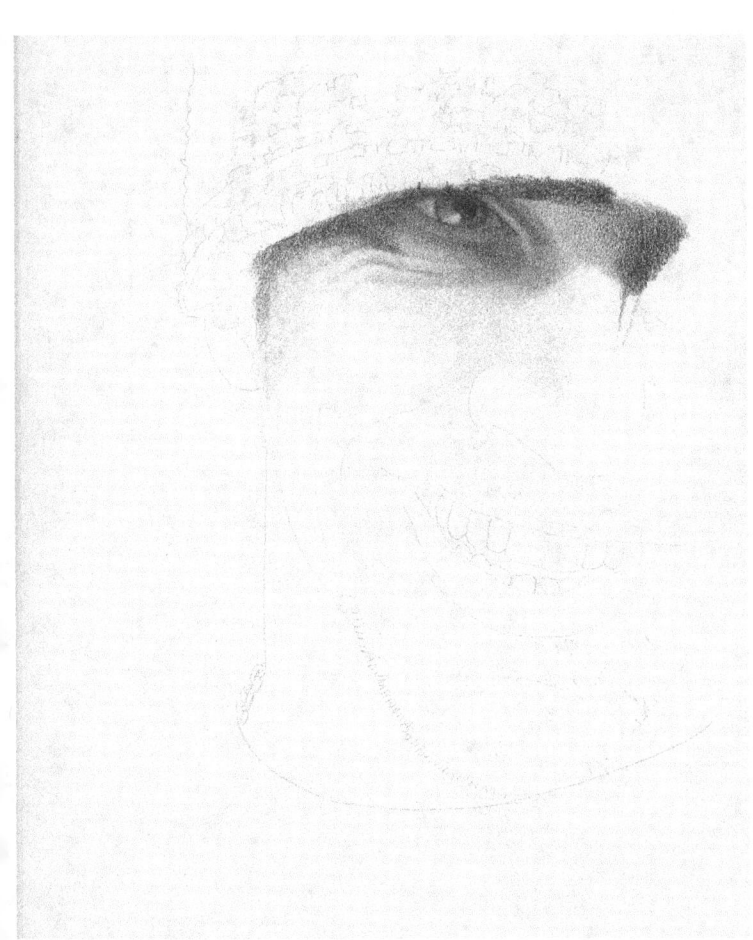
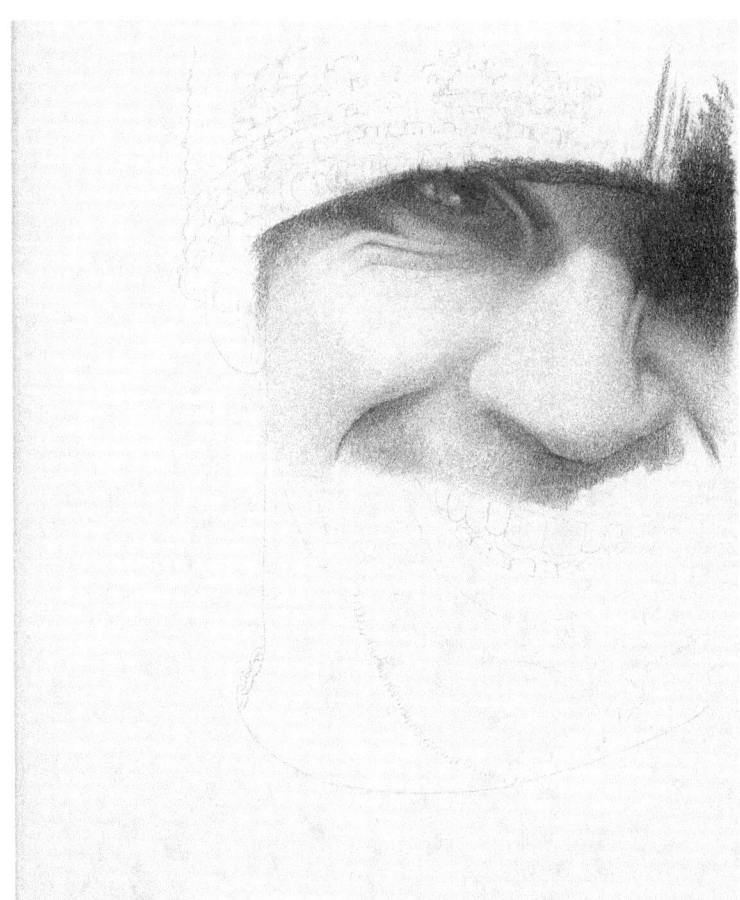
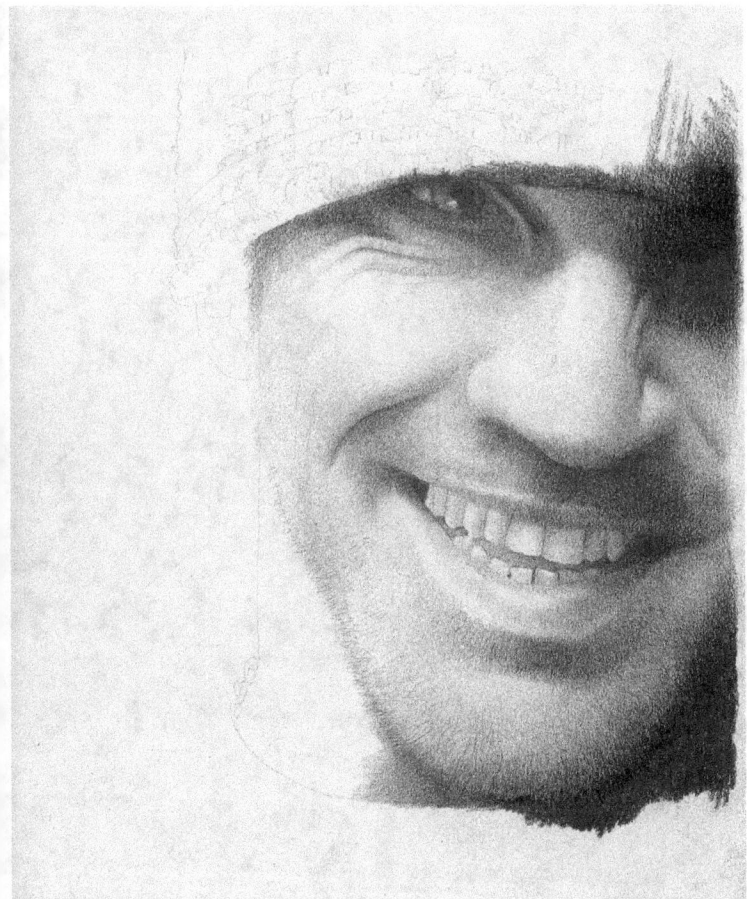
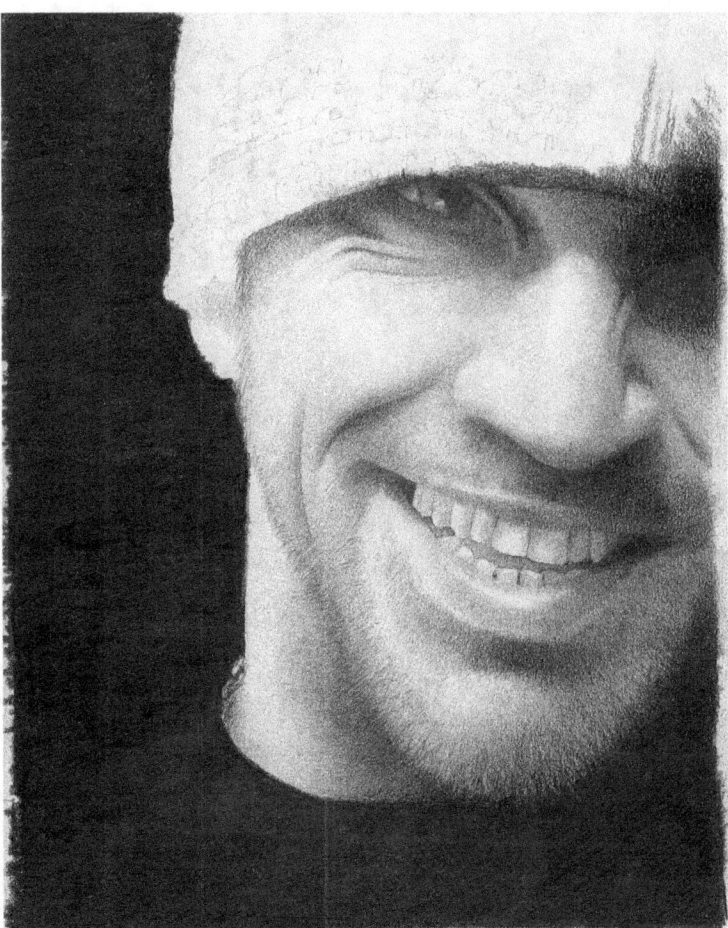

To read more on this drawing of "Robert Charles"
Please see the book: *"Pencil Drawings Volume 2 - a look into drawing men"*

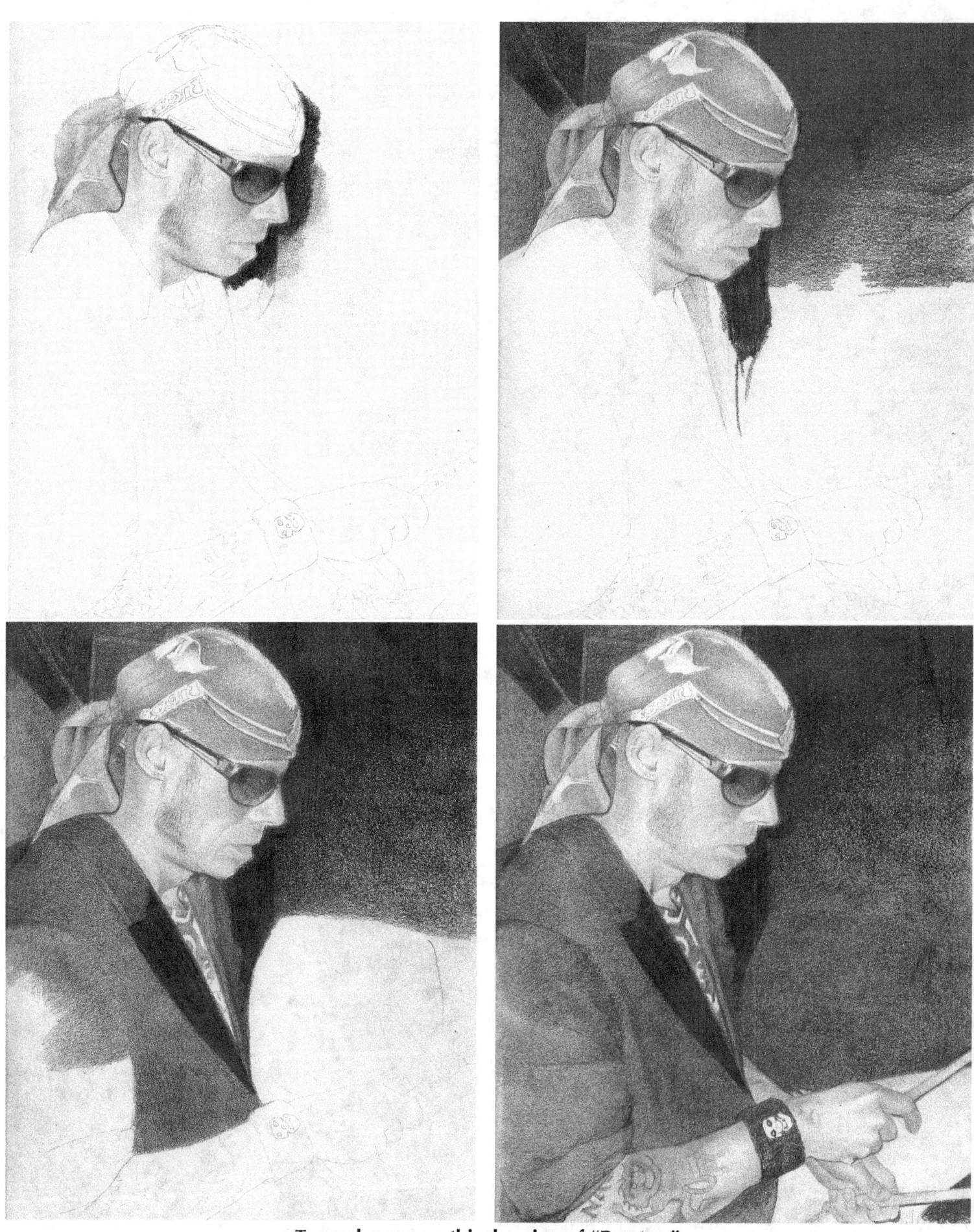

To read more on this drawing of "Preston"
Please see the book:*"Pencil Drawings Volume 2 - a look into drawing men"*

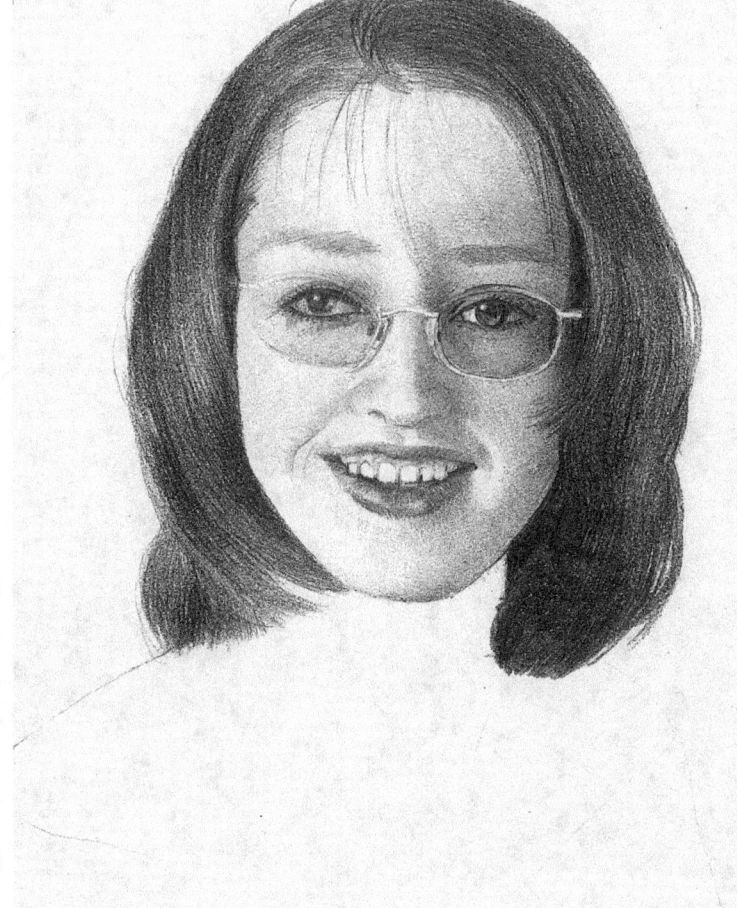
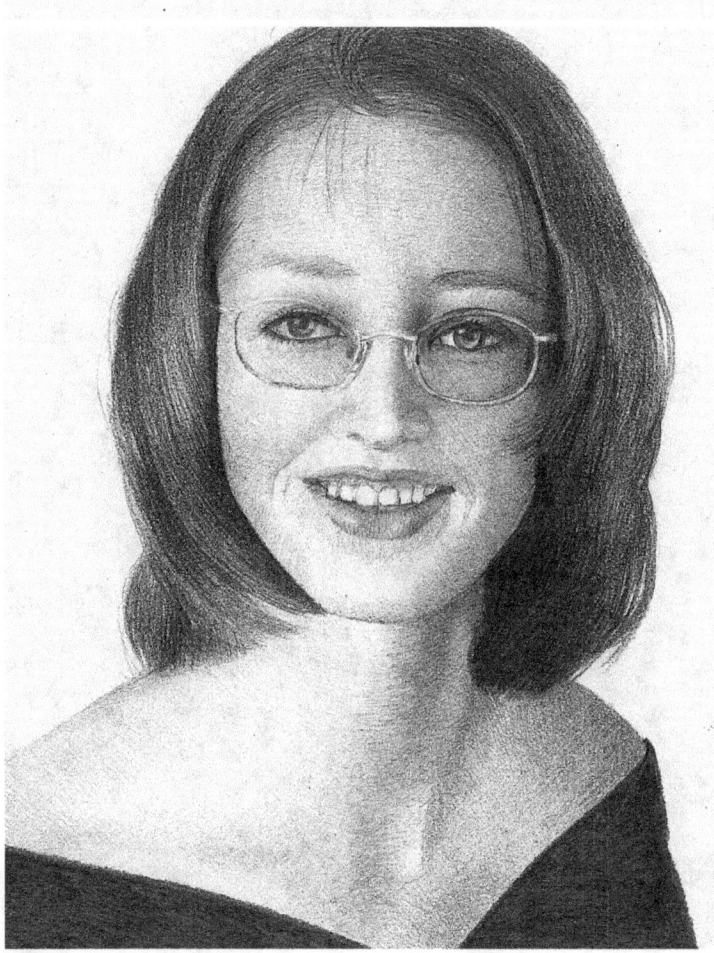

"Rebecca"
4.25" x 6.25" graphite pencil drawing on paper

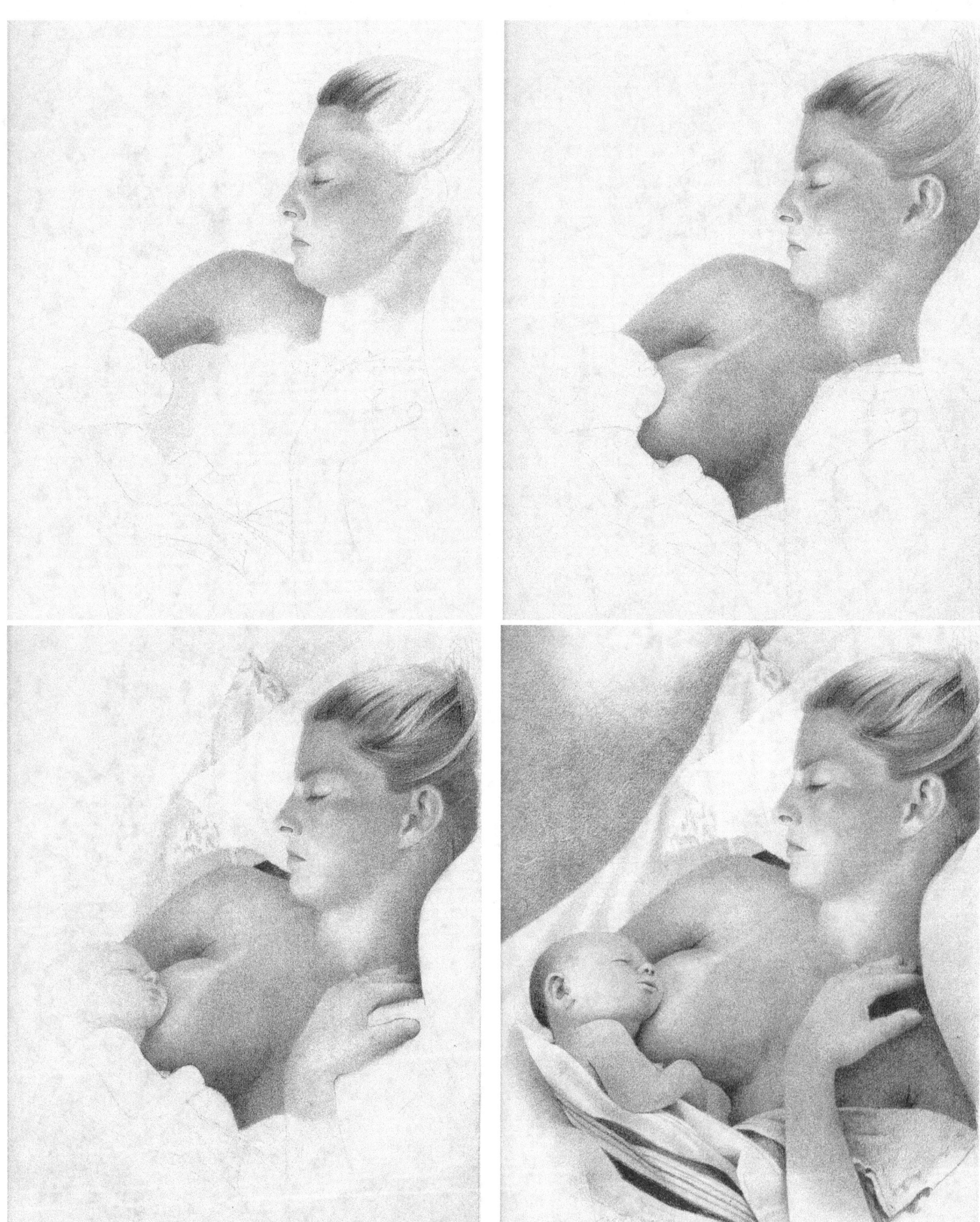

To read more on this drawing of "Rocky and Zander"
Please see the book:*"Pencil Drawings Volume 2 - a look into drawing men"*

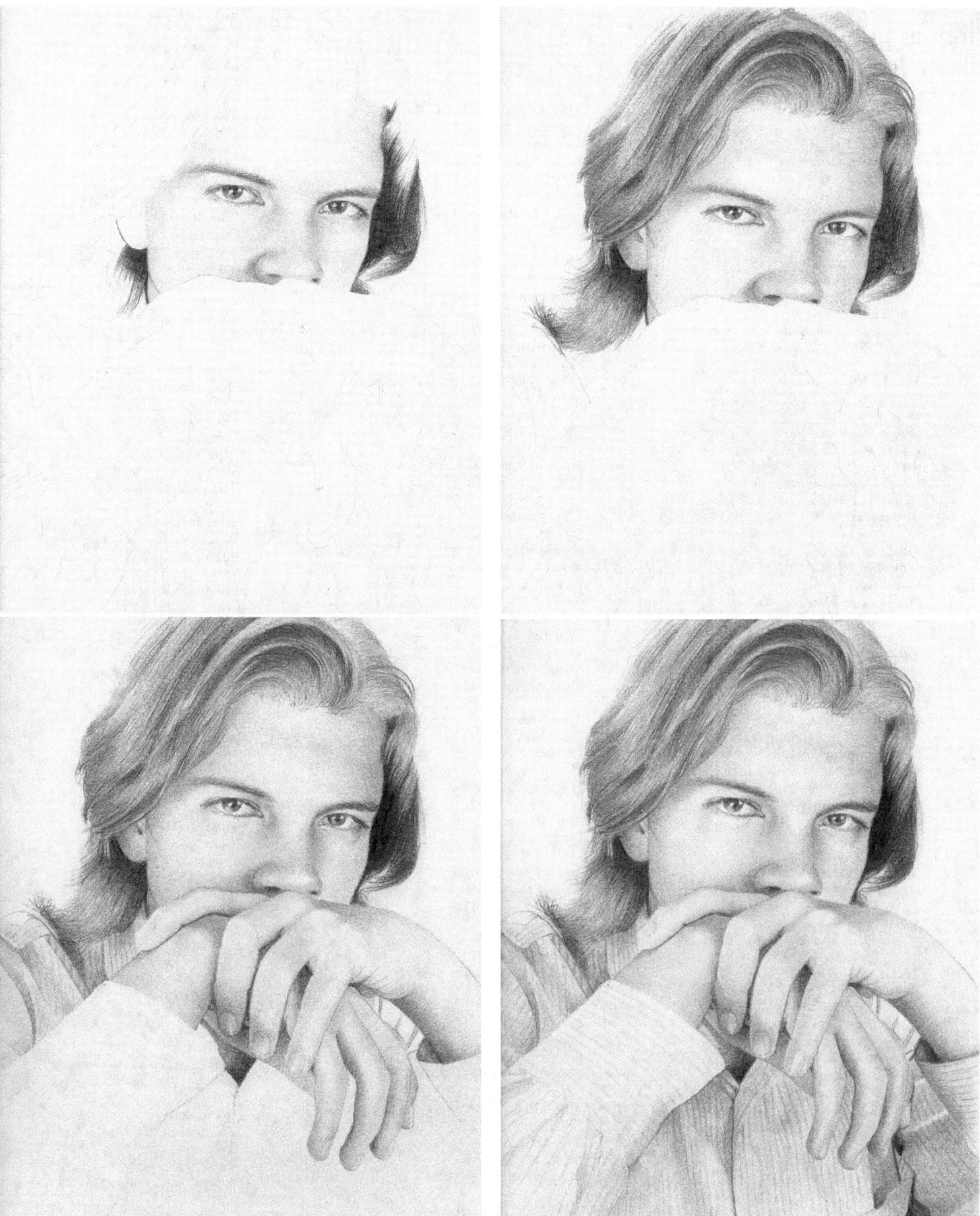

To read more on this drawing of "Stephen"
Please see the book: *"Pencil Drawings Volume 1 - a look into drawing portraits"*

Drawing INDEX: In order of appearance:

Drawing INDEX: In order of appearance:

Drawings In Progress INDEX: In order of appearance:

The following works in progress are some of drawings that are featured in chapters one and two of this book, that I did not go into detail nor shared the process it took to complete each drawing.

For a more in depth and detailed step-by-step progress of the drawings borrowed from *"Pencil drawings - a look into drawing portraits"* and *"Pencil drawings Volume 2 - a look into drawing men"*, each page will indicate in which of my books the specific drawing can be found.

Behind every pencil drawing, is an actual person.
Someone, in some way, who inspire that drawing. Be it the model, a photographer , or in most cases - both

NOTE: Those not listed here either did not provide a bio, or were friends who allowed me to draw.

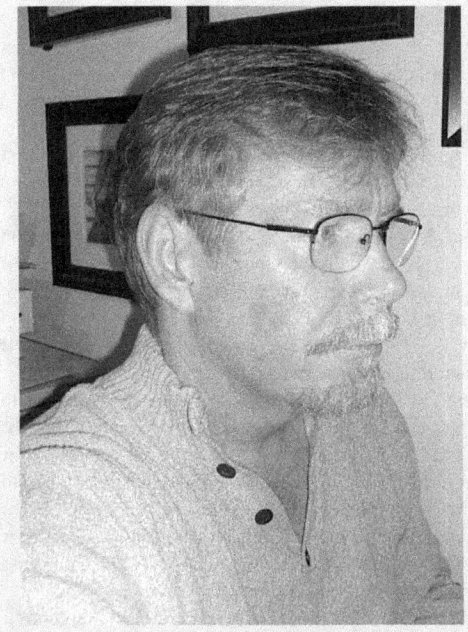

David J. Vanderpool - An award winning graphic artist by day, and a fine arts graphite pencil drawing artist by night, David has kept alive the old tradition of pencil drawing by networking with fellow artist, models and photographers throughout the world, which has allowed him to put together a masterfully crafted portfolio which can be seen at www.paper2pencil.com

Often quoted "I am only as good as the model's I work with" it is clearly seen in his work of not only local friends and fellow artists, but with professional models, singers and photographs who has allowed him to capture their like-ness for several books he has written on pencil drawings, and being able to sell prints and the originals throughout the world.

So what makes his drawing different that most? Each drawing is created with fine lines and crosshatching for shading. Never blending with a standard tool or smear the graphite, unless it's a background seen at a distant. As a self taught artist he discovered that using lighter pencils over the darker shades of gray was perfect for blending as it keeps the drawing from appearing flat, and as the lines wrap abound each muscle the drawing comes to life before the viewer's eyes.

ALECI (photographer)

I like to see myself as a player of light in every form of creativity... dark portraits with a deep inpact of drama are my thing..i hope that you enjoy my works like i do!

www.fotocommunity.com/photographer/aleci/1347983

ANDERSON, GARRETT (model)

Garrett Anderson is a Wisconsin based fitness model, NPC bodybuilding competitor and personal trainer. He has modeled from Puerto Rico to San Francisco for many very talented photographers and advertising clients. Along with modeling Garrett has also done television work in the mid west commercial market. Garrett is very glad to have collaborated with David Vanderpool on this project. He can be reached for future projects at simeon.79@live.com of at his Facebook page www.facebook.com/simeon.79

BOTTO MATT (photographer)

This photo is very special to me and I think will always remain one of my favorites. My Nonna (grand mother in Italian) first came to Australia in 1956 from a simple farming village in the North of Italy in search of a better life. The photo was taken back in 2008 with a simple point & shoot camera. I could talk about the technical aspects of this shot but I think that the main element that makes it what it is, is the interaction and connection between the photographer & subject. I think the reason this photo has the impact that it does is due to the fact that both Nonna and myself were very relaxed at the time the shot was taken. She had complete trust in me, there were no inhibitions or anxiety's, as to how the photo would turn out. The portrait lighting was provided by natural daylight from a single window. Using a more journalistic approach in that I did not direct or pose her, I think has given the shot a natural, un-contrived feel. I feel honoured that I was able to capture it and as equally honoured that David chose to draw it. While I think I'm still discovering my style, I think the ability to create a photo in an unique style is about discovering the right balance of the technical, creative and for portraiture, the all important connection between the photographer & subject.

www.MattBottos.com
www.DefenderOfRock.com

CYE, TERRY (photographer)

My entire existence seems to center on creative endeavors. I am a free-lance photographer with my own studio. I do senior portraits, weddings, and love to cover anything concerning arts and entertainment. I love to build things, last year designed and build onto my studio space, to create an environment what beautiful light. I feel most comfortable working in the earth, planing and toiling in the soil. I see my gardens as living art that are constantly changing each day. I like to listen to classic audio books in the garden. I feel fortunate that I actually make a living doing all the things I love.

http://cyrphoto.blogspot.com/
www.facebook.com/pages/The-Naked-...
www.redbubble.com/people/cyrphoto

DiGENOVA, MATTHEW (model)

Matthew DiGenova came across Josh's work a couple years back and sought out his work to help expand the beginnings of his portfolio. Through this, a wonderful working bond was created, and the birth of several collaborative photo shoots were realized. Matthew DiGenova can be found at his Model Mayhem Page,

www.modelmayhem.com/mattdigenova

DENJIS, WIM (photographer)

I am living in Belgium, The Flemish District, so called "Flanders Fields". My photographic journey began quit early with simple "Practica" and continued during my travel experience. I am especially intrigued by worlds culture, colour and lights, including a photographic study of landscape and peoples lives. I could look at a line of laundry flapping in the wind, a pair of old, hard working couple, a crowd of people on the street, and find it beautiful. Bored and disillusioned with political, empty promises, I would often walking through low class neighborhood of the poorest countries ever and show peoples as they are in simple way. I lived 4 years in North Africa. Due to my work, last few years traveling a lot through China and Vietnam. My photography never had any commercial value for me, I just had hope to touch someone by cosmos of human emotion. Through photography I want to tell everyone that no matter what no one is alone..no one is forgotten in this World. We are all human being belongs to nature no matter what political decision was made, nature still is beautiful and it will be. I would like to capture this beauty as the fact and send it with hope to be available to the public. If you like to know more about my artwork please be free to ask, I'm not so good in description about myself. Best regards, Wim

www.fotocommunity.com/photographer/wim-denijs/792050

FALGA, SANDRA

My name is Sandra Falga, a model, actress, and presenter residing in Barcelona, Spain. After modeling for six years, I have already enjoyed good fortune and success in my career.

I am an on-camera TV and video reporter. This exciting reporting work enables me to pursue both my modeling and acting goals full-time.

As you might expect, I am hard working, determined, and goal-oriented. To further my career, I am continually searching for opportunities to enhance my skills, talent, knowledge, and experience as well as to network with professionals in the fashion, artistic and entertainment industries.

"ONE OF THE SIX SEXIEST SPANISH WOMAN
By ESQUIRE magazine, April 2012
www.sandrafalga.com

FISHER, EDMUND (model)

Edmund Fisher, MD, FACS is one of Bakersfield, California's most respected sources for Plastic Surgery of the Eyes, Nose, Face and Neck. Dr. Fisher also offers Ear Nose & Throat specialty care.

www.facebyfisher.com
www.bakersfieldsinus.com
Facebook http://facebook.com/efishermd

GAGNON, JOSHUA (photographer)

Joshua Gagnon has been creating art his whole life. For the past 4 years that art has been in the form of photography and the exploration of light and shadow. Through this medium he has had the opportunity to work with many talented individuals across a stretch of fields. To view work by Joshua Gagnon, please visit www.JagFotoz.com, and on Model Mayhem at http://www.modelmayhem.com/jagfotoz

JAMES ROBERT (photographer)

Forty years ago I was digging through a course guide for the university I was attending looking for a fine arts class needed to fulfill some required pre-requisites. I chose a photography class and fell in love with this art form. Shortly after the class ended I purchased my first SLR film camera and haven't stopped having fun since.

Along the way I've worked with shooting candid images of people, street scenes and architecture that caught my eye. In addition there was a good amount of scenic and underwater photography as well. It wasn't until 2000 that I came across a few web sites specializing in the male form, something I had always wanted to try. My shoot with Kevin, whose picture is seen here, marks 10 years of working almost exclusively with the male form and learning to post-process the images.

One thing I've learned is to never put your camera down. It takes hours to get a model comfortable working with you so that the images don't look "posed" or "commercial". I much prefer the image to be as natural and relaxed as possible and many good shots come when you aren't planning for them. This image was taken just after we had finished a long set. I wearily sat down on the floor for a five minute break before the next set. Kevin was lying on the floor in front of me and rolled over to face me with this very relaxed yet intense stare. With my camera close at hand I gently raised it up and captured this image.

PANTEA, CRISTINA LAURA (model)

A 23 year old model and photographer from Bucharest, Romania.
http://cristianapantea.weebly.com/
http://krissa85.deviantart.com/
https://twitter.com/#!/CristianaPantea

MUSICK, MIKE (model)

Times are ever changing and the world shifts much like a record moving onto the next song. Making his own groove on the soundtrack of life is Mike Musick, who began jotting down lyrics at the tender age of seven. Growing up in Columbus , Ohio , he learned piano and guitar from his musician mother and,

eventually, went on to study a more structured form of music at Northwestern University in Chicago . Now based in Nashville , Mike is a songwriter who has played with bands all over the country.

"My inspiration comes from my relationship with God." Mike says, "God wants what's best for your life so don't settle for anything less than the best."

These aren't just idle words, but a philosophy he lives by. His record, Honest, brought forth the top-ten single 'America' which is also featured on a PBS film 'The American Southwest' which deals with the water crisis in America. The record's songs 'Scream' and 'Real Big World' are nominated for Hollywood Music Awards.

"Honest is called that for two reasons. It's my own self, becoming honest as an artist with both my musical style and the things I want to say. It's also a commentary on life as a modern day American. One of my favorite songs, off the record, is a song called 'Everybody's Hero.' It's actually about our international policy and how we always have to be everybody's hero." he confides. "Sometimes we overextend ourselves in the world, trying to police everything that's going on. But, I also point out in the song that we need to focus on what we commit to, such as the Iraq war. Most importantly, finish the job. We need to follow through."

If it isn't already obvious, Mike doesn't shy away from jumping right into the problems that plague the world and touch upon issues like politics and religion. "I do a lot of research and study historical stuff and current events. I want to be very involved in what is going on in current culture and I don't mean just pop culture- what's going on in the United States , politically, as well as issues that have to do with human rights, international issues."

Referring to an incident involving recent violence against a young girl in Somalia , Mike speaks passionately, "Someone needs to write a song about that. There are things that need to be talked about. Sometimes, when it's only talked about on the news, it kind of becomes commonplace. Our hearts become hardened to it. The cool thing about music is it can reach to a deeper place. There are different parts of your spirit that are moved. When you hear a song, it moves you, as opposed to just reading something in the paper. I try to take things that I think are important and translate them through music."

www.mikemusick.com
written by Joshua Schrader

NEWMAN, Rev. DANIEL M. , PhD, DD (Editing/proof reader)

Dan is an interfaith minister and holds degrees in Doctor of Philosophy (PhD) and Doctor of Divinity (DD). He is certified as a Prevention Specialist (APS), Risk Reduction Specialist (RRS), and Senior Health Educator for over two decades. Dan is a volunteer counselor and participated as a group facilitator for New Dads sponsored by the National Fatherhood Initiative. He is approved by the Cabinet for Health and Family Services for CEU's listed as HIV/AIDS Professional Education Multi-disciplinary Curriculum and he is certified as a First Aid/CPR/AED Instructor by the National Safety Council Emergency Care Teaching Certificate.

Born in Kentucky and now living in Cincinnati, Ohio, Myrix is a self-taught artist, working in pencil and charcoal. His talent for creating images of hard-working men has not gone unnoticed. Galleries have shown his distinctly masculine images to audiences in locations from San Francisco to Provincetown, from Knoxville to Rapid City, South Dakota. His latest passion is portrait drawing. "His latest show he created a series of portraits, featuring different looks of men.

In 1995 he was ordained by the state of Ohio and 2002 became sole proprietor of Holistic Health Consultant business. April 23, 2012 – In his new book, Grief Behind Bars, author Dan Newman exposes a hidden world of grief and exposes a remarkable personal journey helping inmates. With the execution clock ticking, Newman uncovers deeper truths about death, dying, and grief behind bars. He is an artist, author, humorist, local, regional, national keynote, plenary speaker, workshop provider, and motivational speaker.

GriefBehindBars.com - (513) 542-1900 – dan@griefbehindbars.com

OUANO DAVE

Dave Ouano is a Chicago-based photographer. He has been shooting club and event photos for Windy City Times, Nightspots, Chicago Free Press, ChicagoPride.com, GoGuide, and Pink Triangle Press for over 18 years. He has shot covers for Nightspots and GoGuide, as well as corporate, commercial, and event photography for Domino's Pizza, Dwell Chicago Rentals, Stone Eye Center, Siemens, Hustle Fitness, and the U.S. Green Building Counsel.

Dave's fashion photography has appeared in Fashion Chicago Magazine, Ellements Magazine, the Akira Chronicle, and Linger Magazine. Dave has worked with fashion and fitness models from BMG, Chosen, Factor, Wilhelmina New York, Agency Galatea, and The Rock Agency, and has captured dancers from Gus Giordano, Ron de Jesus, and Corpo dance companies. He has worked with many talented designers, including Amanda Archer, Kaylee Zastrow, Veronica Sheaffer, Cleons, Fraley Le, Stiletto Squad, Thierry Roger, Franc Lloyd Custom Menswear, and Calvin Tran from Bravo's "The Fashion Show". Dave's 16 years of acting, modeling, and voiceover experience may be one reason he is so comfortable working with a variety of models and actors. Dave also has a Bachelors Degree in Marketing from the University of Illinois in Champaign.

Dave Ouano Photography
(773) 860-0162
daveouano@me.com
www.modelmayhem.com/daveouano
www.daveouanophotography.com

RANOGAJEC DARKO (model)

Born and raised in Zurich, Switzerland, and is currently a Swiss citizen. However, both of his parents are from Croatia, which makes him a Croatian at heart. Over 8 years of international modeling, photo shoots, and runway experience in the USA, Italy, Germany and Switzerland have made him skilled and competent in the world of modeling. He has worked with famous fashion and celebrity photographers such as Troy Jensen in Hollywood and Zatac and Maurizio Montani in Milan. Darko is known for his strong ability to engage with the story line and context of a job, no matter what is required. His motto is, "Don't go with the flow, be different", and this is exemplified fully in his charisma, agility, and attitude while performing in front of a camera.

The simplicity of this clean portrait with no styling or posing and the bright look in the eyes might tempt you to think whatever you desire from this guy. www.darko.la

SAWYER, ODESSA (model)

Born in Santa Fe, New Mexico, Odessa Sawyer has been busy creating art in a variety of mediums since she was very young. She studied at the Art Institute of Vancouver, the Art Institute of Seattle and graduated from the Vancouver Film School. Highly influenced by fairy tales, films and fashion, Odessa's work celebrates a whimsical, dreamy and vibrant quality. She works in digital mixed media and utilizes digital painting, photography and traditional pen and pencil. Odessa also dabbles in photography and doll making.

RYAN, TONY

I have for as long as I can remember been deeply passionate about beautiful aesthetics. In 1989 this passion led me to starting up Down Under Creations, a business that is still running now. I commenced as a photographic director and in 1995 took over the photographic duties. I have always loved what I do and am always keen to get deeper and deeper into my passion.

Over the years I have photographed and published images that have been marketed through posters, calendars, magazines, books, cards and also in television documentaries. I have endeavored in this time to present models to look both aesthetically beautiful and have placed equal importance on presenting images where the models project a deep humility.

These days I have a shared passion with photography and writing. I am very open to receiving photographic assignments and also in taking portfolios for those interested. My writing is based on exploring emotions and society beliefs on a broad range of topics.

www.redbubble.com/people/passion
www.leapoffaith.com.au/

VISHNYAKOV, ANDREI

Crazy Russian 'Peter Pan', can't decide what he wants to be when he grows up! In the meantime he plays with photography. Specializes in portrait and figurative work but occasionally branches out into landscape and nature studies. Living in Saint Petersburg is no hindrance as the city offers so many incredible sights. If Russian boys and girls are your weakness or the imperial slendour of St. Petersburg is your dream come true, hopefully the folio of images here will quench your desires, if not, suggestions are welcomed.

http://vishstudio.deviantart.com/
http://facebook.com/vishnyakovpro

WILBY, CORY (model)

Cory Wilby was born and raised in MN, and had always believed that he was put here to do one thing, succeed. Having always tried to be the best or at least excel at everything he did. Be it in art, fitness, or music, whatever it is he is currently perusing there is no top to any mountain he climbs. Ambition is the key to success and accept no limits.

http://facebook.com/cory.wilaby

YOUNG, ACE (model)

Ace Young is an American singer, songwriter, entrepreneur, and actor. He gained national recognition while appearing on the fifth season of American Idol. Young is engaged to marry American Idol season-three runner-up Diana DeGarmo.

After over four years in Los Angeles without a record deal, Young auditioned for American Idol in Denver, Colorado. His televised audition featured him singing Westlife's "Swear it Again." Young was introduced as Brett Young, with the name "Ace" marked in quotations. Later, he told producers he preferred to be called Ace and he was not referred to as Brett on the show again.

After his elimination Young was a guest and performed on MTV's Total Request Live. He was the first Idol contestant to be on MTV directly after elimination. Young also returned home to perform at the Pepsi Center in Denver. He was named one of People Magazine's "Hottest Bachelors" on June 16, 2006. [12] He spent the summer of 2006 on the annual American Idol Top 10 tour, and afterwards released his first single, "Scattered," (co-written with Elvio Fernandes) as a digital download on iTunes. The song reached the Top 50 on the Hot Adult Contemporary sales chart. He also put together a band and started playing gigs around the country.

Young performed at the 2006 Walt Disney Christmas Day Parade along with fellow idol finalists Paris Bennett, Kevin Covais, and Mandisa. He also formed a charity called "Highrollers With Heart" that raised $300,000 to help Children's Hospital in Denver build the Family Hospitality Suite.

Young wrote the chorus for Daughtry's debut single, "It's Not Over." The song was nominated for Best Rock Song at the 50th Annual Grammy Award nominations on December 6, 2007. Along with co-writers, Gregg Wattenberg, Mark Wilkerson, and Chris Daughtry, Young received a songwriting nomination. At the Grammy's they lost the award to Bruce Springsteen's "Radio Nowhere.".

In January 2008, Young was named a Celebrity Ambassador for the Muscular Dystrophy Association (MDA). Young continues to work closely with MDA as a National Association Vice President.[9] He has appeared on the show every year since 2007. In 2011 he hosted the New York MDA telethon. In 2012 he will participate in Labor Day weekend's pre-taped MDA "Show of Strength" telethon.

In April 2008 he released another single, "Addicted," and promoted the song and subsequent video on TNA wrestling. He worked with Bon Jovi producer Desmond Child on his self-titled and self-funded debut album, releasing it independently in July 2008. He wrote seven of the eleven songs on the cd and released it independently to stores and digital retailers.

On May 12, 2008 he appeared on the Fox series Bones alongside season-six American Idol contestant Brandon Rogers. In the episode "Wannabe in the Weeds," Young played an arrogant karaoke singer who was gruesomely murdered. His character sang a Nickleback song, "Far Away." On November 23, 2008, he made an appearance as a bachelor on the VH1 show Rock of Love: Charm School.

Young made his Broadway debut as Kenickie in the revival of Grease on September 9, 2008. He played the role until the show closed January 4, 2009. Young later joined the national tour of Grease in December 2009, this time playing Danny Zuko. He left the tour on February 14, 2010. After "Grease," Young took over the role of Berger in the Broadway revival of Hair, succeeding Will Swenson. Young took over the role in March 2010 and remained with the production until the show closed June 27, 2010

Since Hair, Young has started a music company, called "Young Brothers Entertainment." The new company is partnered with Mailboat Records for digital releases. The company has four acts: Ace Young, Diana DeGarmo, Tha Vill Rachele Royale, and Code 5. Young's single "I Wanna Fall in Love Again" was released on iTunes in May 2012. Young's next project is a cd of original duets with DeGarmo.

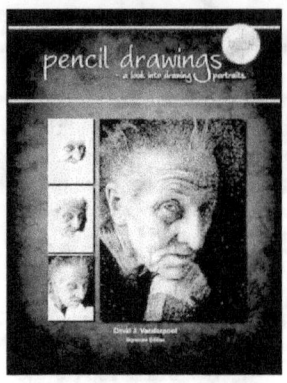

Pencil Drawings - A look into drawing portraits

Pencil Drawings by **David J. Vanderpool**

A rare and often overlooked art form in today's art scene. This collection of masterfully crafted graphite pencil drawings, with over 300 illustrations, shows the step-by-step process it took to complete 16 dynamic graphite drawings.

See each drawing develop and read the artist's thoughts and views on how he crafts each incredible work. This "journal style" book gives the reader unique insight into the creative mind of the artist and takes the reader on a journey from blank page to masterpiece. Featuring a "Question and Answer" sidebar for each drawing. Submitted by fellow artist's and answered by the author and artist of this book.

*ORDER DIRECT AND SAVE:

http://www.lulu.com/spotlight/paper2pencil

First Edition Paperback
Pages: 166
Interior Ink: Black & white
ISBN 9780557680818

List Price: $30.00
Price: $25.50
You Save: $4.50 (15%)
Ships in 3-5 business days

SPECIAL LIMITED SIGNATURE EDITION
First Edition Hardcover *Available only at Lulu.com*
Pages: 166
Interior Ink: Black & white

List Price: $45.00
Price: $38.25
You Save: $6.75 (15%)
Ships in 6-8 business days.

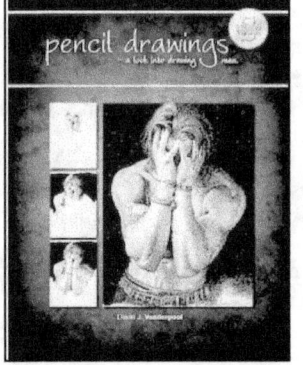

Pencil Drawings - A look into drawing men

Pencil Drawings by **David J. Vanderpool**

The second volume to PENCIL DRAWINGS, by David J. Vanderpool takes where "Portraits" (vol. 1) leaves off. Showing the reader the process it takes to complete 18 portraits few figure drawings men he has encountered through the years. Most as the result of his drawings. Unlike volume one of this series,"Pencil Drawings - a look into drawing portraits", which was presented entirely in a journal-style format, here only the first four drawings featured keep to that format. The remaining fifteen drawings will not only show the step-by-step process it took to complete each drawing, but answers a question that was submitted just for that drawing. With masterfully crafted graphite pencil drawings at their best, this book is an excellent addition to those who have already collected Volume 1. In fact - it's encourage to collect all in the series to have a full understanding on how this artist draws with all lines.

*ORDER DIRECT AND SAVE:

http://www.lulu.com/spotlight/paper2pencil

First Edition Paperback
Pages: 149
Interior Ink: Black & white
ISBN 9781105833656

List Price: $30.00
Price: $25.50
You Save: $4.50 (15%)
Ships in 3-5 business days

SPECIAL LIMITED SIGNATURE EDITION
First Edition Hardcover *Available only at Lulu.com*
Pages: 149
Interior Ink: Black & white

List Price: $45.95
Price: $39.06
You Save: $6.89 (15%)
Ships in 6-8 business days.

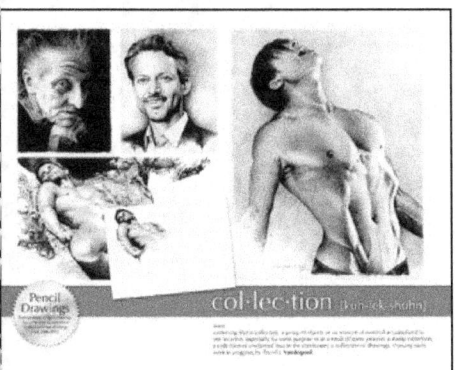
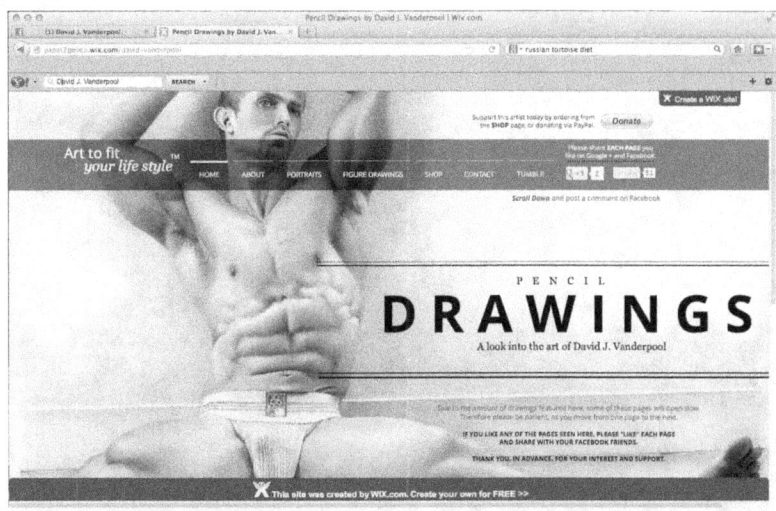
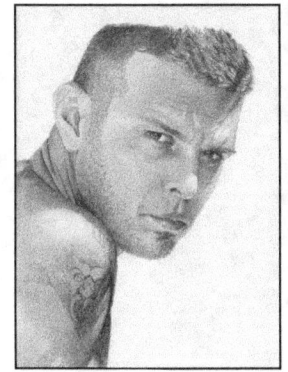 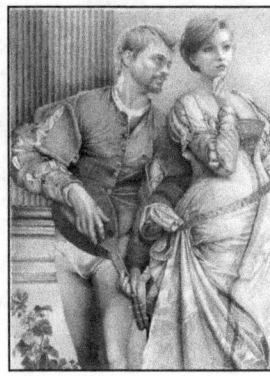 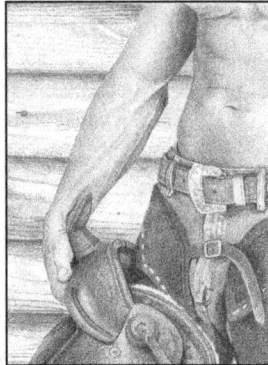 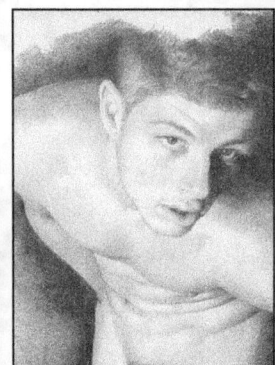 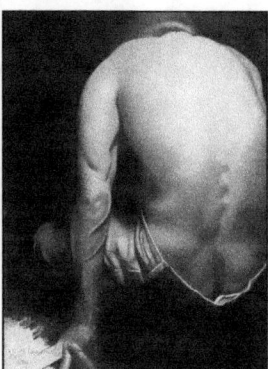